McGraw-Hill's Real Estate Law for Paralegals

The McGraw-Hill Paralegal List

WHERE EDUCATIONAL SUPPORT GOES BEYOND EXPECTATIONS.

Introduction to Law & Paralegal Studies
Connie Farrell Scuderi
ISBN: 0073524638
© 2008

Introduction to Law for Paralegals
Deborah Benton
ISBN: 007351179X
© 2008

Basic Legal Research, Second Edition
Edward Nolfi
ISBN: 0073520519
© 2008

Basic Legal Writing, Second Edition
Pamela Tepper
ISBN: 0073403032
© 2008

Contract Law for Paralegals
Linda Spagnola
ISBN: 0073511765
© 2008

Civil Law and Litigation for Paralegals
Neal Bevans
ISBN: 0073524611
© 2008

Wills, Trusts, and Estates for Paralegals
George Kent
ISBN: 0073403067
© 2008

The Law Office Reference Manual
Jo Ann Lee
ISBN: 0073511838
© 2008

The Paralegal Reference Manual
Charles Nemeth
ISBN: 0073403075
© 2008

The Professional Paralegal
Allan Tow
ISBN: 0073403091
© 2009

Ethics for Paralegals
Linda Spagnola and Vivian Batts
ISBN: 0073376981
© 2009

Family Law for Paralegals
George Kent
ISBN: 0073376973
© 2009

McGraw-Hill's Torts for Paralegals
ISBN: 0073376965
© 2009

McGraw-Hill's Real Estate Law for Paralegals
ISBN: 0073376949
© 2009

Legal Research and Writing for Paralegals
Pamela Tepper and Neal Bevans
ISBN: 007352462X
© 2009

McGraw-Hill's Criminal Law for Paralegals
ISBN: 0073376930
© 2009

McGraw-Hill's Law Office Management for Paralegals
ISBN: 0073376957
© 2009

Legal Terminology Explained
Edward Nolfi
ISBN: 0073511846
© 2009

For more information or to receive desk copies, please contact your McGraw-Hill Sales Representative.

McGraw Hill's Real Estate Law for Paralegals

Lisa Schaffer
Contributing Author

Andrew Wietecki
Contributing Editor

Boston   Burr Ridge, IL   Dubuque, IA   New York   San Francisco   St. Louis
Bangkok   Bogotá   Caracas   Kuala Lumpur   Lisbon   London   Madrid   Mexico City
Milan   Montreal   New Delhi   Santiago   Seoul   Singapore   Sydney   Taipei   Toronto

McGRAW-HILL'S REAL ESTATE LAW FOR PARALEGALS

Published by McGraw-Hill, a business unit of The McGraw-Hill Companies, Inc., 1221 Avenue of the Americas, New York, NY, 10020. Copyright © 2009 by The McGraw-Hill Companies, Inc. All rights reserved. No part of this publication may be reproduced or distributed in any form or by any means, or stored in a database or retrieval system, without the prior written consent of The McGraw-Hill Companies, Inc., including, but not limited to, in any network or other electronic storage or transmission, or broadcast for distance learning.

Some ancillaries, including electronic and print components, may not be available to customers outside the United States.

This book is printed on acid-free paper.

2 3 4 5 6 7 8 9 0 QDB/QDB 14 13 12 11

ISBN   978-0-07-337695-0
MHID 0-07-337695-7

Vice president/Editor in chief: *Elizabeth Haefele*
Vice president/Director of marketing: *John E. Biernat*
Sponsoring editor: *Natalie J. Ruffatto*
Developmental editor II: *Tammy Higham*
Marketing manager: *Keari Bedford*
Lead media producer: *Damian Moshak*
Media producer: *Marc Mattson*
Director, Editing/Design/Production: *Jess Ann Kosic*
Project manager: *Jean R. Starr*
Senior production supervisor: *Janean A. Utley*
Designer: *Marianna Kinigakis*
Media project manager: *Mark A. S. Dierker*
Outside development: *Beth Baugh*
Cover and interior design: *Pam Verros*
Typeface: *10.5/13 Times New Roman*
Compositor: *Aptara, Inc.*
Printer: *Quad/Graphics, Dubuque*
Cover credit: © *iStockPhoto*

Library of Congress Cataloging-in-Publication Data

Schaffer, Lisa.
    McGraw-Hill's real estate law for paralegals / Lisa Schaffer, contributing author ; Andrew Wietecki, contributing editor.
        p. cm.
    Includes indexes.
    ISBN-13: 978-0-07-337695-0 (alk. paper)
    ISBN-10: 0-07-337695-7 (alk. paper)
    1. Real property—United States. 2. Real estate business—Law and legislation—United States. 3. Vendors and purchasers—United States. 4. Conveyancing—United States. 5. Legal assistants—United States. I. Wietecki, Andrew. II. Title. III. Title: Real estate law for paralegals.
KF570.Z9S53 2009
346.7304'3—dc22

                                                    2007038524

The Internet addresses listed in the text were accurate at the time of publication. The inclusion of a Web site does not indicate an endorsement by the authors or McGraw-Hill, and McGraw-Hill does not guarantee the accuracy of the information presented at these sites.

www.mhhe.com

About the Authors

Curriculum Technology

Curriculum Technology works with McGraw-Hill on several projects related to the paralegal series. Curriculum Technology serves education organizations and publishing companies by providing a source of intellectual property development, media, technology, as well as consultation, and research.

Lisa Schaffer, JD, MBA

Contributing Author/Editor

- Bachelor of Arts in History from University of California, Los Angeles
- Juris Doctorate in law from Chapman University School of Law
- Masters in Business Administration from Chapman University
- Advanced Management Certificate from University of California, Riverside
- Executive Management Certificate from University of California, Riverside

Lisa worked in the legal industry for over twenty years in a variety of positions for law firms that specialized in the areas of criminal law, real estate law, corporate law, and personal injury. She served as in-house counsel for regulatory compliance in the legal affairs department of National Water & Power, Inc. doing business in forty-three states.

Lisa taught a variety of courses in paralegal studies for InterCoast Colleges over a period of five years. She was offered and accepted the position of Director of Education. She was later promoted to School Director of the Riverside campus before accepting the position of Chief Administrative Officer for all campuses.

Lisa served as an assistant vice president in the accreditation and licensing department for Corinthian Colleges, Inc.

Andrew Wietecki, JD, MPA

Contributing Editor

- Bachelor of Arts in English from St. Thomas Aquinas College
- Masters in Public Administration from Hamline University, Graduate School
- Juris Doctorate in law from Hamline University, School of Law

Andrew was born and raised in New York City. He has been in the education business for thirteen years, having practiced Real Property Law before that. He has taught at the high-school level in New York City as well as instructing college-level paralegal students. He has been Academic Dean, Legal Program Chair and a college instructor for the past eleven years. Currently, Andrew works in the education field with Curriculum Technology producing a wide variety of learning tools while also tutoring children in English skills.

Amy Eisenhower, JD, BS
Contributing Writers

- Bachelor of Science in English from Wayne State College
- Doctorate in Jurisprudence from the University of South Dakota

Amy was born in Nebraska and has spent much of her life there. She currently resides in Grand Island, Nebraska. Amy earned her Bachelor of Science degree in English from Wayne State College in Wayne, Nebraska and earned her Doctorate in Jurisprudence from University of South Dakota in Vermillion, South Dakota. Amy is a member of both the South Dakota and the Nebraska State Bar.

Amy taught five years of high school English before attending law school. She is currently employed as assistant general counsel for Credit Management, Inc. Amy has been with Curriculum Technology for approximately a year and a half as a senior consultant.

Rastin Ashtiani

- Bachelor of Arts in Psychology from University of California at Irvine
- Doctorate in Jurisprudence from Chapman University

Rastin was born in Los Angeles, California and has spent much of his life living in the Los Angeles area and currently resides in Orange County, California. Rastin earned his Bachelor of Arts degree in Psychology from the University of California at Irvine and earned his Doctorate in Jurisprudence from Chapman University, School of Law in Anaheim, California.

Rastin has worked with the Orange County District Attorney's office and has also worked at the law offices of Dyke Huish. Rastin has been with Curriculum Technology for approximately a year as a consultant for both paralegal and legal projects.

Preface

Real estate law in the United States has a long history, going all the way back to British common law. *McGraw-Hill's Real Estate Law for Paralegals* tracks the evolution of real estate law principles leading up to the current state of real property rights, and also explains the various ownership statutes that exist today.

This text was designed to help prepare students for the practical world of real estate, setting forth the differences in real property (real estate) and personal property. Included in the text are numerous subject areas, ranging from modern-day condominiums, cooperatives, and timeshares to regulations, encumbrances, interests in land, and landlord—tenant relations. This text also introduces contracts, deeds, mortgages, financing, and real estate closings. The variety of subject areas introduces the student to a practical array of topics necessary for success in the real world practice of real estate, while not overwhelming the student with dry, dull, textual material.

McGraw-Hill's Real Estate Law for Paralegals contains twelve chapters along with two appendices. To provide a hands-on approach to learning, each chapter has a recent, applicable case opinion, along with many ancillaries, including charts, tables, figures, and exercises to aid in the student's development.

TEXT DESIGN

Pedagogy

This text has numerous features that take advantage of the varying learning styles that students apply to gain knowledge. Based on the notion that students who apply their newly acquired knowledge often retain it much better than those who do not, this text requires students to apply the knowledge they have acquired. Chapters are designed in a manner that assures the student will have the opportunity to learn the appropriate legal concepts, master the necessary vocabulary, develop legal reasoning skills, and demonstrate knowledge of the material. Each chapter contains the following features:

- **Spot the Issue:** A fact pattern in which the student is asked to "spot" the issue(s) present
- **Legal Research Maxim:** A general statement of a principle in law
- **Case Fact Pattern:** A simple fact pattern including a story and its outcome
- **Research This:** A hands-on assignment designed to develop the student's research skills
- **Eye on Ethics:** A presention of ethical issue(s) related to one or more subjects in the chapter
- **You Be the Judge:** Presentation of a fact pattern and issue with a request that the student "be the judge" and decide on the issue
- **Surf's Up:** Hands-on research presenting the student with numerous Web sites through which surf and gather material
- **Practice Tip:** A tip alerting the student to nuance of law or caveat to a rule

- **Case in Point:** A significant real-life case, included illustrate and expand on the topics discussed in the chapter
- **Portfolio Assignment:** An assignment with which the student can begin, create, and add to a portfolio
- **Vocabulary Builder:** A crossword puzzle for the student to complete, using vocabulary words found in the chapter

The text is written in clear language that engages the student, keeps the reader's interest, and presents information in a variety of styles

OTHER LEARNING AND TEACHING RESOURCES

Supplements

The **Online Learning Center (OLC)** is a Web site that follows the text chapter by chapter. OLC content is ancillary and supplementary germane to the textbook—as students read the book, they can go online to review material or link to relevant Web sites. Students and instructors can access the Web sites for each of the McGraw-Hill paralegal texts from the main page of the Paralegal Super Site. Each OLC has a similar organization. An Information Center features an overview of the text, background on the author, and the Preface and Table of Contents from the book. Instructors can access the instructor's manual and PowerPoint presentations, and Test Bank. Students see the Key Terms list from the text as flashcards, as well as additional quizzes and exercises.

Acknowledgments

Special thanks needs to be given to the reviewers who provided invaluable feedback during the steps to completion of the final draft.

Sally B. Bisson
College of Saint Mary

Elizabeth Eiesland
Western Dakota Technical Institute

Tyiesha Gainey
Tidewater Tech

Victoria Green
Baker College of Allen Park

Vera Peaslee Haus
McIntosh College

Sheila Huber
University of Washington

Angela Masciulli
MTI College

Joy O'Donnell
Pima Community College

Jonathan Politi
Kansas State University

Deborah Walsh
Middlesex Community College

A Guided Tour

McGraw-Hill's Real Estate Law for Paralegals presents students with a clear, easy-to-understand, and exciting text in which they will learn about real property, personal property, and all of the facets inherent in real estate. The text includes a chapter dedicated solely to real estate closings. The students have access to numerous exercises, cases, and hands-on learning assignments (including sample forms) covering topics ranging from "Regulations and Encumbrances" to "Recording Statutes and Examinations." The pedagogy of the book applies three main goals:

- Learning outcomes (critical thinking, vocabulary building, skill development, issues analysis, writing practice).

- Relevance of topics without sacrificing theory (ethical challenges, current law practices, technology application).

- Practical application (real-world exercises, practical advice, portfolio creation).

CHAPTER OBJECTIVES

Upon completion of this chapter, you will be able to:

- Identify the concept of property ownership.
- Understand the difference between real property and personal property.
- Discuss the methods of property ownership.
- Identify the sources of real property law.

Throughout history, property ownership rights and control have been very important. Tribes conquered other tribes for the right to control property. Kings fought with other kings for the right to control property. Countries have gone to war for land. For many people, even the American dream centers on the thought of one day owning their own property. Real property has been and still is a valued commodity in almost all societies. The law of real property involves and regulates almost every aspect of the use and ownership of this commodity. This chapter provides an introduction to the law of real property.

Chapter Objectives

Introduce the concepts students should understand after reading each chapter and provide brief summaries describing the material to be covered.

Spot the Issue

Is a hands-on exercise that presents
students with a fact pattern and
asks them to apply concepts learned
in the chapter to "spot" the issues
present.

SPOT THE ISSUE

Rodney owns a condominium at Main Place Condominiums. Recently, the board has sent notice
that certain regulations have been adopted and added to the rules and regulations of the condominium. These regulations include that an owner cannot have a large dog; trash cans cannot be
kept outside of the individual garage units; guests cannot park on the curbs next to the roadways;
and owners cannot paint the inside of their condominiums the color red. Which regulation would
probably not be within the scope of the board's authority?

Legal Research Maxim

Highlights some of the major
principles in law covered in each
chapter.

LEGAL RESEARCH MAXIM

If the grantee is deceased, the deed is void. Other examples in
which a deed is void may include: a deceased grantor, deceased
heirs of a living person, or a corporation not in existence. However, there are times when a court will reform a deed that would
otherwise be void in order to carry out the grantor's intent. See
*Haney's Chapel United Methodist Church v. United Methodist
Church,* 716 So. 2d 1156 (Ala.1998).

Case Fact Pattern

Describes simple fact patterns and
asks students to apply concepts
learned from the chapter to understand the legal issues at hand.

CASE FACT PATTERN

John and Bob are best friends who both love horses. They
decide to purchase a local ranch and raise horses for sale.
Bob and John want to have an equal interest in the ranch.
They take title to the property as tenants in common, with
each having an equal interest. A few years later, John is
killed in a car accident. John's will indicates that his property
interest in the ranch is to be left to his grown son. Because
John and Bob took title as tenants in common, there exists
no right of survivorship between them.

RESEARCH THIS

Research RESPA to ascertain in more detail what types of transactions are subject to RESPA, as well as who is obligated to perform certain types of duties. How does RESPA protect a consumer financially?

Research This

Gives students the opportunity to investigate issues more thoroughly through hands-on assignments designed to develop critical research skills.

EYE ON ETHICS

It is always important when dealing with real property transactions to check the chain of title carefully in order to ensure that no liens, covenants, or encumbrances are attached to the property of which either party may be unaware. A law office that fails to thoroughly investigate the chain of title could be held liable for malpractice if problems arise from that failure. There are third-party title companies that will, for a fee, examine the chain of title on a property. In addition, the purchase of title insurance helps to provide a source of redress to a party should issues with title be uncovered after the transaction.

Eye on Ethics

Recognizes the importance of bringing ethics to the forefront of paralegal education. It raises ethical issues facing paralegals and attorneys in today's legal environment.

PRACTICE TIP

Whether buying or selling, parties involved in real estate transactions typically employ brokers. Brokers help prospective buyers find a suitable property, help prospective sellers sell their property, and help parties with all the paperwork involved in a real estate transaction. Most states require that an individual take classes and then pass the state's licensing exam in order to become a licensed real estate broker.

Practice Tip

Presents different nuances of the law and caveats to rules to alert student to the intricacies of the law.

Surf's Up

Presents students with numerous and varied Web sites to "surf" and gather additional information on the important legal concepts and issues discussed in each chapter.

SURF'S UP

To learn more about real estate financing, the following Web sites are helpful:
http://www.lendny.com/nymortgagebanker.htm
http://mortgage-x.com.

http://www.fanniemae.com
http://www.ginniemae.gov
http://www.freddiemac.com

You Be the Judge

Places students in the judge's seat. Students are presented with facts from a fictitious case and they use concepts learned from the chapter to make a legal determination.

YOU BE THE JUDGE

Andrew moves into a house next to a college campus, and rents it from the John the landlord for a period of one year, using a written lease. Loud parties with loud music begin to emanate from the Rock 'em Sock 'em fraternity house, located adjacent to the house leased by Andrew. The loud music is heard only on Saturdays and Sundays from 1:00 p.m. until 5:00 p.m. Does Andrew have any grounds to bring a claim against the John for breach of quiet enjoyment? Consider all possibilities in coming to your decision, based on the few facts given.

Chapter Summary

Provides a comprehensive review of the key concepts presented in the chapter.

Summary

The Real Estate Procedures Act (RESPA) is a federal statute that governs all federally guaranteed mortgage loans. RESPA was passed in order to redesign the real estate closing process and protect consumers from the high closing and settlement costs associated with the purchase of property. According to RESPA, all settlement or closing costs must be disclosed to the consumer in advance of the closing. In addition, RESPA eliminates the kickbacks and referral fees that previously plagued the unsuspecting purchasers of real property. RESPA also dictates the maximum amount of funds that may be required to be placed into escrow accounts in order to pay for recurring charges or assessments.

The Truth-in-Lending Act is another act passed by the United States Congress with the intent of protecting the consumer. It protects consumers from inaccurate and unfair billing practices. It also provides for the disclosure of credit terms in a form that is easily read by consumers, so that they can compare the rates from different lenders for a variety of terms.

The Truth-in-Lending Act provides for creditors to make certain disclosures to the consumer or borrower. It affects real estate transactions that are not subject to RESPA. Under the Truth-in-Lending Act, all disclosures must be made prior to the time that the borrower becomes contractually obligated to make payments on the loan.

The Truth-in-Lending Act also provides consumers with the right of rescission. Usually, the right of rescission gives a consumer anywhere from three to five days to change her mind about having contracted for the loan, and allows the borrower to void the transaction without incurring any penalties.

Creditors are required to disclose their interest rates on any loan transaction so that consumers can make informed transactions. The annual percentagerate being assessed on the loan must be disclosed. On some loans the interest rate is set and fixed and does not vary for the life of the loan. For other loans, the interest rate will fluctuate up or down, depending on a predetermined variable to which the interest rate is tied.

Variable interest rates are known as adjustable interest rates and are tied to a particular interest rate index. These rates are usually known as adjustable rate mortgages (ARM). The interest rate index to which these types of loans are tied can be a treasury bill or a prime lending rate. As the index increases or decreases

Key Terms

Caption	Habendum clause	**Key Terms**
Covenant against encumbrances	Indenture	
Covenant for quiet enjoyment	Law of equity	
Covenant of further assurance	Limited warranty deed	
Covenant of warranty	Preamble	
Covenants of title	Quitclaim deed	
Deed	Seal	
Deed poll	Seisin	
Doctrine of merger	Testimonium	
General warranty deed	Void	
Grantee	Voidable	
Grantor		

Used throughout the chapters are defined in the margin and provided as a list at the end of each chapter. A common set of definitions is used consistently across the McGraw-Hill paralegal titles.

Review Questions and Exercises

Review Questions

1. What is the difference between a conventional loan and an insured loan?
2. What is a loan-to-value ratio, and why is it important?
3. What is a VA loan?
4. List six indexes upon which an adjustable-rate mortgage might be based.
5. What is a fixed-rate mortgage?
6. How do a fixed-rate mortgage and an adjustable-rate mortgage differ?
7. What is a construction loan?
8. What is a permanent loan?
9. What is the secondary mortgage market?
10. What is a primary lender?

Emphasize critical thinking and problem-solving skills as they relate to real estate law. The Review Questions focus on more specific legal concepts learned in each chapter. The Exercises introduce hypothetical situations and ask students to determine the correct answers using knowledge gained from studying topics in each chapter.

Portfolio Assignments

PORTFOLIO ASSIGNMENT

The first title insurance company was chartered in 1876. Read and brief *Watson v. Muirhead*, 57 Pa. 161 (1868), the case largely responsible for the development of title insurance.

Ask students to use the skills mastered in each chapter to reflect on major legal issues and create documents that become part of the paralegal's portfolio of legal research. The Portfolio Assignments are useful as both reference tools and as samples of work product.

Vocabulary Builders

Provides a crossword puzzle in each chapter that uses the key terms and definitions from that chapter to help students become more proficient with legal terminology.

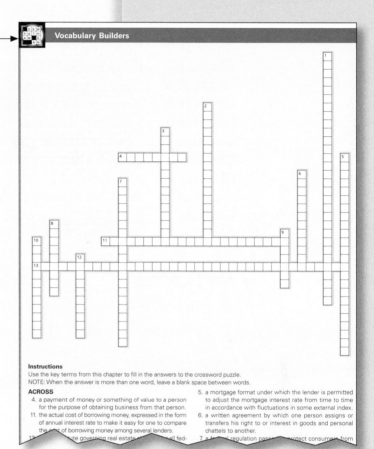

Vocabulary Builders

Instructions
Use the key terms from this chapter to fill in the answers to the crossword puzzle.
NOTE: When the answer is more than one word, leave a blank space between words.

ACROSS
4. a payment of money or something of value to a person for the purpose of obtaining business from that person.
11. the actual cost of borrowing money, expressed in the form of annual interest rate to make it easy for one to compare the cost of borrowing money among several lenders.
13. ~~ute governing real estate~~ ~~all fed-~~

5. a mortgage format under which the lender is permitted to adjust the mortgage interest rate from time to time in accordance with fluctuations in some external index.
6. a written agreement by which one person assigns or transfers his right to or interest in goods and personal chattels to another.
7. ~~a f~~ ~~al regulation pass~~ ~~protect consumers from~~

Case in Point

At the end of each chapter exposes students to real-world examples and issues through a case chosen to expand on key topics discussed in the chapter.

CASE IN POINT

United States District Court,
D. Hawaii.
Samuel Laureano VIERNES and Imelda Legaspi Viernes, Plaintiffs,
v.
EXECUTIVE MORTGAGE, INC; Argent Mortgage Company, LLC; Ameriquest
Mortgage Company; and Lydia Pascual, as an individual, Defendants.
372 F.Supp.2d 576
No. CIV. 04-00212ACKLEK.
Oct. 13, 2004.

BACKGROUND

Mortgagors brought action against mortgage broker, broker's officer, and other defendants, alleging violation of the federal Consumer Credit Protection Act, fraud, intentional infliction of emotional distress, deceptive and unfair trade practices, and breach of fiduciary duty. Mortgage broker defendants moved for summary judgment on federal claim and for **dismissal of state law claims.**
   Holdings: The District Court, Kay, J., held that:
(1) mortgage broker and officer were not "creditors" under Truth-in-Lending Act (TILA) and Regulation Z, and
(2) values of economy, convenience, and fairness all favored court's retention of jurisdiction over state law claims against mortgage broker defendants.
   Summary judgment motion granted; **dismissal motion denied.**
   KAY, District Judge

BACKGROUND

In 2003, Plaintiffs Samuel Laureano Viernes and Imelda Legaspi Viernes sought to refinance the mortgage(s) on their ~~inahu, Haw~~ ~~tiffs used the~~ ~~f De-~~

Plaintiffs filed an Opposition. On October 1, 2004, Defendants filed a Reply to the Opposition. Plaintiffs and Defendants also filed concise statements of fact. On September 24, 2004, Defendants Argent Mortgage and Ameriquest Mortgage filed a statement of no position as to the Motion. A hearing was held on October 12, 2004.
   Defendants Argent Mortgage and Ameriquest Mortgage take "no position" on the motion for summary judgment and dismissal. Argent Mortgage and Ameriquest Mortgage stated at the hearing on October 12, 2004 that they have reached a settlement with Plaintiffs but that Plaintiffs have attempted to repudiate the agreement. These Defendants also stated that they intend to file a motion to enforce the settlement agreement. Should it be determined that there is no settlement, these Defendants have indicated that they will move to assert cross-claims for indemnity and contribution against Executive Mortgage.
   [Text omitted]

DISCUSSION
I. Motion for Summary Judgment on TILA Issues
   The Truth-in-Lending Act ("TILA"), which is contained in Title I of the Consumer Credit Protection Act, as amended (15 U.S.C. § 1601, et seq.), is intended to assure a meaningful disclosure of credit terms so that consumers can compare more readily vari~~ ~~ rms and avoid the~~ ~~rmed use of~~

Brief Contents

Contents

Chapter 1

Introduction to Real Property Law

CHAPTER OBJECTIVES

Upon completion of this chapter, you will be able to:

- Identify the concept of property ownership.

- Understand the difference between real property and personal property.

- Discuss the methods of property ownership.

- Identify the sources of real property law.

Throughout history, property ownership rights and control have been very important. Tribes conquered other tribes for the right to control property. Kings fought with other kings for the right to control property. Countries have gone to war for land. For many people, even the American dream centers on the thought of one day owning their own property. Real property has been and still is a valued commodity in almost all societies. The law of real property involves and regulates almost every aspect of the use and ownership of this commodity. This chapter provides an introduction to the law of real property.

GENERAL ASPECTS OF PROPERTY

The term "**property**" has no real legal meaning. It is an ambiguous term that is used by nonprofessionals to describe a variety of physical items, either tangible or intangible. Ownership describes the relationship between an individual and his property. A right of ownership simply describes a person's right to particular property exclusive of others' rights to the same property. Ownership to property boils down to a person's or an entity's relationship to that property that enables them to control the property with respect to other people or entities. People do not own things; they have a right to possess and control them. The law of property involves a collection of rights of ownership that are typically associated with property. Among those rights is the right to possession. The law associated with real property involves three elements that involve the control of property through ownership. These elements are:

- Exclusivity—the ability to exclude another person from ownership, possession, or use

- Universality—ownership of everything by the state. The state is the origin of all ownership rights.

property
Rights a person may own or be entitled to own, including personal and real property.

1

Right	Effect on Property
Sell	Subject to provisions of an easement or covenant
Mortgage	May have an adverse effect if an easement or covenant causes an inability to obtain maximum financing on favorable terms
Bequeath	Could be subject to the provisions of any easement or covenant
Lease	Enables someone other than the owner to have possession and use of the property for a period of time as defined in the lease
Use and Occupy	Subject to provisions of an easement or covenant
Grade, Fill, or Excavate	Could be prohibited without governmental permission unless minimal effect on property
Install New Permanent Roads or Widen Existing Ones	Often prohibited without governmental permission
Occupy/Use Existing Improvements	Often no restrictions
Construct New Improvements	Major effect if the property has development potential. Governmental permission usually required.
Subdivide and Develop	Sometimes prohibited or may be limited to large tracts, such as 500 acres. Governmental permission usually required.
Farm	Sometimes prohibited, depending on the type and quality of the soil on the property

• Transferability—the ability, recognized by the legal system, to transfer someone's rights in property to someone else

See Figure 1.1 for a description of ownership rights.

All three of these elements associated with ownership rights must be present in a legal system regarding property in order for it to function properly. These elements define the various relationships that exist between people and property. As stated previously, a person is said to hold an interest, or right, in property. The **interest in property** is defined as any right that the law will protect against being violated by others. Interests that are considered inherent in real property are often referred to as a **bundle of rights**. This term emphasizes the fact that property law is not made up of one simple concept of rights, but rather encompasses many rights that the law associates with a person's relationship with property. The law of property concerns a person's ability to possess, transfer, and have access to her property. The theory of a bundle of rights states that ownership of real property embraces a great many rights, such as the right to occupancy; the right to use; the right to sell, bequeath, or transfer; and the right to benefits derived from the occupancy and use of the property. The bundle of rights theory of ownership is often compared to a bundle of sticks. Each stick in the bundle represents a distinct and separate right associated with ownership of the property. These rights may include the rights to use the property, to sell it, to lease it, to enter it, to give it away, and to choose to exercise more than one or none of these rights. Although subject to certain limitations and restrictions, private enjoyment of these rights is guaranteed by law under the United States Constitution.

Two distinct rights that occur throughout the law of property are those of **possession** and **title**. Possession occurs once a person has dominion and control over the property. Title is the formal right of ownership. Title can be held in the name of one person, more than one person, or a legal entity. Title is the legal term that indicates that a person or entity has rights to real property. Most people associate the possession of title as evidence of ownership in real property. Title is typically what the nonprofessional thinks of as ownership.

interest in property
The right that someone may have in specific property.

bundle of rights
The concept of ownership that embraces certain rights of ownership, such as possession, control, use, enjoyment, and disposition.

possession
Having control over a thing with the intent to have and to exercise such control.

title
The right to or ownership in land.

Possession is considered occupation of the land, and that occupation must be demonstrated by visible acts, such as enclosing the property, cultivating crops on the property, constructing structures, and other visible signs of possession. The right of possession is a **right of exclusivity**. The property owner has the right to exclude others from his land.

A landowner also has the right to use her land for profit or pleasure, so long as she does so within the boundaries of the law. An owner of property has the right to dispose of her ownership of the property. The **power of disposition** can occur when the owner sells or leases her property, or it may take place at her death by inheritance or will should she choose to leave her rights in her property to another person or persons as beneficiaries. The law favors the free right to transfer ownership in property. The law will defend the right to transfer ownership in property so long as transfer does not interfere with some important public purpose or private right.

Private property rights are subject to regulation by federal, state, and local governments. These governmental entities have the right to tax, regulate the use of, and take private property for public use.

right of exclusivity
The right to exclude all others from the owner's property.

power of disposition
the ability of an owner to transfer the care and possession of her property to another.

PERSONAL PROPERTY VERSUS REAL PROPERTY

The law recognizes two classifications of property: real and personal. **Real property** relates to land and those things that are more or less permanently attached to the land, such as homes, buildings, and trees. Real property is land, plants growing on the land, and structures that are permanently affixed to the land, as well as mineral deposits that are contained below the land. Real property is not movable. **Personal property** is all property that is not classified as real property. Personal property refers to all other things, such as cars, furniture, stocks, and tools. Personal property is property that is movable. (See Figure 1.2.)

Personal property is property that is movable, transferable, and limited in its duration. It exists independent of its location. Personal property is categorized into two

real property
Land and all property permanently attached to it, such as buildings.

personal property
Movable or intangible thing not attached to real property.

Item	Real Property	Personal Property
Land	YES	
Anything Permanently Affixed to Land		
• Bushes	YES	
• Trees		
• Houses		
• Buildings		
• Mineral deposits		
Movable items		YES
• Lamps		
• Cars		
• Washing machines		
• Stock certificates		
Fixtures	YES	
• May "look" like personal property		
Includes:		
✓ Wallpaper		
✓ Pipes in home		
✓ Central air conditioning	YES	(Air conditioning—window unit) YES
Tangible and Intangible Property		YES

FIGURE 1.2
Differences between Real Property and Personal Property

tangible property
Personal property that can be held or touched, such as furniture or jewelry.

intangible property
Personal property that has no physical presence but is represented by a certificate or some other instrument, such as stocks or trademarks.

gift
Bestowing a benefit without any expectation on the part of the giver to receive something in return and the absence of any obligation on the part of the receiver to do anything in return.

bailment
The delivery of personal property from one person to another to be held temporarily.

fixture
Personal property that has become permanently attached or associated with the real property.

SPOT THE ISSUE

You are going on a trip for a week and you want your dog to be cared for while you are gone. You take the dog to the kennel for it to be cared for in your absence. Is your dog considered property? If so, what type of property? While the dog is in the kennel, what rights to the dog have been transferred to the kennel and by what means has this occurred?

types: tangible and intangible. **Tangible property** can take the form of goods or tangible items of value. Examples of tangible personal property are cars, jewelry, and MP3 players. **Intangible property** is an item that represents something of value. For example, a stock certificate in and of itself may have little value; however, it represents ownership of a share or shares of stock that may be valuable.

Rights to personal property can be transferred. Personal property can be transferred as a **gift** from one person to another. For example, in order to celebrate Martha's graduation from her paralegal program, Martha's grandmother gives her a briefcase. The gift of the briefcase to Martha by her grandmother effectuates a transfer of the property from the grandmother to Martha. A gift of personal property usually transfers possession, ownership, and use of that property. Property can also be transferred by **bailment**. A bailment is the transfer of possession and sometimes the use of a property from one person to another. The laws that govern personal property are expansive and outside the scope of the discussion of this chapter.

Fixtures are items that are attached to the property. While a fixture may resemble personal property, once it is affixed to the land in some manner, it is considered part of the real property. When ownership to the real property is transferred, the fixture is transferred with it. Some of the methods for determining if an item is to be considered a fixture are these:

LEGAL RESEARCH MAXIM

When dealing with issues of real property and the transfer of rights, it is important to determine which items on the property are considered real property and which are personal property. If the determination is not made, items that are someone's personal property may inadvertently be transferred during a real property transaction.

- The way or method that it is attached to the real property. Is the property embedded into the ground, or does it sit on top of the property?
- How the item is adapted without consideration of the real property. For example, an in-ground pool cannot be adapted outside the scope of the property it is attached to. However, an above-ground pool can be moved to and exist outside the real property, so it is considered to be personal property.
- The intent of the person who affixed the property to the land
- The existence of an agreement that determines the nature of the property

CASE FACT PATTERN

John makes furniture for a living. John's tools are an integral part of John's business. John uses a skill saw for making his furniture; it is one of his most important tools. In order to be able to build furniture from his home, John built a workshop in his backyard to house the tools of his trade and to provide a workspace. When building the workshop, John affixed the skill saw to the floor of the workshop with cement so that it would be stable while he worked. Now, John has decided to sell his home and move to another town. What type of property is the skill saw? Will the skill saw be considered personal or real property? Why?

As hinted at above, real property also includes everything beneath the surface of the earth as well as in the air space above the land. An owner of real property typically owns the minerals that exist beneath the surface of the land, such as oil, gas, coal, etc. An owner can also sell the mineral rights separately from the surface of the land, or he can lease them to a company that has the ability to extract them. Usually, the owner will receive royalty payments from the mineral lease. Also, an owner of real property can sell the surface of the land and still maintain the rights to the minerals contained beneath the surface.

The owner of real property also owns the air space above the surface of the land. Air space can be considered a valuable asset if it is located in the center of a city, or it can be valuable because of the views that are seen from the land. Many cities have passed laws that protect an owner's airspace by preventing other owners of real property from planting plants or erecting buildings that might infringe on someone's view from his property.

Trees, plants, and other things that grow in the soil may be considered a part of the real property. Annual crops produced by labor, such as wheat, corn, and soybeans, are considered personal property, as they must be cultivated every year and are not indigenous to the real property. Crops are considered a commodity and are traded on the stock exchange as such. Therefore, they are considered personal property as opposed to real property.

In no jurisdiction can someone own water. A person can own rights to water, but she cannot own the water. A real property owner also has certain rights to water that is located above and below the property. In addition, an owner has certain rights to water that runs through her property. The source of the water determines the rights that a landowner possesses to use that water.

The source of the water dictates to a certain extent what rights an owner of property can claim to the water that is associated with her property. Water is normally categorized into the following areas with the following uses associated with it:

- Groundwater—water that is located beneath the surface of the land. Groundwater can be created by streams that flow underground or by rainwater that collects in pools beneath the surface of the property. An owner of property has the right to utilize groundwater located beneath her property in any way that she chooses, provided that the owner does not cause the groundwater to be diverted so that it harms an adjacent or adjoining property.

- Ocean and lakefront water—water that borders property. Examples are the ocean, lakes, and ponds. An owner of property that borders a body of water has the right to have access to the body of water. The right to access to a body of water that borders property is known as a **littoral right**.

littoral right
Use and enjoyment of water rights concerning properties abutting an ocean, sea, or lake rather than a river or stream.

- Surface water. An owner has the right to use surface water in any manner that she wishes, provided that she does not alter the natural flow of the water or cause damage to another property due to her use. For example, suppose that a landowner's property sits at the base of a hill. When it rains, the runoff of rainwater floods the landowner's barn. The landowner decides to divert the runoff away from her barn. The diversion of the water causes the property below the landowner's property to flood. The landowner is not permitted to divert the water so as to cause her neighbor's property to flood. However, if the landowner decided to reclaim the runoff and use it for watering her gardens, this use would be permitted.

- **Riparian rights**—the right of a property owner to the beneficial use of water from streams, rivers, and natural lakes. These bodies of water are owned by the government and not by individual landowners. However, all owners of properties that adjoin these waterways have equal right to the beneficial use of that water. An

riparian right
The right of every person through whose land a natural watercourse runs to benefit of water as it passes through the person's land, for all useful purposes to which it may be applied.

EYE ON ETHICS

It is very important for paralegals to know their state law as well as the law that governs their jurisdiction. The law governing real property rights is typically mandated by state law. Therefore, if a case involves real property rights such as some of those described above, it is important to thoroughly research your state and local laws in order to determine what rights and duties are provided to owners of real property in that jurisdiction. A legal professional has an ethical duty of competence to research all state and local rules as they pertain to a client's property issue in order to ensure that the client's rights are being adequately represented.

owner does not have the right to interfere with the natural flow of the water. For example, a landowner upstream could not build a dam to collect water thereby diverting the natural flow of the water and thereby deriving more benefit from the use of the water than those property owners that are located downstream.

appropriation
The capture or diversion of water from its natural course or channel and its application to some beneficial use by the appropriator to the exclusion of all other persons.

- **Appropriation**—usually found in the western states where water is scarce, the superior right to use water on the part of the property owner who uses the water first. The date of appropriation establishes a property owner's water rights. The superior right goes to the property owner who utilized the water first. If not enough water exists to serve all of the needs of all of the owners, the first user may use all that he needs while remaining owners may receive only some or none of the remaining water supply. Under appropriation, an owner must show (1) the intent to use the water for a beneficial purpose, (2) the actual diversion of the water from its natural source, and (3) the use of the water for the beneficial purpose within a reasonable amount of time.

RESEARCH THIS

Water rights are typically determined by state law. Research your state's laws and determine what rights a real property owner has with regard to water located on top of, beneath, or running through her property.

METHODS OF ACQUIRING OWNERSHIP TO REAL PROPERTY

There are various methods by which someone can acquire ownership rights to real property. Below is a brief overview of these methods.

Inheritance and Devise

inheritance
The ability to acquire ownership to real property due to a person's kinship to an owner of real property who has died.

intestate
The state of having died without a will.

devise
A disposition of real property by will.

will
A document representing the formal declaration of a person's wishes for the manner and distribution of his or her property upon death.

Inheritance and devise are two methods of ownership transfer that occur at the death of the owner of the property. Inheritance is the passage of title and ownership of real property from the person who dies without a will (**intestate**) to people whom, because of blood or marriage, the law has legally designated as the real property owner's heirs. Each state has its own laws concerning inheritance of real property, and these laws are different from state to state. The law of the state in which the real property is located will govern the transfer of that property between parties.

The acquisition of ownership by **devise** is the passage of title of real property from one who dies with a **will** and designates to whom the property should be left. A will is a legal document that is prepared during the property owner's lifetime that indicates the property owner's intent as to where and how his property is to be disposed of after his death. The will must comply with the state law that governs wills as well as the state law where the real property is located.

Gift

Ownership of real property can be transferred between parties by gift. Once there has been a proper execution and delivery of the deed to the real property and the transfer has been completed, then the gift of the real property is irrevocable. The promise to make a gift of real property is revocable. However, once transfer of the deed to the property has been completed, the process cannot be revoked. A gift is a voluntary transfer to another made gratuitously and without consideration. A promise is not a gift. A promise is a declaration made by one person to another for a good and valuable consideration.

Contract to Sale

Of course, the most common method of property acquisition is through purchase. Property ownership can be obtained by buying the property, and ownership can be transferred by the sale of the property.

Adverse Possession

One of the most coveted real property rights is that of possession, and the law gives substantial protection to this right. In some instances, a person who is not the owner of the property will gain possession of it through unlawful means. If a person obtains possession of a piece of property unlawfully, she is also provided with the right to exclude anyone else from possession of the property except for the true owner of that property. The longer the person continues in unlawful possession of the property, the stronger the presumption is that her possession began lawfully as opposed to unlawfully. If the possession is maintained for a long enough period of time, then the possibility exists that that person who is in unlawful possession of the property will become the legal owner of the property through a process known as **adverse possession**. Adverse possession is a means by which a person may acquire title to property by operation of law. Adverse possession occurs when, after the statute of limitations to bring an action against the unlawful possessor has expired, the title of the real property is considered to be that of the person who is in adverse possession of the property and the original owner loses his ownership to the property.

> **adverse possession**
> The legal taking of another's property by meeting the requirements of the state statute, typically open and continuous use for a period of five to twenty years.

Like most real property laws, those concerning adverse possession vary from state to state. Typically, the person who is the adverse possessor of the property must demonstrate continuous possession of the property for a period of time ranging anywhere from five to twenty years, depending on the state. Most states specify that the possession of the property must be adverse to that of the true owner, which means that the possession exists without the consent or permission of the true owner. Some state laws deem that it is necessary for a person in adverse possession of the property actually to have knowledge that she is in adverse possession of the property. The possession of the property usually must be adverse to that of the true owner; it must be public or out in the open; and it must be continuous, peaceful, exclusive, and uninterrupted.

CASE FACT PATTERN

John is hiking when he comes upon a beautiful valley. On the property, a cabin is situated that appears to have been abandoned for years. John decides that he would like to live on the property. He moves into the cabin and fixes it up. John is aware that he does not own the property and that the cabin belongs to someone else, but he still decides that he is going to live in it. John lives in the cabin continuously for twelve years. The statute of limitations for gaining adverse possession in the state where John resides is ten years. Has John obtained title to the property by adverse possession?

tacking
A term applied especially to the process of establishing title to land by adverse possession, when the present occupant and claimant has not been in possession for the full statutory period, but adds or "tacks" to his own possession that of previous occupants under whom he claims.

quiet title
A proceeding to establish the plaintiff's title to land by bringing into court an adverse claimant and there compelling him either to establish his claim or be forever after estopped from asserting it.

fee simple
An unlimited estate to a person and her heirs and assigns forever, without limitation or condition.

estate
The degree, quantity, nature, and extent of interest that a person has in real and personal property.

conveyance
A transfer.

fee simple determinable
An ownership interest in real property that is created by conveyance containing the words effective to create a fee simple and, in addition, a provision for automatic expiration of the estate upon a stated event.

Multiple periods of possession may be added together or tacked together in order to satisfy the possession requirement of the law. **Tacking** of periods of adverse possession may be allowed if there is evidence of some contractual or blood relationship between the parties that have adverse possession of the property. Tacking is the adding of possession periods by different parties who are in adverse possession of the property. By tacking periods of unlawful possession together for parties who have a contractual or blood relationship, the parties can meet the legal requirements for obtaining title to the property by adverse possession. For example, suppose that John lived in the cabin for eight years. John's son decided that he wanted to live there as well. John's son remains on the property for two more years. By adding the eight years of John's possession with the two years of his son's possession, John and his son meet the requirement to obtain title to the property by adverse possession.

A person in adverse possession of real property will not have any written documentation or written proof of ownership such as a deed. If the person who is in adverse possession of the property wants to sell that property, he may have a difficult time establishing title to that property. The adverse possessor may have to bring an action in the courts known as a **quiet title** action in order to have the courts determine ownership. In an action to quiet title to property, the person in adverse possession of the property essentially has to bring the action against the entire world and challenge anyone out there to come forward and object to the adverse possessor's claim of ownership to the property. Proof of adverse possession will need to be established by affidavits or witnesses as to the time period of the adverse possession of the property, as well as the character and nature of that possession. Was the possession continuous, public, etc.? If the court finds that enough evidence exists to determine that the adverse possessor should be deemed the owner of the property, then the court will issue a judgment stating that the adverse possessor is legally the owner of the property. The judgment issued by the court determining that the adverse possessor is the legal owner of the property can be used in the future to evidence ownership for purposes of the future sale or transfer of the property.

Fee Simple

If you do not want your ownership of real property to be questioned, then you should have an interest in real property that is considered to be in **fee simple**. Fee simple is the ultimate kind of estate or ownership right that an owner can have in real property. Fee simple is also sometimes known as fee simple absolute. Fee simple is a right in real property in which the owner is entitled to the entire **estate**, along with all of the rights thereto. The right to the property encompasses the unconditional powers of disposition of the property during the owner's lifetime as well as after the death of the owner. Fee simple is the ultimate in legal ownership to a property. It is the entire "bundle of rights." The owner keeps all of the sticks in this bundle of rights. Fee simple exists for a potentially infinite period of time. The law presumes that a fee simple estate is created every time that a **conveyance** of the property occurs, unless a lesser estate is mentioned in the conveyance of the property and limits the extent of the estate. Most homes and commercial properties are purchased and owned in a fee simple estate.

Fee Simple Determinable

A **fee simple determinable** is an ownership interest in real property that is limited so that it automatically expires when an event occurs that is stipulated in the deed of the conveyance of the property or in the will that conveys the property. The estate granted in fee simple determinable is similar to an estate in fee simple. An estate in fee simple determinable can be inherited and can last forever, so long as the condition stated in the conveyance is not broken. In simple terms, an estate in fee simple determinable has a condition attached to the conveyance of the property. For example, suppose that Mark conveys a piece of property to Peter with a condition stated in the deed that Peter can have title to the property only if he builds a public park on the land. If Peter builds a house, then the condition is broken, and title to the land could possibly revert back to Mark as a result of the broken condition.

Fee Simple on Condition Subsequent

A **fee simple on condition subsequent** is created when an estate in fee simple is subject to the power of the person who conveyed the estate to recover the conveyed estate on the occurrence of a specific event. However, if the breach of the condition occurs, that does not automatically cause a termination of the fee simple on condition subsequent estate. For example, if Patrick transfers his property to Dana on the condition that it is not used for commercial purposes and then Dana uses the property for commercial purposes, then Patrick has the right to reenter and possess the land due to the breach by Dana of the condition subsequent of not using the property for commercial purposes. The major difference between the fee simple determinable and the fee simple on condition subsequent is that the fee simple determinable automatically expires upon the violation of the specific condition contained in the document that created the estate. In contrast, the fee simple on condition subsequent continues until the estate is terminated by the actions of the **grantor**. Upon termination of the fee simple on condition subsequent, the grantor has the right to reenter the property. At that time, the grantor may transfer the property to another person if she wants to.

Creation of a fee simple determinable or a fee simple on condition subsequent gives the landowner the means of controlling the use of the property after he transfers it to someone else or after her death. If the condition is broken after the grantor's death, sometimes her heirs can reenter the property as a result of the broken condition.

Life Estate

A **life estate** is one that is granted and measured by the life or lives of one or more persons. An estate for life may be for either the life of the owner of the property or the life of some other person or people. The person (or persons) whose life is used as the determinable factor is called the **measuring life**. A life estate can be created by a deed, a will, or an agreement between the parties. At the time of the creation of a life estate, the owner retains or creates either a **reversion** or a **remainder interest**. (See Figure 1.3.)

A reversion exists when the owner grants a life estate to another person, with the condition that the possession of the property will revert, or return, to the owner upon the death of the person who has the life estate.

The owner of the property may grant a life estate to one person and the right of ownership to another person upon the expiration of the life estate. That means that once the person who has the life estate dies, the property will then go to a third person. This is known as a remainder interest. The owner of a life estate is entitled to

fee simple on condition subsequent
A type of transfer in which the grantor conveys fee simple on condition that something be done or not done to the property after the conveyance.

grantor
The person transferring the property.

life estate
An ownership interest in property for a designated period of time, based on the life of another person.

measuring life
Person whose life determines duration of the life estate.

reversion
A future interest under which a grantor retains a present right to a future interest in property that the grantor conveys to another.

remainder interest
The property that passes to a beneficiary after the expiration of an intervening income interest.

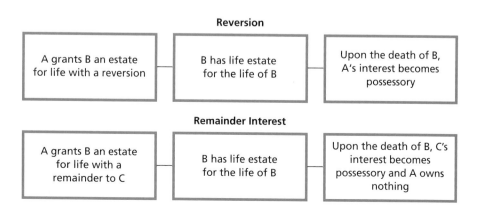

Reversion

| A grants B an estate for life with a reversion | B has life estate for the life of B | Upon the death of B, A's interest becomes possessory |

Remainder Interest

| A grants B an estate for life with a remainder to C | B has life estate for the life of B | Upon the death of B, C's interest becomes possessory and A owns nothing |

FIGURE 1.3
Difference Between Reversion and Remainder Property Interests

the full use and enjoyment of the real property so long as he exercises ordinary care and prudence for the preservation and protection of the property. He must not intend to cause permanent injury to the person who is to be the owner of the real property once the life estate terminates. If the person who has the life estate does not take care of the property, then the life estate owner will be deemed to have committed **waste**. At that point, the life estate terminates, even if the measuring life is still alive. Failure to make needed repairs or improvements on the property may be considered to be acts of waste. There are three kinds of waste under the law:

waste
Deterioration of the property.

1. Voluntary waste is any structural change made to the property that intentionally or negligently causes harm to or depletes the resources of the property unless this depletion is a continuation of some preexisting use for a particular resource, if the land has already been used for that purpose. For example, a mine cannot be placed on the property in order to deplete the property of its mineral resources as that would constitute waste. However, if a mine already existed on the property, the current tenant can continue the use of the mine.

2. Permissive waste is the failure to physically or financially maintain the estate. This includes the failure to make ordinary repairs, pay taxes, or pay interest on the mortgage.

3. Ameliorative waste is an improvement to the estate that changes its character, even if the change actually increases its value. For example, if the tenant tears down a residence and replaces it with a shopping center, the owner can sue the tenant for the cost of restoring the property to its original condition even if the shopping center is of greater value. In the United States, damages for ameliorative waste are not generally awarded. The theory behind this policy is to encourage improvements and economic development.

As a general rule, the person who possesses the life estate is entitled to all income generated from the real property. She is also entitled to possession of the real property during the ownership of the life estate. Life estates are transferable. The owner of the life estate can transfer only that life estate that is subject to the duration of the measuring life. A life estate owner typically has to pay property taxes on the property during the life estate as well as keep the property insured against loss. In addition, the life estate owner must pay any debts secured by the real property.

Estate for Years

estate for years
A type of estate less than a freehold estate, where a person has an interest in land and tenements, and a possession thereof, by virtue of such interest, for some fixed and determinate period of time

An **estate for years** is an estate granted for a fixed period of time. The estate for years continues until the time period for the ownership expires. An estate for years is the second most common form of property ownership, next to the fee simple. An estate for years may be evidenced by a lease. However, many leases are not estates for years. For a lease to be considered to be an estate for years, the lease must clearly state that the ownership to the real property is being conveyed and not just the rights to possession.

YOU BE THE JUDGE

Molly is the mother of Buddy and Frank. Her husband has recently died, and Molly has no place to live. Buddy and Frank own a small house in a neighboring township that they have bought for investment and have been renting to tenants. The tenants moved out shortly before their dad's death. Buddy and Frank have not yet found new tenants for the property. Buddy and Frank now decide that they want to have their mom, Molly, live in the property for the rest of her life. Buddy and Frank grant Molly a life estate in the small house using her own life as the measuring life. After Molly's death, the property will return to Buddy and Frank. Describe the various property interests of Molly, Buddy, and Frank.

Estate at Will

An **estate at will** is an estate that is created by the express or implied agreements of the parties with no fixed term designated. An estate at will can be terminated at any time by either party. An estate at will can also be created by implication. For example, at the expiration of the period of the estate, the possessor of the estate continues to pay rent. If the owner continues to accept the rent of the possessor, the implication is that the estate at will continues.

estate at will
A type of estate less than a freehold estate, where land and tenements are let by one person to another, to have and to hold at the will of the lessor.

SOURCES OF REAL PROPERTY LAW

Much of the law of property has been developed over time from early Anglo-Saxon times. The basis of most of the laws concerning property are found in common law. However, many laws of real property are also found in case law and statutes. The primary source of real property law is case law. The appellate courts of individual states decide issues concerning property law, and those decisions become law in that state. Decisions can vary from one state court to another state court. In addition to case law, states can enact statutes that govern issues concerning real property ownership and rights. Real property rights and ownership are highly regulated by state statutes. State statutes also vary from state to state. If you are going to do work in the area of real property, it is necessary to be familiar with your state's laws regarding real property. The laws in effect in the place where the real property is located are usually the laws that govern the real property issues.

Another source of real property law is the *Second Restatement of Property,* which contains information concerning case law, statutes and other real property legal information. It is a compilation of common law that applies to real property. The *Second Restatement of Property* is not law. It is only a secondary authority that can be reviewed for information and explanation of a real property issue. It should not be cited as a primary source of law. This does not diminish the enormous value that this source provides, but it is not considered the law.

In 1677, the statute of frauds was enacted into English law. The purpose of the statute of frauds was to prevent fraudulent practices in transactions concerning real property. The statute of frauds has been adopted in almost every state and provides that certain real property contracts will not be enforceable unless they are in writing. This is what distinguishes real property contracts from many other forms of contracts not requiring a writing to prove validity. A number of other forms of contracts abide by the statute of frauds as well, including: marriage, certain guaranty loans, and bankruptcy.

PRACTICE TIP

Paralegals are used by law firms, corporations, and governmental agencies in various areas of real property law. Typical activities of a paralegal working in the area of real property can include preparing legal documents, conducting title searches, preparing land descriptions, reviewing leases, and meeting with clients. Real property issues cross over into other areas of law as well, such as family law, wills and trusts, and torts. It is important for an aspiring paralegal to become familiar with real property law concepts and to network within the community.

RESEARCH THIS

Research the law in your state. Determine if your state has adopted the statute of frauds. If so, write down the types of real property contracts that must be in writing to be enforceable under the statute of frauds in your state. Also, research and write down the citation to your state's statute of frauds.

SURF'S UP

The Internet provides a wealth of information on real property issues. Perhaps one of the more interesting Web sites is that of DIRT. DIRT is an e-mail legal discussion group for real estate professionals. DIRT can be located at www.dirt.unkc.edu. Interesting real estate cases are posted almost daily for discussion among the hundreds of real estate lawyers who are members of the group. Look at the daily postings on the site in order to learn what one thousand real estate professionals believe are important real property topics.

PRACTICE TIP

When dealing with real property transactions, it is important to identify the property in question correctly. The description should be able to specify boundaries to the land and distinguish the land from other parcels of land. Every state has set up a system of legal property descriptions. Legal property descriptions are the correct and specific descriptions established by the local government that enable property to be properly identified in legal documents and that ensure that the document is enforceable. Legal descriptions usually describe property in terms of metes and bounds or lot numbers of a recorded plat. These descriptions provide a method by which the property can be properly identified.

Summary

The term "property" has no real legal meaning. It is an ambiguous term that is used by nonprofessionals to describe a variety of physical items, either tangible or intangible. Ownership describes the relationship between an individual and his property. People do not own things; they have a right to possess them. The law of property involves a collection of rights associated with property. Among those rights is the right to possession. The law associated with real property involves three elements: (1) exclusivity—the ability to exclude another person from ownership, possession or use; (2) universality—ownership of everything by the state, so that the state is the origin of all ownership rights; (3) transferability—the ability, recognized by the legal system, to transfer someone's rights in property to someone else.

Two distinct rights that occur throughout the law of property are those of possession and title. Possession exists when a person has dominion and control over the property. Title is typically what the nonprofessional thinks of as ownership. Title is the formal right of ownership. Title can be held in the name of one person, more than one person, or a legal entity.

The law recognizes two classifications of property: real and personal. Real property relates to land and those things that are more or less permanently attached to the land, such as homes, buildings, and trees. Real property is land, plants growing on the land, structures that are permanently affixed to the land, and mineral deposits that are contained below the land. Fixtures are items that are attached to the property. Real property is not movable. Personal property is all property that is not classified as real property. Personal property refers to all other things, such as cars, furniture, stocks, and tools. Personal property is property that is movable.

Inheritance and devise are two methods of ownership transfer that occur at the death of the owner of the property. Inheritance is the passage of title and ownership of real property from the person who dies without a will (intestate) to people whom, because of blood or marriage, the law has legally designated as the real property owner's heirs. Each state has its own laws concerning inheritance of real property, and these laws are different from state to state. The law of the state in which the real property is located will govern the transfer of that property between parties.

Ownership of real property can be transferred between parties by gift. Once there has been a proper execution and delivery of the deed to the real property and the transfer has been completed, then the gift of the real property is irrevocable. The promise to make a gift of real property is revocable. However, once the deed to the property has been properly executed and delivered and the transfer has been completed, the process cannot be revoked.

The most common method of property acquisition is through purchase. Property ownership can be obtained by the purchase of the property, and ownership can be transferred by the sale of the property.

One of the most coveted real property rights is that of possession, and the law gives substantial protection to this right. If a person obtains possession of a piece of property unlawfully, she is also provided with the right to exclude anyone else from possession except for the true owner of that real property. The longer the person continues in possession of the property, the stronger the presumption is that her possession began lawfully as opposed to unlawfully. If the possession is maintained for a long enough period of time, then the possibility exists that that person who is in possession of the property will become the legal owner of the property through a process known as adverse possession. Adverse possession occurs when, after the statute of limitations to bring an action against the possessor has expired, the title of the real property is considered to be that of the person who is in adverse possession of the property.

Tacking is the adding of possession periods by different parties who are in adverse possession of the property. Tacking of periods of possession may be allowed if there is evidence of some contractual or blood relationship between the two parties that have adverse possession of the property.

Fee simple is the ultimate kind of estate or ownership right that an owner can have in real property. Fee simple is also sometimes known as fee simple absolute. Fee simple is a right in real property in which the owner is entitled to the entire estate along with all of the rights thereto. The right to the property encompasses the unconditional powers of disposition of the property during the owner's lifetime as well as after the death of the owner. Fee simple is the ultimate in legal ownership to a property. It is the entire "bundle of rights." Fee simple exists for a potentially infinite period of time. The law presumes that a fee simple estate is created every time that a conveyance of the property occurs unless a lesser estate is mentioned in the conveyance of the property and limits the extent of the estate.

A fee simple determinable is an ownership interest in real property that is limited so that it automatically expires when an event that is stated in the deed of the conveyance of the property or in the will does or does not occur. An estate granted in fee simple determinable is similar to an estate in fee simple. An estate in fee simple determinable can be inherited and can last forever so long as the condition stated in the conveyance is not broken. In simple terms, an estate in fee simple determinable has a condition attached to the conveyance of the property.

A fee simple on condition subsequent is created when an estate in fee simple is subject to the power of the person who conveyed the estate to recover the conveyed estate on the occurrence of a specific event. However, if the breach of the condition occurs, that does not automatically cause a termination of the fee simple on condition subsequent estate.

A life estate is one that is granted and measured by the life or lives of one or more persons. An estate for life may be for either the life of the owner of the property or the life of some other person or people. The person (or persons) whose life is used as the determinable factor is called the measuring life. A life estate can be created by a deed, a will, or an agreement between the parties. At the time of the creation of a life estate, the owner retains or creates a reversion or a remainder interest.

An estate for years is an estate granted for a fixed period of time. The estate for years continues until the time period for the ownership expires. An estate for years is the second most common form of property ownership next to the fee simple. An estate for years may be evidenced by a lease. However, many leases are not estates for years. For a lease to be considered an estate for years, the lease must clearly state that the ownership to the real property is being conveyed and not just the rights to possession.

An estate at will is an estate that is created by the express or implied agreements of the parties with no fixed term designated. An estate at will can be terminated at any time by either party. An estate at will can also be created by implication.

Key Terms

Adverse possession
Appropriation
Bailment
Bundle of rights
Conveyance
Devise
Estate
Estate at will
Estate for years
Fee simple
Fee simple determinable
Fee simple on condition subsequent
Fixture
Gift
Grantor
Inheritance
Intangible property
Interest in property
Intestate

Life estate
Littoral right
Measuring life
Personal property
Possession
Power of disposition
Property
Quiet title
Real property
Remainder interest
Reversion
Right of exclusivity
Riparian Right
Tacking
Tangible property
Title
Waste
Will

Review Questions

1. What is the difference between real property and personal property?
2. Why can't someone own property?
3. Can someone maintain mineral rights to property that he has sold? If so, how?
4. What is a fixture?
5. What is the difference between a fee simple determinable and a fee simple on condition subsequent?
6. Why is a fee simple the best estate to have?
7. What is an estate at will?
8. What is an estate for years?
9. What is a life estate?
10. What is a measuring life?
11. How is waste applicable to a life estate?
12. What is a devise?
13. What is a grantor?
14. How can a possessor of property obtain ownership if she is not legally the owner?
15. What is an action for quiet title?

Exercises

1. Locate your state's codes concerning real property. Look up the codes for life estates and write down the code and section that pertain to the measuring life. What are the factors to consider in your state in determining the measuring life?
2. Looking at your state codes, determine the requirements in order for someone to obtain title to property under a theory of adverse possession. Be sure to include the time period necessary as well as what the nature and character of the possession must be in order to perfect title under adverse possession.

3. Using whatever sources are available to you, locate a case that has to do with the quieting of title under a theory of adverse possession. Brief the case and be prepared to present it to the class. What did the court rule and why?

4. "Was a fixture *always* a fixture," asked Shakespeare. Was it? Explain.

5. In America, do you really ultimately own your private property, even with a deed? Why or why not? Explain.

6. What is the Statute of Frauds? What part in real property transactions does it play and why?

7. Many states are common property states for married individuals. How does this fit into owning real estate and survivorship?

8. Using your own address, whether a house or an apartment in a building, research the title and see who officially owns the piece of property where you live.

PORTFOLIO ASSIGNMENT

As a paralegal in a law firm, you will be responsible for gathering information from clients regarding their real property matters. For this assignment, you are to compose a letter to Mrs. Doris White with the purpose of obtaining information from her regarding her property and her desire to transfer her interests therein. In the letter, include a brief description of the difference between personal and real property, and ask her to identify both of these types of property that are located on her property. Also, provide a description of a fixture and ask her to identify any fixtures. Finally, describe the different types of ownership of property and ask her how she would like to transfer her interests in her property.

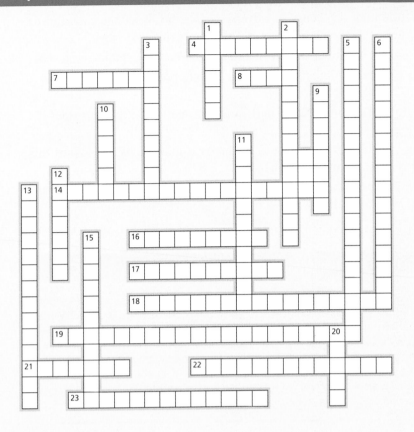

Instructions

Use the key terms from this chapter to fill in the answers to the crossword puzzle.

NOTE: When the answer is more than one word, leave a blank space between the words.

ACROSS

4. A future interest under which a grantor retains a present right to a future interest in property that the grantor conveys to another.
7. An article in the nature of personal property that has been so annexed to the reality that it is regarded as a part of the real property.
8. A voluntary transfer of property to another made gratuitously and without consideration.
14. A method of acquisition of title to real property by possession for a statutory period under certain conditions.
16. Without a will at the time of death.
17. The transfer of title to land from one person, or class of persons, to another by deed.
18. Property that has physical form and substance and can be seen and touched
19. The right that someone may have in specific property.
21. The person by whom a grant is made
22. The capture or diversion of water from its natural course or channel and its application to some beneficial use by the appropriator to the exclusion of all other persons
23. Land, and generally whatever is erected or growing upon or affixed to the land.

DOWN

1. The conveyance of real property by means of a last will and testament.
2. Use and enjoyment of water rights concerning properties abutting an ocean, sea or lake rather than a river or stream.
3. An unlimited estate to a person and his or her heirs and assigns forever without limitation or condition.
5. Property that has no intrinsic and marketable value, but is merely the representative or evidence of value.
6. In a broad and general sense, everything that is the subject of ownership, not coming under the denomination of real estate.
9. A delivery of goods or personal property, by one person (bailor) to another (bailee), in trust until such time that it is returned to the bailor.
10. The degree, quantity, nature, and extent of interest which a person has in real and personal property.
11. The ability to acquire ownership to real property due to a person's kinship to an owner of real property who has died.
12. The term is applied especially to the process of establishing title to land by adverse possession, when the present occupant and claimant has not been in possession for the full statutory period, but adds or "tacks" to his own possession that of previous occupants under whom he claims.
13. The right which every person through whose land a natural watercourse runs has to benefit of water as it passes through her land for all useful purposes to which it may be applied.
15. A proceeding to establish the plaintiff's title to land by bringing into court an adverse claimant and there compelling him either to establish his claim or be forever after estopped from asserting it.
20. The right to or ownership in land

LITTORAL RIGHTS START AT MEAN HIGH WATERMARK

Watts v. Lawrence, 690 So. 2d 1162 (Miss. 1997).

OVERVIEW

The Mississippi Supreme Court recently ruled that waterfront property owners may build certain structures, such as piers and boathouses, subject only to the regulation of the Bureau of Marine Resources (BMR). In doing so, the court held that a waterfront property owner's littoral rights (interests concerning the ocean, sea or lake abutting property) are measured from the mean high watermark. In affirming the greater part of a chancery court decision, the Mississippi Supreme Court rejected the chancery court's attempt to define a littoral property line between neighboring waterfront lots.

BACKGROUND

Defendants David and Deborah Lawrence owned waterfront property adjacent to the Back Bay of Biloxi in Harrison County, Mississippi. They applied for and received a BMR permit to build a pier and a boathouse adjacent to their shoreline. The construction plans included motorized hoists to lift and lower a boat and placed the boathouse more than fifteen feet beyond the high watermark. After driving the pilings but before completion of the boathouse, adjoining property owner James Watts objected to the construction of the boathouse. Watts contended that the Lawrences did not own property possessing littoral rights and as a result were not entitled to build any structure over the water beyond the lot line.

To protest the construction of the boathouse, Watts filed suit against the Lawrences in the Harrison Court Chancery Court seeking a permanent injunction. The chancellor determined that the Lawrence property possessed littoral rights and denied the injunction. In so ruling, the chancellor drew a demarcation line between the littoral property of the parties.

Watts appealed the denial of the injunction. The Lawrences cross-appealed on the decision to establish a line of demarcation.

LITTORAL RIGHTS CLAIM

The Mississippi Code states in pertinent part:
[t]he sole right of . . . erecting bathhouses and other structures in front of any land bordering on the Gulf of Mexico or Mississippi Sound or waters tributary thereto belongs to the riparian owner and extends not more than seven hundred fifty (750) yards from the shore, measuring from the average low water mark.[1]

Under this provision, Watts argued that riparian or littoral rights begin at the "average low water mark." Watts contended that since the land records showed no part of the Lawrence property touching water at the average low water mark, no littoral rights existed.[2] As a result, Watts argued that the Lawrences were not entitled to build any structure over the water. The Lawrences countered that littoral rights begin at the average high water mark, and since the southern boundary of their property touched water at high tide, the land possessed littoral rights. Furthermore, the Lawrences argued that the chancery court's establishment of a littoral property line was inappropriate. In their ruling, the Mississippi Supreme Court noted that Watts's claim that the Lawrence property did not enjoy littoral rights was not supported by case law and was based on a "misguided" interpretation of § 49-15-9.[3]

The high court held that § 49-15-9 did not establish a test for determining whether littoral rights exist but only concerned the extent of such rights once established. The court relied on the case of *Cinque Bambini Partnership v. State,* 491 So. 2d 508, 516-517 (Miss. 1986), in which it held that the state owns the property between the mean low watermark and the mean high watermark in trust for all citizens. The court built on *Cinque Bambini* and ruled for that any property adjacent to the mean high water line, not mean low water, possesses littoral rights.[4] Because the Lawrence property was adjacent to the mean high water line, the court affirmed the determination that the Lawrences had littoral rights.

Having ruled that littoral rights existed, the court turned to the issue of the nature and extent of those rights. The relevant statute (Miss. Code Ann. § 49-15-9) allows, among other things, the building of structures, such as piers and boathouses over the water. However, the statute subjects any such development to the regulation of the Bureau of Marine Resources based on the fact that littoral rights are merely licenses to use property granted by the State and not full-fledged property rights.[5] The Mississippi Supreme Court allowed the Lawrences to continue the construction of the boathouse, because the BMR approved the project via issuance of a permit. In doing so, the Mississippi Supreme Court affirmed the chancery court's denial of the permanent injunction.

LITTORAL PROPERTY LINES

In it effort to resolve the dispute between the neighboring waterfront property owners, the chancery court had established a littoral property line, or line of demarcation, between the litigants' respective water areas.[6] The Mississippi Supreme Court found the lower court's establishment of a demarcation line between the parties' littoral property unnecessary and improper given the BMR's regulatory authority. Since the BMR, through its permit issuance, deemed the boathouse properly placed, a littoral property line was not needed. Accordingly, the Mississippi Supreme Court struck down the chancellor's demarcation line .

Source: *Watts,* 690 So. 2d at 1163. Reprinted with permission of Westlaw.

Chapter 2

Concurrent Ownership

CHAPTER OBJECTIVES

Upon completion of this chapter, you will be able to:

- Identify the requirements for joint tenancy.
- Understand tenancy in common.
- Explain tenancy by the entirety.
- Discuss the role of property under a community property theory.
- Understand the rights and duties of co-owners.

Property may be owned by one person or a group of people. When one person owns the real property, he has the sole right to possession, use, and transfer of the property. He is responsible for all expenses and liabilities associated with the rights of ownership. However, when more than one person owns the same piece of real property, questions arise as to how possession, use, and transfer can occur with more than one person's interest at stake. Also, a question arises as to who is responsible for debts and liabilities. If one person alone holds title to real property, it is called **tenancy in severalty**. Tenancy comes from the French word *tenir*, which means "to hold." A person who holds title in tenancy in severalty holds title alone, with no one else. In contrast, if title is held by more than one person at a time, then this type of ownership is referred to as **concurrent ownership**. This chapter will focus on the various types of concurrent ownership and how these types of ownership deal with the rights and obligations of owning real property.

Most jurisdictions in the United States recognize five types of concurrent ownership. These are

- Joint tenancy
- Tenancy in common
- Tenancy by the entirety
- Community property
- Tenancy in partnership

JOINT TENANCY

Joint tenancy exists when two or more persons own a single, unified interest in a particular piece of real property. Joint tenancy is a form of concurrent ownership that is recognized in most states. Each owner has the right to use, occupy, and possess the

tenancy in severalty
The holding of land and tenements in one person's own right only, without any other person being joined or connected with him in point of interest during his estate therein.

concurrent ownership
More than one individual shares the rights of ownership.

joint tenancy
The shared ownership of property, giving the other owner the right of survivorship if one owner dies.

entire parcel of real property. The right to use or possess the property is held in common with the other joint owners of the property. Under a joint tenancy, each joint owner of the property owns an equal and undivided interest in the whole of the property. No one owner has any rights or interests that are greater than those of any other joint owner. Each owner has the same rights to the property.

One of the most noteworthy characteristics of a joint tenancy is that each joint tenant possesses a **right of survivorship**. The right of survivorship means that if one of the joint tenants (owners) dies, the real property that has been owned jointly by all of them is passed on to the other surviving joint owners. This process will continue until there is a sole survivor from among the original joint tenants; that survivor will then own the entire real property in severalty. For example, three brothers, Matt, Jake, and Todd, decide to buy a piece of property for an investment. After they have owned it for a couple of years, Matt is killed in a motorcycle accident. Because the property was held in joint tenancy with right of survivorship between the brothers, Matt's interest in the property is then absorbed by Jake and Todd. Jake and Todd now own the property jointly. The joint tenancy survives the death of Matt and continues into the future. Suppose that Jake passes away several years later due to cancer. Todd will now be the sole owner in severalty, as all other joint tenants have not survived.

The person who dies does not have the ability to leave her interest in the property to an heir, and her interest does not pass to any heirs via intestacy. Because of the right of survivorship, the interest of the **decedent** passes to the other joint tenants.

A joint tenancy can be created by a deed or a will. When the real property is transferred to two or more persons, the deed will state with express language that they are to take the real property as "joint tenants with the right of survivorship The existence of the interests of more than one person being considered as a single ownership unit rather than as separate interests or individual units is the crux of joint tenancy with the right of survivorship. Under common law requirements, a joint tenancy exists only if four elements are present. These four elements are

- Interest
- Title
- Time
- Possession

Again, all four unities must be present for the creation of a joint tenancy with right of survivorship. Each owner's interest must be identical to that of the other owners, no more and no less. The unity of interest means that each joint tenant must have an identical interest in the property that they share. For example, one joint tenant cannot have a one-quarter interest in the property while the other joint tenant has a three-quarters interest. The interests must be the same and equal. Unity of title means that each ownership interest must stem from the same conveyance of the real property. Each joint tenant must have acquired title by the same deed or will. Unity of **time** means that each ownership interest must have commenced and vested at the same time. Finally, unity of possession means that each joint tenant has a right to possess and enjoy the entire property and each holds the same undivided possession as the others. If any of the four "unities" is not present in a conveyance, the real property interest is not a joint tenancy with right of survivorship, but will be considered a tenancy in common.

A joint tenancy with right of survivorship can be severed. A **severance** of the joint tenancy means that the survivorship component is destroyed. Severance of the joint tenancy typically creates a tenancy in common. There are a number of manners in which a joint tenancy can be severed. For example, if one joint tenant decides to sell

right of survivorship
The right of a surviving joint tenant to take ownership of a deceased joint tenant's share of the property.

decedent
the person who has died.

time
A point in or space of duration at or during which some fact is alleged to have been committed.

severance
The converting of a joint tenancy to a tenancy in common.

partition
The dividing of lands held by joint tenants or tenants in common.

mortgage
An interest in land created by a written instrument providing security for the performance of a duty or the payment of a debt.

tenancy in common
A form of ownership between two or more people where each owner's interest upon death goes to his or her heirs.

testamentary
Pertaining to a will or testament.

PRACTICE TIP

It is important to always distinguish tenancy in common with the terms "common law" or "community property." Each has its own unique characteristics. To recap, tenancy in common is a form of real property ownership. Common law can refer to our case precedent system and also to some of the eastern and southern states, regarding marriage arrangements, not by license, but rather by living together for a statutory time period. Community property refers to a married couple and what each brought into the marriage and property which they acquired together during the marriage.

her interest in the real property, the sale will create a severance of the joint tenancy. If a joint tenant decides to convey his interest in the property to a third person, the joint tenancy will be severed. However, suppose that three joint tenants own a particular piece of property. One of the joint tenants decides to convey her interest to someone else. At that point, the joint tenancy between the remaining two joint tenants will continue, but a tenancy in common will be created between the stranger and the joint tenants. Also, suppose Matt, Bob, and John hold a piece of property as a joint tenancy. Matt decides that he does not want an interest in the property any longer. Matt conveys his interest to Bob. Bob and John remain joint tenants in the property. However, the interest that Matt conveyed to Bob will be held as a tenancy in common with the joint tenancy just as if Bob were a stranger. Think of it as a pie that is divided into three sections. Two-thirds of the pie will remain intact, and the other one-third will be its own slice. Joint tenants can also agree to sever the joint tenancy but remain owners of the property. Property held in joint tenancy can easily be severed in many states.

The common owners, such as joint tenants, may decide to divide the property into separate ownership interests. This process is called **partition**. The process of partitioning may take place by agreement of the common owners or by court action brought by one of the owners. When the common owners agree to partition, separate tracts of the property are usually allocated to each of the owners. Partitioning can also occur through the exchange of deeds executed by all of the common owners.

A lawsuit to partition a particular piece of property can be brought in the court by any of the common owners of that real property. The court will typically divide the property into separate parcels that have a market value equal to each owner's undivided interest in the whole property. If the property is not capable of being divided or the common owners choose not to have the property divided, then the court may order that the property be sold and the proceeds split among the common owners.

In some states, the granting of a mortgage to one joint tenant in which the property is used as collateral can sever the joint tenancy. Typically, this occurs when a particular state views a granting of a **mortgage** as a change in title rather than just a lien on the property. States are also not in agreement as to whether or not the granting of a lease on the property will sever the joint tenancy. Many courts hold that it does not.

TENANCY IN COMMON

A **tenancy in common**, like a joint tenancy, is a form of property ownership in which two or more persons own the same piece of real property. Each tenant in common possesses a separate undivided interest in the real property. Joint tenants take property as a unit, but tenants in common take ownership interests individually. One of the major differences between a joint tenancy and a tenancy in common is that the tenancy in common does not have the right of survivorship. Each tenant in common takes his interest in the property as an individual separate and apart from the other common owners. Since there is no right of survivorship, a tenant in common is allowed to transfer his interest in the real property by **testamentary** instrument. If the tenant in common dies intestate, then his interest will pass under state statute to his descendants. A tenant in common also can convey or lease his undivided interest in a parcel of real property to a third party.

Descendant persons are in the blood stream of the ancestor. A tenancy in common requires only one unity in order to be formed: the unity of possession. Each tenant in common is entitled to possess the whole of the property. However, the tenants may receive their interests at different times, through different instruments. A tenancy in common may be created by deed, lease, devise, or bequest, or by intestacy.

TENANCY BY THE ENTIRETY

In common law, a husband and wife are considered as one person. The concept of owner property under tenancy by the entirety identifies that the assets of a married couple are unified and become the property of both through marriage. Under the concept of **tenancy by the entirety**, a married couple is treated as a single person, and the couple owns the property as a single unit. Tenancy by the entirety is created at the time that the married couple takes title to the property. It cannot be created if one person owns property and then is later married. So long as the couple remains married, the property cannot be sold or mortgaged unless the spouses do so together. A divorce will convert a tenancy by the entirety into a tenancy in common. After the divorce, each party will own a half interest in the real property. In order for a tenancy by the entirety to be formed, the same four unities that are required for a joint tenancy must be present. Again, those unities are interest, title, time, and possession. For example, Paul and Samantha have been married for four years. They decide that they are going to buy their first house. They find a house for sale that is owned by John. Paul and Samantha make John an offer on the house which he accepts. Upon the close of escrow, title to the property is transferred from John to Paul and Samantha together as a married couple. Paul and Samantha now hold the house under tenancy by the entirety. In contrast, suppose Paul were not married to Samantha at the time he purchased the house from John. John would convey the house to Paul as the owner. When Paul subsequently married Samantha, Paul would still own the house and Samantha would not have an ownership interest because Paul and Samantha were not married at the time the title was conveyed.

tenancy by the entirety
A form of ownership for married couples, similar to joint tenancy, where the spouse has right of survivorship.

Like a joint tenancy, a tenancy by the entirety contains a right of survivorship. On the death of one spouse, the surviving spouse owns the whole of the real property. In addition, there is no severance of a tenancy by the entirety. So long as the husband and wife are alive and married, neither can sever the tenancy by the entirety. Only in the event of a divorce is the tenancy by the entirety severed. Twenty-three states recognize tenancy by the entirety. Other states are community property states and recognize property under those statutes.

LEGAL RESEARCH MAXIM

Tenancy by the entirety and joint tenancy are very similar, with some states not using tenancy by the entirety any more and resorting to joint tenancy, even for married individuals. Which states still use tenancy by the entirety?

COMMUNITY PROPERTY

Eight states recognize marital property rights and interests as **community property**. The states that recognize community property are

- Arizona
- California
- Idaho
- Louisiana

community property
All property acquired during marriage in a community property state, owned in equal shares.

- Nevada
- New Mexico
- Texas
- Washington

The basic assertion of a community property system is that all property acquired during the marriage is the result of the joint efforts of both the husband and the wife. As such, each of the parties has an equal interest in that property, and that interest is held jointly. During the marriage, all property acquired either individually or jointly by the husband and/or the wife is held by them as a community property except for property handed down by inheritance and individual gambling winnings. Property that is not part of the community is called **separate property**. Any property owned by either the husband or the wife before marriage or that has been acquired by either spouse as a result of a gift, inheritance, bequest, or devise is considered to be outside the community and is separate property. Income obtained from separate property remains the separate property of the spouse to whom the separate property belongs unless that income is **commingled** with community property. For example, if Bob owned a house prior to the marriage and that house is rented out, Bob can keep the rents from the house so long as he maintains them in separate accounts from his joint bank account with his wife. If Bob deposits the rents into the joint bank account, those funds are then commingled with community property and will be considered part of the community.

See Figure 2.1 for a comparison of the different types of ownership.

separate property
Property owned by a married person in his or her own right during the marriage.

commingle
To combine funds or properties into a common fund or stock.

Type	Community Property	Tenancy in Common	Joint Tenancy	Tenancy by the Entirety
Definition	Property held by husband and wife	Property held by two or more persons	Property held by two or more individuals	Property held by husband and wife
Creation	Operation of law	By express act or failure to act	Express intention along with the four unities	Taking title during marriage
Possession	Equal right of possession	Equal right of possession	Equal right of possession	Equal right of possession
Title	Usually as joint tenancy with husband and wife both listed	Each co-owner has a separate legal title and undivided interest	One title to property with each tenant considered owner of whole with undivided equal interests	One title in the marital unit
Conveyance	No restrictions	Each co-owner's interest may be conveyed separately	Conveyance of one co-owner terminates tenancy	Cannot be conveyed without consent of spouse
Survivorship	No right of survivorship	No right of survivorship	Right of survivorship	Right of survivorship
Creditor Rights	Subject to creditor claims to each co-owner's interest	Co-owner's fractional interest may be sold to satisfy claims	Joint tenant's interest subject to execution sale and tenancy is then broken	Only a creditor of both spouses can execute on property
Presumption	All property obtained during marriage is owned by the community	All interests equal unless specified	Must be expressly stated	Automatic when both names are on deed

FIGURE 2.1   Types of Ownership

YOU BE THE JUDGE

Sophie and Ernie have been married for fifteen years. There have been problems throughout the marriage, and finally, after a long and bitter fight, Sophie and Ernie decide to seek a divorce. Together, Sophie and Ernie own a four-bedroom home on one acre of land located in Anytown, Arizona. In addition, Ernie owned a condominium before he and Sophie were married. Ernie rents the condominium and deposits the rental income into the couple's joint savings account. During the marriage, Sophie's parents died and left her the family home. Sophie also rents out the home, but maintains the rental income in a bank account separate from the couple's joint bank account. During the divorce proceeding, the court determines that the family home located in Anytown, Arizona, is deemed to be community property and orders it sold and the proceeds split 50/50 between Ernie and Sophie. The condominium is determined to be Ernie's separate property, since it was acquired prior to the marriage. However, the rental income from the property is considered community property, because it has been commingled into the couple's joint savings account. Sophie's parents' home is determined to be Sophie's separate property because she obtained it through inheritance. The rental income from that property is deemed to be separate property, because Sophie has been maintaining the rental income in a bank account separate from the couple's joint accounts. What type of property ownership do you think exists in the state where Ernie and Sophie are getting divorced?

SPOT THE ISSUE

You work for a real property attorney. Client Joanne Barker calls to say that she is interested in changing the title on her property to include her grown children's names. She asks you what the procedures are for changing title in this jurisdiction, and also asks you where she should file. You are thoroughly familiar with the procedures. Should you answer her questions?

Property that is considered to be community property is owned equally by both husband and wife. Therefore, community property means that each party in the marriage has a one-half interest in any property acquired during the marriage. Neither the husband nor the wife can convey the property without the other's consent. If the parties divorce, the property of the marriage is usually divided equally and is deemed to be owned by the husband and wife as tenants in common. The real property may be partitioned if possible. All property acquired during marriage is presumed to be community property. Upon the death of one of the spouses, one-half of that spouse's community property interest will go to benefit the surviving spouse. In some jurisdiction, upon the death of one of the spouses, the other spouse will retain all of the community property. Community property law is almost completely formed by statutes. Each state's statutes vary from those of other community property states.

DOWER AND CURTESY

At common law, a widow was not automatically the heir of her husband's estate. If the husband died without a will, the wife could be left homeless and without a means to support herself. The property would go to the eldest son, who might or might not support his father's wife. The concept of **dower** was created in order to provide a means of support for the wife and any younger siblings. Therefore, the law in some states provides for a dower, which is an interest in real property of the husband by his widow, to give her a means of support after the death of her husband. A dower interest can be either a life estate or a fee simple interest and some undivided fraction of the real property that the husband owned during the marriage. The requirements for a dower are these:

dower
The provision that the law makes for a widow out of the lands or tenements of her husband, for her support and the nurture of her children.

- A valid marriage
- Ownership of the real property by the husband during the marriage
- Death of the husband before the wife

A dower interest is created at the time the couple is married. However, the interest is not realized until the time of the death of the husband.

Curtesy is similar to dower except that it deals with the rights of the husband after the wife dies. The husband is entitled to a life estate in each piece of real property in which the wife held an interest during the marriage provided such an interest was inheritable. The requirements for curtesy are these:

curtesy
A life estate by which in common law a man held property of his deceased wife if children were born during the marriage.

- A valid marriage
- Ownership of the real property by the wife during the marriage
- Death of the wife before the husband
- The existence of children that were born alive to the couple

Most states have abolished or altered both dower and curtesy.

ELECTIVE SHARE

elective share
Statutory provision that a surviving spouse may choose between taking that which is provided for her in her husband's will, claiming dower, or taking her statutorily prescribed share.

The modern view has provided for an **elective share** (also known as a forced, or statutory, share in many jurisdictions) to be taken by the spouse instead of the concept of dower and curtesy. Under an elective share statute, upon the death of a spouse, the remaining spouse has the right to renounce the will and take an elective share of the deceased spouse's property as determined by statute. Under an elective share principle, one spouse cannot disinherit another spouse.

The following is an excerpt from Florida concerning a surviving spouse's right to an elective share.

> *732.201 **Right to elective share.**—The surviving spouse of a person who dies domiciled in Florida has the right to a share of the elective estate of the decedent as provided in this part, to be designated the elective share.*

RIGHTS, DUTIES, AND LIABILITIES

Whenever a co-ownership situation such as the ones that have been discussed above exists, each common owner has a right to enter on the commonly owned real property and take possession of the whole property. Each common owner has rights equal to those of the other common owners to do the same thing. A common owner of real property may use and enjoy the property as if she were an owner in severalty. A common owner is permitted to occupy as well as use every portion of the real property at all times and in all situations. A common owner has the right to extract the minerals from the land, cut timber, or participate in any other such activities. A common owner also has a right to a proportionate share of any income produced by these activities. A common owner is held to a standard of reasonable care and must take

 EYE ON ETHICS

A legal assistant cannot practice law. He can only work under the authority and supervision of a practicing attorney. Therefore, it is illegal for a legal assistant to provide any legal advice concerning any real property or divorce issues. A legal assistant who is working on his own can only fill out documents; he cannot advise a client as to the content of the forms. To do so would be considered to be the unauthorized practice of law. A legal assistant who works in real property needs to be careful not to cross that line. It is important to remember that legal assistants can only fill out documents at the client's or attorney's direction; they cannot offer their advice as to the selection of the documentation that is necessary for the matter.

care of the real property as an ordinarily prudent person would take care of her own property in the same or similar circumstances.

A common owner is responsible for expenses on the property in proportion to his respective interest in the real property. Any common owner who pays more than his share of the common expenses is entitled to have the other common owners reimburse him in proportion to their shares for the amount paid over and above his own share. The right to reimbursement is called the right of **contribution**.

A common owner may enforce her right of contribution against other common owners by way of lien on the other common owners' interest in the real property. If the lien is not paid by the other common owners, then it can be paid at the time of the sale of the real property. As stated before, common owners have the right to transfer or encumber their own interest in the real property. Any deed executed by a common owner will be treated as conveying only her own undivided interest in the property. One common owner does not have the authority to rent, grant an easement across, sell, or mortgage the property without the consent of the other common owners. The debts of a single common owner will bind her interest in the property but will not affect the other common owners who own the property.

contribution
The right of one who has discharged a common liability to recover of another also liable, the aliquot portion that he ought to pay or bear.

RESEARCH THIS

Research your state's laws and determine whether or not your state considers a mortgage as a transfer of title to real property and, if so, whether the granting of a mortgage will sever a joint tenancy. Also, determine whether your state considers the granting of a lease on the property to be a severance of a joint tenancy ownership in that property.

Property may be owned by one person or a group of people. When one person owns the real property, he has the sole right to possession, use, and transfer of the property. He is responsible for all expenses and liabilities associated with the rights of ownership. However, when more than one person owns the same piece of real property, questions arise as to how possession, use, and transfer can occur with more than one person's interest at stake. Also, a question arises as to who is responsible for debts and liabilities. If one person alone holds title to real property, it is called tenancy in severalty. Tenancy comes from the French word *tenir,* which means "to hold." A person who holds title in tenancy in severalty holds title alone with no one else. However, if title is held by more than one person at a time, then this type of ownership is referred to as concurrent ownership.

Joint tenancy exists when two or more persons own a single, unified interest in a particular piece of real property. Joint tenancy is a form of concurrent ownership that is recognized in most states. Each owner has the right to use, occupy, and possess the entire parcel of real property. The right to use or possess the property is held in common with the other joint owners of the property. Under a joint tenancy, each joint owner of the property owns an equal and undivided interest in the whole of the

Summary

property. No one owner has any rights or interests that are greater than those of any other joint owner. Each owner has the same rights to the property.

One of the most noteworthy characteristics of a joint tenancy is that each joint tenant possesses a right of survivorship. The right of survivorship means that if one of the joint tenants (owners) dies, the real property that has been owned jointly by all of them is passed on to the other surviving joint owners. This process will continue until there is a sole survivor from among the original joint tenants; that survivor will then own the entire real property in severalty.

The common owners, such as joint tenants, may decide to divide the property into separate ownership interests. This process is called partition. The process of partitioning may take place by agreement of the common owners or by court action brought by one of the owners. When the common owners agree to partition, separate tracts of the property are usually allocated to each of the owners. Partitioning can also occur through the exchange of deeds executed by all of the common owners.

A tenancy in common, like a joint tenancy, is a form of property ownership in which two or more persons own the same piece of real property. Each tenant in common possesses a separate undivided interest in the real property. Joint tenants take property as a unit, but tenants in common take ownership interests individually. One of the major differences between a joint tenancy and a tenancy in common is that the tenancy in common does not have the right of survivorship. Each tenant in common takes his interest in the property as an individual separate and apart from the other common owners. Since there is no right of survivorship, a tenant in common is allowed to transfer his interest in the real property by testamentary instrument. If the tenant in common dies intestate, then his interest will pass under state statute to his descendants. A tenant in common also can convey or lease his undivided interest in a parcel of real property to a third party.

In common law, a husband and wife are considered as one person. Under the concept of tenancy by the entirety, a married couple is treated as a single person, and the couple owns the property as a single unit. So long as the couple remains married, the property cannot be sold or mortgaged unless the spouses do so together. A divorce will convert a tenancy by the entirety into a tenancy in common. After the divorce, each party will own a half interest in the real property. In order for a tenancy by the entirety to be formed, the same four unities that are required for a joint tenancy must be present: interest, title, time, and possession.

The basic assertion of a community property system is that all property acquired during the marriage is the result of the joint efforts of both the husband and the wife. As such, each of the parties has an equal interest in that property and that interest is held jointly. During the marriage, all property acquired either individually or jointly by the husband and/or the wife is held by them as a community property. Property that is not part of the community is called separate property. Any property owned by either the husband or the wife before marriage or that has been acquired by either spouse as a result of a gift, inheritance, bequest, or devise is considered to be outside the community and is separate property. Income obtained from separate property remains the separate property of the spouse to whom the separate property belongs, unless that income is commingled with community property.

Under an elective share statute, upon the death of a spouse, the remaining spouse has the right to renounce the will and take an elective share of the deceased spouse's property as determined by statute. Under an elective share principle, one spouse cannot disinherit another spouse.

Whenever a co-ownership situation like the ones that have been discussed above exists, each common owner has a right to enter on the commonly owned real property and take possession of the whole property. Each common owner has rights equal to those of the other common owners to do the same thing. A common owner of real property may use and enjoy the property as if she were an owner in severalty. A common owner is permitted to occupy as well as use every portion of the real property at all times and in all situations. A common owner has the right to extract the minerals from the land, cut timber, or participate in any other such activities. A common owner also has a right to a proportionate share of any income produced by these activities. A common owner is held to a standard of reasonable care and must take care of the real property as an ordinarily prudent person would take care of her own property in the same or similar circumstances.

Key Terms

Commingle
Community property
Concurrent ownership
Contribution
Curtesy
Decedent
Dower
Elective share
Joint tenancy
Mortgage

Partition
Right of survivorship
Separate property
Severance
Tenancy by the entirety
Tenancy in common
Tenancy in severalty
Testamentary
Time

Review Questions

1. What is ownership in severalty?
2. What is the most significant feature of a joint tenancy?
3. What are the four unities required for a joint tenancy, and why are they important?
4. How can a co-owner enforce his right of contribution?
5. How is a tenancy in common different than a joint tenancy?
6. What is partition?
7. In tenancy by the entirety, how do the husband and wife take title?
8. Describe the differences between community property and tenancy by the entirety as they relate to real property interests.
9. How is property typically divided in a community property state?
10. Under what circumstances is property considered a spouse's separate property in a community property state?
11. What is dower and how does it operate?
12. What is curtsey?
13. What is an elective share?
14. Describe how the right of survivorship works.
15. Explain the differences between the right of survivorship under a joint tenancy as opposed to a tenancy by the entirety.

Exercises

1. You are working as a legal assistant for a law firm that handles real estate law. You are working with Kurt, who wishes to purchase a house from Sam. When the title search report comes to the law firm, you notice that the house is owned not only by Sam, but by Bertha, Sam's wife, as well. What precautions do you need to take when preparing any contracts for Kurt to purchase this property?

Research your state's laws and determine if the property that has both Sam and Bertha's names on title would be held in joint tenancy, community property or tenancy by the entirety in your jurisdiction.

2. Oscar owns Whitecap. Oscar dies, leaving the property to his three children, Arnold, Betty, and Cathy, as tenants in common. Arnold purchased Kathy's interest. The property is a single-family home. Arnold moves into the home and uses the property as his principal residence. Betty has now demanded to live in the home as well. If Arnold refuses, will a judge order Arnold to share the house with Betty? Research the various types of ownership rights that exist in your jurisdiction in order to determine if Arnold will have to share the house with Betty. Explain why.

3. Describe the advantages and disadvantages of holding property under tenancy in common, joint tenancy, tenancy by the entirety, and community property. If you were buying a piece of property with a family member, how would you want to take title and why?

4. One afternoon, two gentlemen come in and want a deed drawn up for a piece of property they are purchasing. Both of them want tenancy by the entirety listed as the form of ownership. Can you do that in your state? Research and explain fully.

5. ABC Corporation wants to purchase a piece of property with another party, A.B.C.D. LLC. How would you list the form of ownership on the deed? Which form would you use and why?

6. Can someone's estate (person is deceased) be listed as an owner on a deed? If so, in what form of ownership? Explain your answer.

7. Why do people say they have a mortgage when they own a house? Is it the home-owner or the bank that has the mortgage? Who holds the loan?

 PORTFOLIO ASSIGNMENT

Visit your county clerk's office and interview your county clerk regarding what percentage of deeds from the year 2000 forward are deeds which disclose ownership by (1) joint tenancy and (2) tenancy in common.

Vocabulary Builder

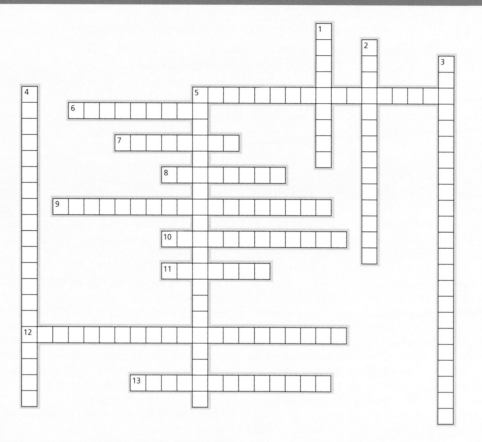

Instructions

Use the key terms from this chapter to fill in the answers to the crossword puzzle.

NOTE: When the answer is more than one word, leave a blank space between the words.

ACROSS

5. a form of ownership whereby each tenant holds an undivided interest in property.
6. the converting of joint tenancy to a tenancy in common.
7. an interest in land created by a written instrument providing security for the performance of a duty or the payment of a debt.
8. the person who has died.
9. property owned in common by husband and wife, each having an undivided one-half interest by reason of their marital status.
10. the right of one who has discharged a common liability to recover of another also liable.
11. succession to the ownership of an estate by inheritance, or by any act of law.
12. the right to property of the living one of two or more persons after the death of the other or others.
13. type of ownership of real property by two or more persons in which each owns an undivided interest in the whole and attached to which is the right of survivorship.

DOWN

1. the dividing of lands held by joint tenants, coparceners, or tenants in common.
2. statutory provision that a surviving spouse may choose as between taking that which is provided for her in her husband's will, claiming dower or taking her statutorily prescribed share.
3. tenancy which is created between a husband and wife and by which together they hold title to the whole with right of survivorship so that, upon death of either, the other takes the whole, to the exclusion of the heirs of the deceased.
4. the holding of land and tenements jointly by more than one person.
5. one who holds land and tenements in his own right only, without any other person being joined or connected with him in point of interest during his estate therein.

SHARON L. WENGEL, a/k/a SHARON L. GROBBEL,
Plaintiff-Counterdefendant-Appellant, v JAMES WENGEL,
Defendant-Counterplaintiff-Appellee.
No. 263657
COURT OF APPEALS OF MICHIGAN
February 28, 2006, Decided

[Text omitted]

I. FACTUAL BACKGROUND, ALLEGATIONS, AND PROCEDURAL HISTORY

Plaintiff and defendant met in 1972. The two became romantically involved, and defendant moved into plaintiff's home. In 1974, the parties moved into the disputed property, which was placed solely in plaintiff's name. Defendant maintained that he subsequently made improvements to the property and assisted with household expenses. In 1981, plaintiff, who had changed her name but had not married defendant, transferred the property to defendant and herself "as joint tenants with full rights of survivorship." Defendant contended that he continued to make improvements to the property. In 1985, the parties had a disagreement, and defendant moved out of the home. Defendant alleged in his counterclaim that plaintiff ejected him from the property and has exercised exclusive control and possession of the property. According to defendant, plaintiff refused to provide him with the rental value of the property and refused to sell the property. Defendant also alleged that plaintiff wrongfully retained possession of approximately $ 25,000 of his personal property.

Plaintiff alleged that, after defendant left the home, she told him that she intended to retain possession of the property and that "he should have his name removed from the property." According to plaintiff, defendant refused to do so and told her that he wanted $ 25,000 to release his interest. Plaintiff asserted that she has had exclusive physical possession of the property since 1985. She further maintained that, since 1985, she has performed all the maintenance, made all the mortgage payments, and solely paid the taxes with respect to the residence. Defendant does not appear to dispute these claims.

On May 12, 2004, plaintiff filed this action to quiet title. Plaintiff claimed that she had obtained exclusive title to the property through adverse possession because she had been in possession of the property since 1985 and the possession was actual, visible, open, notorious, exclusive, continuous, and uninterrupted for the requisite 15-year statutory period. Plaintiff also claimed that she should be awarded possession of the property because she conveyed an interest in the property to defendant in 1981, in exchange for defendant's agreement to live together and share all expenses, including the mortgage, taxes, insurance, and upkeep, but defendant refused to contribute toward any of the expenses and, therefore, the agreement failed for lack of consideration. Defendant's counterclaim alleged claims for partition and sale of the real property, conversion of his personal property, and recovery of reasonable rental damages.

The trial court granted summary disposition in favor of defendant with respect to plaintiff's claim of adverse possession. The trial court also dismissed, without prejudice, plaintiff's alternate theory to quiet title, which is best described as a breach of contract claim, and the court dismissed defendant's counterclaim without prejudice.

[Text omitted]

II. GENERAL PRINCIPLES OF ADVERSE POSSESSION

The basis for a claim of adverse possession is found in MCL 600.5801, which provides, in pertinent part:

No person may bring or maintain any action for the recovery or possession of any lands or make any entry upon any lands unless, after the claim or right to make the entry first accrued to himself or to someone through whom he claims, he commences the action or makes the entry within the periods of time prescribed by this section.

Generally, an action for the recovery or possession of land must be brought within 15 years after it accrues. MCL 600.5801(4); *Kipka v Fountain*, 198 Mich. App. 435, 438; 499 N.W.2d 363 (1993). The *Kipka* panel, addressing the principles of adverse possession, stated:

A claim of adverse possession requires clear and cogent proof that possession has been actual, visible, open, notorious, exclusive, continuous, and uninterrupted for the statutory period of fifteen years.

Other cases additionally indicate that the possession must be hostile and under cover of a claim of right. *McQueen v Black*, 168 Mich. App. 641, 643; 425 N.W.2d 203 (1988), quoting *Connelly v Buckingham*, 136 Mich. App. 462, 467–468; 357 N.W.2d 70 (1984). "The term 'hostile' as employed in the law of adverse possession is a term of art and does not imply ill will"; rather, hostile use is that which is "inconsistent with the right of the owner, without permission asked or given," and which use "would entitle the owner to a cause of action the intruder.

III. CONCURRENT OWNERSHIP AND GENERAL PRINCIPLES REGARDING JOINT TENANCIES WITH FULL RIGHTS OF SURVIVORSHIP

In Michigan, there are five common types or forms of concurrent ownership that are recognized relative to the ownership of real property, and those are tenancies in common, joint tenancies, joint tenancies with full rights of survivorship, tenancies by the entireties, and tenancies in partnership. 1 Cameron, *Michigan Real Property Law* (3d ed), Concurrent Ownership, § 9.1, p 310; see also *Albro v Allen*, 434 Mich. 271, 275; 454 N.W.2d 85 (1990)

All conveyances and devises of land made to two or more persons shall be construed to create a tenancy in common, and not a joint tenancy, unless expressly declared to be a joint tenancy; however, this rule does not apply to mortgages, nor to grants or devises made in trust, made to executors, or made to a husband and wife. *MCL 554.44 and MCL 554.45.*

In *Albro, supra,* our Supreme Court addressed the issue whether a tenant holding real property with a cotenant as joint tenants with full rights of survivorship can convey a life estate interest to a third person without the cotenant's consent. The Court undertook an extensive analysis of the characteristics of joint tenancies, both ordinary joint tenancies and joint tenancies specifically granting the rights of survivorship. A standard or ordinary joint tenancy is characterized by the four unities, which are (1) unity of interest, (2) unity of title, (3) unity of time, and (4) unity of possession. *Id.* at 274. The chief characteristic of such a joint tenancy is the right of survivorship, which means that upon the death of one of the joint tenants, the surviving tenant(s) takes or assumes ownership of the whole estate. *Id.* at 274–275.

On the other hand, a joint tenancy with full rights of survivorship is created by express language directly referencing words of survivorship as contained in the granting instrument, and this tenancy is composed of a joint life estate with dual contingent remainders.

The *Albro* Court reached the following conclusion:

The interest which was conveyed by the deed to Carol Allen and Helen Albro "as joint tenants with full rights of survivorship" was a joint life estate with dual contingent remainders. The contingent remainder of either cotenant may not be destroyed by any act of the other.

With this background on adverse possession and concurrent forms of ownership, we now proceed to our discussion and analysis regarding the interplay of the two.

IV. DISCUSSION AND ANALYSIS

In *Campau v Campau*, 45 Mich. 367; 8 NW 85 (1881), Our Supreme Court, reiterating its previous ruling in the case, indicated that ownership by adverse possession may be obtained by a tenant against his or her cotenant in the context of a tenancy in common.

As reflected in *Campau,* a claim of adverse possession by a tenant against a cotenant, both sharing ownership interests in the property at issue, is not comparable to the usual scenario in which adverse possession arises, because, in the typical case, the person claiming adverse possession is occupying or possessing property to which he or she has no legal right to possess and which is titled in the name of another, making it easier to identify and determine hostile occupation, as compared to a situation in which there exists concurrent ownership.

Accordingly, there is a presumption, in the context of a claim of adverse possession, that a tenant who occupies and possesses the premises recognizes and is honoring the rights of any cotenants to similarly possess and occupy the property unless there is evidence of acts or declarations that clearly establish the contrary and that unambiguously provide notice to the cotenants of an effort to displace or exclude them from the premises in violation of their property rights such that a cause of action arises. See *Krueger v Hackley Union Nat'l Bank & Trust Co*, 5 Mich. App. 362, 365–366; 146 N.W.2d 691 (1966).

In *Krueger, supra* at 366–367, this Court stated:

The law of adverse possession as between cotenants is thoroughly discussed in 82 ALR2d 5, where at pp 23 and 24 the author of that annotation summarizes:

"A cotenant, whether a tenant in common or a joint tenant, may undoubtedly hold the common premises adversely to his cotenant or cotenants, and in such fashion as eventually to ripen his claim into title against them, even though his possession was commenced amicably as a cotenant. To establish that his possession was adverse he must show that at the time in question he was personally, or by tenant or agent, in actual possession of the premises, or of the particular and sufficiently defined part of the premises to which he makes claim, that he intended an actual adverse possession operative as of that time, that he did in fact hold and claim the premises adversely, and lastly, that his cotenant or cotenants had knowledge or notice of that fact.

It is abundantly clear from the case law that a tenant can acquire sole ownership of property by invoking the doctrine of adverse possession against a cotenant or cotenants, where the estate is a tenancy in common, although there is a heightened level of proof necessary to establish the claim.

The specific question posed to us today, is whether the doctrine of adverse possession can be extended to equally apply in joint tenancies with full rights of survivorship.

We begin our examination of this issue by focusing on the life estate interest that is created when property is held jointly with rights of survivorship. As indicated in *Albro, supra* at 275, a joint tenancy with full rights of survivorship is composed of a joint life estate with dual contingent remainders. "Estates in lands are divided into estates of inheritance, *estates for life,* estates for years, and estates at will and by sufferance." MCL 554.1 (emphasis added).

Therefore, plaintiff's 1981 conveyance of the property to herself and defendant as "joint tenants with full rights of survivorship" gave each of them a possessory, freehold estate with an immediate right to occupy the property. The joint life estate would cease upon the death of either party, leaving the surviving party the whole estate in fee simple. MCL 600.5801 provides that a person may maintain an action to recover property within 15 years after the claim first accrued. Accordingly, when defendant was disseised or wrongfully deprived of the property in 1985, at which time he had a right of possession, the 15-year period of limitations began ticking with respect to defendant's opportunity to initiate a civil action, whether through summary proceedings or standard proceedings, to recover possession.

Moreover, a ruling that one may adversely possess property against the holder of a life estate finds support in the case law. We first note that it is well settled that the life estate itself is freely transferable. *Albro, supra* at 280. In *Watkins v Green*, 101 Mich. 493, 497; 60 NW 44 (1894), our Supreme Court ruled that a tenant is not precluded from establishing adverse title against a cotenant, and it recognized that a life estate interest can be lost by adverse possession. Additionally, a life tenant, such as plaintiff, may, in general and without reaching any interest in remainder, establish a claim for adverse possession. See *Felt v Methodist Educational Advance*, 251 Mich. 512, 516–517; 232 NW 178 (1930). 263–264.

For the reasons stated above, we hold that a life estate interest can be lost by adverse possession and that it can be lost in the context of a joint tenancy with full rights of survivorship.

In relation to their time of enjoyment, estates are divided into estates in possession and estates in expectancy; and estates in expectancy, denominated as future estates and reversions, exist where the right to possession is postponed until a future date. MCL 554.7, MCL 554.8, and MCL 554.9. "A future estate is an estate limited to commence in possession at a future day, either without the intervention of a precedent estate, or on the determination, by lapse of time or otherwise, of a precedent estate, created at the same time." MCL 554.10. A remainder is created when a future estate is dependent upon the precedent estate. MCL 554.11. Future estates are contingent "whilst the person to whom, or the event upon which they are limited to take effect remains uncertain." MCL 554.13. Valid future estates are not void on the basis of the probability or improbability of the contingency. *MCL 554.26.* "When a remainder on an estate for life . . . shall not be limited on a contingency, defeating or avoiding such precedent estate, it shall be construed as intended to take effect only on the death of the first taker[.]" MCL 554.29. "Expectant estates are descendible, devisable and alienable, in the same manner as estates in possession." MCL 554.35. Contingent remainders are not possessory estates. *Albro, supra* at 284–285. n8 Although a joint tenant with rights of survivorship can achieve partial partition through conveyance of the life estate, the partition does not affect the contingent remainders. *Id.* at 282, 287. Furthermore, "[a] cotenant's contingent remainder cannot be destroyed by an act of the other cotenant." *Id. at 276*; see also *Townsend v Chase Manhattan Mortgage Corp*, 254 Mich. App. 133, 136; 657 N.W.2d 741 (2002) (no act of a cotenant can defeat the other cotenant's right of survivorship).

With respect to life estates in general, a contingent remainder cannot be destroyed by any act of the holder of the preceding life estate. *Albro, supra* at 279. Our Supreme Court in *Rendle, supra* at 44, similarly noted that the established general rule is that a life tenant's possession cannot be adverse to a remainderman. A life tenant cannot acquire adverse rights against any remaindermen, nor hold the property adversely to the remaindermen before the end of the life estate. *Lowry, supra* at 682. The *Lowry* Court adopted the following rationale from *Allison v White*, 285 Ill 311, 323; 120 NE 809 (1918):

"The possession of land by a tenant for life cannot be adverse to the remainder-man or reversioner, and the possession of a grantee of the life estate, even under a deed purporting to convey the fee, cannot be adverse so as to set the Statute of Limitations in operation against the remainder-man or reversioner.

A contingent remainderman does not have a present right of possession that "would entitle [him or her] to a cause of action against the intruder." *Mumrow, supra* at 698.

No expectant estate can be defeated or barred by any alienation or other act of the owner of the intermediate or precedent estate, nor by any destruction of such precedent estate by disseizin, forfeiture, surrender, merger, or otherwise.

In *Lowry, supra* at 684, the Court noted that "this statute was enacted to abrogate the common-law rule, under which it was possible for a life tenant to defeat a contingent remainder by a deed of feoffment with livery of seizin."

The statutes and the case law make clear that the contingent remainder interest held by defendant in the case at bar could not be destroyed by adverse possession because a claim to recover possession of the property on the basis of said interest, or defendant's status as a remainderman, would not accrue, if at all and at a minimum, until the occurrence of the contingency, which is plaintiff's death, or, in other words, the expiration of the precedent estate. A life tenant's possession cannot be adverse to a remainderman. The 15-year statutory period would not commence running against defendant until a cause of action accrued in which defendant sought to enforce his rights as the holder of the contingent remainder, which interest, at the time of plaintiff's death, would vest and leave defendant with a fee simple. Only if defendant failed to commence an action within 15 years of plaintiff's death, against whomever might conceivably be adversely possessing the property, if indeed anyone did so, might defendant's interest in the property be lost by adverse possession. While plaintiff could adversely possess defendant's life estate interest in the property, she could not adversely possess his contingent remainder interest.

We have contemplated an attempt to distinguish the case from the referenced case law and statutes on the basis that defendant is not only a remainderman, but a life estate holder, as opposed to situations where the remainderman does not have any present possessory interest whatsoever and has nothing to do with the property during the lifetime of the life estate holder. Thus, defendant had some property interest that was potentially subject to adverse possession as soon as he was excluded from the property, and the period of limitations began running on enforcing that interest, yet he failed to act. We further hold that plaintiff established as a matter of law a claim for adverse possession as it pertained to defendant's life estate. Not only must a tenant show possession that was actual, visible, open, notorious, exclusive, continuous, hostile, and uninterrupted for the statutory period, *Kipka, supra* at 439 (excludes "hostile"); *McQueen, supra* at 643 (includes "under a claim of right") the tenant must intend to possess the premises to the exclusion of his or her cotenant, and the cotenant must have knowledge or notice of this intent as clearly evidenced by acts or declarations, *Taylor, supra* at 588-589; *Donohue, supra* at 90–91; *Weshgyl, supra* at 23; *Krueger, supra* at 365–366. With respect to the element of hostility, this simply means that the possession must be inconsistent with the rights of the owner. *Mumrow, supra* at 698.

Here, we first note that defendant's answer to plaintiff's complaint does not reference paragraph 9 of the elements listed. Next, defendant stated in his counterclaim that plaintiff "ejected [him] from the premises and exercised exclusive control and possession to the subject property." Defendant further asserted that plaintiff "has refused the sale of the described property and has had the full and unfettered possession of the entire property[.]" Defendant additionally claimed that plaintiff refused to give him the reasonable rental value of his interest in the property for which he sought compensation dating back to 1985. Even with respect to defendant's allegations regarding personal property contained in the home, he contended that plaintiff "has exercised dominion and control" over personal property. In defendant's trial brief, he stated, "In 1985, . . . the plaintiff made the defendant leave the home[.]" Moreover, in his appellate response brief, defendant makes no claim that, factually, the elements of adverse possession were not established; rather, he focuses solely on the legal argument that adverse possession is inapplicable where there exists a joint tenancy with full rights of survivorship.

V. CONCLUSION

We hold that the doctrine of adverse possession is available to the occupying tenant to defeat the ousted cotenant's life estate interest held in the property. We further hold, however, that the ousted life tenant's contingent remainder cannot be destroyed through adverse possession by the occupying life tenant because the statutory period to file an action to recover the property relative to that particular interest cannot commence, at a minimum, until the contingency occurs, i.e., the claim accrues at the death of the occupying life tenant, here plaintiff, which would mark the expiration of the precedent estate. In regard to defendant's life estate interest, the trial court erred in finding that plaintiff could not establish adverse possession for lack of hostility, and erred in granting defendant's motion for summary disposition, where the record reflects, as a matter of law, that the elements of adverse possession were admitted and satisfied, even observing a heightened level of proof. But, also as a matter of law, defendant's contingent remainder in fee simple remains intact.

We reverse in part, affirm in part, and remand for entry of judgment in favor of plaintiff with regard to adverse possession of defendant's life estate interest and for entry of judgment in favor of defendant relative to his contingent remainder. We do not retain jurisdiction.

/s/ William B. Murphy

/s/ Kirsten Frank Kelly

Source: 2006 Mich. App. LEXIS 5152006 Mich. App. LEXIS 515 Reprinted with the permission of Lexis Nexis.

Chapter 3

Condominiums, Cooperatives, and Timeshares

CHAPTER OBJECTIVES

Upon completion of this chapter, you will be able to:

- Define "condominium".

- Understand cooperative property ownership.

- Discuss timeshare arrangements.

As urban areas become increasing more populated and land increasingly scarcer, American property ownership has gone upward. By building vertically, property owners could increase the number of units that they could rent per parcel of property. Eventually, multi-story dwelling units began to be sold instead of rented. As a result, condominiums and cooperatives were created. Condominium ownership is now seen throughout the United States.

CONDOMINIUMS

condominium
Form of property ownership in which the owner owns an individual unit in a multi-unit building and is a tenant in common with other individual unit owners in the common areas.

common areas
Those portions of the condominium property that are owned in common by all of the owners of units in the condominium.

A **condominium** is a type of ownership of property that allows the homeowner to hold title to a specifically designated unit in a multi-story residential dwelling. Condominium ownership is a combination of both individual and joint ownership interests. Besides individually owning their own dwelling units, condominium owners have joint ownership and control over the **common areas** of the property as well. The common areas typically include the exterior walls of buildings, stairwells, elevators, walks, yards, roofs, entryways, and pool areas, just to name a few. The common areas are areas of the property that are used by all of the individual condominium owners and are jointly owned and maintained by them as well. Basically, any area of the property that can be utilized by any of the condominium owners is designated as a common area.

Condominiums did not exist in common law; therefore, they have been created by statutes. The laws that govern and define condominium ownership have been developed by each state and are both statutory and contractual in nature. The person or entity that develops the condominium must prepare a comprehensive set of contractual

- Master Deed
- Declaration of Condominium
- Bylaws
- Articles of Incorporation
- Purchase and Sale Agreements
- Plats and Plans Map
- Rules and Regulations

FIGURE 3.1
Documents Needed to Establish a Condominium

covenants, known as the **condominium declaration**, that governs the condominium ownership. The condominium declaration sets forth the specific rights and obligations of each individual condominium unit owner. It controls the governance of the condominium. The declaration is recorded in the county recorder's office where the condominium is located, and each condominium owner is bound by the terms contained therein.

A condominium can be created either by purchasing an apartment building and converting it into a condominium or by developing and constructing a new condominium. In either situation, the developer is required by state law to establish rights, rules, and regulations for the governance of the condominium. The developer must also prepare a **plat** description that shows the size and location of all individual units. The plat description will designate all common areas as well. A **homeowners' association** needs to be established that will govern the condominium property upon the final completion and sale of all of the units by the developer. (See Figure 3.1. for a listing of documents needed to establish a condominium property)

Perhaps the most important document in the creation of a condominium is the condominium declaration. The declaration is also sometimes called the *master deed*. As stated above, the declaration is prepared and signed by the condominium developer and recorded with the county recorder in the county where the condominium is to be located.

A condominium declaration usually contains the following items:

- Name of the condominium
- Legal description of the entire real property that is to be the condominium
- Description of all common areas
- Creation of a governing body for the condominium or the requirement that one be created
- Limitations or restrictions on the power of the condominium
- Allocation of a share of liability for common area expense to each condominium unit
- Statement of all restrictive covenants in the general use of the units and common areas
- Description of how the condominium can be expanded
- Statement of how the condominium can be terminated

The homeowners' association is formed as a nonprofit corporation, with each individual unit owner having one vote in the issues concerning the homeowners' association. Since the homeowners' association is a form of corporation, in order to be legal, it must file **articles of incorporation** with the secretary of state in the state in which the condominium is located. The articles of incorporation usually include the following:

- Name of the association
- Purpose of the association

condominium declaration
A legal document required by state condominium acts to create a condominium.

plat
A map of a specific land area, such as a town, section, or subdivision, showing the location and boundaries of individual parcels of land subdivided into lots, with streets, alleys, easements, units, etc.

homeowners' association
An association of people who own homes in a given area, formed for the purpose of improving or maintaining the quality of the area.

articles of incorporation
The basic charter of an organization, written and filed in accordance with state laws.

- Period of duration for the corporation
- Initial directors of the corporation
- Registered agent and registered office of the corporation for service of process
- Criteria for becoming a member of the association and the name of the initial incorporator

Bylaws must also be adopted by the homeowners' association. The bylaws of a condominium govern the day-to-day operations of the complex. The bylaws normally include the following items:

- Selection of the board of directors
- How and when meetings are to be held and conducted
- The manner in which officers are to be appointed or elected
- How votes are to be counted
- The governance of the corporation
- Regulation of the common areas
- Rights and responsibilities of unit owners
- Assessment and collection of monthly charges and other relevant issues

Bylaws are not required to be recorded with the secretary of state. However, they must be provided to each purchaser of a condominium unit prior to the time of purchasing the unit. A developer usually retains control of the condominium association until all of the individual units have been sold or some percentage of the units has been sold.

The costs and expenses of operating a condominium are paid for by the individual condominium owners. Costs and expenses usually include taxes on the common areas, maintenance and repair of the common areas, and insurance.

Taxes on individual condominium units are paid by the individual unit owners. Each individual unit owner is responsible for the maintenance and repairs on his individual unit. Each individual condominium owner is also liable for injuries sustained by people as a result of his failure to maintain his premises. Taxes on common areas are paid by the association and are a joint debt of all of the individual owners. The joint responsibility for payment of expenses is accomplished by the use of an **assessment** against each individual owner's unit. The assessment is used to pay that individual unit owner's share of the joint liabilities. The amount of the assessment is determined by the homeowners' association. If the assessment is not paid by a unit owner and that owner becomes delinquent, the association may be able to enforce its collection by filing a lien against the individual unit for unpaid assessments. The association can enforce this lien by having the condominium unit foreclosed on and sold for the purpose of paying the lien for the unpaid assessment. Unpaid assessments

PRACTICE TIP

It is important to have a potential buyer of a condominium review important documents before making her purchase, so that she understands the parameters of the rules, regulations, and ownership of her unit. Important documents for a potential buyer to review include, but are not limited to, the following:

- Bylaws
- Minutes of past meetings
- Financial statements
- Budgets
- Purchase and sale agreement
- Rules and regulations
- Insurance documentation

SPOT THE ISSUE

Rodney owns a condominium at Main Place Condominiums. Recently, the board has sent notice that certain regulations have been adopted and added to the rules and regulations of the condominium. These regulations include that an owner cannot have a large dog; trash cans cannot be kept outside of the individual garage units; guests cannot park on the curbs next to the roadways; and owners cannot paint the inside of their condominiums the color red. Which regulation would probably not be within the scope of the board's authority?

YOU BE THE JUDGE

Michelle is interested in purchasing a condominium unit in the Shady Elm Condominium complex. Michelle purchases a three-bedroom, two-bath end unit. Prior to the close of the purchase of the unit, Michelle is provided with the bylaws of the complex. In the bylaws, Michelle learns that she is to pay an assessment of $120.00 per month to cover her portion of the costs and expenses incurred by the homeowners' association. In addition, Michelle learns that homeowners' association meetings are held on the first Tuesday of every month in the clubhouse by the pool. Officers are elected once a year for a one-year term. Michelle thinks that she may want to run for office. Applications for nominations will be due to be submitted to the board of directors of the homeowners' association two months after she moves in. What would happen to Michelle if she became delinquent in paying her monthly assessment as stated in the bylaws for the condominium?

are also imposed on a purchaser of a unit if the assessments are unpaid at the time of purchase by the new owner.

Condominium owners also are **jointly and severally liable** for damage or harm caused to person or property in connection with the common areas. Because each individual owner is a joint owner of the common areas, each owner is held liable. For example, suppose a visitor trips and falls as a result of a broken sidewalk area in the decking around the pool. The visitor breaks her leg. The pool area of the condominium complex is considered a common area, because it is used by all owners and they all own it jointly. As a result, the visitor may sue all owners individually and together in order to recover damages, because the condominium owners own and control the common areas of the complex individually and together as a whole. **Liability insurance** that insures both the individual unit owners and the association will handle any issues that may arise in this regard. Liability insurance is paid for by the association out of the assessment paid to the homeowners' association by each of the individual unit owners.

Condominium ownership is a form of individual property ownership. Like all property ownership, the condominium owner is free to sell, gift, devise, rent, or otherwise transfer his interest in his individual condominium unit. Such transfers are usually accomplished without restriction, unless some specific restriction is stated in the condominium declaration.

joint and several liability
Shared responsibility, apportioned between all of the defendants, but in no case can the plaintiff recover more than 100 percent of the damages awarded.

liability insurance
That type of insurance protection which indemnifies one from liability to third persons, as contrasted with insurance coverage for losses sustained by the insured.

LEGAL RESEARCH MAXIM

Sometimes property can be owned by a trust. A trust is a legal entity created by a grantor for the benefit of designated beneficiaries. A trust may designate a trustee to manage any property owned by the trust for one or more beneficiaries. A trust property can own a condominium. It is important when researching ownership interests in property to be aware that the legal entity of a trust can own property.

COOPERATIVES

Cooperatives are different from condominiums. Belonging to a cooperative is considered an ownership in personal property and not real property. Cooperatives can be found in areas along the East Coast. A cooperative is a corporation. It owns the land, the building, and all common areas associated with the cooperative. A person who wants to become an owner in the cooperative will purchase shares of stock from the cooperative corporation. The number of shares purchased determines the percentage of the cooperative that is owned. The shares of stock in the cooperative enable the stockholder to possess but not to own a unit in the cooperative. The stockholder is able to enter into a long-term lease for her cooperative unit with the cooperative corporation. A cooperative owner is a tenant under a long-term lease with the cooperative corporation as well as an owner in the landlord cooperative corporation.

The general overseeing of the cooperative is conducted by all of the owners of the cooperative. However, a cooperative is governed by a board that is responsible for the financial status and the physical aspects of the property. The board will review all

cooperative
A form of ownership of real property in which a corporation owns a multiunit building and leases living space in the building to the shareholders of the corporation.

Jeronimo is a local merchant and wants to move into a local cooperative on the eastern seaboard. Jeronimo has found an owner in the cooperative who is willing to sell her shares. Jeronimo makes a decent living; he is financially sound but is not wealthy. However, Jeronimo can afford to purchase the cooperative shares. The board of the cooperative refuses to approve Jeronimo due to his lower economic status. Can the board of the cooperative refuse to approve the sale of shares to Jeronimo?

prospective tenants to see if they will fit into the cooperative. If a shareholder wishes to sell his shares in the cooperative, the prospective buyer must first be approved by the board.

The units are owned by the cooperative corporation and not the shareholders; therefore, financing for a unit is made through the cooperative, and a shareholder will pay an assessment to the board to cover the costs of the financing. Should a shareholder default on paying his assessment, then the remaining shareholders in the cooperative must make up the shortfall.

Difference between Cooperatives and Condominiums

The difference between a cooperative and a condominium is that a condominium has few or no restrictions on transferability and can be traditionally financed. A cooperative must be financed through the cooperative corporation and has restrictions placed on transferability through a board review of the purchaser.

TIMESHARES

timeshare
A form of shared property ownership, commonly in vacation or recreational condominium property, wherein rights vest in several owners to use property for specified periods each year.

With property costs rising, the days of owning a second vacation home have gone by the wayside. Increasingly **timeshares** have taken the place of vacation homes. A timeshare is a form of property ownership that enables the owner to have intermittent use

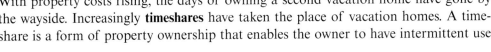

RESEARCH THIS

Since most laws vary from state to state, it is important to know your jurisdiction and the laws that apply to that jurisdiction. Research the issue of timeshares under your state laws. What restrictions or requirements does your state place on the sale and ownership of timeshares? A potential timeshare purchaser must be aware of the pitfalls that can occur in such a transaction. Sometimes, timeshare transactions are fraught with frauds and scams. Using a Web site such as www.mexicantimesharefraud.com, discuss the fraudulent issues that can be found in such a transaction if a buyer is not careful.

EYE ON ETHICS

Criminal remedies can be sought against a legal assistant who engages in the unauthorized practice of law. Therefore, it is very important to guard against any perception or misunderstanding that may lead the public to believe that you are an attorney. Always identify yourself as a legal assistant. Have your title printed clearly on your business cards. Also, make sure that any correspondence that is attributed to you clearly states that you are not an attorney. Do not render legal advice or appear to be representing a client. For example, a paralegal negotiating an agreement between parties in a real estate transaction is engaging in the unauthorized practice of law. A paralegal cannot give legal advice.

of the property at specified periods of time during the year. For example, a person purchases a timeshare in Jackson Hole, Wyoming, because she likes the skiing there. The timeshare gives the holder the right to use a home or condominium at the ski resort area for a limited period each year.

Timeshares are regulated by state law. The purchaser of a timeshare is entitled to a period of **rescission** after the timeshare contract has been signed. The purchaser is also entitled to a full disclosure of the operation of the timeshare.

rescission
Mutual agreement to early discharge or termination of remaining duties.

Summary

A condominium is a type of ownership of property that allows the homeowner to hold title to a specifically designated unit in a multi-story residential dwelling. Condominium ownership is a combination of both individual and joint ownership interests. Besides individually owning their own dwelling units, condominium owners have joint ownership and control over the common areas of the property as well. The common areas typically include the exterior walls of buildings, stairwells, elevators, walks, yards, roofs, entryways, and pool areas, just to name a few. The common areas are areas of the property that are used by all of the individual condominium owners and are jointly owned and maintained by them as well. Basically, any area of the property that can be utilized by any of the condominium owners is designated as a common area.

Condominiums did not exist in common law; therefore, they have been created by statutes. The laws that govern and define condominium ownership have been developed by each state and are both statutory and contractual in nature. The person or entity that develops the condominium must prepare a comprehensive set of contractual covenants, known as the condominium declaration, that govern the condominium ownership. The condominium declaration sets forth the specific rights and obligations of each individual condominium unit owner. It controls the governance of the condominium. The declaration is recorded in the county recorder's office where the condominium is located, and each condominium owner is bound by the terms contained therein.

The homeowners' association is formed as a nonprofit corporation, with each individual unit owner able to have a vote in the issues concerning the homeowners' association. Since the homeowners' association is a form of corporation, in order to be legal, it must file articles of incorporation with the secretary of state in the state where the condominium is located.

Cooperatives are different from condominiums. Belonging to a cooperative is considered an ownership in personal property and not real property. Cooperatives can be found in areas along the East Coast. A cooperative is a corporation. It owns the land, the building, and all common areas associated with the cooperative. A person who wants to become an owner in the cooperative will purchase shares of stock from the cooperative corporation. The number of shares purchased determines the percentage of the cooperative that is owned. The shares of stock in the cooperative enable the stockholder to possess but not to own a unit in the cooperative. The stockholder is able to enter into a long-term lease for his cooperative unit with the cooperative corporation. A cooperative owner is a tenant under a long-term lease with the cooperative corporation as well as an owner in the landlord cooperative corporation.

Timeshares are a form of shared property ownership. Usually people vacation in timeshares during periods of time to which they are assigned use of the timeshare. Timeshares are regulated by state law.

Key Terms

Articles of incorporation
Assessment
Bylaws
Common areas
Condominium
Condominium declaration
Cooperative

Homeowners' association
Joint and Several Liability
Liability Insurance
Plat
Rescission
Timeshare

Review Questions

1. What is a common area?
2. What is a timeshare?
3. List five items that should appear in a condominium declaration.
4. How are common area costs and expenses paid in a condominium property ownership situation?
5. What is a cooperative?
6. Where do articles of incorporation need to be filed?
7. List five items that would probably be found in bylaws.
8. What is a homeowners' association?
9. What remedy is available to a homeowners' association if a condominium owner fails to pay her assessment?
10. When is a condominium purchaser to receive a copy of the bylaws?
11. What is a lien?
12. Who governs a condominium?
13. Does a cooperative owner own his property?
14. If you were purchasing property from a cooperative, what would be the process?
15. What happens if someone fails to pay his assessment in a cooperative?

Exercises

1. Write a memorandum discussing the advantages and disadvantages of both condominiums and cooperatives. Express your opinion as to which situation would be a better choice of property interest given the laws in your state.
2. Research your state laws. Write a memorandum as to the requirements that must be in a condominium declaration for your state.
3. Briefly discuss why a person might want to purchase a cooperative instead of a condominium unit. What are the pros and cons of both?
4. Condominiums and cooperatives can be new construction or the conversion of an existing structure into units. Are there any advantages and/or disadvantages to either new construction or the conversion of an existing structure? Please explain.
5. Do cooperative owners of stock have a deed to their personal living unit? What does guarantee them the right to possess the unit? Please explain your answer fully.

6. Can existing owners of condo units and/or coop units, holding a deed or a stock certificate, respectively, determine whether or not you can purchase a unit in their building? Please explain.

7. Does a condominium owner own any part of the condominium common area? If so, how does she determine how much she does own? Is there a tax deduction on her federal and state income tax return for the part she does own, if any? Please explain.

8. Does living in a condominium or cooperative unit present an opportunity for a lifestyle different from that one would have in a detached, single-family home? Explain what some of the daily changes in your life would be if you opted to purchase a condo or coop rather than a house.

PORTFOLIO ASSIGNMENT

Using the Internet, find a sample lease agreement. You can use Web sites such as www.hud.gov to find sample lease agreements. Prepare a sample residential lease agreement for a fictitious condominium unit. Fill out the entire document as though you were preparing it for your supervising attorney. You can make up the information required for the condominium unit, owner, and renter, but use information that would appear to be realistic.

Vocabulary Builder

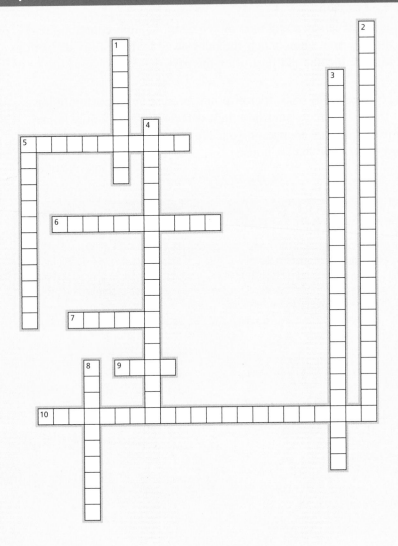

Instructions

Use the key terms from this chapter to fill in the answers to the crossword puzzle.

NOTE: When the answer is more than one word, leave a blank space between the words.

ACROSS

5. a form of ownership of real property in which a corporation owns a multi-unit building and leases living space in the building to the shareholders of the corporation.

6. a form of property ownership in which the owner owns an individual unit in a multi-unit building and is a tenant in common with other individual unit owners in the common areas.

7. regulations, ordinances, rules, or laws adopted by an association or corporation or the like for its internal governance.

8. a map of a specific land area, such as a town, section, or subdivision, showing the location and boundaries of individual parcels of land subdivided into lots, with streets, alleys, casements, units, etc.

9. an association of people who own homes in a given area, formed for the purpose of improving or maintaining the quality of the area.

DOWN

1. a form of shared property ownership, commonly in vacation or recreational condominium property, wherein rights vest in several owners to use property for specified periods each year.

2. a legal document required by state condominium acts to create a condominium.

3. the basic instrument filed with the appropriate governmental agency on the incorporation of a business.

4. that type of insurance protection which indemnifies one from liability to third persons as contrasted with insurance coverage for losses sustained by the insured.

5. that portion of the condominium property that is owned in common by all of the owners of units in the condominium.

8. the process of ascertaining and adjusting the shares respectively to be contributed by several persons toward a common beneficial object according to the benefit received.

Blachy v. Butcher, 129 F. App'x 173 (6th Cir. 2005); 2005 U.S. App. LEXIS 6445;
95 A.F.T.R.2d (RIA) 1854, *aff'ing* 2003 U.S. Dist. LEXIS 6139 (W.D. Mich. 2003),
appl'n granted, 2005 U.S. App. LEXIS 18467 (6th Cir. Mich., Aug. 24, 2005), *cert. denied,*
2005 U.S. LEXIS 5782 (U.S. 2005)

I. HISTORY

A. Factual history

Alexander Butcher ("Alexander") and his wife Rosemary Butcher ("Rosemary") sought to develop resort condominiums in northern Michigan through Little Traverse Development Company ("LTDC"), a Michigan corporation owned solely by Alexander. On June 30, 1978, Cedar Cove, a Michigan limited partnership in which Alexander was a partner, conveyed four parcels of land, consisting of approximately 100 acres in Little Traverse Township, to Alexander and Rosemary for the price of $ 640,000. By warranty deed dated July 6, 1978, Mr. and Mrs. Butcher conveyed two of these four parcels (40.81 acres in total) to LTDC. Both the June 30 and July 6 deeds were recorded on July 12, 1978. That same day, Alexander signed a warranty deed in his capacity as president of LTDC, conveying the unmortgaged portion of the property, consisting of 17.83 acres, back to Mr. and Mrs. Butcher as tenants by the entirety. This deed was recorded on July 14, 1978.

At Alexander's request, Lawyers Title issued a title commitment to LTDC for the full 40.81 acres on July 18, 1978. Lawyers Title failed to discover the 17.83 acre conveyance from LTDC back to Mr. and Mrs. Butcher. As a result, the title commitment erroneously listed LTDC as the owner of all 40.81 acres—including the 17.83 acres that had been conveyed to Mr. and Mrs. Butcher.

On November 1, 1978, Alexander, on behalf of LTDC, executed a master deed creating Harbor Cove Phase II on the entire 40.81 acres. From 1981 to 1984, LTDC constructed and sold condominiums on portions of the acreage that included the 17.83 acres. Nine of those condominiums were sold to the plaintiffs or their predecessors-in-interest.

On May 8, 1984, Alexander formed H.C. Development Company ("HCDC"). He was the majority stockholder, president, and a director of this new corporation. In late October of 1984, Alexander signed a warranty deed on behalf of LTDC, purporting to convey 12.60 of the 17.83 acres to HCDC. Alexander, as president of HCDC, then signed a master deed creating Harbor Cove Phase III on the 12.60 acres. He granted Northwestern Savings and Loan Association a mortgage on this acreage to secure a construction loan. After Lawyers Title issued a title commitment for the transaction, HCDC constructed condominiums on the development. HCDC began selling the condominiums in December of 1985. Three of these condominiums were sold to the plaintiffs or their predecessors-in-interest.

In the deeds conveying the condominiums to the plaintiffs, Alexander, acting as president of both LTDC and HCDC, represented that one or the other of those entities held title to the particular condominium being sold. He also stated under oath on several occasions that LTDC was the owner of the Phase II property and that HCDC was the owner of the Phase III property.

In August of 1988, the Internal Revenue Service ("IRS") issued an assessment against Mr. and Mrs. Butcher for approximately $ 61,000 in unpaid federal income taxes that arose from the taxable year 1986. On September 9, 1988, the United States, acting on behalf of the IRS, filed a tax lien against Mr. and Mrs. Butcher's property seeking to attach Rosemary's and Alexander's interest in the 17.83 acres.

On March 1, 1991, Rosemary filed for bankruptcy. The **condominium owners**—who had been paying the property taxes on the 17.83 acres over the years—subsequently learned of the July 12, 1978, conveyance from LTDC to Mr. and Mrs. Butcher. On September 17, 1991, Rosemary amended her bankruptcy schedules to claim ownership of the 17.83 acres. Prior to that date, Mr. and Mrs. Butcher had taken no action to claim title to any portion of the property. Alexander quitclaimed his interest in the 17.83 acres to Rosemary on October 31, 1991. Alexander died in December 1991.

B. Procedural history

Rosemary filed her Chapter 7 bankruptcy petition in the United States Bankruptcy Court for the Eastern District of Michigan. Seven and a half months later, Lawyers Title and the **condominium owners** to whom Lawyers Title issued title insurance policies sued Alexander, LTDC, HCDC, and the IRS in Emmet County Circuit Court, Michigan. The plaintiffs did not sue Rosemary because she was under the protection of the bankruptcy court.

On November 18, 1991, the IRS removed the state court action to the United States District Court for the Western District of Michigan. The district court stayed the Western District case while the plaintiffs pursued an adversary proceeding in Rosemary's bankruptcy case. In both actions, the plaintiffs sought a constructive trust.

Subsequent to Alexander's death in late 1991, Rosemary and Robert Butcher (Rosemary's brother-in-law and co-personal representative of Alexander's estate) moved the district court to dismiss the plaintiff's case because Alexander's estate had not been substituted as a party following his death. The plaintiffs responded by moving to transfer venue to the bankruptcy court. On August 16, 1993, the district court denied the motion to dismiss, holding that the order staying the district court action pending the adversary proceeding in the bankruptcy court tolled the time limit for substituting the estate of Alexander into the suit under Rule 25(a)(1) of the Federal Rules of Civil Procedure. The district court also granted the plaintiffs' motion to transfer venue to the Bankruptcy Court for the Eastern District of Michigan.

The plaintiffs' Western District case and Rosemary's bankruptcy proceeding were consolidated on November 18, 1993, in the bankruptcy court. On February 11, 1994, the bankruptcy court substituted Rosemary and Robert Butcher for Alexander.

In late November of 1994, the bankruptcy court granted the plaintiffs' motion for summary judgment and imposed a constructive trust over the 17.83 acres for the **condominium owners'** benefit. The bankruptcy court also concluded that the constructive trust related back to 1978, thus predating and superseding the IRS's 1988 tax lien.

The defendants appealed the bankruptcy court's ruling to the United States District Court for the Eastern District of Michigan. On July 31, 1995, the bankruptcy court's award of summary judgment to the plaintiffs was reversed by the district court. The district court's decision was based upon the case of, in which this court held that a bankruptcy court may not impose a constructive trust over estate property. *See id.* at 1452–53. Because of *In re Omegas Group*, the district court concluded that the proper remedy would be to have the debt declared nondischargeable. The case was then remanded to the bankruptcy court.

The bankruptcy court transferred the plaintiff's claim for a constructive trust over Rosemary's nonbankruptcy interest—the interest she acquired from Alexander—back to the Western District of Michigan. It also lifted the automatic stay in order to permit the plaintiffs to name Rosemary as a defendant and to add a fraudulent conveyance claim.

After the case was transferred back to the Western District, the parties filed cross-motions for summary judgment. The district court granted the plaintiffs' motion, concluding that a constructive trust was appropriate. The district court further ruled that the Butchers' arguments relating to standing, jurisdiction, and the statute of limitations were meritless. The court held that a constructive trust arose on July 12, 1978, the date LTDC conveyed the 17.83 acres to Rosemary and Alexander. Because the district court retroactively applied the constructive trust as of that date, it concluded that the 1988 federal tax lien was subordinate to the plaintiffs' interest in the property and therefore ineffective.

The Butchers filed a motion for reconsideration, arguing that a constructive trust should not have been imposed over Rosemary's nonbankruptcy interest because she had not been served with a summons and a copy of the amended complaint. The district court acknowledged this oversight and ordered the plaintiffs to serve Rosemary with a summons and a copy of the amended complaint within fourteen days. It further ordered Rosemary to file a response, setting forth her reasons why a constructive trust should not be imposed over her nonbankruptcy interest in the 17.83 acres. Additionally, the United States filed a motion to clarify and reconsider, arguing that the district court appeared to be placing the constructive trust over Rosemary's bankruptcy and nonbankruptcy interests alike. The Butchers filed a supplemental motion for reconsideration arguing that summary judgment should be denied, but acknowledging that Rosemary's attorney had received a summons and a copy of the amended complaint pursuant to an agreement with opposing counsel. Rosemary then filed a response, setting forth her opposition to the constructive trust.

Other than finding that the constructive trust was overbroad, the district court rejected all of the arguments in the motion for reconsideration, the supplemental motion for reconsideration, and the Government's motion to clarify. Because the scope of the constructive trust was unclear, the district court declared in a supplemental order that the scope of the constructive trust would be limited to the nonbankruptcy portion of Rosemary's overall interest in the 17.83 acres. The Butchers

filed another motion to reconsider, and the district court denied it. The Butchers appealed.

On appeal, this Court held that the district court had jurisdiction over the nonbankruptcy portion of Rosemary's interest in the 17.83 acres; that the interest in the property Rosemary received from Alexander in October 1991 was not part of her bankruptcy estate; that neither Alexander's quitclaim deed nor his death extinguished the constructive trust claim; that the owners and Lawyers Title had standing to bring the constructive trust claim; that removal to federal court was proper despite the fact that the owners and Lawyers Title had named the IRS as a defendant rather than the Government; that the constructive trust claim was not time-barred; and that summary judgment was proper as to Rosemary. *See Blachy*, 221 F.3d. at 905–10. The Court upheld the imposition of the constructive trust on Rosemary's nonbankruptcy interest in the 17.83 acres but found that the constructive trust did not defeat the federal tax lien. *See id.* at 903–06. After unsuccessfully petitioning this Court for a rehearing, Rosemary filed an unsuccessful petition for writ of certiorari. *See Blachy v. Butcher*, 532 U.S. 994, 121 S.Ct. 1653, 149 L.Ed.2d 636 (2001). On January 3, 2003, Rosemary moved the district court to reconsider pursuant to Federal Rule of Civil Procedure 60(b)(4), (5), and (6). She alleged that the district court lacked subject matter and personal jurisdiction. She requested relief from the district court's December 16, 1998, summary judgment order and its March 10, 1999, motion for reconsideration. The district court denied Rosemary's motion because it was untimely and the arguments she made would not have changed the case's outcome. The district court also held that Rosemary's motion was an improper attempt to get a lower court to alter a higher court's ruling. Lastly, the district court noted that all of the arguments Rosemary presented in her motion had been previously raised and rejected by itself and this Court.

Rosemary moved for reconsideration of the order denying her motion for Rule 60(b) relief. She also argued that Alexander had not conveyed his entireties interest in the property to her when he quitclaimed in October 1991. The district court denied Rosemary's motion for the reasons stated in its March 17, 2003, order. Lawyers Title moved for sanctions and the district court awarded it the attorneys' fees and expenses incurred in responding to Rosemary's meritless motion. The Butchers timely appealed.

[Text omitted]

ANALYSIS

A. The Butchers' Appeal of the Rule 60(b) Motion

Rule 60(b)(6) is properly invoked only in "unusual and extreme situations where principles of equity *mandate* relief." *Olle v. Henry & Wright Corp.*, 910 F.2d 357, 365 (6th Cir. 1990). District courts can allow Rule 60(b) motions only for the following reasons: 1) mistake, inadvertence, surprise, or excusable neglect; 2) newly discovered evidence which by due diligence could not have been discovered in time to move for a new trial under Rule 59(b); 3) fraud, . . . misrepresentation, or other misconduct of an adverse party; 4) the judgment is void; 5) the judgment has been satisfied, released, or discharged, or a prior judgment upon which it is based has been reversed or otherwise vacated, or it is no longer equitable that the judgment should have prospective application; or 6) any other reason justifying relief from the operation of the judgment. The motion shall be made within a reasonable time, and for reasons (1), (2), and (3) not more than one year after the judgment, order, or proceeding was entered or taken.

Fed. R. Civ. P. 60(b).

Rosemary sought reconsideration pursuant to Rule 60(b)(4), (5), and (6), alleging that the district court lacked removal jurisdiction; no court had jurisdiction over the acreage because it was still being held in tenancy by the entirety at the time suit was originally filed; Lawyers Title defrauded the court by making various factual misstatements; the Michigan state court had exclusive jurisdiction because Alexander's interest in the acreage was part of his probate estate; Lawyers Title lacked standing or a right of subrogation; and Appellees' counsel, the United States, and the bankruptcy trustee defrauded the court and Rosemary by arranging for the federal tax lien to be paid from the proceeds of the sale of the 17.83 acres held in the bankruptcy estate.

These claims, like all claims under Rule 60(b)(4), (5), and (6), must be filed "within a reasonable time." *Id.* The flexible nature of this time frame is not unlimited. In fact, the Court has held that a motion filed pursuant to Rule 60(b)(4)and (6) is untimely where more than three years have passed between the time the motion was filed and judgment was entered. *See Ohio Cas. Ins. Co. v. Pulliam*, 1999 U.S. App. LEXIS 14136, No. 96–6522, 1999 WL 455336, *2 (6th Cir. June 23, 1999).

The district court entered summary judgment against Rosemary on December 14, 1998, and entered its final order on March 10, 1999. Rosemary did not file her Rule 60(b) motion until January 3, 2003. Rosemary argues that this was not an unreasonable length of time given that the bankruptcy portion of the proceedings did not end until October 6, 2002. However, Rosemary's Rule 60(b) motion did not seek reconsideration of the bankruptcy court's order; rather, her motion was aimed at the district court's 1998 and 1999 orders. Because the district court's orders were the subject of Rosemary's motion, their entry dates are the relevant marks by which to measure the timeliness of Rosemary's motion. More than three years passed between the time the district court entered its orders and the time Rosemary filed her Rule 60(b) motion. This is an unreasonable delay. *See Pulliam,* 1999 U.S. App. LEXIS 14136, 1999 WL 455336, at *2. Thus, the district court properly denied Rosemary's Rule 60(b) motion as untimely.

In addition to being untimely, Rosemary's claims are meritless. As this Court explained on the previous appeal, the district court had subject matter jurisdiction, removal was appropriate, and Lawyers Title had standing to sue pursuant to the subrogation clause in its title insurance policy. *See Blachy,* 221 F.3d at 906–10. These conclusions barred the district court from granting relief for these claims. *See United States v. Real Property Numbered as 429 S.Main Street,* 906 F.Supp. 1155, 1159 (S.D. Ohio 1995) ("A district court . . . does not have jurisdiction to alter an appellate ruling where the appellate court has already considered and rejected the basis for relief cited in the Rule 60(b) motion."). Moreover, the Butchers' Rule 60(b) motion did not argue that the case was improperly removed or that the Michigan state court had exclusive jurisdiction. This Court does not generally hear issues raised for the first time on appeal. *See Bailey v. Floyd County Bd. of Educ.,* 106 F.3d 135, 143 (6th Cir. 1997). The Butchers do not set forth any reason for the Court to depart from the general rule.

Finally, the Butchers cannot establish fraud upon the court. Fraud upon the court is conduct: 1) on the part of an officer of the court; 2) that is directed to the judicial machinery itself; 3) that is intentionally false, willfully blind to the truth, or is in reckless disregard for the truth; 4) that is a positive averment or a concealment when one is under a duty to disclose; 5) that deceives the court. *See Demjanjuk v. Petrovsky,* 10 F.3d 338, 348 (6th Cir. 1993). The Butchers do not discuss any of these elements or apply them to the facts of the case. Even if they had, any fraud related to the sale and distribution of assets in 2001 and 2002 could not have invalidated the district court's 1998 and 1999 orders.

B. Sanctions

The district court sanctioned Rosemary and her counsel, Robert Butcher, jointly pursuant to Rule 11 and 28 U.S.C. § 1927. This Court reviews the district court's imposition of these sanctions for abuse of discretion. *See Tropf v. Fid. Nat'l Title Ins. Co.,* 289 F.3d 929, 936 (6th Cir. 2002) (discussing Rule 11); *Ridder v. City of Springfield,* 109 F.3d 288, 298 (6th Cir. 1997) (citation omitted) (discussing § 1927).

In this Circuit, "the test for imposition of Rule 11 sanctions is whether the individual's conduct was reasonable under the circumstances." *See Tropf v. Fid. Nat'l Title Ins. Co.,* 289 F.3d 929, 939 (quotation omitted); *see also Pittman v. Michigan Corrections Organization,* 123 Fed. Appx. 637, 2005 WL 65516, *3 (6th Cir. 2005). Rule 11(b) provides that:

By presenting to the court (whether by signing, filing, submitting, or later advocating) a pleading, written motion, or other paper, an attorney or unrepresented party is certifying that to the best of the person's knowledge, information, and belief, formed after an inquiry reasonable under the circumstances,—

(1) it is not being presented for any improper purpose, such as to harass or to cause unnecessary delay or needless increase in the cost of litigation;

(2) the claims, defenses, and other legal contentions therein are warranted by existing law or by a nonfrivolous argument for the extension, modification, or reversal of existing law or the establishment of new law;

(3) the allegations and other factual contentions have evidentiary support or, if specifically so identified, are likely to have evidentiary support after a reasonable opportunity for further investigation or discovery; and

(4) the denials of factual contentions are warranted on the evidence or, if specifically so identified, are reasonably based on a lack of information or belief.

After "notice and a reasonable opportunity" to respond are given, a court may sanction a party, attorney, or law firm, that has violated or is responsible for violating Rule 11(b). See Fed. R. Civ. P. 11(c).

Here, the district court sanctioned Rosemary because her Rule 60(b) motion was "objectively unreasonable." Such a characterization is patently sound. After all, Rosemary's claims had been rejected in some form or fashion by the district court and the Sixth Circuit alike. Thus, the district court correctly determined that Rosemary did not have a good faith basis for filing her Rule 60(b) motion. Sanctions were, therefore, appropriate under Rule 11(b)(2). The district court also found that sanctions were appropriate under § 1927. Section 1927 provides that any attorney "who so multiplies the proceedings in any case unreasonably and vexatiously may be required by the court to satisfy personally the excess costs, expenses, and attorneys' fees reasonably incurred because of such conduct." 28 U.S.C. § 1927.

As the foregoing section of this opinion attests, Rosemary's Rule 60(b) motion was objectively meritless. Its untimeliness and baselessness were obvious. Similarly, there can be no doubt that the Appellants' litigation strategy vexatiously and unreasonably multiplied these proceedings. From the time this case entered the federal court system in 1991 through the present date, Rosemary has not obtained a single successful judgment. She and her counsel, Robert Butcher, have contested issues they had no business contesting and, in the course of their conduct, earned the sanctions the district court imposed under Rule 11 and § 1927.

The Butchers' conduct persists even on appeal. Upon a separately filed motion or notice from a court, Federal Rule of Appellate Procedure 38 allows a court to award "just damages and single or double costs to the appellee." Fed. R. App. P. 38. Sanctions are appropriate under Rule 38 where litigation is frivolous, where "the result is obvious or where the appellant's argument is wholly without merit." *See Pieper v. Am. Arbitration Ass'n*, 336 F.3d 458, 465 (6th Cir. 2003).

The Appellees move the Court to sanction the Butchers pursuant to Rule 38 and § 1927 and the Court has a difficult time imagining a case where sanctions would be more just. The result of the Butchers' appeal was obvious since their arguments were either untimely, could not be raised for the first time to this Court, or were objectively meritless. The Butchers must bear the consequences of their actions and be deterred from further folly.

Conclusion

We AFFIRM the district court's decision. Furthermore, we GRANT the Appellees' motion for sanctions on appeal under Rule 38 and § 1927. Appellees shall file an affidavit within fifteen days of this order setting forth the hourly rates of its counsel and the number of hours spent in defending this appeal.

[Footnotes omitted]

Source: Blachy v. Butcher, 129 Fed. App'x 173; 2005 U.S. App. LEXIS 6445. Reprinted with the permission of LexisNexis.

Chapter 4

Regulations and Encumbrances

CHAPTER OBJECTIVES

Upon completion of this chapter, you will be able to:

- Identify public regulations on land.

- Explain zoning.

- Understand the power of eminent domain.

- Discuss the types of private encumbrances.

Many property owners face restrictions on their properties that prevent them from being able to do something on those properties. Perhaps you want to build a commercial retail center on your property, only to find that your property is zoned for residential use only. Or, you want to put a second story on your home, but you find the building codes prevent you from doing so. This chapter will discuss some of the restrictions that are attached to and binding on real property.

ENCUMBRANCE

Most urban property is burdened or restricted by some type of **encumbrance**. But what is an encumbrance? An encumbrance is a claim, lien, charge, or liability that is attached to the real property and is binding on that property. An encumbrance provides for the interests of another person or entity to be attached to the property. An encumbrance can reduce the value of the land or obstruct the unrestricted use of the property by the owner. Encumbrances typically include zoning restrictions, restrictive covenants, money judgments, taxes, mortgages, easements, and licenses. Encumbrances are attached to the property by a written instrument and can be discovered by a title examination of the property, as they are typically recorded and will show up in the **chain of title**. Chain of title usually refers to the recorded sequence of transactions by which title has passed from a sovereign to the present claimant. It includes instruments that will be picked up by a title search.

encumbrance
A claim or liability that is attached to property and may decrease its value.

chain of title
Record of successive conveyances, or other forms of alienation, affecting a particular parcel of land, arranged consecutively, from the government or original source of title down to the present holder.

 LEGAL RESEARCH MAXIM

When running title searches, encumbrances, liens, easements, and such are found on Schedule B to the title report, while the property description is found on Schedule A. Property descriptions found on Schedule A many times begin with a landmark in the area to begin measuring boundaries, such as this: "beginning at the large tree on northwest corner," or "beginning at the large boulder facing the north end of the field. . . ."

PUBLIC REGULATIONS

condemnation
The determination and declaration that certain property is assigned to public use, subject to reasonable compensation.

The Fifth Amendment of the United States Constitution provides the federal government with the ability to "take" private property for the benefit of the public health and welfare. The ability to take private property is made binding on the states by the Fourteenth Amendment. **Condemnation** is the exercise of eminent domain by the government. If the government wishes to condemn private property for public use, it must comply with procedures which assure property owners due process of law. The power given to the federal and state governments by the Constitution to be able to promote and protect the public welfare also gives the government the right to impose restrictions such as zoning regulations, building codes, subdivision regulations, environmental protection laws, and other restrictions on private property owners. All of these restrictions are imposed under the power to promote the health and welfare of the public. Some of the public restrictions imposed on private property owners will be discussed below.

ZONING

zoning
The division of a region, such as a county, city, or town, by legislative regulation into districts, and the prescription and application in each district of regulation having to do with structural and architectural design of buildings within designated districts.

euclidean zoning
Type of zoning based on district and use.

The main type of public regulation of land use in the United States is **zoning**. Various levels of governmental entities can establish zoning regulations that restrict the use of real property that is owned by private landowners. Zoning is accomplished primarily at the local or municipal level of government. The main objective of zoning is to improve living and working conditions in populated areas by preventing the rights of one property owner from interfering with or impinging upon the rights of other property owners.

One of the most important types of zoning is **Euclidean**, or use, **zoning**. Use zoning enables a municipality to be divided into districts. Only certain types of uses of the land are permitted within certain districts. For example, certain districts may be zoned for industrial purposes. Zoning restrictions will prohibit the construction of residential dwellings within the industrial district. Districts are graded from "highest" (single-family residences) to "lowest" (worst kind of industry). Euclidian zoning would allow a single-family house to be built in a commercial district, but would not allow the commercial use of a building located in a residential district.

Spot zoning refers to zoning amendments that are invalidated as legislative acts not supported by rational basis. The term applies to zoning changes which result in a use classification that is inconsistent with surrounding uses. The burden of demonstrating that a zoning amendment is spot zoning lies with the party attacking the ordinance.

variance
A license or official authorization to depart from a zoning law.

The Standard State Zoning Enabling Act authorizes the appointment of a board of adjustment. A board of adjustment may grant a **variance** when a strict application of a zoning ordinance would result in substantial and undue hardship upon the developer of the property and if such a variance would not result in substantial detriment to the public good and would not substantially impair the purpose of the zoning plan and/or ordinance. When granting a variance, zoning boards may impose reasonable conditions. Zoning boards may not, however, condition a variance upon use of the property by the

RESEARCH THIS

Euclidean zoning is named after the case that brought the issue of district zoning to the United States Supreme Court for the first time. Research the cases *Village of Euclid v. Ambler Realty Co.*, 272 U.S. 365 (1926) and *Nectow v. City of Cambridge*, 277 U.S. 183 (1928).

What were the facts of each case? What was the holding of each case? How did the court's ruling in *Euclid* affect zoning in the United States? What did the court decide about the zoning ordinance under scrutiny in *Nectow*?

original applicants only. Thus, a variance "runs with the land." See *St Onge v. Donovan,* 71 N.Y.2d 507, 522 N.E.2d 1019, 527 N.Y.S.2d 721 (1988).

Another type of zoning restriction is that of density. Density requirements are used to maintain the appearance of a community while providing a means to ensure that public facilities, such as parks, sewers, and schools, are not overburdened by too many people in one area. Density restrictions can be achieved by establishing minimum lot sizes for homes, requiring that structures be set back from the street, and establishing minimum square footages for homes and height limits on other structures.

Zoning is considered constitutional so long as the zoning restriction shows some reasonable association to the public welfare. If a zoning regulation is found to be unreasonable or not properly associated with the public welfare, it may be considered to be a "taking" of the real property of a private owner. In such situations, the owner may be entitled to compensation or to having the zoning regulation **voided**.

- Zoning consists of dividing a city or county into districts
- Dictating within each district the types of structures and building designs that structures can have if they are located in the district
- Establishing uses for the buildings within each district

Zoning is a legislative process that requires procedural **due process**. The Fourteenth Amendment provides that no state shall "deprive any person of life, liberty, or property without due process of law." This means that there are certain restrictions placed on the means by which a zoning activity may be taken. For example, notice must be given to all interested parties regarding a zoning issue. Notice can be given by running a notice in the local newspaper. Once notice is given, typically a public hearing is held to air views and obtain public comments. Landowners as well as other interested parties are given the opportunity to speak at the public hearing. Governmental officials are required to present evidence to support the proposed zoning classifications. Once the hearing has been completed, the zoning classification is voted on, usually by the city or county council where the proposed zoning restriction is to take affect. A property owner cannot appeal a zoning decision or classification in a court of law. A court generally will not overturn the government's vote on a zoning issue unless clear evidence of abuse by the government exists.

When zoning for a particular area is changed, there can be existing land uses in the area that do not conform to the zoning change. These existing uses are called nonconforming uses. Since outlawing existing uses would be determined to be a violation of due process, most zoning ordinances provide for either (1) a grant to the land user of the preexisting use a period within which he may continue the nonconforming use; or (2) permission for the use to continue indefinitely. These nonconforming uses typically are permitted to continue so long as they do not expand. Some zoning statutes provide for the termination of nonconforming uses over a period of time. Zoning ordinances are enforced through injunction.

BUILDING CODES AND SUBDIVISION

Zoning ordinances can also be enforced by the issuance of building permits through the use of **building codes**. A building permit will be refused unless the proposed improvement and its intended use comply with zoning. Building codes represent the police power that is given to local governmental entities in order to protect the public good. Building codes may regulate construction methods and techniques, as well as the types of materials that are to be used in construction or improvements on structures. Most cities and counties do not permit a building to be constructed and occupied without the proper permits having been obtained and a final inspection by the building department.

void
Describing a transaction that is impossible to enforce because it is invalid.

due process
In real estate law, protection of one of two types: procedural, which provides a person a guarantee to fair procedures; and substantive, which protects a person's property from unfair governmental interference or taking.

PRACTICE TIP

If you decide to concentrate on real property in your career as a paralegal, be sure to build a bond with the County Clerk's office or County Recorder's office of your area, as you will be dealing with those entities on a regular basis.

building codes
Laws, ordinances, or governmental regulations concerning fitness for habitation, setting forth standards and requirements for the construction, maintenance, operation, occupancy, use, or appearance of buildings, premises, and dwelling units.

Another method by which local governments can regulate land use is through **subdivision**. Subdivision is the process by which vacant land is developed for residential purposes. Subdivision provides for the layouts of streets and the availability of land for public parks. Subdivision laws also usually require that streets and sewers be provided for and approved in advance by the local government.

Subdivision is obviously different from zoning. Subdivision regulates the layout of the land. Zoning regulates the types of buildings that may be constructed, as well as the uses of the land.

HISTORIC AND ENVIRONMENTAL PRESERVATION

Municipalities also control land use through **historic preservation**. Historic preservation seeks to maintain a common style of historical or architectural interest in a specified area. In such designated areas, no alterations, demolition, or new construction can occur without permits and prior approval being obtained.

In addition to the designation of historical districts, a particular building or structure may be declared a historical landmark. A municipality may determine that a particular building or structure needs to be preserved due to its unique or unusual historical or architectural importance. Historical preservation can be at the local, state, or federal level.

Governmental entities can regulate land use for environmental concerns as well. Environmental laws can regulate broad environmental concerns on the land, such as use of automobiles, operation of factories, and other activities that may be outside the scope of traditional real property law. The federal government regulates environmental quality of real property through legislation such as the Environmental Protection Act, Federal Water Pollution Control Act, and Federal Resource Conservation and Recovery Act. Through this legislation, the federal government imposes strict restrictions, uses, and fines on individuals who damage the environment of real property. **Master plans** can be a valuable tool for housing, industry, and recreation facilities, as they generally include projected environmental impact.

POWER OF EMINENT DOMAIN

Eminent domain is the power of federal, state, and local governments to take private property for public use. With the right of private ownership in the United States also comes the fact that property is held subject to a perpetual repurchase option by the United States, the various states, the counties, cities, and other governmental agencies. The Constitution does provide a landowner with legal safeguards in order to protect the landowner from the harsh consequences of eminent domain. The government is not permitted to exercise its right of eminent domain without first establishing that the private property is needed for a **public use**.

Public use is construed quite broadly by the courts. So long as the government's use is rationally related to a conceivable public purpose, the requirement is satisfied. **Urban renewal** has been determined to be a public use, even though the building may be operated by a private agency. For example, Duke owns a building in an economically depressed area of Anytown. Anytown decides that it wants to take Duke's building under its power of eminent domain under the theory of urban renewal. Anytown is successful in its eminent domain and obtains the property. Anytown decides to allow a private developer to turn the building into upscale trendy apartments that will be managed and operated by the developer.

The Fifth Amendment of the Constitution states: "[N]or shall private property be taken for public use without just compensation." One of the most litigated aspects of eminent domain is the value of the property being taken. The courts have generally

subdivision
The division of a lot, tract, or parcel of land into two or more lots, tracts, parcels, or other divisions of land for sale or development.

historic preservation
An ordinance that prohibits the demolition or exterior alteration of certain historic buildings or of all buildings in a historic district.

master plan
A municipal plan for housing, industry, and recreational facilities.

eminent domain
The power to take private property for public use by the state, municipalities, and private persons or corporations authorized to exercise functions of public character.

public use
A use that confers some benefit or advantage to the public; it is not confined to actual use by the public.

urban renewal
Redevelopment plans indicating a relationship to such local objectives as appropriate land uses, improved traffic, public transportation, public utilities, recreation, community facilities, and other public improvements.

SPOT THE ISSUE

Mr. Smith received a notice informing him about a hearing set in 2 months to decide a taking issue of Mr. Smith's property by the government for public use. Mr. Smith was worried that he might lose his home. This was a very old property needing a lot of work, but nonetheless famous in his area, because of the Underground Railroad's use of his cellar; his ancestors had used the house to shelter slaves escaping to the North before and during the Civil War. Does Mr. Smith have to lose the property to the government? Spot the issue.

determined that the value of the property should be measured as the fair market value of the land at the time of the taking. The **fair market value** is based on the highest and best use that may be made of the property.

Before the government can take private property, the property owner is entitled to due process of a notice as well as a hearing. At the hearing, a property owner can have legal representation and can submit evidence that the taking of the property by the government is not necessary for public use, or that the compensation being offered for the property is unreasonable and not at fair market value or based on the highest and most profitable use. The government can take private property for many uses. Some of the uses include constructing public streets, sewer facilities, airports, and government buildings; slum clearance; redevelopment projects; etc.

The government also has the power to encumber a property through its right to tax real property that is located within its jurisdictional boundaries. Property taxes can be found at the county and city levels. If the tax is measured on the value of the real property being taxed, it is called an **ad valorem tax**.

Most governments have a period of time designated as a tax year. Property taxes need to be paid within this specified tax year. The taxes become a **lien**, or debt charged against the real property, on the first day of the tax year. Tax liens have a priority over any mortgage or other property interests on the property and are paid before all other debts, liens, or claims. Tax liens can be enforced by foreclosure and sale of the real property by public authority. Governments can levy special assessments against real property owners for the costs of things, such as grading, curbing, paving, and sewer and water lines, that benefit a person's real property. Special assessments are enforceable by foreclosure and public sale of the real property.

Before a judgment in a lawsuit affecting title to real property is handed down, a party may record a *lis pendens*. This puts later claimants on notice of claims to be litigated concerning the property. Wills and affidavits of heirship of an intestate may also be recorded.

PRIVATE ENCUMBRANCES

Private encumbrances are encumbrances that are voluntarily created by private individuals who have transactions in some manner that involve real property. The most common forms of private encumbrances are liens, mortgages, and covenants.

A **judgment lien** is a money debt that is attached to a particular piece of property. When a property owner is sued for a sum of money and loses, a judgment may be issued by the court in favor of the person suing the property owner. The person who has been awarded the judgment can place a lien on the property in order to secure the debt. This means that before the property is sold, the lien is paid. Judgment liens do not officially become liens on the property until they have been recorded with the county recorder's office in the county in which the property is located.

fair market value
The amount that a willing buyer would pay for an item that a willing seller would accept.

ad valorem tax
A tax imposed on the value of the property.

lien
A legal right or interest that a creditor has in another's property.

lis pendens
(Latin for "a pending lawsuit") a notice, recorded in the chain of title to real property, required or permitted in some jurisdictions to warn parties that certain property is the subject of litigation, and that any interests acquired during the pendency of the suit are subject to outcome.

judgment lien
An encumbrance that arises by law when a judgment for the recovery of money is docketed and that attaches to the debtor's real estate located in the county in which the judgment is docketed.

Judgment liens remain attached to the property until they have been paid or they expire after a prescribed period of time. Typically, a judgment lien terminates after anywhere between seven and fourteen years. For example, in California, a judgment lien terminates after ten years have passed.

mechanic's lien
A claim created by state statutes for the purpose of securing priority of payment of the price or value of work performed and materials furnished in erecting, improving, or repairing a building or other structure, and as such attaching to the land as well as buildings and improvements erected thereon.

Mechanic's liens are different from judgment liens in that they are liens that are prescribed by statute. A mechanic's lien is attached to a piece of property in order to secure payment for work that has been performed on the property or to secure payment for materials that have been used for construction, repair, or alteration on the property.

A mechanic's lien usually cannot be sought until the work has been performed on the property or the material has been used on the property. The lien is not perfected until a notice of lien has been filed with the county recorder in the county in which the property is located. Most states require that the notice of lien be recorded with the county recorder within a reasonable period of time after the completion of the work on the property. A reasonable period of time is typically between 60 and 120 days. A notice of lien requires the following elements:

claimant
One who claims or asserts a right, demand, or claim.

- The amount of the lien
- The name of the **claimant**

EYE ON ETHICS

It is always important when dealing with real property transactions to check the chain of title carefully in order to ensure that no liens, covenants, or encumbrances are attached to the property of which either party may be unaware. A law office that fails to thoroughly investigate the chain of title could be held liable for malpractice if problems arise from that failure. There are third-party title companies that will, for a fee, examine the chain of title on a property. In addition, the purchase of title insurance helps to provide a source of redress to a party should issues with title be uncovered after the transaction.

SURF'S UP

To find more resources concerning real property issues, a legal assistant can turn to the Internet. Several Web sites exist that are dedicated strictly to the practice of law. These dedicated Web sites can be a great resource for information. The following are two popular Web sites:

www.megalaw.com
www.findlaw.com

- The name of the owner of the property
- A description of property that the lien is being attached to
- The notarized signature of the claimant

Mortgages are also a form of private encumbrance. In a mortgage, a property owner uses the real property as security against a loan for money. Mortgages will be discussed in further detail in a later chapter.

Another method for restricting the use of property is through a **covenant**. Landowners can use covenants to restrict the use of their property. Restrictive covenants may be in the form of stated restrictions found in the deeds of conveyance used to convey the property. Restrictive covenants are also found in documents that are recorded against the property with the county recorder where the property is located. A private restrictive covenant is used in an attempt to control the development or use of the property so as to try to enhance the value of the owner's lot or share in the property.

A restrictive covenant is usually enforced by an injunction issued by a court. Enforcement of the covenant may be brought by any person who bought the property with notice of the restrictions and in reliance on those restrictions.

mortgage
An interest in land created by a written instrument providing security for the performance of a duty or the payment of a debt.

covenant
A promise of two or more parties written into a conveyance of land, usually a deed, binding either party to the other that something be done or not be done.

Summary

An encumbrance is a claim, lien, charge, or liability that is attached to real property and is binding on that property. An encumbrance provides for the interests of another person or entity to be attached to the property. An encumbrance can reduce the value of the land or obstruct the unrestricted use of the property by the owner. Encumbrances typically include zoning restrictions, restrictive covenants, money judgments, taxes, mortgages, easements, and licenses. Encumbrances are attached to the property by a written instrument and can be discovered by a title examination of the property, as they are typically recorded and will show up in the chain of title.

The Fifth Amendment of the United States Constitution provides the federal government with the ability to "take" private property for the benefit of the public health and welfare. The ability to take private property is made binding on the states by the Fourteenth Amendment. The power given to the federal and state governments by the Constitution to be able to promote and protect the public welfare also gives the government the right to impose on private property owners restrictions such as zoning regulations, building codes, subdivision regulations, environmental protection laws, and other restrictions.

The main type of public regulation on land use in the United States is zoning. Various levels of governmental entities can establish zoning regulations that restrict the use of real property that is owned by private landowners. Zoning is accomplished primarily at the local or municipal level of government. The main objective of zoning is to improve living and working conditions in populated areas by preventing the rights of one property owner from interfering with or impinging on the rights of other property owners.

Zoning is a legislative process that requires procedural due process. The Fourteenth Amendment provides that no state shall "deprive any person of life, liberty, or property without due process of law." This means that there are certain restrictions placed on the means by which a zoning activity may be taken. For example, notice must be given to all interested parties regarding a zoning issue. Notice can be given by running a notice in the local newspaper. Once notice is given, a public hearing typically is held to air views and obtain public comments. Landowners as well as other interested parties are given the opportunity to speak at the public hearing. Governmental officials are required to present evidence to support the proposed zoning classifications. Once the hearing has been completed, the zoning classification is voted on, usually by the city or county council where the proposed zoning restriction is to take affect. A property owner cannot appeal a zoning decision or classification in a court of law. A court generally will not overturn the government's vote on a zoning issue unless clear evidence of abuse by the government exists.

Zoning ordinances can also be enforced by the issuance of building permits through the use of building codes. A building permit will be refused unless the proposed improvement and its intended use comply with zoning. Building codes represent the police power that is given to local governmental entities in order to protect the public good. Building codes may regulate construction methods and techniques as well as the types of materials that are to be used in construction or improvements on structures. Most cities and counties do not permit a building to be constructed and occupied without the proper permits having been obtained and a final inspection by the building department.

Another method by which local governments can regulate land use is through subdivision. Subdivision is the process by which vacant land is developed for residential purposes. Subdivision provides for the layouts for streets and the availability of land for public parks. Subdivision laws also usually require that streets and sewers be provided for and approved in advance by the local government.

Municipalities also control land use through historic preservation. Historic preservation seeks to maintain a common style of historical or architectural interest in a specified area. In such designated areas, no alterations, demolition, or new construction can occur without permits and prior approval being obtained.

Eminent domain is the power of the federal, state, and local governments to take private property for public use. With the right of private ownership in the United States also comes the fact that property is held subject to a perpetual repurchase option by the United States, the various states, the counties, cities, and other governmental agencies. The Constitution does provide a landowner with legal safeguards in order to protect the landowner from the harsh consequences of eminent domain. The government is not permitted to exercise its right of eminent domain without first establishing that the private property is needed for a public use.

Government also has the power to encumber a property through its right to tax real property that is located within its jurisdictional boundaries. Property taxes can be found at the county and city levels. If the tax is measured on the value of the real property being taxed, it is called an ad valorem tax.

A judgment lien is a money debt that is attached to a particular piece of property. When a property owner is sued for a sum of money and loses, a judgment may be issued by the court in favor of the person suing the property owner. The person who has been awarded the judgment can place a lien on the property in order to secure the debt. This means that before the property is sold, the lien is paid. Judgment liens do not officially become liens on the property until they have been recorded with the county recorder's office in the county in which the property is located.

Mechanic's liens are different from judgment liens in that they are liens that are prescribed by statute. A mechanic's lien is attached to a piece of property in order to secure payment for work that has been performed on the property or to secure payment for materials that have been used for construction, repair, or alteration on the property.

Restrictive covenants may be in the form of stated restrictions found in the deeds of conveyance used to convey the property. Restrictive covenants are also found in documents that are recorded against the property with the county recorder where the property is located. A private restrictive covenant is used in an attempt to control the development or use of the property so as to try to enhance the value of the owner's lot or share in the property.

Key Terms

Ad valorem tax
Building codes
Chain of title
Claimant
Condemnation
Covenant
Due process
Eminent domain
Encumbrance
Euclidean zoning
Fair market value
Historic preservation

Judgment lien
Lien
Lis pendens
Master plan
Mechanic's lien
Mortgage
Public use
Subdivision
Urban renewal
Variance
Void
Zoning

Review Questions

1. Define "covenant."
2. What is a zoning regulation?
3. What is a Euclidean zoning regulation?
4. What is the difference between a zoning ordinance and a building code?
5. What is eminent domain?
6. Which part of the Constitution gives the government the power of eminent domain?
7. What is a judgment lien?
8. Describe what a mechanic's lien is and how it is enforced.
9. What is the purpose of subdivision regulation?
10. How are private restrictive covenants enforced?
11. What is an ad valorem tax?
12. What are the elements that are required for a notice of lien?
13. Why is historic preservation important?
14. How does the government preserve historic areas?
15. What is an encumbrance?

Exercises

1. Dude operates a movie theater along a freeway located in the city of Snap. For over twenty years, Dude had a billboard on the edge of his property advertising the current movies playing at the theater. Then, the Snap City Council enacted a zoning ordinance that barred billboards from being displayed anywhere in the city. The "preexisting uses" section of the ordinance provides that any nonconforming use must be phased out within five years of the ordinance. Dude has sued to overturn the ordinance as applied to him, arguing that while Snap has the right to ban billboards, it may not require him to remove an existing billboard, because this constitutes a taking of his property without due process. Will Dude prevail?

2. Research your state's requirements for filing a mechanic's lien. Prepare a mechanic's lien for construction work performed on the property at 1234 Elm Street, Your City, State, Zip for the amount of $43,000. You are the claimant, and your teacher is the property owner. Make sure that you follow all necessary procedures for filing a claim, and use the proper local forms.

3. Look up your local county recorder's Web site on the Internet. Find out what needs to be done in order to attach a judgment lien on the property. Prepare a memorandum detailing the steps necessary for perfecting a judgment lien. Use the address given in question 2 as the property address.

4. In the past few years, there have been major challenges launched against certain government entities throughout the United States, regarding eminent domain. Research past news and court records and determine which specific issue has recently received a lot of press regarding the taking of property.

5. Research when, *in the United States,* the practice of recording documents relating to real property began.

6. Did Native American tribes and nations view property as we do or as the first arriving Europeans did when they arrived here in North America? What was their concept of boundaries, encumbrances, covenants, and ownership of land? Was it the same as our notions? Explain.

 PORTFOLIO ASSIGNMENT

Visit your County Clerk's Office or County Recorder's Office and research the piece of property you live at. Determine whether or not your property has ever had a lien of any kind placed upon it.

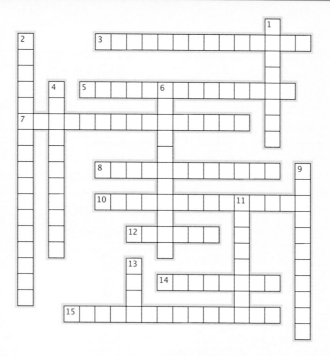

Instructions

Use the key terms from this chapter to fill in the answers to the crossword puzzle.

NOTE: When the answer is more than one word, leave a blank space between the words.

ACROSS

3. the power to take private property for public use by the state, municipalities, and private persons or corporations authorized to exercise functions of public character.

5. a tax imposed on the value of the property.

7. a claim created by state statutes for the purpose of securing priority of payment of the price or value of work performed and materials furnished in erecting, improving, or repairing a building or other structure, and as such attaching to the land as well as buildings and improvements erected thereon.

8. the determination and declaration that certain property is assigned to public use, subject to reasonable compensation.

10. laws, ordinances, or governmental regulations concerning fitness for habitation, setting forth standards and requirements for the construction, maintenance, opertion, occupancy, use or appearance of buildings, premises, and dwelling units.

12. the division of a region, such as a county, city or town, by legislative regulation into districts and the prescription and application in each district of regulation having to do with structural and architectural design of buildings within designated districts.

14. is an interest in land created by a written instrument providing security for the performance of a duty or the payment of a debt.

15. record of successive conveyances, or other forms of alienation, affecting a particular parcel of land, arranged consecutively, from the government or original source of title down to the present holder.

DOWN

1. a license or official authorization to depart from a zoning law.

2. the price in cash, or its equivalent, that the property would have brought at the time of taking, considering its highest and most profitable use.

4. a claim or liability that is attached to property and may decrease its value.

6. (Latin for "a pending lawsuit") a notice, recorded in the chain of title to real property, required or permitted in some jurisdictions to warn parties that certain property is the subject of litigation, and that any interests acquired during the pendency of the suit are subject to outcome.

9. a municipal plan for housing, industry, and recreational facilities.

11. a restriction inserted in a conveyance of land, on the part of the grantor, and binding herself for the completeness, security, and continuance of the title transferred to the grantee.

13. a legal right or interest that a creditor has in another's property.

RANDY L. HOFFER, Plaintiff-Appellant, v. DAVID CALLISTER and BECKY CALLISTER, husband and wife; SCOTT STEWART and SANDRA G. STEWART, husband and wife; and JUDITH E. WILSON, an individual, Defendants-Respondents. SCOTT STEWART and SANDRA G. STEWART, husband and wife, Counterclaimants, v. RANDY L. HOFFER, Counterdefendant. JUDITH E. ALLEN, formerly known as JUDITH E. WILSON, an individual, Counterclaimaint, v. RANDY L. HOFFER, Counterdefendant. JUDITH E. ALLEN, formerly known as JUDITH E. WILSON, Cross Claimant, v. DAVID CALLISTER and BECKY CALLISTER, husband and wife; SCOTT STEWART and SANDRA G. STEWART, husband and wife, Cross Defendants. JUDITH E. ALLEN, formerly known as JUDITH E. WILSON, an individual, Third Party Plaintiff, v. RICHARD N. CHILD, BARBARA V. CHILD and DOES 1 through 10, Third Party Defendants.

SUPREME COURT OF IDAHO
137 Idaho 291; 47 P.3d 1261; 2002 Ida. LEXIS 71

May 6, 2002, Filed

KIDWELL, Justice

This dispute calls for this Court to determine whether zoning violations, if proven, may constitute **encumbrances** on the title to real property. Randy L. Hoffer (Hoffer) brought this claim for damages against David and Becky Callister and Scott and Sandra G. Stewart (Callister and Stewart), who sold property to him, and Defendant Judith E. Allen, formerly known as Judith E. Wilson (Wilson), Callister and Stewart's predecessor, for breach of contract and breach of deed warranties against **encumbrances**. The district court granted summary judgment in favor of the defendants, finding that zoning violations are not **encumbrances** and that, based on the clear language of the contract, there was no breach. Hoffer appealed, and we affirm the decision of the district court.

FACTS AND PROCEDURAL BACKGROUND

In 1979, Wilson purchased real property in Ada County, Idaho, from Richard and Barbara Child. When Wilson purchased the property it was being used as a mobile home park (the park), and it contained twenty-seven mobile home spaces. On July 29, 1994, Wilson sold the park to Callister and Stewart pursuant to a real estate contract (Wilson contract), which required Callister and Stewart to make monthly installment payments to Wilson over the course of approximately thirty-five years. Wilson executed a warranty deed in favor of Callister and Stewart.

On August 31, 1995, Callister and Stewart sold the park to Hoffer, assigning their rights under the Wilson contract to Hoffer (assignment contract). Hoffer paid Callister and Stewart cash for their interest and assumed their contract with Wilson. Wilson consented to the assignment and assumption. Callister and Stewart executed a warranty deed in favor of Hoffer.

In the spring of 1999, prospective tenants in the mobile home park advised Hoffer that they could not get permits from Ada County for placement of mobile homes in the park. Hoffer investigated, and he discovered that Ada County was asserting that only sixteen spaces were allowable in the park under relevant zoning restrictions. The County subsequently amended its position to allow for nineteen spaces. Based upon the pleadings, briefs, and affidavits, it is undisputed that Hoffer never had any discussions with Wilson or Callister

and Stewart concerning the park's zoning status prior to purchasing the property. It is also undisputed that neither Wilson nor Callister and Stewart had any actual knowledge that Ada County was asserting a possible zoning violation until they were informed of this by Hoffer in 1999. There is no contention that any of the defendants made any representations to Hoffer about the number of spaces allowed in the park or any possible zoning restrictions or violations.

At the outset of this case, Ada County was maintaining the position that the park may contain only nineteen spaces and that Hoffer can reach this number through attrition, as homes are removed from the park over time.

Hoffer instituted this action against Wilson and Callister and Stewart on December 28, 1999, seeking damages for a loss in value of the property, based on the reduction in income he alleged would result from his loss of six rental spaces. He alleged claims for breach of contract and breach of deed warranties against Wilson, and a claim for breach of deed warranties against Callister and Stewart. Alternatively, he sought rescission of the contracts and restitution, based on mutual mistake. Wilson and the Stewarts filed counterclaims against Hoffer, and Wilson filed a cross-claim against Callister and Stewart and a third-party claim against the Childs. The cross-claim, third-party claim, and counterclaims are not at issue in this appeal. No jury trial was requested. Subsequently, Wilson and Callister and Stewart filed motions for summary judgment on Hoffer's claims. Hoffer filed a cross-motion for summary judgment. The district court granted summary judgment in favor of the defendants, dismissing Hoffer's claims, because the court found that, as a matter of law, zoning violations are not **encumbrances**. The district court also found that, under the clear and unambiguous language of the Wilson contract, there was no breach. Hoffer has appealed the district court's denial of his breach of warranty claims, but he does not argue on appeal that the contracts should be rescinded due to mutual mistake.

ANALYSIS

A. An Existing Zoning Violation is not an Encumbrance.

It has never been judicially determined that there was a zoning violation in this case. The district court granted summary judgment in favor of the defendants, dismissing Hoffer's claims, because the court found that, as a matter of law, zoning violations are not **encumbrances**. Hoffer appeals from that decision, arguing that, as a matter of law, an existing zoning violation can constitute an **encumbrance** on the title to real property. This Court exercises free review over issues of law. *Bouten Constr. Co.*, 133 Idaho at 760, 992 P.2d at 755.

The specific question of whether a zoning violation is an **encumbrance** appears to be an issue of first impression in this state. This is also the paramount issue in this case, because Hoffer's causes of action for breach of deed warranties and breach of contract—except for his claim related to paragraph 8 of the Wilson contract—are dependent upon a finding that the alleged zoning violations, if proven, are **encumbrances**.

Chapter 6, Title 55 of the Idaho Code governs transfers of real property. Section 55-613 provides, in its entirety: "The term '**encumbrances**' includes taxes, assessments, and all liens upon real property." This Court has indicated that I.C. § 55-613 is inclusive, rather than exclusive, and that the law may recognize other types of **encumbrances** that are not specified in the statute:

Aside from [this] statutory provision [], an **encumbrance** may otherwise be defined to be any right or interest in land to the diminution of its value, but consistent with the free transfer of the fee. It does not depend upon the extent or amount of diminution in value, but embraces all cases in which the owner does not acquire the complete dominion over the land which his grant apparently implies.

Hunt v. Bremer, 47 Idaho 490, 494, 276 P. 964, 965 (1929). This Court has more recently stated that "the covenant of title is breached when there are hostile titles, superior in fact to those of the grantor." *Koelker v. Turnbull*, 127 Idaho 262, 265-66, 899 P.2d 972, 975-76 (1995).

As the language from these cases makes clear, an **encumbrance** that does not fit within one of the categories enumerated in I.C. § 55-613 must be a right, interest, or hostile title relating to the land. We find no Idaho authority for the proposition that zoning ordinances or zoning violations generally create such rights, interests, or hostile titles. Additionally, while this Court has not addressed the particular question posed in this case, it has held that privately imposed land use restrictions are not **encumbrances**. *See Middlekauff v. Lake Cascade, Inc.*, 103 Idaho 832, 834, 654 P.2d 1385, 1387 (1982) (Middlekauff I). In *Middlekauff I*, the plaintiffs were the owners of parcels in a subdivision in Valley County, Idaho. At the time the parcels were sold to the plaintiffs, the developer promised that one specific parcel would always be kept open as a common recreational area for use by all of the owners in the subdivision. During the developer's bankruptcy proceedings, the bankruptcy court approved a transfer of the common area to a third party, "free and clear of all liens and **encumbrances**." *Id.* at 833, 654 P.2d at 1386. The third party then prevented the common use of the property, and the buyers of the subdivision parcels brought suit. The third party claimed that the conveyance approved by the bankruptcy court granted them title free of the use restriction, because the restriction was an **encumbrance**. This Court held that the third party did not take title to the property free of the use restriction because the interest that the subdivision property owners had in the common use of the parcel was not an **encumbrance**. *Id.* This Court affirmed

that holding in *Middlekauff v. Lake Cascade, Inc.*, 110 Idaho 909, 916, 719 P.2d 1169, 1176 (1986) (*Middlekauff II*).

We decline to extend the traditional scope of a general warranty against **encumbrances** in such a manner as to include zoning matters. To expand the concept of **encumbrance** as urged by Hoffer would create uncertainty and confusion in the law of conveyancing and title insurance. Neither a title search nor a physical examination of the premises would have disclosed the alleged violation. The better way to deal with violations of zoning **regulations** is by contract provisions, which can give the purchaser full protection in a situation like this one.

We hold that a zoning violation of the type alleged in this case does not constitute an **encumbrance** on the title of real property. We do not address the possible situation in which a zoning violation existing at the time of sale would be so egregious as to substantially or completely destroy the value of the property and render the buyer's title practically meaningless. The district court's decision to grant summary judgment in favor of the defendants is affirmed regarding Wilson's claims that hinge on the definition of "**encumbrance**."

B. Summary Judgment in Favor of the Defendants on Hoffer's Claim for Breach of Contract Warranties Other than Warranties Against Encumbrances was Proper.

Although we have found that the zoning violations alleged in this case are not **encumbrances**, Hoffer might still prevail on his breach of contract claim against Wilson if there was a breach under paragraph 8 of the Wilson contract, which contains warranties that do not hinge on the definition of "**encumbrance**." Paragraph 8 provides, in relevant part:

Buyer is acquiring the property "as is." To the best of her knowledge, Seller warrants as follows:

No violation exists with respect to the property of any . . . local law [or] ordinance.

There are no claims, causes of action, or other litigation or proceeding existing, pending, contemplated, threatened or anticipated. . . .

Based upon the record and the briefs, there is no dispute that Wilson did not have any actual knowledge of the alleged zoning violations. Hoffer argues that the inclusion of the language "to the best of her knowledge" makes the contract ambiguous, creating an issue of fact. Additionally, he argues that by using the language "to the best of her knowledge" Wilson warranted that she had checked the public record and that whatever appeared in the record did not indicate, to the best of her knowledge, any violation. However, this is not a reasonable interpretation of the simple language at issue. The district court properly interpreted the contract language as follows:

"The language of the contract, however, is clear and unambiguous. It states that the warranties are made to the best of seller's knowledge. It does not say the seller has searched the public record, or that no actual violation exists, or that the buyer may rely on this warranty to stop researching on his own. In fact, the contract states that the buyer is taking the property "as is" and that there are no warranties that the property is fit for any particular purpose. Because of the clear language of the contract, I find Plaintiff has no claim for breach of contract based on these provisions."

We agree. The warranties contained in paragraph 8 are not ambiguous and did not create a jury question as to their meaning. They clearly apply only to zoning violations or anticipated litigation that Wilson knew about, and they included no warranty that Wilson had checked all of the public records regarding the property. Because there are no allegations that Wilson actually knew of the zoning violations, there can be no breach. Therefore, the district court's decision to grant summary judgment in favor of the defendants on Hoffer's breach of contract claim is affirmed.

CONCLUSION

A zoning violation of the type alleged in this case does not constitute an **encumbrance** on the title to real property. Paragraph 8 of the Wilson contract limits its warranties against zoning violations to those within Wilson's knowledge, and Hoffer did not allege that Wilson ever had actual knowledge of the zoning violations. Summary judgment dismissing Hoffer's claims was appropriate, and the decision of the district court is affirmed. Attorney fees and costs on appeal are awarded to the respondents.

Chief Justice TROUT, Justices SCHROEDER, WALTERS, and EISMANN Concur.

Source: *2002 Ida. LEXIS 71.* Printed with the permission of LexisNexis.

Chapter 5

Nonpossessory Interests

CHAPTER OBJECTIVES

Upon completion of this chapter, you will be able to:

- Understand the concept of an easement.
- Identify the four ways easements are granted.
- Explain the termination of an easement.
- Discuss the purpose of a license.
- Understand the concept of a covenant.
- Understand the concept of an equitable servitude.

Nonpossessory interests in land concern the various rights that one may have in the land of another. Most nonpossessory interests in land are usually those that involve either the privilege of one person to use another person's land or promises concerning another person's land. Nonpossessory interests in land do not allow someone to have an ownership interest in another's property; instead, they answer the question, "Who may use and restrict the use of the land?" Most properties have some type of nonpossessory interest that is associated with them. This chapter will discuss some of the types of nonpossessory interests.

EASEMENTS

An **easement** is perhaps the most common nonpossessory interest associated with real property. An easement is the privilege that one person may have to use the property of another. An easement may be either affirmative or negative in nature. An easement is considered an encumbrance on the property on which the easement is located. Easements are considered affirmative in nature if they entitle the holder of the easement to be able to do a physical act on the property of another. Most easements are affirmative in nature. For example, Jeb owns a piece of property behind Peter's piece of property. In order for Jeb to enter his property, he must cross Peter's property. Peter grants Jeb an affirmative easement so that Jeb has the privilege to physically cross Peter's property in order to access his own.

Easements can also be negative in nature. A negative easement is one that enables the holder to prevent the landowner from making certain uses of her land. Negative easements are not very common. A person in possession of a negative easement does not have the right to enter a landowner's property. For example, using the example above, suppose that Peter's property is right next to the ocean and Jeb's property is

easement
The right of a nonowner of real property to use the real property of another for a specific purpose.

appurtenant easement
An easement created to benefit a particular piece of real property.

easement in gross
An easement created that grants the owner of the easement the right to use a piece of real property for a particular purpose.

dominant tenement
A piece of real property that is benefited by an easement appurtenant.

servient tenement
A piece of real property on which an easement appurtenant is located.

utility easement
The right of utility companies to lay lines across the property of others.

profit
A right exercised by one person in the soil of another, accompanied with participation in the profits of the soil thereof.

profit à prendre
[French for "profit to take"] A right or privilege to go on another's land and take away something of value from its soil or from the products of its soil.

behind Peter's. Jeb may possess a negative easement that prevents Peter from building any structures that may obstruct Jeb's view of the ocean. If Peter does attempt to build a structure, Jeb does not have the right to enter Peter's property to prevent him from doing so. Jeb will have to obtain an injunction to prevent Peter from building any structures that may obstruct Jeb's view.

Easements are divided into two categories: **easements appurtenant** and **easements in gross**. An appurtenant easement is one that benefits the holder with a privilege to a particular piece of land. The piece of land benefited by the easement is called the **dominant tenement**. The piece of land on which the easement is located is known as the **servient tenement**. Using the example above, Peter's land would be the servient tenement, because the easements are located on Peter's land. Jeb's land would be the dominant tenement, as Jeb's land benefits from using Peter's land because Jeb can access his property, as well as prevent Peter from building any structures that would obstruct Jeb's view of the ocean. If a parcel of land that is the dominant tenement, such as Jeb's, is sold, the easement will transfer automatically to the new landowner, even if the deed does not specifically mention the easement. For an easement to be considered appurtenant, its benefit must be intimately connected to a particular piece of property. In the example above, the easement granting Jeb the right of way over Peter's land is intimately connected to Jeb's property, because, without it, Jeb would not be able to access his property. Easements are assumed to be appurtenant unless there are clear facts to the contrary.

An easement in gross is the opposite of an easement appurtenant, in that it does not benefit a particular piece of real property. The easement is considered to be personal to the holder of the easement. While an appurtenant easement passes with the transfer of the dominant tenement, an easement in gross is connected to a person, so it usually does not transfer with the property. For example, suppose that Mary has a pool on her property and Betty does not. Mary tells Betty that she may come over and use the pool any time she would like to. Mary grants Betty this privilege strictly based on their friendship and not on any ownership interests or property interests. The easement in gross granted to Betty is personal to Betty only, and will not transfer or cannot be assigned to anyone else. Utility companies often possess easements in gross; these do not depend on the ownership of a surrounding estate. **Utility easements** are quite common.

Another method of nonpossessory interest in land is that of a **profit**, sometimes called a **profit à prendre**. A profit is the right to go onto another's land for the purpose of removing the soil or a product of the soil. Therefore, if someone possesses a profit in the land of someone else, he may be entitled to mine the minerals on the land, drill for oil, or capture or hunt wild animals. All of these are examples of a profit.

CASE FACT PATTERN

In *Willard v. First Church of Christ, Scientist,* plaintiffs filed an action to quiet title to a lot against First Church of Christ. The Willards had become aware of an easement clause several months after purchasing the lot in question. The previous owner had bought the lot to provide the church with parking and sold it only because she was assured the church could continue to use it thereafter. The trial court found that although the previous owner had intended to convey an easement appurtenant to the church, the clause used was ineffective, because it invalidated the common law rule that one cannot "reserve" an interest in property for a third party. On appeal the judgment was reversed, and the court held that when there is substantial evidence that the parties intended to convey an easement, an easement can be created in favor of a third party.

Creation of Easements

An easement may be created in four ways. The four ways to create an easement are

- By an express grant
- By implication
- By necessity
- By prescription

Express Grant

An easement can be created by an express grant, which is usually accomplished by a writing. An easement that is expressly granted is typically done by a deed or will. An **express easement** is expressly granted in writing and describes the use of the easement and the property on which the easement is located. The easement is also signed by the grantor of the easement, witnessed, notarized, and delivered to the grantee of the easement.

The grantor of the easement must be the owner of the property on which the easement is located. The grantor cannot convey an easement for any length of time that is longer than the grantor's ownership of the servient tenement. A title examination of the grantor's real property is conducted to determine what rights the grantor of the easement has to the real property. A mortgage or a trust deed that is secured by the property where the easement is located and that is recorded before the express grant of the easement will have priority over the easement. This means that if the mortgage or the deed of trust goes into **default** and is foreclosed, the **foreclosure** will end the easement.

Implied Easement

An **implied easement** can occur when two parties are situated in such a manner that an easement is created without any express language. If certain requirements are met, the court may find that, based on the actions of the two parties, an easement exists. The requirements for an implied easement are as follows:

- The property is being divided so that the owner of a parcel is either selling it or retaining part of it, or is subdividing the property and selling different pieces of it to different people.
- The use for which an implied easement is being asserted existed prior to the severance of the property.
- The easement was apparent and continuous prior to the severance.
- The easement is reasonably necessary to the enjoyment of the dominant tenement.

Implied easements are based on a theory that when real property is severed and conveyed, the conveyance of the property contains everything that is necessary for the beneficial use and enjoyment of the property. An implied easement may also be

express easement
An easement expressly granted in writing and describing the use of the easement and the property on which the easement is located.

default
An omission or failure to perform a legal or contractual duty.

foreclosure
A termination of all rights of the mortgagor or her grantee in the property covered by the mortgage.

implied easement
An easement that is created by the conduct of the parties to the easement and not by written agreement or express language.

 SPOT THE ISSUE

Susan owns a lot that is bordered on the south by a public road. The lot is bordered on the north by a dirt path that is impassable at certain times of the year. Thus, during the winter, Susan often drives from her house on the north half of her lot to the public road bordering the south end of the lot, via a private road she built that runs through the entire lot, from north to south. Susan then sells the house and only the north half of the property to Sam. Will Sam be able to continue to use the private road when reasonably necessary to reach the public road, even though it runs through the piece of property that he did not purchase?

reserved by the grantor of the property for the grantor's own benefit against the property that is being received by the grantee. In creating an implied easement, the law states that it must occur at the time of the severance of the property and cannot occur at some subsequent time.

LEGAL RESEARCH MAXIM

For a prescriptive easement to exist, each state requires a different time period in which a party was using the land as an easement without permission from the owner.

adverse possession
method of acquiring title to real property by possession for a statutory period under certain conditions.

prescriptive easement
A right to use another's property that is not inconsistent with the owner's rights and that is acquired by a use, open and notorious, adverse, and continuous for the statutory period.

easement by necessity
An easement that is indispensable to the enjoyment of the dominant estate.

easement by estoppel
A court-ordered easement created from a voluntary servitude after a person mistakenly believed the servitude to be permanent and acted in reasonable reliance on the mistaken belief.

Prescriptive Easement

An easement can be created by **adverse possession**. A **prescriptive easement** is created when a person uses the property of another without the permission of the owner for a period of time.

People who acquire a prescriptive easement do not obtain possession or control over the property. There are no ownership rights associated with a prescriptive easement, as there are with adverse possession. The holder of a prescriptive easement uses the property only for a particular use or purpose. The prescriptive easement enables the holder to continue to use the property for the same purpose. A prescriptive easement can be obtained over any private property. However, a person may not obtain a prescriptive easement over any property that is owned by a governmental entity.

A prescriptive easement must be adverse to the owner of the property to which it is located; however, the use does not need to be hostile, as is a requirement of adverse possession. If the owner of the property gives her permission to the use prior to the prescriptive easement's taking effect, then the prescriptive easement will end. The prescriptive easement must be used and enjoyed on a continuous and uninterrupted basis throughout the statutory period. The use does not need to be exclusive; the property can be used by others as well. If at any time before the expiration of the term required to create a prescriptive easement the prescriptive use is interrupted or stopped by the servient tenement, then the prescriptive easement is not created. The use leading to a claim of a prescriptive easement must be open, visible, and notorious. The use must be apparent in order to constitute the landowner's possession of the knowledge and opportunity to interrupt the use. Periods of use can be tacked together in order to meet the statutory requirement to create a prescriptive easement in the same manner that tacking is used in adverse possession. Once created, the prescriptive easement is perpetual. Prescriptive easements are appurtenant and can be transferred with the dominant tenement.

Easement by Necessity

Sometimes two parcels of land are situated in such a way that an easement over one piece is necessary for the enjoyment of the other. Most states will provide a person who does not have access to a public road or street the right to obtain an easement to cross over the adjacent land in order to gain access to the roadway. Such an easement is called an **easement by necessity**. The most common example of an easement by necessity occurs when one parcel of land is landlocked by others and an easement must be granted in order to allow the landlocked parcel access to the roadway. An easement by necessity will last only so long as the easement is necessary. For example, if two properties are landlocked and one uses an easement by necessity over the other, but subsequently a roadway is built so that the property is no longer landlocked, then the necessity is no longer in effect. An easement by necessity requires that fair compensation be paid to the landowner of the servient tenement. Easements by necessity are created by operation of law. A similar type of easement is an **easement by estoppel**, which is ordered by the court after a person mistakenly believes an easement was given voluntarily to her by the landlord (voluntary servitude) and believes it to be permanent and acts in reasonable reliance on that mistaken belief.

PRACTICE TIP

When researching title reports, it is standard practice to find easements listed on Exhibit B of a report.

Termination of Easements

Once it has been determined that an easement has been created, it is important to then find out if the easement has been terminated, to decide whether the easement holder still has a right to use the easement. Easements can terminate for a variety of reasons, including release, merger, severance, abandonment, and destruction. For instance, the parties may agree to terminate the easement after a certain period of time. If the purpose for which the easement is granted is no longer relevant, then the easement may no longer be necessary and can terminate. If the two properties, the dominant and the servient tenements, are merged into one estate, then any easement located on one will no longer be necessary and will terminate. If the person who holds the easement abandons it, then the easement will terminate. An easement will continue until it is terminated by the operation of law. Easements are interests in property even though they are nonpossessory interests; therefore, they cannot be revoked by the grantor. If the easement were revocable, then it would be a license.

LICENSES

A **license** is a right to use the landowner's land; however, the landowner has the right to revoke the privilege. This power of revocability is what differentiates a license from an easement. The difference between a license and an easement is that an easement is a nonpossessory property interest and a license is the permission to perform a certain act upon another's land. A license can be created either orally or in writing, or it can be implied from the conduct and activities of the parties.

For an example of a license, imagine that Dr. Jones owns an acre of land in the country. On her land is a lake stocked with trout. Dr. Jones' coworker, Bob Ducket, loves to fish. Dr. Jones tells Bob that he can use the lake to fish whenever he would like. Dr. Jones has granted a license to Bob to fish. Dr. Jones can just as easily revoke the fishing privilege whenever she wishes.

license
A personal privilege to do some particular act or series of acts on lands without possessing any estate interest therein; it is ordinarily revocable at the will of the licensor and it is not assignable.

COVENANTS

A **covenant** is a promise that may attach to the land. A covenant is a contract between two parties, but if it meets certain requirements, it is binding against any person who later buys the land to which the covenant is attached. Most covenants that run with the land involve a promise by one party to pay for certain gains or a promise to do or not to do something with the land.

A covenant can be either a benefit or a burden to the land. A covenant "runs with the land," which means that the provisions of the covenant limit not only the person who originally obtained the deed that contained the covenant, but every subsequent titleholder thereafter. In order for a covenant to be a burden on the property and run with the land, it must have the following requirements:

covenant
An agreement, convention, or promise of two or more parties, by deed in writing, signed, and delivered, by which either of the parties pledges himself to the other that something is either done, or shall be done, or shall not be done, or stipulates for the truth of certain facts.

- The promise has to be enforceable between the original parties to the agreement.
- The original parties must have intended for the promise to run with the land.
- The burden must be related to and concern the promisor's land.
- There must be a transfer of land between the promisor and the promisee, along with a succession of the land from promisor to the promisor's assignee.

For a benefit to run with the land, it has to have the same requirements as those stated above, except that the benefit does not have to have an assignee that will succeed to the promisor's land.

In order for a subsequent purchaser to be bound by a covenant, she must have notice of the covenant. Notice needs to be actual (appearing in the deed) or implied

Mary owns a large tract of land that was left to her by her family. She decides to sell off some of the parcels. Mary wishes the land to remain single-family residential, so she puts a statement in the deed stating that the property is to remain residential and that no multi-family dwelling units can be built on the property. Fredrick buys two of the parcels of the property from Mary, fully aware of the covenant that runs with the land. Frederick holds onto the parcels for many years as an investment. After ten years, Frederick decides to sell one of the parcels. He sells a parcel to Marcelo. Marcelo buys the property with the covenant on the deed. Marcelo builds an apartment building on the property. Frederick, who still possesses the other parcel of land subject to the same covenant, sues Marcelo for monetary damages. Why will Marcelo not be able to successfully defend Frederick's suit?

---

restrictive covenant
Private agreement that restricts the use or occupancy of real property.

(appearing in the record books of the county recorder's office where the property is located). **Restrictive covenants** are commonly encountered in residential real estate transactions such as deeds or leases. Such a covenant is generally a private agreement that restricts the use or occupancy of real property. For example, a restrictive covenant may specify architectural styles that may be used.

One who seeks to enforce a covenant may seek damages in the form of monetary relief as a result of the breach of the covenant.

EQUITABLE SERVITUDE

equitable servitude
An agreement stipulating building restrictions and restrictions on the use of land that may be enforced in equity.

specific performance
The remedy of requiring exact performance of a contract in the specific form in which it was made, or according to the precise terms agreed upon.

An **equitable servitude** is the same as a covenant, except that the remedies sought for a breach are different. If a breach of a covenant occurs, the injured party may seek monetary damages from the court. However, if an equitable servitude is breached, the injured party may seek only the remedy of an injunction, or **specific performance**.

Equitable servitudes are created by means of a writing just like a covenant. However, unlike a covenant, an equitable servitude may be created by implication. For example, if it can be determined that in a subdivision there was a common scheme, such as a plan including no multi-family dwelling units, then an equitable servitude may be implied. In order to be bound by an equitable servitude, a person who acquires the property must have notice of the servitude. Notice can be actual, as when it is stated in a deed, or by investigation, through a visual inspection of the property.

Equitable servitudes run with the land just as covenants do. The major differences between covenants and equitable servitudes are these:

privity
Mutual or successive relationships to the same right of property, or such an identification of interest of one person with another as to represent the same legal right.

- A covenant must be created by a writing. An equitable servitude may be created by implication.
- **Privity** need not exist for an equitable servitude, whereas privity is necessary for a covenant.
- Notice for an equitable servitude may be accomplished by investigation.
- The remedy for an equitable servitude is an injunction or specific performance. The remedy for a breach of a covenant is monetary damages.

Homeowners may be required to convey an implied servitude to a homeowner's association. A homeowner's association has an undivided interest in the common areas of the property. Research the laws in your state and determine how a homeowner's association can enforce a breach of the equitable servitude against a homeowner in the complex.

EYE ON ETHICS

Most legal documents concerning property transactions such as deeds and/or mortgages require that the documents be either witnessed or notarized. A legal assistant who goes to work for a law firm that practices in real estate or real property law should become readily familiar with which types of documents require witnessed signatures or notarization. A legal assistant should always insist that he will not witness or notarize documents unless he actually sees the person whose signature is to be witnessed or notarized sign the document.

SURF'S UP

The Internet is a tremendous resource for learning about real property law. Two helpful Web sites that deal with real property law are:

Legal Information Institute: http://www.law.cornell.edu/topics/real_property.htmlREALTOR.com: http://www.realtor.com/

Unlike easements, profits, and licenses, which are grants of an affirmative right to use land belonging to another, covenants and equitable servitudes are restrictions on the right to use land. Easements, by definition, will "run with the land," while covenants and equitable servitudes will "run with the land" only if certain requirements are met.

Summary

An easement is perhaps the most common nonpossessory interest associated with real property. An easement is the privilege that one person may have to use the property of another. It may be either affirmative or negative in nature and may be considered an encumbrance on the property on which the easement is located. Easements are often affirmative in nature. This means that they entitle the holder of the easement to perform a physical act on the property of another.

Easements are divided into two categories: easements appurtenant and easements in gross. An easement appurtenant is one that benefits the holder with a privilege to a particular piece of land. The piece of land benefited by the easement is called the dominant tenement. The piece of land on which the easement is located is known as the servient tenement.

An easement in gross is the opposite of an appurtenant easement, in that it does not benefit a particular piece of real property. The easement is considered to be personal to the holder of the easement. While an appurtenant easement passes with the transfer of the dominant tenement, an easement in gross is connected to a person, so it usually does not transfer with the property.

Another method of nonpossessory interest in land is that of a profit, sometimes called a profit à prendre. A profit is the right to go onto another's land for the purpose of removing the soil or a product of the soil. Therefore, if someone possesses a profit in the land of someone else, she may be entitled to mine the minerals on the land, drill for oil, or capture or hunt wild animals.

Easements are often defined by the ways in which they were created. An easement can be created by an express grant, which is usually accomplished by a writing. An example would be an easement created by a deed or will. The easement that is expressly granted is in writing and describes the use of the easement and the property on which the easement is located. It is also signed by the grantor of the easement, witnessed, notarized, and delivered to the grantee of the easement.

An implied easement can occur when two parties are situated in such a manner that an easement is created without any express language. If certain requirements are met, the court may find that, based on the actions of the two parties, an easement exists and no writing is necessary for the easement to be enforceable.

An easement can also be created by adverse possession. A prescriptive easement is created when a person uses the property of another without the permission of the owner for a period of time. People who acquire prescriptive easements do not obtain possession or control over the property. There are no ownership rights associated with a prescriptive easement, as there are with adverse possession. The holder of a prescriptive easement uses the property only for a particular use or purpose. The prescriptive easement enables the holder to continue to use the property for the same purpose. A prescriptive easement can be obtained over any private property; however, a person may not obtain a prescriptive easement over any property that is owned by a governmental entity.

Sometimes two parcels of land are situated in such a way that an easement over one piece is necessary for the enjoyment of the other. Most states will provide a person who does not have access to a public road or street the right to obtain an easement to cross over the adjacent land in order to gain access to the roadway. Such an easement is called an easement by necessity. The most common example of an easement by necessity occurs when one parcel of land is landlocked by others and an easement must be granted in order to allow the landlocked parcel access to the roadway. An easement by necessity will last only so long as the easement is necessary.

A license is a right to use the landowner's land; however, the landowner has the right to revoke the privilege. This power of revocability is what differentiates a license from an easement. The difference between a license and an easement is that an easement is a nonpossessory property interest and a license is the permission to perform a certain act upon another's land. A license can be created either orally or in writing, or it can be implied from the conduct and activities of the parties.

A covenant is a promise that may attach to the land. A covenant is a contract between two parties, but if it meets certain requirements, it is binding against any person who later buys the land to which the covenant is attached. Most covenants that run with the land involve a promise by one party to pay for certain gains or a promise to do or not do something with the land.

An equitable servitude is the same as a covenant, except that the remedies sought for a breach are different. If a breach of a covenant occurs, the injured party may seek money damages from the court. However, if an equitable servitude is breached, the injured party may seek only a remedy of an injunction or specific performance. Unlike easements, profits, and licenses, which are grants of an affirmative right to use the land, covenants and equitable servitudes are restrictions on the right to use the land.

Key Terms

Adverse possession
Covenant
Default
Dominant tenement
Easement
Easement appurtenant
Easement by estoppel
Easement by necessity
Easement in gross
Equitable servitude
Express easement

Foreclosure
Implied easement
License
Prescriptive easement
Privity
Profit
Profit à prendre
Restrictive covenant
Servient tenement
Specific performance
Utility Easement

1. Explain the differences between an appurtenant easement and an easement in gross.
2. What is the difference between an easement in gross and a license?
3. Identify the four ways that an easement can be created.
4. Define an implied easement.
5. Explain the difference between a covenant and an equitable servitude.
6. What is a license?
7. What is an easement by necessity?
8. What are the requirements for a covenant?
9. What is a prescriptive easement?
10. What is a dominant tenement?
11. What happens to an easement when the dominant and servient tenements merge?
12. What is privity?
13. What does it mean to "run with the land"?
14. How might a person obtain notice of an equitable servitude?
15. What does it mean to be landlocked?

1. You are a legal assistant in a law firm that practices real property law. Your supervising attorney has a client who is trying to negotiate an easement for a driveway across his neighbor's property in order to provide easier access to his residence. Your supervising attorney has asked you to prepare the easement documentation. What information will you need?
2. Research the laws in your state concerning how to obtain an easement by necessity. Write a memorandum on the requirements and the processes involved.
3. Barbara and Stan are adjacent landowners in a residential area. Both believe that swimming pools are unsightly and a mosquito breeding ground. Therefore, they agree, in writing and signed by both parties, that neither will permit a swimming pool to be installed on their properties. Four years later, Stan sells his property to Bill. Bill checks the county recorder's office prior to the purchase of the property and finds no evidence of any agreement. Furthermore, the deed of conveyance shows no evidence of any agreement. Bill builds a pool on the property. If Barbara brings an action against Bill for breach of a covenant or servitude, what will the court find?
4. What types of real property may have many covenants attached to them? Give an example.
5. What are the differences between an easement by necessity and an implied easement? Are there any similarities? If so, what are those similarities?
6. Are there any licenses on the property you grew up on? Research whether or not there are any. If so, list what they are and why they exist.
7. What is needed to claim an easement by adverse possession or prescriptive easement? Are the requirements different for each state or not?
8. Research the requirements for becoming a notary public in your state. What are your state's requirements?

 PORTFOLIO ASSIGNMENT

Take a trip down to your County Clerk's Office and research the address you live at, whether a house or apartment building. Are there any records of written easements on the property/parcel in question? If so, what are they? Are there any easements by necessity on the property/parcel in question? If so, what are they?

Vocabulary Builder

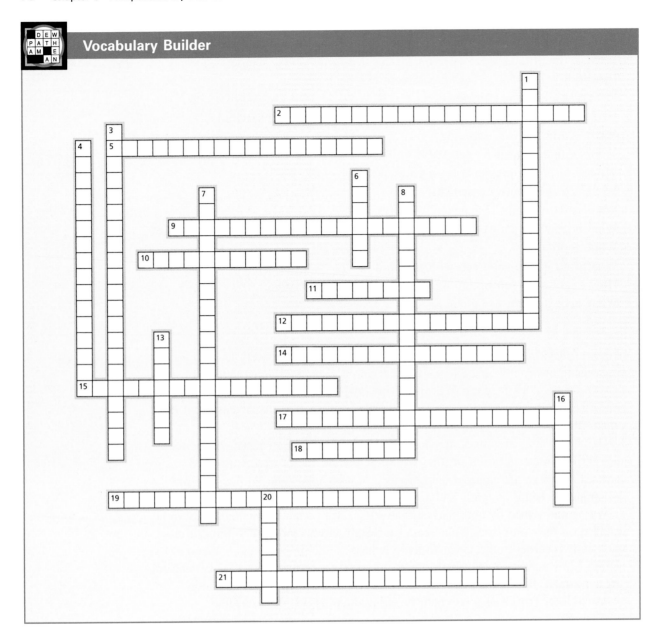

Vocabulary Builder

Instructions

Use the key terms from this chapter to fill in the answers to the crossword puzzle.

NOTE: When the answer is more than one word, leave a blank space between words.

ACROSS

2. a court-ordered easement created from a voluntary servitude after person mistakenly believing the servitude to be permanent, acted in reasonable reliance on the mistaken belief.

5. a method of acquiring title to real property by possession for a statutory period under certain conditions.

9. the remedy of requiring exact performance of a contract in the specific form in which it was made or according to the precise terms agreed upon.

10. a termination of all rights of the mortgagor or her grantee in the property covered by the mortgage.

11. the right of a nonowner of real property to use the real property of another for a specific purpose.

12. a piece of real property on which an easement appurtenant is located.

14. an easement that is created by the conduct of the parties to the easement and not by written agreement or express language.

15. an easement created that grants the owner of the easement the right to use a piece of real property for a particular purpose.

17. an agreement stipulating building restrictions and restrictions on the use of land that may be enforced in equity.

18. an agreement, convention, or promise of two or more parties, by deed in writing, signed, and delivered, by which either of the parties pledges himself to the other that something either is done, or shall be done, or shall not be done, or stipulates for the trust of certain facts.

19. an easement created to benefit a particular piece of real property.

21. a private agreement that restricts the use or occupancy of real property.

DOWN

1. an easement expressly granted in writing and describing the use of the easement and the property on which the easement is located.

3. an easement that is indispensable to the enjoyment of the dominant estate.

4. A right or privilege to go on another's land and take away something of value from its soil or from the products of its soil.

6. a right exercised by one person in the soil of another, accompanied with participation in the profits of the soil thereof.

7. a right to use another's property that is not inconsistent with the owner's rights and that is acquired by a use, open and notorious, adverse, and continuous for the statutory period.

8. a piece of real property that is benefited by an easement appurtenant.

13. a personal privilege to do some particular act or series of acts on lands without possessing any estate interest therein; it is ordinarily revocable at the will of the licenser and it is not assignable.

16. an omission or failure to perform a legal or contractual duty.

20. mutual or successive relationships to the same right of property, or such an identification of interest of one person with another as to represent the same legal right.

Kleen et al. v. West Fork Billabong
2003 ML 1091, 2003 Mont. Dist. LEXIS 2790,
March 13, 2003, Decided

FACTUAL BACKGROUND

This action arises out of a complaint filed by Plaintiffs on June 13, 2001 requesting declaratory and injunctive relief regarding easement rights concerning an airport runway and tie-downs located in part on Defendants' real property. The airport runway in question has been known as the "Shook Mountain Landing Strip" and "The West Fork Airport," and is presently identified on aviation maps and charts as "West Fork." It has historically existed and been utilized on what is now Lot 7B of Certificate of Survey ("COS") # 5379R (originally part of Lot 7 of COS # 1075) and Lots 4 and 5 of COS # 1075. The airport is listed in the U.S. Department of Transportation, Federal Aviation Administration Publication named the "Airport/Facility Directory" (under Conner-West Fork Lodge) as a privately-owned airstrip for public use, and the runway is shown to be 2,520 feet in length.

Plaintiffs contend they purchased their properties in large part because they own and operate airplanes, and Plaintiffs' free use of the airstrip was an important consideration for them.

On or about May 14, 2001, Defendants (or some of them) placed a post and pole fence across the runway at approximately 625 feet from the northeast end of the runway that made the runway unusable for Plaintiffs and potentially hazardous for all persons attempting to land at or take off from the airport. Defendants further threatened to conduct activities on the airstrip which are inconsistent with its use as an airfield, such as holding an antique automobile show in mid-June, 2001, and closure of the airport during certain months of the year.

On July 26, 2001, the parties filed a Stipulation to Mutual Preliminary Injunction in which the parties agreed the Defendants would not fence the runway and would repair the post holes in the runway left from their post and pole fence; the parties would be enjoined from placing or permitting anything on the runway easement which creates any hazard for aviation; the parties would be enjoined from all non-aviation use of the runway easement; and the use of the easement premises shall be exclusively for airport purposes and uses as stated in the Easement Grant dated November 6, 1981 pending further order of the Court. The Court approved the Stipulation on August 6, 2001.

On August 17, 2001, Defendants filed their answer and counterclaim, in which they request declaratory judgment on the parties' easement rights under the Easement Grant; declaratory relief on the parties' legal obligations for administering, operating, and maintaining the airstrip and assumption of liability; and injunctive relief of non-aviation use by the Plaintiffs.

PARTIES' CONTENTIONS

In their motion for partial summary judgment, Plaintiffs move the Court to enter judgment that: (1) the Easement Grant limits the use of the easement area exclusively to airport uses; and (2) the Easement Grant does not limit the aviation use of the airstrip to any time, season, month, time of year, or weather conditions.

Defendants counter in their response that Plaintiffs have incorrectly interpreted the granting language, which they allege contains a drafting error that violates Mont. Code Ann. §§ 70-17-105 and 111(1), with the result that Defendants, as servient tenement holders, are not subject to the easement restrictions as are Plaintiffs as dominant tenement holders, but rather are subject to the general rule that servient tenement holders are entitled to make any use of the servient estate that does not unreasonably interfere with enjoyment of the servitude.

Defendants, in their motion for partial summary judgment, request the Court to enter judgment that: (1) Defendants are not easement holders over that portion of the easement premises existing over their property, but are easement holders over that portion of the easement premises existing over the property of Plaintiff Merle E. Kleen; (2) Defendants' use of the easement premises existing over Defendants' property is non-exclusive; (3) Defendants are not subject to the exclusive use limitations prescribed in Section 3 regarding those portions of the easement premises owned by Defendants, but are subject to the exclusive use limitations regarding those portions of the easement premises owned by Plaintiff Kleen; (4) Defendants' use of that portion of the easement premises existing across Defendants' land is subject only to the general rule that the holder of a servient estate is entitled to make any use of the servient estate that does not unreasonably interfere with enjoyment of the servitude; therefore, Defendants' use of snowmobiles on that portion of the landing strip on Defendants' land during the winter months does not constitute interference with Plaintiffs' enjoyment of the servitude; and (5) while the runway exists solely upon Defendants' land as illustrated by COS # 1075, the runway easement includes airspace over portions of Parcels 4 and 5 owned by Plaintiff Kleen and must remain clear; therefore, no fence can be placed at the end of the West Fork Runway.

Plaintiffs agree: (1) that Defendants do not have an easement on their own land; (2) that Defendants have access to their own property within the easement premises for airport purposes; (3) that COS # 1075 illustrated the location of the runway at the time it was surveyed in June-July, 1976; and (4) that Defendants are obligated to keep their land and airspace unobstructed for ingress and egress of aircraft.

Plaintiffs disagree with Defendants' contentions: (1) that COS # 1075 illustrates the correct location of the current easement premises on the basis that the 1981 Easement Grant changed the location of the runway; (2) that Defendants are not subject to the requirement that the easement premises across their land be used exclusively for airport purposes; (3) that Defendants' use of their property is subject only to the common law restriction that they not unreasonably interfere with Plaintiffs' enjoyment of the easement; and (4) that Defendants' use of snowmobiles on the landing strip when it is snow-covered is not interference with Plaintiffs' enjoyment of the easement.

OPINION

In interpreting the meaning of an easement grant, contract principles apply. *Mularoni v. Bing,* 2001 MT 215, P32, 306 Mont. 405, P32, 34 P.3d 497, P32. Construction and interpretation of written agreements are questions of law for the court to decide. Id. The breadth and scope of an easement are determined upon the actual terms of the grant. Id.; Mont. Code Ann. § 70-17-106.

The Easement Grant provides in relevant part:

A. Grantors are the owners of certain real property situated in Ravalli County, Montana, which includes the "easement premises" hereinafter described; the property affected by the easement premises is either the following or part thereof: [Parcels 4, 5, and 7, COS # 1075]

B. There exists over and across said real property an airport known as the Wilcox-Shook Mountain Resort Airport by the Department of Transportation, United States of America. The easement premise is one and the same as said airport and is described as follows:

Those certain runway easements and tie-down area across said Parcels 4, 5, and 7, as described on Exhibit "A" attached hereto.

C. By prior written agreements the Grantors have granted certain easements for use of the easement premises, which by this instrument they desire to create an easement for said airport and give written and recorded effect thereto, and define the existing boundaries of the easement premises and the respective rights therein . . .

NOW, THEREFORE, for valuable consideration, receipt and sufficiency of which is hereby acknowledged [sic], the following grants, agreements, covenants, and restrictions are made:

1. Each Grantor hereby grants to the other Grantors, and to the owner of each parcel, Parcels 1 though 13, inclusive, Certificate of Survey No. 1075, records of Ravalli County, Montana, a non-exclusive easement for use of the easement premises and the air over same as an airport for the ingress, egress and tie-down of one (1) airplane only for each of the above-described parcels. This grant is appurtenant to each of said parcels.

2. All tie-downs shall be built as far Westerly as practically possible in the tie-down area.

3. Use of the easement premises shall be exclusive for airport purposes and uses set forth above (Paragraph 1).

4. All provisions of this instrument, including the benefits and burdens, run with the land and are binding upon and enure to the heirs, assigns, successors, tenants and personal representatives of the parties hereto.

5. Any party may enforce this instrument by appropriate action and should he or she prevail in such litigation, he or she shall recover as part of his or her costs a reasonable attorney's fee.

6. The use of the airport and tie-down shall be free to grantee hereunder.

PLAINTIFFS' MOTION FOR PARTIAL SUMMARY JUDGMENT

A. The Easement Grant limits the use of the easement area exclusively to airport uses.

Plaintiffs contend the terms of the Easement Grant limit the use of the easement area exclusively to airport uses. Paragraph 1 spells out the non-exclusive easement granted by each grantor to the other grantors and to the owner of each of the parcels in the subdivision "for use . . . as an airport for the ingress, egress and tie-down of one (1) airplane only for each of the above-described parcels." This non-exclusive, or common, easement grant allows the servient landowner, or grantor, to share in the benefit of the easement. Paragraph 3 provides that "[u]se of the easement premises shall be exclusive for airport purposes and uses set forth above (Paragraph 1)." The Court determines that the plain language of the Easement Grant provides for an easement which is limited exclusively to airport uses. Thus, the easement premises may not be used by any grantee for purposes other than airport uses.

Plaintiffs contend that all owners of Parcels 1 through 13 (COS # 1075 shows only 11 parcels in the subdivision; the subdivision had apparently been further divided into 13 parcels by the time the 1981 Easement Grant was filed) are recipients of the easement grant, and therefore all owners are subject to the limitations of the easement set forth in Paragraphs 1 and 3, which limit use of the easement exclusively to airport purposes. Plaintiffs argue that another way to analyze the Easement Grant is to find that it contains "restrictive covenants" or "negative easements," and that while the grantors granted the right to use land for airport purposes, they also restricted the land's use to those airport purposes by use of "mutual restrictions."

The Court notes that the grantors in the Easement Grant, while purporting to grant a nonexclusive easement to the owner of each parcel in the subdivision, in effect could lawfully grant an easement to only those subdivision owners other than themselves. "An easement is always distinct from the right to occupy and enjoy the land [**12] itself." 25 Am. Jur. 2d Easements and Licenses § 2 (1996). The general rule that a person cannot have an easement in his own land is codified at Mont. Code Ann. § 70-17-05: "A servitude thereon cannot be held by the owner of the servient tenement." The Court determines that the intent (and effect) of the owners of Parcels 4, 5, and 7 (the parcels on which the airport lies) in Paragraph 1 was to grant an easement for use of the airport to all other owners within the subdivision. The owners of the parcels on which the airport lies are the servient tenement owners, and all other owners are the dominant tenement owners. The "non-exclusive easement," as stated above, allows the servient tenement owners to share in the benefit, or use, of the easement. Only the dominant tenement owners are subject to the use limitations of the Easement Grant. It is a well-settled rule that the servient tenement owner(s) may make use of the land in any lawful manner that he chooses, which use is not inconsistent with and does not interfere with the use and right reserved to the dominant tenement owners." *Titeca v. State,* 194 Mont. 209, 214, 634 P.2d 1156, 1160 (1981). [**13]

In conclusion, the Court determines that the Easement Grant limits the use of the easement area by dominant tenement owners exclusively to airport uses, and may not be used by any servient tenement owner for any use that is inconsistent with or interferes with any use and right reserved to the dominant tenement owners.

B. The Easement Grant does not limit the aviation use of the airstrip to any time, season, month, time of year, or weather conditions.

Plaintiffs contend the terms of the Easement Grant do not limit the aviation use of the airstrip to any time, season, month, time of year, or weather conditions, and therefore, Defendants do not have the right to close the airport during the winter months or at any other time. The Court agrees. No provision in the Easement Grant limits or restricts use of the airstrip to any particular time, season, month, time of year, or weather conditions. Plaintiffs should prevail on this portion of their motion for partial summary judgment.

II. DEFENDANTS' MOTION FOR PARTIAL SUMMARY JUDGMENT

Defendants are not easement holders over that portion of the easement premises existing over their property. However, Defendants are easement holders over that portion of the easement premises existing over the property of Plaintiff Merle E. Kleen.

The Court agrees with Defendants' contention that they are not easement holders over that portion of the easement premises existing over their property, but are easement holders over that portion of the easement premises existing over the property of Plaintiff Kleen. Likewise, Plaintiff Kleen is not an easement holder over that portion of the easement premises existing over his property, but is an easement holder over that portion of the easement premises existing over the property of Defendants.

B. Defendants' use of the easement premises existing over Defendants' property is "nonexclusive", therefore Defendants are not excluded from the easement premises existing over Defendants' property.

Defendants contend the terms of the Easement Grant indicate that the grantors intended to retain their ability to use the easement premises even after allowing the easement grantees to use the easement. The Court agrees. The term "non-exclusive easement" in Paragraph 1 is by definition an easement allowing the servient landowner to share in the benefit of the easement. The Court rephrases Defendants' language in B. above in its determination that Defendants are not excluded from the easement premises existing over their property, but retain their ability to use the easement premises by virtue of the non-exclusive easement grant.

C. Because Defendants are not easement holders over that portion of the easement premises existing on Defendants' property, Defendants are not subject to the exclusive use limitations prescribed in Section 3 for those portions of the easement premises owned by Defendants. However, Defendants are subject to the exclusive use limitations for those portions of the easement premises owned by Plaintiff Merle E. Kleen.

Defendants attempt to support this legal conclusion by arguing that the term "non-exclusive easement" in Paragraph 1 and the term "exclusive" in Paragraph 3 are "directly contradictory

and thus, absolutely irreconcilable." The Court finds no merit in Defendants' argument and no relationship between it and the legal conclusion they request. The "non-exclusive easement," or common easement, in Paragraph 1 addresses the holders of the easement and has been interpreted above. The term "exclusive" in Paragraph 3 addresses the use of the easement and limits it to "airport purposes and uses set forth [in Paragraph 1]." As the Court has previously determined, Defendants, as easement holders over that portion of the easement premises existing over the property of Plaintiff Kleen, are subject to the use limitations of Paragraph 3. Defendants, as servient tenement owners of that portion of the easement premises existing over their own property, are subject to the general rule that they may use the easement premises for any use that is not inconsistent with or does not interfere with any use and right reserved to the dominant tenement owners.

D. Defendants' use of that portion of the easement premises existing across Defendants' land is subject only to the general rule that the holder of a servient estate is entitled to make any use of the servient estate that does not unreasonably interfere with enjoyment of the servitude. Therefore, Defendants' use of snowmobiles on the West Fork Airport landing strip - in the winter months, solely upon Defendants' land within the boundary of the landing strip illustrated by COS # 1075 and at times when the landing strip is covered by snow - does not constitute interference with Plaintiffs' enjoyment of the servitude.

The Court has already concluded that Defendants, as servient tenement owners, are governed by the general rule that they may use the servient estate in any manner that does not interfere with the use and enjoyment of the easement holders. However, based on this legal determination, the Court is unable to conclude that Defendants' use of snowmobiles on the easement premises during the winter does not constitute interference with Plaintiffs' enjoyment of the servitude. Defendants' argument that the airport is closed during the winter months is supported by language in their own brochure advertising the West Fork Lodge which states that the airport is closed from November 30th until March 1 st; the handwritten words "Closed Nov 31 st [sic] until April 1st) across the bottom of the relevant page in the U.S. Department of Transportation, FAA, Airport Master Record (AFD Eff Date 07-15-1999); and affidavits from Rick Magee and Roy Shook. Rick Magee, owner of the West Fork Lodge and Airport from 1992-1995 and in 1999, states that he closed the airport every winter during his tenure by calling "the FAA office in Great Falls," and that twice a year usually in January and/or February, publicly advertised snowmobile racing was held on the airstrip. He contends the airport was closed "between approximately end of November until early May." Roy Shook, the founder of the Shook Mountain Airport and owner for 15 years, states that during his tenure:

[n]o aircraft ever flew into, or took off from the airstrip using skis. The airstrip was only used in the winter when it was plowed. My standard management practice for operating the airstrip was to keep the airstrip open at all times. However, I closed the airport for maintenance or when the snow was too deep for safe operation of the airstrip . . .

Based on the evidence presented by the Defendants, it appears that airport closures did occur at times during the winter months at the behest of the airstrip owners, and at times, snowmobile racing was held on the premises. However, sporadic historical use does not define the scope of easement rights. Defendants present no evidence that Plaintiffs concurred with the decisions to close the airport. Plaintiffs contend they have never agreed to airport closure for non-airport activities. Mere disagreement, however, is not enough; Plaintiffs must show that Defendants' closure of the airport during winter months constitutes interference with Plaintiffs' use of the easement. The Court can think of possibilities in which winter airport closure could conceivably interfere with Plaintiffs' use of the easement, were Plaintiffs, for example, to acquire snow removal equipment in order to keep the airport operable throughout the winter, or were the snow so sparse during a winter that Plaintiffs could make use of the airport without snow-removal equipment. Furthermore, the Court notes that merely because no aircraft has ever flown into the airstrip using skis does not preclude the possibility that one may do so.

The Court determines there is a factual dispute as to whether snowmobile racing on the easement premises during the winter months constitutes interference with the Plaintiffs' enjoyment of the easement, and for this reason, concludes this portion of the motion should be denied.

Certificate of Survey # 1075, incorporated by reference in Section 1 of the Easement Grant, illustrates that the runway of the West Fork Airport exists solely upon Defendants' property. However, the runway easement described in Exhibit A of the Easement Grant indicates that the airspace must remain clear over the indicated portions of parcels 4 and 5 owned by Merle E. Kleen. Therefore, no fence can be placed at the end of the West Fork Runway.

The illustration of the runway on COS # 1075 is irrelevant to the issue above; the easement premises are determined by the legal description of the easement premises found in Exhibit "A", attached to and filed with the Easement Grant. According to the legal description, the easement lies across portions of Parcels 4, 5, and 7 of COS # 1075. No fence or other obstruction may block any portion of the easement, regardless of which parcel that portion lies upon. Interestingly, while it was Defendants' May 14, 2001 placement of a post and pole fence across the easement premises which caused Plaintiffs to file their complaint in this matter on June 13, 2001, Defendants are now requesting the Court to rule that no fence can bar the runway. The Court agrees that no fence or other obstruction may bar any portion of the easement premises. The Court notes that Plaintiffs agree, as well.

ORDER

IT IS THEREFORE ORDERED that judgment regarding the Motion for Partial Summary Judgment filed by Plaintiffs' Kleen, et al. is hereby rendered as follows:

Part A is GRANTED to the extent that the Easement Grant limits the use of the easement area by dominant tenement owners exclusively to airport uses, and may not be used by any servient tenement owner for any use that is inconsistent with or interferes with any use and right reserved to the dominant tenement owners.

Part B of the Motion for Partial Summary Judgment is GRANTED.

IT IS FURTHER ORDERED that judgment regarding the Motion for Partial Summary Judgment filed by Defendants West Fork Billabong, L.L.C. and Peter Dobbs is hereby rendered as follows:

Part A of the Motion for Partial Summary Judgment is GRANTED.

Part B of the Motion for Partial Summary Judgment is GRANTED to the extent that Defendants are not excluded from the easement premises existing over their property, but retain their ability to use the easement premises by virtue of the non-exclusive easement grant.

Part C of the Motion for Partial Summary Judgment is GRANTED.

Part D of the Motion for Partial Summary Judgment is DENIED.

Part E of the Motion for Partial Summary Judgment is GRANTED.

[Footnotes omitted]

Source: 2003 Mont. Dist. LEXIS 2790. Reprinted with permission from LexisNexis.

Chapter 6

Landlord and Tenant

CHAPTER OBJECTIVES

Upon completion of this chapter, you will be able to:

- Identify and describe the various types of tenancy.
- Understand the rights and duties of the tenant.
- Discuss the landlord's duties under a lease.
- Explain tort liability of the landlord and the tenant.
- Discuss assignments and subleases.

The number of Americans that can realistically own their own homes has been declining in recent years. As such, the laws involving the rights, duties, and obligations of persons involved in nonfreehold estates grow and become more important. Property is divided into freehold estates and leasehold, or nonfreehold, estates. This chapter will discuss the issues and concerns surrounding leasehold estates.

leasehold
An estate in real property held by a tenant under the lease.

lease
Any agreement that gives rise to a relationship of landlord and tenant or lessor and lessee.

landlord
The lessor of property.

tenant
A person, or a corporation, who rents real property from an owner; also called a lessee.

lessor
One who rents property to another.

lessee
One who rents property from another.

mitigate
To lessen in intensity or amount.

acceleration clause
Provision that requires a debtor to pay off a balance sooner than the scheduled due date if some specified event occurs.

LEASES

A **leasehold** is a possessory interest in property, but it is not an ownership interest. A leasehold is rooted in feudal times and stems from the idea that it is a tenant who holds under a landlord. It is created by the terms of a **lease**. The lease determines the rights and obligations between the **landlord** and the **tenant**. The lease describes the relationship between the parties as lessor and lessee. Leaseholds are nonfreehold estates and the most notable types include: the periodic tenancy, the tenancy for years, the tenancy at will, and the tenancy at sufferance. Like all contracts, a lease will determine who the parties are, the terms under which the relationship will take shape, the period of time for the relationship, and the rights to termination, and will include the signatures of the parties. As is the case in many breach of contract actions, if a tenant breaches the lease (contract), the landlord is required to **mitigate** his own damages. Additionally, a lease may contain an **acceleration clause**, which, upon a default by the lessee, requires that all payments due during the life of the lease be made immediately.

The legal relationship between a landlord and a tenant involves both contract and property law. The landlord—tenant agreement is typically embodied in the written lease. This lease, though not explicitly a contract, is generally subject to interpretation involving contract law principles.

There are many differences between residential and commercial leases. Residential tenants receive the benefit of many rights not received by commercial tenants. For example, for commercial tenants there are no implied rights of habitability; the privacy protections of entry by landlord laws do not apply; and many rights that are not waivable in residential tenancies may be waived. (See Figure 6.1 for a sample of a residential lease.)

Nonfreehold estates are known for an important characteristic, in that each normally includes a duty on the tenant's part to pay rent. A nonfreehold estate does not include a possessory interest in land. In addition, a leasehold is considered to be personal and not real property. Also, for the term of the lease, the tenant is entitled to exclusive possession of the property.

A landlord may sell, gift, devise, or otherwise transfer her interest in the leased property. The new landlord cannot alter the terms of the lease during the period of the lease unless the lease specifically provides for such modification. A tenant's right to transfer possession of the leased premises to another depends on the terms of the lease. A tenant can sometimes assign or sublease his rights.

VARIOUS TYPES OF TENANCY

If a lease is to be for more than one year, the lease must be in writing. Typical leases have a set period of time during which they are in effect, and then provide an option to renew. There are four types of leaseholds that may be created. These leaseholds are

- Tenancy for years
- Periodic tenancy
- Tenancy at will
- Tenancy at sufferance

Tenancy for Years

A **tenancy for years** is created when the landlord and the tenant agree on a specific duration for the lease. A tenancy for years is the most common type of leasehold. The tenancy for years is an estate in the property for a fixed period of time. The fixed period of time can be from six months to several years. The key feature of a tenancy for years is that the beginning and ending dates are fixed and computable. At common law, there was no set limit as to the number of years the term may run, however today, some states have enacted statutes which limit the duration of the term.

In a tenancy for years, no notice is needed to terminate the leasehold. Since the lease has a specified end date, the leasehold simply ends on the last day of the lease, and the tenant is required to vacate the premises. For example, Lois is a freshman at the local state university. She enters into a lease agreement to lease an apartment for the duration of her stay at the school, which is four years. At the end of the four-year period, the lease will automatically terminate on the specified day. A landlord may terminate the lease at an earlier date if the tenant fails to pay rent, or the tenant may, under certain jurisdictions, surrender the property to the landlord at an earlier date.

Periodic Tenancy

A **periodic tenancy** is a tenancy created when a lease specifies intervals at which payments are due, but does not specify how long the lease is for. The periodic tenancy will continue from one period to the next automatically, unless one of the parties terminates at the end of a notice period. At common law, six months notice was required to terminate a year-to-year tenancy, however today, many jurisdictions only require thirty days notice to terminate the lease. A periodic tenancy can be created

nonfreehold estate
A lease agreement.

PRACTICE TIP

Landlord—tenant law is derived from both statutory and common law sources. A number of states base their statutory law on the Uniform Residential Landlord and Tenant Act created by a commission attempting to achieve uniformity across the states.

tenancy for years
The temporary use and possession of lands or tenements not the tenant's own, by virtue of a lease or demise granted to him by the owner, for a determinate period of time, as for a year or a fixed number of years.

periodic tenancy
Tenancy in which the tenant is a holdover after the expiration of a tenancy for years.

FIGURE 6.1   **Sample Lease**

SAMPLE LEASE OR RENTAL AGREEMENT

By this agreement made at _____, PA on the _____ day of
_____, 20____, the Landlord _____ and
the Tenant _____ agree as follows:

1. PROPERTY

The Landlord hereby leases to Tenant for the term of this agreement

a. the property located at:

| _____ | _____ | _____ |
| No. | Street Name | Unit No. |

| _____ | _____ | _____ |
| City | State | Zip |

and

b. the following furniture and appliances on that property:

_____

_____

2. TERM

The term of this lease is for _____, beginning on _____, and ending on _____.
At the expiration of said term, the lease will automatically be renewed for a period of one month unless
either party notifies the other of its intention to terminate the lease at least one month before its expiration date.

(or)

At the expiration of said term, the lease will expire unless the tenant gives a written notice at least 15 days before the termination date of the lease. Thereafter, the lease will automatically be renewed for periods of one month until either party notifies the other of its intention to terminate the lease. The notice of termination will be in writing and will be effective on the next rental date no less than 30 days after the date of the notice.

3. RENT

Tenant agrees to pay rent in the amount of _____ per month, each payment due on the _____ day of each month and to be made at:

| _____ | _____ | _____ | _____ |
| Address | City | State | Zip |

4. UTILITIES/SERVICES

Landlord agrees to provide the utilities and services indicated:
_____ electricity   _____ gas   _____ water
_____ garbage collection   _____ snow removal   _____ other

Contd...

FIGURE 6.1   **Sample Lease** *Contd...*

5.   **DEPOSIT**

Tenant has paid a deposit of $_____ of which Landlord acknowledges receipt. Upon regaining possession of the property, Landlord shall refund to Tenant the total amount of the deposit less any damages to the property, normal wear and tear expected, and less any unpaid rent.

6.   **REFUND PROCEDURE**

Forwarding Address—Tenant shall provide Landlord with a forwarding address at which the Landlord can send him/her the deposit refund.

Landlord shall return the entire deposit to Tenant within 15 days after retaking possession; or shall return so much of the deposit as exceeds any damages done to the property during the Tenant's residence, normal wear and tear expected, and any unpaid rent. If the Landlord returns any amount less than the full deposit, he/she shall also provide a written itemized list of damages and charges.

Tenant maintains the right to sue Landlord for any portion of the deposit not returned to him/her which the tenant believes he/she is entitled.

7. **INVENTORY CHECKLIST**

The Tenant is provided with an Inventory Move-In Checklist attached to this lease. The Tenant shall note the conditions of each item on the checklist and return a copy to the Landlord within 10 days after taking possession. If the Landlord objects to inclusions of any item, he/she shall notify the Tenant in writing within 10 days. The Tenant and Landlord shall note the condition of each item on the checklist after the Tenant returns possession to the Landlord and shall give a copy to the other party.

The Landlord may not retain any portion of the Security Deposit for damages noted in the Move-Out Checklist to which the Landlord did not object.

8. **THE PARTIES ALSO AGREE**

A. Tenant shall not sublease nor assign the premises without the written consent of the Landlord (but this consent shall not be withheld unreasonably).

B. The Landlord may not enter the premises without having given tenant at least 24 hours notice, except in case of emergency. Landlord may enter to inspect, repair, or show the premises to prospective buyers or tenants if notice is given.

C. Tenant agrees to occupy the premises and shall keep the same good condition, and shall not make any alternations thereon without the written consent of the landlord.

D. Landlord agrees to regularly maintain the building and grounds in a clean, orderly, and neat manner. Landlord further agrees not to maintain a public nuisance and not to conduct business or commercial activities on the premises.

E. Tenant agrees not to use the premises in such a manner as to disturb the peace and quiet of other tenants in the building. Tenant further agrees not to maintain a public nuisance and not to conduct business or commercial activities on the premises.

F. Tenant shall, upon termination of this Agreement, vacate and return the dwelling in the same condition that it was received, less reasonable wear and tear, and other damages beyond the Tenant's control.

G. Any alternations to this Agreement shall be in writing and signed by all parties. We, the undersigned, agree to this Lease:

LANDLORD	TENANT
_____	_____
Signature	Signature
_____	_____
Typed Name	Typed Name
_____	_____
Address	Address
_____	_____
Signature	Signature
_____	_____
Typed Name	Typed Name
_____	_____
Address	Address

by express agreement or by inference. Additionally, the death of either the landlord or the tenant generally has no effect on the duration of a term of years or periodic tenancy. Periodic tenancies are created

- When an express agreement exists
- By implication, when the lease is from year to year or month to month without any specified ending date
- By operation of law, if the tenant remains in possession after the termination of a tenancy for years

For example, suppose Lois stays in her apartment past the four-year period of time. She continues to pay the specified rent, and the landlord continues to accept her checks. A periodic tenancy has been created by inference as a result of both of their actions. A periodic tenancy from year to year may be created by a tenant's act of holding over after the expiration of a term of years because by remaining on the leased property after the end date of a lease, such a tenant then gives the landlord the option of treating the tenant as a trespasser or simply continuing to treat the individual as a tenant. Even if a landlord initially chooses to treat the individual as a trespasser, but then fails to take any action to eject the tenant in question, courts will typically hold that the landlord constructively agreed to continue the lease month-to-month.

Tenancy at Will

tenancy at will
The holding of premises by permission of the owner or landlord, but without a fixed term.

A **tenancy at will** is a lease that may be terminated at any time by either party. A tenancy at will has no stated duration. A tenancy at will must be created by an express writing. It may be terminated at any time without notice, or it can terminate by operation of law. However, some modern statutes do require a period of notice such as thirty days. For example, Corpus Corporation is conducting a specific market analysis study, and its employees need to complete numerous focus group studies. The studies are to last approximately four months. Corpus Corporation does not have the

FIGURE 6.2
Leaseholds

Leaseholds	
Tenancy for years	Has a specific time for beginning and ending and ends automatically
Periodic tenancy	Has no specific termination date; automatically renews; and notice is required for termination
Tenancy at will	Either party may terminate at will; at common law no notice is required; today modern law may still require 30 days notice
Tenancy at sufferance	Often results after an eviction and it can result in the creation of a periodic tenancy

requisite space in its building to conduct these studies. However, the adjacent building has additional space available. The owner of the adjacent building agrees to allow Corpus Corporation to use a portion of the building for the focus group studies in exchange for a payment of the utilities that are consumed for each month that Corpus uses the space. The studies last four months, and the tenancy at will ends. Corpus is responsible for the utilities only during the time that the focus group studies were being conducted.

Tenancy at Sufferance

A **tenancy at sufferance** is a tenancy created when a tenant retains possession of property after the expiration of another tenancy or a life estate without the owner's consent. In order to end the lease, the landlord has to take steps to **evict** the tenant. The landlord has two choices when a tenant holds over:

* To evict the tenant
* To hold the tenant to another term as a tenant

(See Figure 6.2 for a comparison of the four types of leaseholds.)

TENANTS' RIGHTS AND DUTIES

The tenant has the legal right to possession of the premises as soon as the leasehold commences. A tenant also has the right to **quiet enjoyment** of the leased premises. If the landlord interferes with or enables a third person to interfere with the tenant's use of the premises, then a breach of the covenant of quiet enjoyment will have occurred. For example, if the landlord leases a house adjacent to a tenant and then proceeds to have loud, wild parties next door that disturb the tenant, then this is a breach of the quiet enjoyment of the property by the landlord.

A tenant has a duty and obligation to pay rent. If a tenant abandons the premises, he will not be relieved of his duty to pay rent through the end of the lease period. However, most jurisdictions do require a landlord to mitigate his or her damages in such a situation. That is, if a tenant abandons the premises before the end of the lease

tenancy at sufferance
A tenancy that arises when one comes into the possession of property by lawful title, but wrongfully holds over after the termination of her interest.

evict
In civil law, to recover anything from a person by virtue of the judgment of a court or judicial sentence.

quiet enjoyment
The possession of real property with the assurance that the possession will not be disturbed by superior title.

YOU BE THE JUDGE

Andrew moves into a house next to a college campus, and rents it from the John the landlord for a period of one year, using a written lease. Loud parties with loud music begin to emanate from the Rock 'em Sock 'em fraternity house, located adjacent to the house leased by Andrew. The loud music is heard only on Saturdays and Sundays from 1:00 p.m. until 5:00 p.m. Does Andrew have any grounds to bring a claim against the John for breach of quiet enjoyment? Consider all possibilities in coming to your decision, based on the few facts given.

period, the landlord must use reasonable efforts to find a new tenant. Sometimes the lease is surrendered, that is, the tenant gives up the lease before the end of the term and the landlord accepts the tenant's offer. In this situation, the tenant will have no further obligation to pay rent.

The tenant has the responsibility to keep the premises in good repair and not to commit waste or damage the premises. The tenant cannot use the premises for illegal purposes. If he does, then the landlord has the right to terminate the lease and sue for damages. A tenant also has a duty to behave reasonably when he uses the premises. The duty involves things such as the following:

security deposit
Money deposited by a tenant with the landlord as security for full and faithful performance by the tenant of the terms of the lease, including damages to premises.

- The tenant must not unreasonably disturb other tenants.
- The tenant must obey reasonable regulations established by the landlord.
- The tenant must abide by health and building codes as they relate to the tenant's use of the premises.
- The tenant must not commit waste.

LEGAL RESEARCH MAXIM

Learn about the laws regarding the landlord—tenant relationship at www.uslandlord.com/laws.

LANDLORD'S DUTIES UNDER A LEASE

In most leasehold situations, the tenant is required to make a **security deposit** to the landlord that can be equal to the amount of one or two months' rent. The purpose of the security deposit is to offset the damages caused by the tenant should the tenant breach the lease.

If the tenant fails to pay rent, the landlord has the right to terminate the lease and evict the tenant from the premises. On the other hand, a landlord has the following duties under a lease:

constructive eviction
Option of a tenant to leave and surrender premises without penalty, because while not depriving tenant of possession, the landlord has made the premises untenantable through disrepair or some act rendering the premises unlivable.

- Duty to deliver possession of the premises to the tenant
- Duty not to interfere with the tenant's right to quiet enjoyment
- Duty to maintain the leased premises in good repair, including an implied warranty of habitability

If the landlord cannot keep the premises in good repair, the tenant may be able to leave the premises, without consequences, because of a doctrine known as **constructive Eviction**.

CASE FACT PATTERN

Bob leases, *in writing*, an apartment to Amy for one year, with rent payable on the first of every month. A week goes by and leaks and cockroaches begin to come through the ceilings in three rooms. The apartment has a total of five rooms. Written and verbal letters and messages are sent to Bob, certified delivery. This continues to happen over the next two months, and now the toilet no longer functions properly. Each time a person flushes the toilet, water sprays out of it into the neighboring bathtub. Notices from Amy go out again to Bob. Again, nothing happens. Amy moves out after another month of no action (*now three months into the lease*) and no contact from Bob. Bob sues in court to recover the security deposit and nine remaining months of rent. Bob loses, based on valid constructive eviction by Amy. It is important to keep in mind that a breach of the covenant of quiet enjoyment most be considered substantial for a tenant to be successful under a theory of constructive eviction. For example, Fred lives in Apartment 2A. Barney lives in apartment 2B. Barney regularly has parties that go late into the night and the excessive noise frequently prevents Fred from sleeping. Fred complains to the landlord but the parties and the noise continue. Fred would likely not be able to successfully assert constructive eviction in this instance as the interference would not be considered substantial.

TORT LIABILITY OF LANDLORDS AND TENANTS

During the period of time that a tenant is in possession of the premises, she is treated as though she is the owner for tort liability purposes. Many jurisdictions hold that a general duty of due care is owed by the possessor of land to any occupants, provided they are not trespassing. At common law, the tenant had an implied duty to make needed minor repairs to the leased property. Specifically, this meant that the tenant was to keep the property in the same general condition as it was at the beginning of the lease term. For example, a tenant would be expected to fix a broken window. This duty to repair has largely disappeared as, in modern times it is believed that the landlord should maintain the premises. The implied duty of habitability suggests that it is the landlord's duty to repair. However, residential leases may be written in a manner that makes the tenant responsible for making minor repairs to the property, and commercial leases almost always require the tenant to make needed repairs that fall outside of what is often referred to as "fair wear and tear."

Some jurisdictions still abide by the common law distinctions of licensee and invitee. Common law also held landlords liable for tenant injuries only if the landlord was negligent in the performance of his or her duties. If a **licensee**, or social guest, enters the premises, the tenant has a duty to warn the visitor of any dangerous conditions of which the tenant is aware. If an **invitee** comes onto the tenant's premises for business purposes, the tenant owes the invitee a duty of reasonable care. The tenant is not required to warn the invitee of any dangers that she is aware of, but the tenant is required to make a reasonable inspection of the premises in order to discover defects and to take reasonable steps to correct these defects. A tenant has no duty of care to a **trespasser**. (See Figure 6.3 for distinctions among trespassers, licensees, and invitees.)

Landlords owe a duty of reasonable care to tenants and third parties not to negligently cause them injury. The landlord will be held liable if he conceals from or fails to disclose to the tenant a dangerous existing defect at the commencement of the lease. The landlord will also be held liable for areas that are retained under the landlord's control, such as common areas, lobbies, elevators, and corridors. The tenant may have a right to use these areas, but they are under the control of the landlord, and the landlord has a duty to take reasonable care to keep these areas safe.

If the landlord makes repairs to the premises, he will be held liable if those repairs are made negligently. Landlords have a duty to keep the premises in a habitable and safe condition.

Federal law prohibits discrimination in housing and the rental market. The Fair Housing Act, enacted in 1968, prevents landlords, real estate companies, and other entities from making housing unavailable because of race or color, religion, sex, national origin, familial status, or disability. The federal government may bring lawsuits when there is reason to believe that discrimination has occurred.

licensee
One known to be on the premises but whose presence gives no benefit to the property owner.

invitee
Person wanted on the premises for a specific purpose known by the landowner.

trespasser
One who intentionally and without privilege enters another's property.

Party	Distinctions
Trespassors	Those who enter property without permission
Licensees	Those entering with permission such as social guests in a tenant's home
Invitees	Those entering with permission for the purpose for which the property is maintained such as customers in a tenant's place of business

FIGURE 6.3 Distinctions among Trespassers, Licensees, and Invitees

SPOT THE ISSUE

George owns and manages Welcoming Winds apartment complex. His tenants include families of several different races and religions, and he welcomes nontraditional families. Valerie, who is blind, fills out a rental application for Welcoming Winds, but her application is denied. She asks George why her application was not accepted. George kindly says that he would not feel comfortable having her live alone in an apartment. and advises her she would be better off living with a good friend or family member.

ASSIGNMENT AND SUBLEASE

assignment
The transfer of the rights to receive the benefit of contractual performance under the contract.

sublease
A lease executed by the lessee of land or premises to a third person, conveying the same interest that the lessee enjoys, but for a shorter term than that for which the lessee holds.

assignee
The party to whom the right to receive contractual performance is transferred.

sublessee
A third party who receives by lease some or all of the leased property from a lessee.

Unless the parties have agreed to the contrary, either party has the right to transfer her interest in the premises. The law prefers that property is freely alienable; however, the alienability of a leasehold may be restricted by the written lease. An **assignment** is the transfer of all rights that the tenant may possess under the lease. If a tenant transfers anything less than the entire interest in the premises, a sublease occurs. A **sublease** is a transfer of a portion of the rights that a tenant possesses under the lease. The landlord has the right to transfer her interest in the property by virtue of a sale of the property or a lease of the premises.

The major factor of an assignment is that it establishes a new landlord—tenant relationship between the assignee and the original party, who did not assign her rights. A sublease does not establish a new landlord—tenant relationship. An assignment is the transfer by the tenant of her entire interest in the leased premises. The tenant will transfer the entire remaining length of the term in the lease to the **assignee**. If the tenant transfers any interests that are less than her entire interest in the leased premises, then the tenant has created a sublease.

When an assignment of the lease is made, the assignee becomes primarily obligated to the landlord for the rental payment. A sublease conveys some or all of the leased property for a shorter term that that of the lessee, who retains a reversion in the lease. The tenant will not escape contractual liability for the payment of rent simply by assigning the lease. The tenant can be relieved of any contractual liability for the payment of rent only if a release of his liability in this regard is executed between the tenant and the landlord. When the tenant subleases the premises, the tenant becomes the landlord for the sublessee. The tenant and the sublessee are contractually obligated to each other.

RESEARCH THIS

Research the California case of *Becker v. IRM Corp.*, 698 P.2d 116 (1985). This case views a landlord's duty to inspect leased premises for dangerous conditions differently than is stated in common law. What obligations does the California court impose on the landlord regarding the inspection of leased premises for dangerous conditions?

EYE ON ETHICS

Most leases are forms. Most law firms have form files that contain existing leases. It is unethical for a legal professional to charge a client for the entire cost of the creation of a lease as if it were a new work product when a form is used and the information simply changed for the client. It is ethical to charge the client just for the time it took to customize the form for that particular client.

Landlord and tenant law affects many people in the United States. There are many resources available on the Internet that are helpful resources in the area of landlord-tenant law. Some of these Web sites are:

http://www.law.cornell.edu/topics/landlord_tenant.html
http://www.nolo.com/lawcenter/index.cfm
http://www.tenantnet.com/

Summary

A leasehold, sometimes known as a nonfreehold estate, is a possessory interest in property, but it is not an ownership interest. It is created by the terms of the lease. The lease determines the rights and obligations between the landlord and the tenant and describes the relationship between the parties as lessor and lessee. Like all contracts, a lease determines who the parties are, the terms under which the relationship will take shape, the period of time for the relationship, and the rights to termination, and includes the signatures of the parties.

A tenancy for years is created when the landlord and the tenant agree on a specific duration for the lease; it is the most common type of leasehold and extends over a fixed period of time. The key feature of a tenancy for years is that the beginning and ending dates are fixed and computable.

A periodic tenancy is created when a lease specifies intervals at which payments are due, but does not specify how long the lease is for. It will continue from one period to the next automatically, unless one of the parties terminates at the end of a notice period. A periodic tenancy can be created by express agreement or by inference.

A tenancy at will is a lease that may be terminated at any time by either party, as it has no stated duration. It must, however, be created by an express writing.

A tenancy at sufferance is a tenancy created when a tenant retains possession of property after the expiration of another tenancy or a life estate without the owner's consent. In order to end the lease, the landlord has to take steps to evict the tenant.

A tenant has the legal right to possession of the premises as soon as the leasehold commences. He also has the right to quiet enjoyment of the leased premises. If the landlord interferes with or enables a third person to interfere with the tenant's use of the premises, then a breach of the covenant of quiet enjoyment will have occurred.

A tenant has a duty and obligation to pay rent. If a tenant abandons the premises, she will not be relieved of her duty to pay rent through the end of the lease period. The tenant also has the responsibility to keep the premises in good repair and to not commit waste or damage the premises. If a tenant does not pay rent or fails at any of her other responsibilities, the landlord then has the right to terminate the lease and sue for damages. A tenant also has a duty to behave reasonably when she uses the premises.

A landlord also has duties under a lease: (1) duty to deliver possession of the premises to the tenant; (2) duty not to interfere with the tenant's right to quiet enjoyment; and (3) duty to maintain the leased premises in good repair, including an implied warranty of habitability.

During the period of time that a tenant is in possession of the premises, he is treated as though he is the owner for tort liability purposes. If a licensee enters the premises, the tenant has a duty to warn the visitor of any dangerous conditions that the tenant is aware of. If an invitee comes onto the tenant's premises for business purposes, the tenant owes the invitee a duty of reasonable care. The tenant is not required to warn the invitee of any dangers that he is aware of, but the tenant is required to make a reasonable inspection of the premises in order to discover defects and to take reasonable steps to correct these defects. A tenant has no duty of care to a trespasser.

Unless the parties have agreed to the contrary, either party has the right to transfer her interest in the premises. An assignment is the transfer of all rights that the tenant may possess under the lease. A sublease is a transfer of a portion of the rights that a tenant possesses under the lease. The landlord has the right to transfer her interest in the property by virtue of a sale of the property or a lease of the premises.

Key Terms

Acceleration clause
Assignee
Assignment
Constructive Eviction
Evict
Invitee
Landlord
Lease
Leasehold
Lessee
Lessor
Licensee

Mitigate
Periodic tenancy
Quiet enjoyment
Security deposit
Sublease
Sublessee
Tenancy at sufferance
Tenancy at will
Tenancy for years
Tenant
Trespasser

Review Questions

1. What is a leasehold?
2. List the duties of a tenant.
3. List the duties of a landlord.
4. What is the difference between an assignment and a sublease?
5. What is a tenancy in years?
6. What is significant about a tenancy at will?
7. List the four types of tenancies and their most significant features.
8. What is a security deposit?
9. How is a periodic tenancy created?
10. What is a tenancy at sufferance?
11. What can a landlord do if a tenant holds over the term of the lease?
12. What is an assignee?
13. How is it that a tenant can still be liable for rental payments on a lease if he has assigned his rights and interest in the leased premises?
14. What duty does a tenant have to an invitee?
15. What is an eviction?

Exercises

1. On December 1, Lilia and Thomas orally agreed that Thomas would lease Lilia's premises for the sum of $800 per month. No specified term was set. Thomas took possession of the property on January 1. What type of tenancy have the parties created?
2. Research your local state laws and determine what a landlord must do in order to evict a tenant. Prepare the necessary court forms and pleadings that would be used to initiate such an eviction process. Use yourself as the tenant and your teacher as the landlord.

3. Obtain a form lease that would be valid in your jurisdiction. Using yourself as the tenant and your teacher as the landlord, prepare a lease for a tenancy for years at a rental rate of $1,400 per month.

4. Dawn and Howard agreed that Dawn would rent a townhouse from Howard for a period of one year. A written lease stating the term was signed by both parties. Two months into the lease, after losing her job, Dawn moves in with her sister. Howard tells Dawn she must continue paying rent until the expiration of the lease term. Is Howard obligated to look for another renter? Why or why not?

5. Claire leases a small restaurant. Some of the chairs in the restaurant are in poor repair. Agnes Andrews comes in one afternoon for a cup of coffee and a piece of pie. The chair she is sitting on breaks underneath her. She sustains a broken hip. Discuss Claire's tort liability? Would Agnes be a licensee or an invitee?

6. Landlord Lizard verbally agrees to lease Tommy Tenant a 4-bedroom apartment for a 1-year term at $1,200 per month, due on the first of the month. Tommy Tenant moves in with no problems. Four months later, leaks begin to permeate the structure and Tommy's apartment from an adjacent building. Tommy complains in writing and verbally to Landlord Lizard and his concerns fall on deaf ears. Two months later, Tommy moves out claiming constructive eviction. Does he have a claim based on the facts given? Go back to the beginning of the exercise and read entire problem over again thoroughly before coming to a conclusion.

7. Carol the Carpetbagger leases an apartment from Linda Landlord. Everything is legal and binding between them. Unbeknownst to Linda, Carol subleases her apartment to Timid Theresa. Timid Theresa has a guest over, Bad Luck Betty. Approaching the front door, Bad Luck Betty slips and trips on a piece of cement that broke away due to the rain storms the area had almost 2 months ago, and breaks her kneecap. Has a tort been committed and, if so, who is responsible for damages to Bad Luck Betty's broken kneecap?

8. What duties, if any, does a landlord owe to possessors of easements, gas meter person, mail carrier, telephone cable person?

 PORTFOLIO ASSIGNMENT

Using a form downloaded from www.dhcr.state.ny.us/ora/, the New York Rent Administration, create a residential lease lasting one year between Rosie Renter and Larry Landlord.

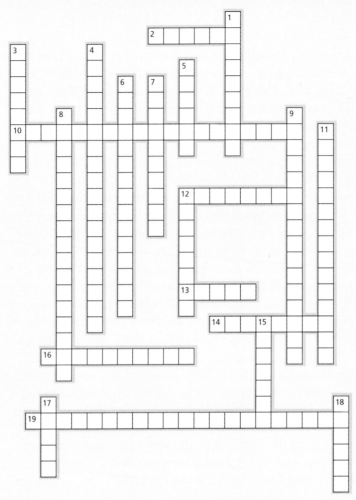

Instructions

Use the key terms from this chapter to fill in the answers to the crossword puzzle.

NOTE: When the answer is more than one word, leave a blank space between words.

ACROSS

2. one who rents property from another.
10. a provision that requires a debtor pay off a balance sooner than the scheduled due date if some specified event occcurs.
12. the owner of an estate in land, or a rental property, who has leased it to another person, called a tenant.
13. in civil law, to recover anything from a person by virtue of the judgment of a court or judicial sentence.
14. one to whom property rights or powers are transferred by another.
15. one who intentionally and without privillege enters an-othhers property.
19. a tenancy that arises when one comes into the posses-sion of property by lawful title, but wrongfully holds over after the termination of her interest.

DOWN

1. an estate in real property held by a tenant under the lease.
3. to make less severe or intense.
4. an estate which does not include a possessory interest in land.
5. one who has temporary use and occupation of real property.

6. the possession of premises by permission of the owner or landlord, but without a fixed term.
7. the act of transferring to another all or part of one's property, interest, or rights.
8. the temporary use and possession of lands or tene-ments not the tenant's own, by virtue of a lease or de-mise granted to him by the owner, for a determinate period of time, as for a year or a fixed number of years.
9. generic term descriptive of a tenancy from week to week, month to month, or year to year.
11. the possession of real property with the assurance that the possession will not be disturbed by superior title.
12. one who has permission to enter or use another's premises; a social guest.
15. one who has an express or implied invitation to enter or use another's premises, such as a business visitor or a member or the public to whom the premises are held open.
17. any agreement that gives rise to a relationship of land-lord and tenant or lessor and lessee.
18. One who rents property to another.

SANTA FE TRAIL NEIGHBORHOOD REDEVELOPMENT CORP v. W.F. COEN & COMPANY
COURT OF APPEALS OF MISSOURI, WESTERN DISTRICT
154 S.W.3d 432; 2005 Mo. App. LEXIS 113
January 25, 2005, Opinion Filed

OPINION: Appellants, Dr. Henrik A. Knudsen and his wife Rogene F. Knudsen, appeal a judgment of the Circuit Court of Jackson County in their civil action for apportionment and distribution of an award of damages which was paid into the registry of the court after certain real property they owned was condemned. The Knudsens claim the trial court erred in distributing a part of the award to Respondent, Dr. Joan R. Walker, since Dr. Walker was not entitled to any distribution whatsoever. We reverse and remand for entry of a new judgment in favor of Dr. Walker.

The underlying facts of this case are undisputed. In 1965, the Knudsens purchased real estate located at 1520 South Noland Road in Independence, Jackson County, Missouri ("the Property"). The Property, on which a building had been constructed, was used as a dental office beginning in 1967, and Dr. Knudsen practiced dentistry there until he retired in 2001. In 1977, the Knudsens built an addition onto the front of the building, connecting to the building's existing plumbing and electrical systems. The reception room for the dental offices in the building was located in the front of the building and was shared by everyone in the building. There was a parking lot in the rear of the building that was also shared by the occupants of the building, as well as by patients.

At some point prior to 1996, Appellants began renting space in the building to another dentist, Dr. Branstetter. At this time, Dr. Walker worked for Dr. Knudsen. Dr. Branstetter subsequently sold his dental practice to Dr. Walker, who, on November 15, 1996, entered into a written agreement with the Knudsens to occupy the office space that had formerly been occupied by Dr. Branstetter. Pursuant to the terms of the agreement, Dr. Walker took possession of her office space in the building on November 15, 1996.

The written agreement between the Knudsens and Dr. Walker ("the Agreement") was titled "PROFESSIONAL OFFICE LEASE AGREEMENT." It was signed by the Knudsens as "Landlords" and by Dr. Walker as "Tenant," and throughout the text of the Agreement, the Knudsens were referred to as "landlord" and Dr. Walker was referred to as "tenant." The Agreement provided that it was a contract to "lease" and "rent" office space in the building to Dr. Walker, who agreed to "accept the Leased Premises in [their] present condition and as suited for the uses intended by" her. That intended use was specified in the Agreement, which further provided that "the Leased Premises shall be used for a professional office space."

The professional office space leased to Dr. Walker pursuant to the Agreement was described as "office space consisting of 1,164 square feet, more or less," and was further described as comprising "approximately 46.6% of the total leasable space within the office building." The diagrams attached to the Agreement indicate that the leased space included a common reception area and a common area in the basement that were to be shared by all occupants. The Agreement also provided that the Knudsens would maintain the building's rear parking lot, which Dr. Walker and her patients were permitted to use.

The Agreement expressly provided that "this contract shall create the relationship of Landlord and Tenant between the parties thereto" and that "Landlord gives to Tenant exclusive control of the Leased Premises." In addition, the Agreement gave Dr. Walker the right to "assign this lease or sublease all or portions of the Leased Premises to others if such operation is within the purposes for which the Leased Premises may be used," as long as she obtained the prior written consent of the Knudsens, which was not to be unreasonably withheld.

The Agreement specified an initial lease term of five years at a basic monthly rental rate of $ 775 per month, and required Dr. Walker to pay a $ 775 security deposit for the leased space. The term of the Agreement as initially executed was from November 15, 1996, to November 14, 2001. The Agreement also specified that Dr. Walker had the option to renew the lease for an additional five-year term upon giving written notice to the Knudsens of her intent to do so at any time prior to three months before the end of the original term of the lease. If renewed, the basic monthly rental rate, during each subsequent year following the end of the original five-year term of the Agreement, was to incrementally increase by an amount related to the increase in the Consumer Price Index (CPI) as computed and published by the United States Department of Labor Statistics for the area encompassing the Property.

In addition to the rent and security deposit, Dr. Walker agreed to pay 46.6% of all monthly utility bills for the Property, as well as all ad valorem personal property taxes resulting from her occupancy thereof. She also agreed to pay for glass breakage, sign damage, and environmental cleanup, disposal, inspections, and fines, if any, and to maintain the leased space in good order and repair, excepting only those repairs expressly required to be made by the Knudsens. Dr. Walker further agreed to maintain, throughout the lease term and at her own expense, a general liability insurance policy covering the leased space, in amounts not less than $ 100,000 per person and $ 300,000 per occurrence for bodily injury claims and not less than $ 50,000 for property damage claims. Finally, Dr. Walker agreed not to store any substances containing components designated as hazardous, dangerous, toxic, or harmful without the prior written consent of the Knudsens.

On December 5, 2000, Dr. Walker's attorney sent a letter to the Knudsens via certified mail giving them timely notice of Dr. Walker's desire and intent to renew the Agreement for a second five-year term. On June 1, 2001, Dr. Knudsen retired and sold his dental practice to a third party, Dr. Rodger Suchman.

Dr. Suchman wished to rent, as a month-to-month tenant only, the office space previously occupied by Dr. Knudsen in the building, and although this space was slightly larger than the space being rented to Dr. Walker, the rental fee was set at $ 775 per month, which, after the CPI adjustment provided for in the renewed Agreement between the Knudsens and Dr. Walker, was slightly less than the basic monthly rental rate then being paid by Dr. Walker for the office space she was occupying.

On August 30, 2001, a Petition for Condemnation was filed by the Santa Fe Trail Neighborhood Redevelopment Corporation ("Santa Fe") requesting, among other things, that all of the real property owned by the Knudsens which was situated in the Martha's Vineyard Subdivision be condemned as blighted and in need of redevelopment. This included not only the Property, but also an adjacent vacant lot owned by the Knudsens. On November 14, 2001, the trial court entered an order condemning both pieces of real estate.

On March 11, 2002, pursuant to a stipulation between the Knudsens and Santa Fe, the trial court entered a consent judgment reflecting that the Knudsens had agreed to accept the sum of $ 275,000 in full satisfaction and release of their claim for damages arising from Santa Fe's condemnation of the Martha's Vineyard Subdivision real estate owned by the Knudsens. Santa Fe was ordered to pay $ 275,000 into the court registry as damages for the takings by Santa Fe, and the trial court also ordered Santa Fe to pay "reasonable tenant moving expenses."

On March 21, 2002, Santa Fe deposited $ 275,000 into the court registry. Although the November 14, 2001 order of condemnation expressly granted Santa Fe the right to take possession of the condemned real estate at that time, Santa Fe did not exercise this right. Instead, Dr. Walker continued in uninterrupted possession and control of her office space in the building on the Property until she vacated the premises on December 31, 2002.

As authorized by § 523.053.1, on March 25, 2002, the Knudsens filed a motion requesting that the condemnation damage award be apportioned to reflect the respective legal interests of both themselves and Dr. Walker in the Property, a copy of which they served on Dr. Walker. Although this motion described Dr. Walker as a "tenant" of the Property who was "entitled to [receive] moving expenses" from Santa Fe under the terms of the March 11, 2001 consent judgment and acknowledged that Dr. Walker claimed a leasehold interest in the Property pursuant to the Agreement, the motion further requested an order commanding the court clerk to disburse to the Knudsens all of the $ 275,000 being held in the court registry.

On March 28, 2002, Dr. Walker filed a response to the Knudsens' motion in which she claimed a bonus value leasehold interest in the condemnation proceeds pursuant to the renewed Agreement and requested that the trial court retain the proceeds in the registry "until such time as the Court can determine the interest of the various claimants to this sum." On April 28, 2003, the trial court entered an order of partial distribution in which it directed, in accordance with a stipulation between the parties, that the sum of $ 225,000 be paid to the Knudsens out of the registry and that the remaining $ 50,000, which was still the subject of a dispute between the Knudsens and Dr. Walker, be placed in an interest-bearing bank account until further order of the court.

In November 2003, the trial court held a hearing on the Knudsens' motion for apportionment and distribution and received evidence presented by the Knudsens and Dr. Walker. Dr. Walker presented the testimony of an expert real estate appraiser, William Davis, while the Knudsens also presented the competing testimony of another expert real estate appraiser, Larry Witt. After considering this and other evidence, on December 12, 2003, the trial court entered a judgment finding that with regard to the Property in question, Dr. Walker's proportionate share of the condemnation damages that had been paid into the registry by Santa Fe was $ 47,000. On January 12, 2004, the trial court issued an amended judgment finding that Dr. Walker was also entitled to recover the interest that had accrued on her $ 47,000 proportionate share, leading to the instant appeal.

The Knudsens raise five points on appeal, which we will address out of their original order. In their second point, the Knudsens claim the trial court erred in apportioning any part of the condemnation damage award to Dr. Walker because she did not have a compensable interest in the Property in that the Agreement was merely a license revocable at will, not a lease creating a landlord-tenant relationship. We disagree. While the Knudsens are correct that one whose right to enter real estate owned by another is merely a license does not have a compensable legal interest in the property if it is subsequently condemned, under the plain terms of the Agreement, Dr. Walker was clearly a lessee, not merely a licensee.

In order for one to have a compensable interest in a condemnation proceeding, "the interest held [in] the property for which compensation must be rendered . . . must consist of some definite right of domination in and over the [property], such as the right of user, or exclusion, or disposition. Other than to show their express intent, it matters not what the parties themselves call their agreement. *Friend v. Gem Int'l, Inc.*, 476 S.W.2d 134, 137 (Mo. App. E.D. 1971). "Rather, the nature of the relationship depends upon how it fits within the standards set by the law." *Id.* "The denomination of an instrument as a 'license' or a 'lease' by the parties cannot alter or affect its true nature. *Id.*

A lease is generally regarded as a conveyance or grant of an estate in real property for a limited term with conditions attached.

Thus an "'estate' in the leasehold context requires simply a conveyance of a lessor's interest in real property for a limited term." *Chubb Group of Ins. Cos. v. C.F. Murphy & Assocs., Inc.*, 656 S.W.2d 766, 778 (Mo. App. W.D. 1983).

A license is only a privilege to enter certain premises for a specific purpose. In contrast, a lease is "any agreement which gives rise to relationship of landlord and tenant" and said "contract is for exclusive possession of tenements for a determinate period." A landlord-tenant relationship is created when: (1) there is reversion in the landlord; (2) creation of an estate in the tenant either at will or for a term less than that which the landlord holds; (3) transfer of exclusive possession and control of the tenant; and (4) a contract.

Whether a particular agreement is a lease or a license depends on whether or not it shows the intention to establish the relation of landlord and tenant, such intention being determined from a consideration of the entire instrument, and the circumstances under which it was made. . . . Definiteness of the space to be occupied is one of the criteria for determining whether the instrument is a lease.

Johnson, 592 S.W.2d at 857-58 (internal quotation marks omitted).

Applying the facts to this well-developed body of Missouri law, it is clear that the contractual Agreement between the Knudsens and Dr. Walker was a lease creating a landlord-tenant relationship and a leasehold estate, rather than merely a revocable license. Dr. Walker's actions of paying the security deposit and making regular monthly rental payments to the Knudsens, along with her actual continuous possession and control of the office space for the purposes authorized by the terms of the Agreement, fulfilled the express intention of the parties that Dr. Walker enjoy exclusive possession and control thereof during the term of the Agreement. The Agreement further granted Dr. Walker the right to assign her interests under the Agreement or sublease all or any portion of the office space to a third party for similar uses upon prior written consent of the Knudsens, which consent was not to be unreasonably withheld. These factors are all inconsistent with the grant of only a license, because one of the essential characteristics [of a license] is the absence of the right to possession of the land." *Friend*, 476 S.W.2d at 138.

In addition, the Agreement nowhere states that it could be revoked at the whim or pleasure of the Knudsens. This, too, is entirely inconsistent with a mere license, because "the essential attribute of a bare license is the right of the grantor to freely revoke it any time." *Kansas City Area Transp. Auth. v. Ashley*, 485 S.W.2d 641, 644 (Mo. App. W.D. 1972). For this reason, if no other, it can hardly be said that Dr. Walker occupied the office space as only a licensee.

Notwithstanding all this, the Knudsens cite the Agreement as providing that "no estate shall pass out of the Landlord," claiming that Dr. Walker thereby contracted away her right to claim any estate in the Property - even a leasehold. However, as noted by Dr. Walker, while those words do indeed appear in the Agreement, they have been taken out of their proper context. Accordingly, we hold that the Agreement between the Knudsens and Dr. Walker was not merely a revocable privilege to enter the Property for a specific purpose, but a fully executed lease which had been properly renewed, by Dr. Walker and at her option, for a new five-year term nearly nine months before Santa Fe commenced condemnation proceedings. Point denied.

In their first point, the Knudsens argue the trial court erred in apportioning any part of the condemnation damage award to Dr. Walker because she did not have a compensable interest in the Property in that the Agreement had terminated since it provided that the lease term ceased at the time actual possession of the Property was taken by Santa Fe. We disagree, because under the plain terms of the Agreement, Dr. Walker's right to recover her proportionate share of the condemnation damages paid into the registry by Santa Fe was not impaired or extinguished.

Where, as here, a tract being condemned is subject to a leasehold interest and a single award of damages is made without regard to the lessee's claim, that amount may be allocated between the owner of the fee interest and the owner of the leasehold interest pursuant to the procedure provided in § 523.053. *State ex rel. Mo. Highway & Transp. Comm'n v. Rantz*, 43 S.W.3d 436, 440 (Mo. App. S.D. 2001).

Under Missouri law, the general rule is that "damages in condemnation require the fact finder to measure the value of the property prior to the taking against its value after the taking. The date of the taking is the date upon which the condemnor pays the [damage] award into court." *State ex rel. Mo. Highway & Transp. Comm'n v. Starling Plaza P'ship*, 832 S.W.2d 518, 520 (Mo. banc 1992) (internal citations omitted). Moreover, "ownership of property for purposes of a condemnation action is determined at the time the petition in condemnation is filed." *Id.* at 521. Accordingly, to have a compensable interest in a condemnation award of damages, any claimant thereto must show that it had an interest in the condemned property at the time the condemnor commenced condemnation proceedings. *Ticor Title Ins. Co. v. Land Clearance for Redevelopment Auth. of Kansas City*, 729 S.W.2d 236, 238 (Mo. App. W.D. 1987).

Nevertheless, the Knudsens claim that the Agreement itself divested Dr. Walker of any legally compensable interest she might otherwise have had in the Property. They rely on the following provision of the Agreement:

CONDEMNATION: If the Leased Premises, or any portion thereof should be condemned by any legally constituted authority for any purpose, then the term of this lease shall cease from the date when possession thereof is taken, and rental shall be accounted for as between Landlord and Tenant as of said date. Such termination, however, shall be without prejudice to the rights of either Landlord or Tenant, to the extent of their respective interest, to recover compensation and damage caused by condemnation from the condemnor. Neither party shall have any rights in any award made to the other by any condemnation authority, notwithstanding termination of this lease.

The Knudsens claim that by agreeing to this provision, Dr. Walker "contracted away any rights that she might have otherwise had to share in any condemnation proceeds" under Missouri law. Since "the interpretation to be given a contract on undisputed facts is a question of law," *Stotts v. Progressive Classic Ins. Co.*, 118 S.W.3d 655, 662 (Mo. App. W.D. 2003), our review of this issue is *de novo*. City of Harrisonville v. Pub. Water Supply Dist. No. 9, 49 S.W.3d 225, 230 (Mo. App. W.D. 2001). "The cardinal principle of contract interpretation is to ascertain the intention of the parties and to give effect to that intent. The terms of a contract are read as a whole to determine the intention of the parties and are given their plain, ordinary, and usual meaning." *Dunn Indus. Group, Inc. v. City of Sugar Creek*, 112 S.W.3d 421, 428 (Mo. banc 2003) (internal citation omitted).

The first sentence of the condemnation clause provides that vis-a-vis the two parties to the lease, the term of the lease was to come to an end and the final rental payment to be determined, not upon the date condemnation proceedings commenced or the leased premises were condemned, but when Santa Fe *took actual possession thereof*. The second sentence provides that notwithstanding this, "such termination . . . shall be without prejudice to the rights of either Landlord or Tenant, to the extent of their respective interest, to recover compensation and damage caused by condemnation from the condemnor." This means that neither party's right to recover damages from Santa Fe for its respective compensable interest in the condemned Property was to be impaired, compromised, or eliminated by the lease termination provision contained in the first sentence. Finally, the third sentence provides that, again notwithstanding the lease termination provision contained in the first sentence, neither party "shall have any rights in any award made to the other by any condemnation authority." This simply means that neither the Knudsens nor Dr. Walker had any rights in any award of condemnation damages made to the other by Santa Fe.

Here, the Agreement does not call for termination of the lease upon the date of the taking of the property by the condemnor. Instead, the Agreement provided that the term of the lease (and Dr. Walker's continued obligation to pay rent to the Knudsens) was to come to an end when the condemnor (Santa Fe) *took actual possession of the condemned Property* (which did not take place until some time after December 31, 2002), *not at the time of the taking* (which took place on March 21, 2002, more than nine months earlier). Because the lease was still in full force and effect at the time of the taking, which, as noted *supra,* is the critical date for determining damages in condemnation, *Bi-State* is inapposite. Furthermore, and even more critically, unlike the lease in *Bi-State,* the Agreement contained a separate clause expressly providing that Dr. Walker's right to recover damages from Santa Fe for her leasehold interest in the condemned Property was not to be prejudiced by the lease termination provision. Thus, it cannot be said that she thereby affirmatively waived or surrendered her right, as a leaseholder under Missouri law, to her proportionate share of the condemnation damage award. Rather, the manifest intent of the parties to the Agreement was that, with regard to the "rights of either Landlord or Tenant, to the extent of their respective interest, to recover compensation and damage caused by condemnation from the condemnor," the Agreement should be construed as if there had been no lease termination clause at all. Indeed, in *Bi-State,* the court declared: "*Absent a termination clause*, the lease terminates because the leasehold interest has been appropriated for public use, thus giving rise to a right of compensation."

For these reasons, we hold that the trial court properly concluded that the Agreement's condemnation clause did not operate to impair or extinguish Dr. Walker's right, under Missouri law, to recover her proportionate share of the condemnation damages paid into the registry by Santa Fe. Point denied.

In their third point, the Knudsens claim the trial court erred in entering judgment in favor of Dr. Walker for the amount of the bonus value computed by her expert witness, William Davis, since the evidence he relied on "to establish both market rent and contract rent was based upon incorrect figures, irrelevant facts and improper methodologies."

The proper measure of damages for condemnation of a lessee's interest in real property is the bonus value of the unexpired term of the lease as measured by the difference between the market rental and the contract rental for the use and occupancy of the affected leasehold. *Doernhoefer,* 389 S.W.2d at 784. In Doernhoefer, the Missouri Supreme Court discussed the factors to be considered in determining the market value of a leasehold:

The value of the leasehold should be determined from the testimony of qualified expert witnesses as that value which a buyer under no compulsion to purchase the tenancy would pay to a seller under no compulsion to sell, taking into consideration the period of the lease yet to run, including the unexercised right of renewal, the favorable and unfavorable factors of the leasehold estate, the location, type and construction of the building, the business of the tenant, comparable properties in similar neighborhoods, present market conditions and future market trends, and all other material factors that would enter into the determination of the reasonable market value of the property.

389 S.W.2d at 784. In reviewing the admissibility of such evidence on appeal, "we are mindful that the trial court is allowed wide latitude in the admission of evidence because it is presumed that it will not give weight to that evidence which is incompetent. It is, therefore, difficult to base reversible error on the erroneous admission of evidence in a court-tried case." The conflicting opinions of experts in condemnation cases such as this "must be weighed by the trier of fact and considered in light of matters such as the knowledge, experience, and attention given to the case. Whether an expert's opinion is based upon and supported by facts in evidence sufficient to support that opinion is a question of law for the court." *Boatmen's Trust,* 857 S.W.2d at 457 (internal citations omitted).

As mentioned *supra,* during the apportionment hearing, Dr. Walker presented the testimony of William Davis, who had been in the appraisal business for 45 years and who opposing counsel stipulated was an expert in his field. Davis conducted an appraisal of Dr. Walker's leasehold interest in the Property and prepared a report setting forth his findings and the basis therefor. This report was admitted into evidence at the hearing.

Davis indicated that he had conducted his appraisal pursuant to the regulations and rules of ethics of the Appraisal Institute and that he had followed uniform standards of professional practice in preparing the appraisal. He testified that he had conducted a careful inspection of both the inside and outside of the building that included taking photographs and making measurements. He also testified that, based upon his measurements, Dr. Walker was actually using a greater amount of square footage than was approximated in the Agreement.

Davis explained that his methodology in appraising Dr. Walker's leasehold interest consisted of first determining the market rent that should be attributed to the leasehold interest and then subtracting the contract rent actually paid for the leasehold interest. Davis acknowledged that Missouri courts commonly refer to this difference as the "bonus value." Davis further indicated that, in appraising the value of a leasehold, it is important to distinguish between the "leasable space" and the "adjusted leasable space." In essence, based on measurements he had made which were described in drawings set forth in his report, he explained that the adjusted leasable space for the Property in question included both the space that was leased to Dr. Walker for her exclusive use and the common areas that were shared by all tenants of the building. Davis testified that he arrived at the adjusted leasable space by determining the square footage that was used exclusively by Dr. Walker, determining the square footage of the area that Dr. Walker shared with other occupants of the building, and then reducing the shared square footage by a percentage to reflect the fact that the area was shared. He ultimately arrived at a final figure of 1197.2 square feet for the adjusted leasable space for the Property.

In determining market value for Dr. Walker's leasehold interest, Davis considered eleven comparable properties that were also being leased for use as dental offices. Davis first determined the rent for each of the eleven comparable properties. He then adjusted these rents to reflect differences between the comparable properties and Dr. Walker's leasehold, taking into account the following factors: (1) whether the dental equipment in the leased premises was installed by the lessor or the lessee; (2) the location of the leased property; (3) the age of the leased property; (4) the condition and design of the leased property; and (5) who paid utilities under the lease. After making these adjustments and accounting for other relevant data, Davis arrived at an average annual market rent of $ 14.25 per square foot. He then reduced this amount by an additional seven percent to account for lease vacancy rates and the general creditworthiness of dentists, arriving at an average annual rental rate of $ 13.25 per square foot and an average monthly rental rate of $ 1.10417 per square foot.

Having arrived at an average monthly market rental rate of $ 1.10417 per square foot, Davis then determined the difference between this average market rate and the actual contract rate under the Agreement. In determining the amount that Dr. Walker was to pay in rent under the Agreement, Davis took into account the CPI adjustment called for by its terms. He then projected this difference over the term of the lease, including both renewal periods, and, using what he testified to be an appropriate discount factor under the circumstances of seven percent, discounted these amounts to present value to arrive at a final bonus value. Based on these calculations, Davis determined that the bonus value of Dr. Walker's leasehold was $ 47,262.88, which he rounded down to $ 47,000 for the sake of simplicity.

The Knudsens also presented testimony of an expert real estate appraiser, Larry Witt. Witt agreed that the proper method for determining bonus value is to compare the contract rate to the market rate, adjusting the comparable properties for factors such as age and location. While Witt identified two comparable properties that he had used in his appraisal, neither of these properties was being used as a dental office at the time of his appraisal. Witt also expressed his disagreement with both the comparable properties used by Davis and Davis' assessment of the value of those properties. In conjunction with Witt's testimony, counsel for the Knudsens attempted to use an exhibit that set forth the CPI figures issued by the U.S. Department of Labor, but the trial court refused to admit this exhibit into evidence because counsel had failed to establish a foundation for its admission—a ruling the Knudsens do not challenge on appeal. On rebuttal, Davis indicated that he did not believe Witt's comparable properties provided an adequate basis for appraising the value of Dr. Walker's leasehold because Witt's appraisals were not sufficiently similar to the lease in question. In particular, Davis noted that Witt's comparable properties were not being used as dental offices while Davis' comparable properties were all being used as dental offices at the time of his appraisal.

Davis explained his reason for using certain CPI figures and Witt explained why he thought different CPI figures ought to apply. The trial court evidently accepted Davis' CPI figures.

From the foregoing discussion of the evidence, it is readily apparent that Davis' methodology was consistent with the factors set forth by our Supreme Court in *Doernhoefer,* and the trial court did not abuse its discretion or otherwise err in relying upon that evidence. Point denied.

In their fourth point, the Knudsens argue that the trial court erred in entering an *in personam* judgment against them and in favor of Dr. Walker since eminent domain actions are *in rem* proceedings and all judgments entered thereon must normally be rendered *in rem* against the condemnation proceeds, rather than *in personam* against one or more of the parties. Although this is a highly technical deficiency, we agree.

"In Missouri it is well settled that eminent domain proceedings are *in rem* rather than *in personam* proceedings, and that when an award is made and paid into the registry of the court, the fund is substituted for the land and becomes the *res*." *State ex rel. State Highway Comm'n of Mo. v. Eilers,* 445 S. W.2d 374, 376 (Mo. 1969). Thus, Santa Fe's condemnation action was an *in rem* proceeding, and when the $ 275,000 damage award was deposited by Santa Fe into the court's registry, it was substituted for the condemned property and became the *res* of the condemnation action. *Id.*

There is no question that the trial court's original judgment of December 12, 2003, and its amended judgment of January 12, 2004, were both rendered against the Knudsens in personam. The relevant portion of the original judgment reads as follows: "IT IS THEREFORE ORDERED, ADJUDGED AND DECREED that Joan Walker be awarded judgment against Henrik A. Knudsen and Rogene Knudsen in the amount of $ 47,000 and for costs herein." The amended judgment contains identical language, except that it added an award of the "interest accrued" on the amount awarded to Dr. Walker during the seven and a half months that had elapsed since the remaining $ 50,000 portion of the total condemnation award of $ 275,000 had been deposited into an interest-bearing bank account by order of the trial court.

Based on the record before us, there is nothing to suggest that the $ 50,000 previously retained in the court's registry is not still there. Consequently, both the original and amended judgments are void and the cause must be reversed and remanded to the trial court for its entry of a proper in rem judgment against the res.

If, on motion by the Knudsens, the entire $ 275,000 damage award had been distributed to them prior to the § 523.053 apportionment hearing, the trial court would have had jurisdiction to enter an in personam judgment against them and in favor of Dr. Walker for the amount due her as a result of the taking of the bonus value of her leasehold by Santa Fe. Since this did not occur here, we reject Dr. Walker's claim that the in rem condemnation proceeding was converted to one in personam merely because the Knudsens filed a motion requesting payment to them of the entire amount of the damage award.

For this reason, we reverse and remand with instructions that the trial court enter a new judgment not inconsistent with this opinion. On remand, the trial court is instructed to enter a proper in rem judgment in favor of Dr. Joan R. Walker in the amount of $ 47,000, plus 94% ($ 47,000/$ 50,000) of the interest which has accrued on the funds in the court's registry. Likewise, the trial court is further instructed to enter a proper in rem judgment in favor of Dr. Henrik A. Knudsen and Rogene F. Knudsen in the amount of $ 3,000, plus 6% ($ 3,000/$ 50,000) of the interest which has accrued on the funds in the court's registry.

Joseph M. Ellis, Judge

SOURCE: 2005 Mo. App. LEXIS 113. Reprinted with the permission of LexisNexis.

Chapter 7

Contract for Sale

CHAPTER OBJECTIVES

Upon completion of this chapter, you will be able to:

- Understand the importance of a contract.
- Define the requirements of a contract for sale.
- Discuss marketable title.
- Identify the remedies available for default of a contract for sale.

The buying and selling of real estate is accomplished by virtue of a contract. The negotiation of the terms of the deal are set forth and memorialized in a contract before the purchase or sale. This chapter will examine the legal document that effectuates a purchase or sale of real property: the contract.

THE IMPORTANCE OF A CONTRACT

Statute of Frauds
A collective term describing various statutes stipulating that no suit or action shall be maintained on certain classes of contracts or engagements unless there shall be a note or memorandum thereof in writing signed by the party to be charged or by his authorized agent.

contract
A legally binding agreement between two or more parties.

The **Statute of Frauds** is applicable in all states and is applicable to any sale or purchase of an interest in real property. The statute originated in England during the 17th century, where its purpose was to prevent fraud. The Statute of Frauds requires that in order to be enforceable in a court of law the sale and/or transfer of an interest in real property must be accomplished with a written document, or **contract**. In addition to the transfer of property ownership, leases of more than one year must be in writing as well. Most jurisdictions allow oral leases of land for terms of less than one year. To meet that statutory writing requirement of the Statute of Frauds, the contract should

- be an actual writing; be signed by the party against whom the contract is being enforced; and
- contain all the essential terms of the agreement.

The writing does not have to be a contract to satisfy the Statute of Frauds. It can be a letter, a check, a memo, a pleading, or any other writing so long as the writing contains the requisite elements. If no sufficient writing exists, then neither party to a land transaction may enforce the contract against the other. The Statute of Frauds often results in parties being unable to enforce a contract that they have made and relied upon. Because this so often results in an unjust result, the part performance doctrine has been created as an exception to the rule. This exception allows courts to enforce a contract in equity even if there is not a sufficient writing to satisfy the Statute of Frauds. It is important to remember that the part performance doctrine is just a substitute for a writing. Parties must still prove the needed elements of a contract existed before successfully enforcing it.

To Satisfy the Statute of Frauds, a writing must contain the following elements:

1. The names of the parties or some other identification of them
2. An identification of the land
3. Words expressing an intent to sell the property
4. Most American statutes require a writing be signed by the party to be charged though a few statutes require "the vendor" to sign.

FIGURE 7.1
Necessary Elements of a Writing

Payment of either all or a large part of the purchase price, taking possession of the property, and the making of substantial improvements on the land are all acts that can cause courts to use the part performance doctrine to enforce a contract made otherwise unenforceable by the Statute of Frauds. However, most courts do require a combination of at least two of such acts and a few courts even require the existence of all three. Of course, the three acts discussed are ones that only the purchaser can perform. Still, some courts permit the seller to use the purchaser's acts to prove a contract existed. (See Figure 7.1 for the necessary elements a "writing" must have to satisfy the Statute of Frauds.)

RESEARCH THIS

Research your state's laws and codes with regard to the Statute of Frauds. What types of contracts need to be in writing in your state, and why? Do contracts that transfer an interest in real estate have to be in writing to be enforceable? Since most laws vary from state to state, it is important to know your jurisdiction and the laws that dictate which contracts need to be in writing to be enforceable.

Once a property has been identified and the parties have agreed to the terms, the contract memorializes the agreement between the parties and all of the terms of that agreement. But why is a contract for sale important? There are several reasons that a contract for sale is important. First, it satisfies the Statute of Frauds. In addition, banks and other financial institutions will not lend money unless they have identified all of the terms of a transaction. Financial institutions want definitive terms and understandings between the parties. They do not want the money they lend to be in jeopardy. And the most important way of memorializing an agreement between the parties is through a contract. The buyer of a property will not commit to purchase the property unless he is sure that the financial institution is willing to commit the dollars necessary to complete the purchase. Buyers will not commit to paying hundreds of thousands of dollars for a piece of property unless the financing is secure and the deal is memorialized. The seller of the property wants to close the transaction, so she also has incentive to have the terms of the agreement memorialized in a contract. Contracts for sale are often referred to as "earnest money contracts." This is because a purchaser of property generally pays a portion of the purchase price at the time the contract is signed. This payment can be held directly by the seller, or else by the real estate broker or a lawyer in a trust account until the closing. Such a deposit is not a legal necessity but it is frequently used because it provides a powerful incentive for the buyer to go through with the sale.

In order for a real estate contract to be valid, it must have the following elements:

- the parties must have legal capacity;
- mutual agreement must exist between the parties;
- consideration must be present;
- the contract must be for a lawful purpose; and
- a written agreement must exist.

PRACTICE TIP

Whether buying or selling, parties involved in real estate transactions typically employ brokers. Brokers help prospective buyers find a suitable property, help prospective sellers sell their property, and help parties with all the paperwork involved in a real estate transaction. Most states require that an individual take classes and then pass the state's licensing exam in order to become a licensed real estate broker.

legal capacity
The right of persons to come into court and be bound by their own agreements.

mutual agreement
A meeting of the minds on a specific subject, and a manifestation of intent of the parties to do or refrain from doing some specific act or acts.

offer
A promise made by the offeror to do (or not to do) something provided that the offeree, by accepting, promises or does something in exchange.

acceptance
An agreement to the terms of an offer, creating a binding contract.

consideration
Something of value received by a promisor from a promisee.

equitable title
Title that indicates a beneficial interest in property and that gives the holder the right to acquire formal legal title.

contract for the sale of land
A contract that calls for conveyance of interest in real estate and requires a writing signed by a party sought to be charged as being within the Statute of Frauds.

Legal capacity means that the parties to the agreement may legally be bound by the agreement. Therefore, minor children and individuals who are mentally incompetent are not considered to have legal capacity, and contracts that they enter into may not be enforceable. Thus, a sixteen-year-old who enters into a contract to buy real property cannot be legally bound by the agreement. However, it is important to remember that the other party, assuming he or she has legal capacity, is bound by the contract should the minor choose to follow through with the agreement.

A **mutual agreement** must have occurred between the parties; in other words, a "meeting of the minds" must exist between the parties. One party must have made an **offer**, and there must be an **acceptance** of that offer by the other party. A contract must also have **consideration** pass from one party to the other party. Consideration can be anything of value, including money.

In order for a contract to be enforceable, it must be made for a lawful purpose. The American judicial system will not uphold a contract that commits a crime or where the activity is otherwise illegal. Illegal activities are against public policy. For example, Internet gambling is illegal in most areas. Therefore, a contract whereby two people wish to establish an Internet gambling business will be held as unenforceable, as it is based on an unlawful purpose.

Finally, real estate contracts are subject to the Statute of Frauds, as well as to other statutory requirements, and need to be in writing.

CONTRACT FOR SALE

A land sale contract is the agreement to sell property whereby the seller retains legal title to the property until the purchaser has made the requisite payment for the property (see Figure 7.2). The seller will transfer **equitable title** to the property only after the purchaser has paid the amount set forth in the contract. After the purchaser pays the amount stated in the contract, then the deed is recorded and the fee title is transferred to the new owner. This installment method of contracting is usually found in contracts for sale. (See Figure 7.3 describing the difference between equitable title and legal title.)

Contracts for the sale of land involve two steps. First, the contract to sell or purchase land is signed and specifies a date for the closing of the deal. Second, at the closing of the deal, the seller gives the buyer a deed to the property and the buyer gives the seller the agreed-upon consideration for the property. In order for a contract for sale to meet the Statute of Fraud requirements, every essential element of the agreement must be expressed therein. The essential elements for a contract for sale are these:

- The identity of the parties to the sale
- An outline of the rights and obligations of the parties
- The signatures of the parties that are to be bound by the agreement
- A legal description of the property to be conveyed
- The stated purchase price

CASE FACT PATTERN

Monique agreed to sell real property to Judy. The written contract stated, "I agree to sell my farm." If the evidence showed that Monique owned only one farm and that this farm was indeed the subject of the parties' agreement, most courts will enforce the contract, despite the somewhat vague legal description. See *Seabaugh v. Sailer*, 679 S.W.2d (Mo.App.1984).

Real Estate Purchase Contract

We agree to purchase the Real Estate commonly known as [property address goes here], belonging to [Seller's name goes here], for the Sum of :_____
_____ ($_____) Payable 10% nonrefundable down payment on the day of sale and the balance due within thirty days. [You can change the down payment and time for closing] Closing shall take place on or before [Closing date goes here}. Real Estate taxes will be prorated to the day of closing. Buyer will be responsible for paying all installments thereafter. Buyer will have possession on or before [Agreed upon possession date goes here].

Buyer hereby waives the right to lead-based paint inspection if the property was built prior to 1978.

Property is being purchased as is, subject to all easements of record, restrictive covenants of record as to the use and improvement of said property, applicable regulations imposed by any planning or zoning board, or any unpaid assessments due hereafter. Time is of the essence and this is an irrevocable offer to purchase with no contingencies. In the event the purchaser fails to perform according to the terms of this contract, the down payment shall be forfeited as partial liquidated damages, and not as a penalty, without effecting any of the Seller's further remedies.

Improvements and fixtures permanently installed and fixed to the real estate are included in the sales price.

Indemnification and release: Purchasers hereby release the Sellers from any and all liability relating to any defect or deficiency affecting said real estate, which release given shall survive the closing of this transaction. The purchasers have made all inspections and agree to purchasing the property "as is and where is".

The Seller acknowledges receipt of the down payment, and if in the form of a personal check, by the purchaser's signatures below, this contract shall constitute a personal demand note guaranteeing the negotiability of this check. Should the Seller be required to sue to collect the check, court costs and attorney's fees will be at the purchaser's expense.

The undersigned purchasers have read the entire contents of this contract and expressly agree that all terms and conditions of the purchase are included herein, and acknowledge receipt of a copy.

Printed as to appear on deed: _____

_____ SS# _____

Purchaser's signature _____ Date _____

Printed as to appear on deed: _____

SS# _____Purchaser's signature: _____

Date _____ Address: _____

_____ Phone: _____

The Seller's agree to sell the above real Estate on these terms.

Seller: _____ Date _____

Seller: _____ Date _____

FIGURE 7.2
Sample Real Estate Purchase Contract

TYPES OF TITLE

Equitable Title	A title that indicates a beneficial interest in property and that gives the holder the right to acquire formal legal title
Legal Title	A title that evidences apparent ownership but does not necessarily signify full and complete title or a beneficial interest.

FIGURE 7.3
Types of Title

LEGAL RESEARCH MAXIM

Assume that a plaintiff/seller finds himself in disagreement with a defendant/buyer regarding the agreed-upon purchase price of the residence which the defendant agreed to buy from the plaintiff. The plaintiff claims that the defendant orally agreed to pay $80,000. The defendant claims he agreed to pay only $60,000. The plaintiff takes his claim to court. He loses. Why?

parole evidence rule
A court evidentiary doctrine that excludes certain types of outside oral testimony offered as proof of the terms of the contract.

performance
The successful completion of a contractual duty.

breach
A violation or infraction of a law or an obligation.

escrow
A legal document or property delivered by a promisor to a third party to be held by the third party for a given amount of time or until the occurrence of a condition.

Each party must be identified in the contract, and most American statutes require that the party to be charged must sign it. Because of the statute of frauds, a contract for the sale of land may not be considered valid unless it is memorialized in writing and signed by the interested parties. The **parole evidence rule** prevents parties from modifying their agreements by evidence that adds to, varies, or contradicts the terms of the writing.

The rights and obligations of the parties must be included in the contract. Some of the rights and obligations will include a time period within which each party must complete **performance**, the closing date, the date the contract was executed, and the terms regarding method of payment. The contract should also state that the conveyance of the property by deed will occur once the purchase price is paid. Lastly, a provision should be included stating the rights a party has in the event that the other party fails to fulfill her obligations and commits a **breach** of contract.

The description of the property must be sufficiently clear as to what property is the subject of the agreement. The price must be stated and is usually either a reasonable price or the market price.

ESCROW

Escrow is a legal device by which an objective, unbiased, third party (the escrow officer) is brought in and acts as stakeholder for both buyer and seller and handles the distribution of funds. Essentially, the purpose of the escrow agent is to ensure that both the buyer and the seller fulfill their individual promises to each other. In some jurisdictions, real estate brokers can also be escrow agents. All parties involved in a land transaction want to be certain that all terms and conditions of the contract are met before any money or property is exchanged. Before closing, the escrow agent will collect all of the necessary information. This information includes, but is not limited to, the conditions of the sale, related insurance policies, and loan documents. After all the necessary steps have been taken by the escrow agent, the closing can then proceed.

LISTING CONTRACTS

There are several different kinds of listing contracts, the most common being the "exclusive right to sell" (see Figure 7.4). "The open listing," "the exclusive agency listing," and "the one-time show" are also types of listing contracts. An open listing is typically used by those attempting to sell their home without listing it with a real estate company. It gives a real estate agent the right to bring a prospective buyer to view a property, but that is about all. A "one-time show" listing is similar to an open listing. It is most generally used by real estate agents who are showing an FSBO (for sale by owner) home to one of their clients. In this situation, the seller signs the agreement, which identifies the prospective buyer and promises the real estate agent a commission should that particular buyer purchase the property.

An "exclusive agency" listing permits a real estate agent to list and market a property and guarantees the agent a commission if the house sells through any real estate agent or company. The listing also allows sellers to seek out buyers on their own. This is not a commonly used or popular type of listing agreement. In this type of agreement, there is not much incentive for an agent to spend money marketing the property in question, because the agent is guaranteed a commission.

FIGURE 7.4
**Exclusive Right
to Sell**
Source: ALLLAW.com

EXCLUSIVE RIGHT TO SELL

This agreement is entered into this _____ day of _____, 20__ by and between _____, (Owner) and _____, (Broker). For and in consideration of Broker's services to be rendered in listing for sale and in undertaking to sell or find a purchaser for the property hereinafter described, the parties understand and agree that this is an exclusive listing to sell the real estate located at: _____. The minimum selling price of the property shall be_____ dollars ($), payable on the following terms:

Broker is authorized to accept and hold a deposit in the amount of _____ dollars ($) as a deposit and to apply such deposit on the purchase price.

If said property is sold, traded or in any other way disposed of by Broker or by anyone else within the time specified in this listing, it is agreed to and understood that Broker shall receive from the sale or trade of said property as Broker's commission _____ percent (%) of the purchase price.

Should said property be sold or traded within____ days after expiration of this listing agreement to a purchaser with whom Broker has been negotiating for the sale or trade of the property, then said commission shall be due and payable on demand.

Owner agrees to furnish a certificate of title showing a good and merchantable title of record, and further agrees to convey by good and sufficient warranty deed or guaranteed title on payment in full.

The listing contract shall continue until midnight of the _____ day of _____, 20__.

_____
Owner
I accept this listing and agree to act promptly and diligently to procure a buyer for said property.

_____
Broker

In the "exclusive right to sell" listing contract, the listing agent will work to market the property to other agents who are working for prospective buyers. Those other agents will show your home to their clients who are looking to buy. No matter which agent sells the property, the listing agent will still earn a commission. This type of listing contract is the only type many real estate agents will accept.

MARKETABLE TITLE

Title refers to the **ownership** of real property. Title is evidence of ownership. When a person buys or sells real property, title is transferred from one person or entity to another. A **marketable title** is title that can be transferred from one party to another without the likelihood that any claims against the title will be made by other parties. Sometimes the term "merchantable" is used in the place of "marketable." In *Peatling v. Baird* 213 P.2d 1015 the Court held that "a marketable title to real estate is one which is free from reasonable doubt, and a title is doubtful and unmarketable if it exposes the party holding it to the hazard of litigation." When a person sells real property, there is an **implied warranty** that the title to the property is marketable. Marketable title is reasonably free of encumbrances and other title defects that could lead to litigation. It is assumed that if someone places a property on the market to sell, he has marketable title. You cannot transfer what you do not have; therefore, you must have marketable title. This theory is critical to a real estate transaction, as a potential purchaser generally expects to receive property to which no one else can make a claim. Purchasers of real property do not expect their ownership interests to be challenged after the completion of the transaction. Even if a contract for sale

title
The right or ownership in land.

ownership
The right to possess a thing allowing one to use and enjoy property, as well as the right to convey it to others.

marketable title
Title that transfers full ownership rights to the buyer.

implied warranty
An unwritten warranty that is normally and naturally included by operation of law that applies to the goods to be sold.

doesn't address marketability of title, the law will imply that title must be marketable. A marketable title is not perfect but any defects in it must be relatively minor such that a reasonable buyer or a lender would not object to it.

unmarketable title
A title that a reasonable buyer would refuse to accept because of possible conflicting interests in or litigation over the property.

An **unmarketable title** may exist if the seller possessed title, but lost it in a legal proceeding. Title can also be unmarketable if there is some type of blemish in the chain of title that makes ownership interests unclear. This can happen if the title has been forged or obtained by fraud. Sometimes a title obtained by adverse possession may be held to be unmarketable unless there are circumstances that clearly establish the adverse possession. In addition, a mortgage, judgment lien, or mechanic's lien can make a title unmarketable. If there is any litigation that threatens the land's clear title and such litigation has a reasonable chance of success, the title will be considered unmarketable. However, if the litigation has no real rational basis or reasonable likelihood of success, then the title will remain marketable.

Other reasons that a title may be unmarketable include the following:

- Variations in the names on the deed on record
- Misdescription of the property
- Defective creation of the deed, so that it is not recordable
- Lack of capacity in the grantor
- Adverse possession
- Mortgages on the property
- Liens recorded against the property
- An easement, if it reduces the full enjoyment of the property
- Use restrictions
- Zoning violations

Instances where the courts have held that a title has not been rendered unmarketable include an easement known to the purchaser, a lack of legal access, and the presence of hazardous waste on property. In these situations, Courts ultimately held that although such factors generally do affect the market value of property, they do not in fact affect the marketability of title and would not provide satisfactory justification for the rescission of a contract.

A title for a parcel of property is considered to be marketable in a contract for sale unless the contract specifically states that a third party has a claim to the property. In every contract for sale of real property, there is an implied provision that the seller possesses good and marketable title and that the purchaser will receive good and marketable title to the property upon completion of the transaction. If the purchaser discovers that

 SPOT THE ISSUE

Blanca is selling her vacation home in Utah. It is located near all of the best ski resorts. Jack inspects the property, loves the location, and decides that he wants to purchase the home. After a few weeks of negotiation, Blanca and Jack reach an agreement on a purchase price for the home of $250,000. Blanca sells Jack the home. The contract declares that Blanca holds marketable title to the property. After tendering the purchase price to Blanca, Jack receives a letter from an attorney stating that a business called Mike's Sewer and Septic holds a lien on the property due to the fact that the business performed thousands of dollars of septic tank work on the property and has not been paid. Mike's Sewer and Septic had filed a mechanic's lien on the property before the sale. Blanca has failed to provide Jack with marketable title. Jack has his attorney contact Blanca to say that Jack is rescinding the contract for sale and wants the return of all monies paid on the home. Will Jack be able to rescind the contract? Will Blanca have to return all monies paid to her for the property?

the seller has failed to provide marketable title to the property, the purchaser may be able to **rescind** the contract. If the purchaser is allowed to rescind the contract, she can back out of the sale and receive a refund for any monies paid toward the purchase of the property. Because title defects are not always apparent, buyers typically purchase title insurance to indemnify themselves against any damage or loss arising from a title defect. Most lenders typically require a that borrower purchase title insurance.

rescind
Cancel; revoke; terminate.

DISCLOSURES

When selling a house, one may be obligated to disclose problems that could materially affect the property. In most states, it is illegal to deliberately conceal major physical defects, and the seller must make **disclosures** to the buyer. These disclosures cover areas such as the age and condition of the structure, including the plumbing, heating, and electrical systems; any existing easements, shared driveways, and fences; any additions or structural alterations made to the property, especially those made without a building permit; any soil or flooding problems; any zoning violations; any homeowners' association obligations or deed restrictions; and any known nuisances. For example, if the seller of a property is aware that a basement floods in heavy rains, such information should be disclosed to prospective buyers. Many states require that sellers make written disclosures on the physical condition of the property. Generally a broker will give a prospective seller an agency disclosure form to use because real estate agents are responsible for informing their principal (seller) of the disclosure requirements. The disclosure statement covers matters that are within the personal knowledge of the seller as well as matters that could be made known through a reasonable inspection of the property in question. The statement is to be given to any prospective buyers as soon as possible and must be given before any transfer of title. See Figure 7.5 for a sample disclosure statement from the State of North Carolina.

disclosure
Act of disclosing; revelation.

REMEDIES FOR BREACH

If one of the parties fails to perform under the contract, the injured party can seek redress against the breaching party. Generally, changes in the value of the property in question occurring after the breach are considered irrelevant. The injured party can seek one of the following remedies after a breach of contract: specific performance, money damages, rescission, or liquidated damages.

specific performance
A remedy requiring exact performance of a contract in the specific form in which it was made, or according to the precise terms agreed upon.

Specific Performance

The remedy of **specific performance** is an **equitable remedy**. Specific performance requires that the breaching party perform the obligations as stated in the contract. The law states that real property is unique; therefore, because of a property's uniqueness, the breaching party must be required to perform under the contract because a remedy at law would be inadequate. The court orders the breaching party to perform.

equitable remedy
Non-monetary remedy fashioned by the court using standards of fairness and justice.

YOU BE THE JUDGE

Max and Martha have put their house up for sale. Mike and Michelle would like to buy it. Max and Martha know that the house is in a flood plain; however, they have lived in the house for twenty years and have never had a problem. Max and Martha decide there is no reason to tell Mike and Michelle about the flood plain, because it has never affected them during their ownership of the house. They fill out the disclosure statement and intentionally fail to indicate that the property is located within the flood plain. Mike and Michelle purchase the house. Two months later, the basement floods after heavy rains causing extensive damage.

FIGURE 7.5   **Residential Sample Disclosure Form from the State of North Carolina**

STATE OF NORTH CAROLINA
RESIDENTIAL PROPERTY DISCLOSURE STATEMENT
INSTRUCTIONS TO PROPERTY OWNERS

1.   G.S. 47E requires owners of residential real estate (single-family homes and buildings with up to four dwelling units) to furnish purchasers a property disclosure statement. This form is the only one approved for this purpose. A disclosure statement must be furnished in connection with the sale, exchange, option and sale under a lease with option to purchase (unless the tenant is already occupying or intends to occupy the dwelling). A disclosure statement is not required for some transactions, including the first sale of a dwelling which has never been inhabited and transactions of residential property made pursuant to a lease with option to purchase where the lessee occupies or intends to occupy the dwelling. For a complete list of exemptions, see G.S. 47E-2.

2.   You must check one of the boxes for each of the 20 questions on the reverse side of this form.

   a.   If you check "Yes" for any question, you must describe the problem or attach a report from an engineer, contractor, pest control operator or other expert or public agency describing it. If you attach a report, you will not be liable for any inaccurate or incomplete information contained in it so long as you were not grossly negligent in obtaining or transmitting the information.

   b.   If you check "No", you are stating that you have no actual knowledge of any problem. If you check "No" and you know there is a problem, you may be liable for making an intentional misstatement.

   c.   If you check "No Representation", you have no duty to disclose the conditions or characteristics of the property, even if you should have known of them.

   *   If you check "Yes" or "No" and something happens to the property to make your Statement incorrect or inaccurate (for example, the roof begins to leak), you must promptly give the purchaser a corrected Statement or correct the problem.

3.   If you are assisted in the sale of your property by a licensed real estate broker, you are still responsible for completing and delivering the Statement to the purchasers; and the broker must disclose any material facts about your property which they know or reasonably should know, regardless of your responses on the Statement.

4.   You must give the completed Statement to the purchaser no later than the time the purchaser makes an offer to purchase your property. If you do not, the purchaser can, under certain conditions, cancel any resulting contract (See **"Note to Purchasers"** below). You should give the purchaser a copy of the Statement containing your signature and keep a copy signed by the purchaser for your records.

Note to Purchasers: If the owner does not give you a Residential Property Disclosure Statement by the time you make your offer to purchase the property, you may under certain conditions cancel any resulting contract and be entitled to a refund of any deposit monies you may have paid. To cancel the contract, you must personally deliver or mail written notice of your decision to cancel to the owner or the owner's agent within three calendar days following your receipt of the Statement, or three calendar days following the date of the contract, whichever occurs first. However, in no event does the Disclosure Act permit you to cancel a contract after settlement of the transaction or (in the case of a sale or exchange) after you have occupied the property, whichever occurs first.

---

5.   In the space below, type or print in ink the address of the property (sufficient to identify it) and your name. Then sign and date.

Property Address: ———————————————————————————————————

Owner's Name(s): ————————————————————————————————————
Owner(s) acknowledge having examined this Statement before signing and that all information is true and correct as of the date signed.

Owner Signature: ——————————————————————————— Date ——————————

Owner Signature: ——————————————————————————— Date ——————————
Purchaser(s) acknowledge receipt of a copy of this disclosure statement; that they have examined it before signing; that they understand that this is not a warranty by owner or owner's agent; that it is not a substitute for any inspections they may wish to obtain; and that the representations are made by the owner and not the owner's agent(s) or subagent(s). Purchaser(s) are encouraged to obtain their own inspection from a licensed home inspector or other professional.

Purchaser Signature: ——————————————————————————— Date ——————————

Purchaser Signature: ——————————————————————————— Date ——————————

contd...

FIGURE 7.5   Residential Sample Disclosure Form from the State of North Carolina *contd...*

Property Address/Description: _____

_____

[Note: In this form, "property" refers only to dwelling unit(s) and not sheds, detached garages or other buildings.]

Regarding the property identified above, do you know of any problem (malfunction or defect) with any of the following:

	Yes*	No	No Representation

1. FOUNDATION, SLAB, FIREPLACES/CHIMNEYS, FLOORS, WINDOWS (INCLUDING STORM WINDOWS AND SCREENS), DOORS, CEILINGS, INTERIOR AND EXTERIOR WALLS, ATTACHED GARAGE, PATIO, DECK OR OTHER STRUCTURAL COMPONENTS including any modifications to them?......... ☐ ☐ ☐
   a. Siding is ☐ Masonry ☐ Wood ☐ Composition/Hardboard ☐ Vinyl ☐ Synthetic Stucco ☐ Other _____ .... ☐
   b. Approximate age of structure? _____ ☐

2. ROOF (leakage or other problem)?.. ☐ ☐ ☐
   a. Approximate age of roof covering? _____ ☐

3. WATER SEEPAGE, LEAKAGE, DAMPNESS OR STANDING WATER in the basement, crawl space or slab?........ ☐ ☐ ☐

4. ELECTRICAL SYSTEM (outlets, wiring, panel, switches, fixtures etc.)? ·········· ☐ ☐ ☐

5. PLUMBING SYSTEM (pipes, fixtures, water heater, etc.)? ························· ☐ ☐ ☐

6. HEATING AND/OR AIR CONDITIONING? ·································· ☐ ☐ ☐
   a. Heat Source is: ☐ Furnace ☐ Heat Pump ☐ Baseboard ☐ Other_____ .... ☐
   b. Cooling Source is: ☐ Central Forced Air ☐ Wall/Window Unit(s) ☐ Other_____ .... ☐
   c. Fuel Source is: ☐ Electricity ☐ Natural Gas ☐ Propane ☐ Oil ☐ Other _____ ☐

7. WATER SUPPLY (including water quality, quantity and water pressure)?·········· ☐ ☐ ☐
   a. Water supply is: ☐ City/County ☐ Community System ☐ Private Well ☐ Other _____ .... ☐
   b. Water pipes are: ☐ Copper ☐ Galvanized ☐ Plastic ☐ Other _____ ☐ Unknown .... ☐

8. SEWER AND/OR SEPTIC SYSTEM?.. ☐ ☐ ☐
   a. Sewage disposal system is: ☐ Septic Tank ☐ Septic Tank with Pump ☐ Community System ☐ Connected to City/County System ☐ City/County System available ☐ Straight pipe (wastewater does not go into a septic or other sewer system [note: use of this type of system violates state law]) ☐ Other _____ .... ☐

9. BUILT-IN APPLIANCES (RANGE/OVEN, ATTACHED MICROWAVE, HOOD/FAN, DISHWASHER, DISPOSAL, etc.)?·········· ☐ ☐ ☐

Also regarding the property identified above, including the lot, other improvements, and fixtures located thereon, do you know of any:

10. PROBLEMS WITH PRESENT INFESTATION, OR DAMAGE FROM PAST INFESTATION OF WOOD DESTROYING INSECTS OR ORGANISMS which has not been repaired?············· ☐ ☐ ☐

11. PROBLEMS WITH DRAINAGE, GRADING OR SOIL STABILITY OF LOT?·········· ☐ ☐ ☐

12. PROBLEMS WITH OTHER SYSTEMS AND FIXTURES: CENTRAL VACUUM, POOL, HOT TUB, SPA, ATTIC FAN, EXHAUST FAN, CEILING FAN, SUMP PUMP, IRRIGATION SYSTEM, TV CABLE WIRING OR SATELLITE DISH, OR OTHER SYSTEMS? ·········· ☐ ☐ ☐

13. ROOM ADDITIONS OR OTHER STRUCTURAL CHANGES ? ·········· ☐ ☐ ☐

14. ENVIRONMENTAL HAZARDS (substances, materials or products) including asbestos, formaldehyde, radon gas, methane gas, lead-based paint, underground storage tank, or other hazardous or toxic material (whether buried or covered), contaminated soil or water, or other environmental contamination)?·········· ☐ ☐ ☐

15. COMMERCIAL OR INDUSTRIAL NUISANCES (noise, odor, smoke, etc.) affecting the property? ·········· ☐ ☐ ☐

16. VIOLATIONS OF BUILDING CODES, ZONING ORDINANCES, RESTRICTIVE COVENANTS OR OTHER LAND-USE RESTRICTIONS? ·········· ☐ ☐ ☐

17. UTILITY OR OTHER EASEMENTS, SHARED DRIVEWAYS, PARTY WALLS OR ENCROACHMENTS FROM OR ON ADJACENT PROPERTY? ·········· ☐ ☐ ☐

18. LAWSUITS, FORECLOSURES, BANKRUPTCY, TENANCIES, JUDGMENTS, TAX LIENS, PROPOSED ASSESSMENTS, MECHANICS' LIENS, MATERIALMENS' LIENS, OR NOTICE FROM ANY GOVERNMENTAL AGENCY that could affect title to the property? ·········· ☐ ☐ ☐

19. OWNERS' ASSOCIATION OR "COMMON AREA" EXPENSES OR ASSESSMENTS? ·········· ☐ ☐ ☐

20. FLOOD HAZARD or that the property is in a FEDERALLY-DESIGNATED FLOOD PLAIN? ·········· ☐ ☐ ☐

* If you answered "Yes" to any of the above questions, please explain (Attach additional sheets, if necessary): _____

_____

_____

Owner Initials and Date	Owner Initials and Date
Purchaser Initials and Date	Purchaser Initials and Date

Specific performance can be ordered against either the seller or the purchaser, depending on which party breaches the contract. A court can enforce the obligations of each party by an order of specific performance by a judicial conveyance of the property or through an order holding the defendant in contempt until he or she performs the contract. There are situations when specific performance is not available. Specific performance cannot be sought if granting it would lead to undue hardship or unfairness to one party. Also, specific performance will not be granted to a seller if he did not have marketable title to convey. For example, in *Langemeier v. Urwiler Oil & Fertilizer, Inc.* 660 N.W.2d 487 (Neb. 2003), the court held that if a seller does not have title to the property in question or has previously sold it to another party who is not within the court's power, then specific performance will be unavailable.

Money Damages

If one party breaches an agreement, the injured party can sue for money damages. The legal theory behind the awarding of money damages is that an injured party should be placed into the same situation she would be in if the contract had been performed. The amount of money awarded is typically the difference between the contract price and the market value of the property.

Rescission

There are two forms of rescission. The first is the voluntary agreement between the parties where they agree to "unwind" the contract. The second is a court order in response to a breach of contract with a goal of putting the parties back into the position they were in before the existence of the contract. Rescission operates under a theory opposite to that of money damages or specific performance. Instead of trying to place the injured party in the position he would have been if the contract had been performed, rescission attempts to place the party in the position he would have been in had the contract not come to fruition. As stated above, rescission allows the injured party to back out of the deal and to be reimbursed for any monies paid or expenses incurred.

Liquidated Damages

liquidated damages
An amount of money agreed upon in the original contract as a reasonable estimation of the damages to be recovered by the nonbreaching party. This amount is set forth in the contract so the parties have a clear idea of the risk of breach.

Liquidated damages constitute a certain amount of money, agreed to by both parties, that is to be paid should one of the parties breach the contract. Liquidated damages are enforceable by the court so long as the amount that is agreed upon is reasonable and represents a realistic figure that may have occurred should the parties have elected actual money damages. If the amount is so large as to constitute a penalty against one of the parties, the court will not enforce that clause of the contract. If a liquidated damages clause is in the contract, this is typically the only legal remedy available to the injured party. In the majority of land contracts, where the buyer has made an earnest money deposit, if the buyer later breaches the contract, the deposit will then be turned over to the seller.

 EYE ON ETHICS

Oftentimes, an earnest money deposit is required to hold a piece of real property while the terms of the contract for sale can be agreed upon and memorialized. Sometimes, this deposit is given to an attorney to hold in trust until there is a meeting of the minds on the terms of the sale. Monies received from clients should never be commingled in the general account of the attorney. Monies received from clients should be held in a separate client trust account until such time as they need to be tendered for the deal or are earned for services rendered by the attorney.

SURF'S UP

Many terms that are involved in real property law can be difficult to memorize or do not lend themselves to common definitions. The Internet provides vast resources that can help explain and define legal real property terms. One Web site that is particularly helpful for researching real property law issues can be accessed at this address:

www.law.cornell.edu/topics/real_estate.html

Time of Performance

Although it is not required that parties of a contract set a date of performance within the contract, if they do not do so, a court will generally find that a reasonable time of performance was intended. Often the contract sets a time which either is or is not "of the essence." In the absence of the phrase "of the essence," a court will assume that time is not of the essence unless other circumstances known to both parties indicate that the time of performance is indeed significant. If time is not of the essence a party who performs late will still be able to enforce a contract unless the performance was unreasonably late. If a contract provides that time is of the essence, then a late performance by one party will completely excuse the other party from performance. Additionally, if time was not made of the essence originally, either party may make it so if done in a reasonable amount of time.

Summary

Most real estate transactions are accompanied by contracts of sale. Because of the Statute of Frauds, the sale and/or transfer of an interest in real property must be accomplished with a written document to be enforceable. A contract serves as that writing requirement.

In order to form a contract, a mutual agreement must have occurred between the parties. In other words, a "meeting of the minds" must exist between the parties. One party must have made an offer, and there must be an acceptance of that offer by the other party. A contract requires that consideration pass from one party to the other. Consideration can be anything of value, including money.

A land sale contract is the agreement to sell property whereby the seller retains legal title to the property until the purchaser has made the requisite payment for the property. The seller will transfer equitable title to the property only after the purchaser has paid the amount set forth in the contract. After the purchaser pays the amount stated in the contract, then the deed is recorded, and the fee title is transferred to the new owner. This installment method of contracting is usually found in contracts for sale.

Contracts for the sale of land involve two steps. First, the contract to sell or purchase land is signed and specifies a date for the closing of the deal. Secondly, at the closing of the deal, the seller gives the buyer a deed to the property, and the buyer gives the seller the agreed-upon consideration for the property.

Title refers to the ownership of real property. Title is evidence of ownership. When a person buys or sells real property, title is transferred from one person or entity to another. A marketable title is a title that can be transferred from one party to another without the likelihood that any claims against the title will be made by other parties. When a person sells real property, there is an implied warranty that the title to the property is marketable. Marketable title is reasonably free of encumbrances and other title defects that could lead to litigation. It is assumed that if someone places a property on the market to sell, she has marketable title.

If one of the parties fails to perform under the contract, the injured party can seek redress against the breaching party. The injured party can seek one of the following remedies: specific performance, money damages, rescission, or liquidated damages.

Key Terms

Acceptance	Marketable title
Breach	Mutual agreement
Consideration	Offer
Contract	Ownership
Contract for sale of land	Parole evidence rule
Disclosure	Performance
Equitable remedy	Rescind
Equitable title	Specific performance
Escrow	Statute of frauds
Implied Warranty	Title
Legal capacity	Unmarketable title
Liquidated damages	

Review Questions

1. What are the elements for a valid contract?
2. What is the Statute of Frauds, and why is it important to contracts for sale?
3. What is specific performance?
4. When are liquidated damages used as a remedy for a breach of a contract for sale?
5. Why is consideration important for a contract?
6. Define mutual agreement.
7. List five items that would make a title unmarketable.
8. What is the implied covenant of marketable title?
9. What are the two steps involved in contracts for sale of land?
10. What is rescission?
11. What is the legal theory behind specific performance and money damages?
12. What is the legal theory behind rescission?
13. What is an offer?
14. What is acceptance?
15. What is an equitable remedy?

Exercises

1. Rico and Sam have entered into a contract for the sale and purchase of a piece of property. Sam has agreed to a purchase price of $120,000. The property has a value of $150,000. Sam fails to perform on the contract. What is the amount of money damages to be awarded to Rico? If Rico fails to perform, what is the amount of money damages that could be awarded to Sam?

2. Research your state laws. Write a memorandum as to the requirements for enforcing a liquidated damages clause in a contract for sale of real property.

3. Using Exercise 1 above, obtain a sample contract for sale of land, and prepare the contract for Sam and Rico. Make sure that you research your state laws to ensure compliance with the laws in your jurisdiction. The address of the property is the address of your school.

4. Locate real estate disclosure forms for your state. Write a memorandum explaining what the law requires a seller disclose. Smith agreed to sell land to Johnson for $150,000. Subsequently, the land's value rose to $250,000. If Smith then refused to complete the sale what amount of damages would Johnson be entitled to?

5. Sarah and Bonnie entered into an oral contract under which Bonnie agreed to buy Sarah's lakefront cabin. Bonnie paid $1,000 earnest money, moved into the cabin, and immediately spent $2,000 fixing the cabin up. Then Bonnie changed her mind about the transaction, moved out of the cabin, and refused to complete the sale. Can Sarah still enforce the contract?

6. Steve contracted to sell his house to Tony. Nothing was said in the contract as to the status of the title. A title search later revealed a restrictive covenant, enforceable by the neighboring owners, against operation of any commercial activity within the house. Tony had planned to open a tattoo parlor and refused to complete the purchase. Can Steve enforce the contract?

7. A contractor constructed a 300-unit luxury apartment building and placed the units up for sale. Victor signed a contract to purchase one of the units but soon afterwards, his job transferred him to a different city and he refused to complete the purchase. The contractor now seeks specific performance. What is the likely result and why?

 PORTFOLIO ASSIGNMENT

Your supervising attorney's new client wants to sell the residence that he built thirty-five years ago. Using the sample disclosure statements provided in the text (see Figure 7.3), write a one- to two-page memo for your supervising attorney detailing a seller's disclosure requirements. Be sure to include also what happens if the seller is not truthful in making disclosures, and whether the seller is responsible for disclosed defects.

United States District Court,
W.D. Virginia,
Big Stone Gap Division.
Ron BAKER, Plaintiff,
v.
JIM WALTER HOMES, INC., Defendant.
No. 2:05CV00059.
July 19, 2006.

Background: Purchaser brought action in state court against home builder, alleging that builder had breached an oral contract to sell purchaser a model home from builder's lot. After removing action to federal court based on diversity of citizenship and amount in controversy, builder moved for summary judgment.

Holding: The District Court, Jones, Chief Judge, held that alleged oral contract for sale of model home was a contract for the sale of real estate, such that action was barred by Virginia's real estate statute of frauds.

Motion granted.

JONES, Chief Judge.

In this diversity case, I find that the plaintiff's action is barred by the Virginia statute of frauds.

The plaintiff, Ron Baker, filed suit in the Circuit Court of Scott County, Virginia, against the defendant, Jim Walter Homes, Inc. ("Jim Walter Homes"), alleging that the defendant had breached a "valid oral contract" to sell the plaintiff a two-story model home from the defendant's lot. The defendant thereafter removed the action to this court, based on diversity of citizenship and amount in controversy. See 28 U.S.C.A. § 1441(a) (West 1994).

Jim Walter Homes has now moved for summary judgment pursuant to Federal Rule of Civil Procedure 56, asserting, among other things, that the action is barred by the applicable statute of frauds. The issues have been briefed and argued and the Motion for Summary Judgment is ripe for decision.

The uncontested facts as shown by the summary judgment record are as follows.

Jim Walter Homes is a "contract home builder" that has "model homes built on a display lot for public inspection." A prospective customer may thus view the various model homes on the display lot and decide whether to have Jim Walter Homes build the selected model for the customer on the customer's land. In the present case, Jim Walter Homes had built four model homes as well as a construction office on a display lot that it had rented in Kingsport, Tennessee. The lease of the lot was shortly to run out and Jim Walter Homes decided to sell the model homes and the office to buyers who would remove them from the lot. Otherwise, the owner of the lot would have obtained the buildings.

The plaintiff Baker purchased three of the model homes and the construction office, each pursuant to a written contract, and moved them from the lot. The fourth and remaining model home is the subject of this case. Baker claims that Jim Walter Homes, through its agent, Jim Meadows, orally agreed to the sell this model home to him for the price of $1,000. Under the alleged terms of this contract, Baker was to remove the

house from the lot and place it on other land by way of "partial demolition and use of a house mover." Jim Walter Homes denies that there was any agreement to sell the model home. In addition, it asserts that the alleged oral contract is unenforceable by virtue of either the Virginia statute of frauds relating to real estate or the Uniform Commercial Code ("UCC") statute of frauds relating to the sale of goods.

The parties agree that Virginia law applies. See Stein v. Pulaski Furniture Corp., 217 F.Supp. 587, 588–89 (W.D.Va.1963) (holding that Virginia statute of frauds applies to federal diversity action in Virginia, even if contract made outside Virginia).

The Virginia real estate statute of frauds bars any action "upon any contract for the sale of real estate" unless it is in writing. Va.Code Ann. § 11-2(6) (Michie 1999). Land or real estate "includes everything belonging or attached to it, above and below the surface." *Stuart v. Pennis*, 91 Va. 688, 22 S.E. 509, 510 (1895). Similarly, the UCC statute of frauds makes unenforceable any oral contract for the sale of goods for the price of $500 or more. See Va.Code Ann. § 8.2-201(1) (Michie 2001).

Baker concedes that there is no writing that qualifies under either statute of frauds. However, he argues that the real estate statute of frauds does not apply because the model home in question was not real estate and that the UCC statute of frauds does not apply because Jim Walter Homes has admitted that a contract for sale was made. See Va.Code Ann. § 8.2-201(3)(b) (Michie 2001) (providing that the contract is enforceable "if the party against whom enforcement is sought admits in his pleading, testimony or otherwise in court that a contract for sale was made, but the contract is not enforceable under this provision beyond the quantity of goods admitted").

Summary judgment is appropriate if there are no material facts in dispute and the moving party is entitled to judgment as a matter of law. See Fed.R.Civ.P. 56(c); *Celotex Corp. v. Catrett*, 477 U.S. 317, 322, 106 S.Ct. 2548, 91 L.Ed.2d 265 (1986). For the reasons that follow, I find the plaintiff's action is barred and judgment must be entered for the defendant.

Because I decide the case based on the statute of frauds, it is not necessary for me to decide any other ground for summary judgment in favor of the defendant.

In arguing that the real estate statute of frauds does not apply, Baker relies on the decision in *Pardee & Graham Real Estate, Inc. v. Schulz Homes Corp.*, 259 Va. 398, 525 S.E.2d 284 (2000). However, that case does not help the plaintiff. There, the Virginia court held that an oral contract for a commission on the sale of a custom home to be built on a lot already owned by the home buyer was not covered by the real estate statute of frauds. The court reasoned that since the home had not yet been built, it could not be considered "real estate" within the meaning of the statute of frauds, noting that "[g]enerally, 'contracts to erect buildings or other structures upon land are not within the statute [of frauds], although the structures when completed will be real estate.' " *Id.* at 286–87 (quoting 9 Samuel Williston & Richard A. Lord, A Treatise on the Law of Contracts § 25.15 (4th ed.1999)).

In the present case, the model home had already been built when the alleged contract was made.

Moreover, a UCC provision, Va.Code Ann. § 8.2-107(1) (Michie 2001), is controlling. That statute provides that "[a] contract for the sale of . . . a structure or its materials to be removed from realty is a contract for the sale of goods within this title if they are to be severed by the seller. . . ." *Id.* An Official Comment to this UCC section states that

[i]f the buyer is to sever, such transactions are considered contracts affecting land and all problems of the Statute of Frauds and of the recording of land rights apply to them. Therefore, the Statute of Frauds section of this Article does not apply to such contracts though they must conform to the Statute of Frauds affecting the transfer of interests in land.

UCC § 2-107 official comment 1 (1972).

While the official comments to the UCC are not binding on Virginia courts, they "are frequently helpful in discerning legislative intent." *Halifax Corp. v. First Union Nat'l Bank*, 262 Va. 91, 546 S.E.2d 696, 703 (2001).

Other courts have applied UCC § 2-107(1) to similar facts. See *652 *Denton v. Clove Valley Rod & Gun Club*, Inc., 95 A. D.2d 844, 464 N.Y.S.2d 203, 204 (1983) (holding that oral contract for buyer to purchase and remove historical home from land was governed by UCC § 2-107(1) and barred by real estate statute of frauds); *Rosen v. Hummel*, 47 A.D.2d 782, 365 N.Y.S.2d 79, 81 (App.Div.1975) (holding that oral contract for buyer to enter on land and dismantle and carry off "a structure" was controlled by § 2-107 and barred by real estate statute of frauds); see also *Williston & Lord*, supra, at § 26:13 (explaining that while at common law a contract to sell and deliver a house was a contract for the sale of goods, UCC § 2-107(1) changes that rule where the buyer, rather than the seller, is to sever the structure).

Baker argues that it was not intended that the model home be considered as real estate. He has submitted copies of the written contracts for his purchase from Jim Walter Homes of the other display models located on the lot. Two of these written contracts state that "Buyer is purchasing only the display model home and fixtures attached to that house. The property on which the model is located is not a part of the sale."

It is true that UCC § 2-107(2) provides that things other than structures that are attached to land and which can be severed without material harm to the realty, are treated as goods, regardless of whether the buyer or the seller is to sever the item. See Va.Code Ann. § 8.2-107(2) (Michie 2001); *Williston & Lord*, supra, at § 26:12 (noting that for the purposes of the statute of frauds and other purposes, "certain mobile homes and modular homes . . . and . . . certain other prefabricated metal or other buildings" may be treated as goods rather than as realty).

The defendant Jim Walter Homes, which has the burden of proof of the affirmative defense of the statute of frauds, has not presented precise evidence surrounding the construction of the model home in question. See *State Highway & Transp. Comm'r v. Edwards Co.*, 220 Va. 90, 255 S.E.2d 500, 503 (1979) (holding that intention of party making the annexation is the prime consideration in determining whether personal property has become reality, which intent may be inferred from the nature of the property, its purpose, and the mode of annexation). Nevertheless, it is sufficiently clear from the summary judgment record that the model home was a "structure" and thus UCC § 2-107(1) applies. See *Condon Bros., Inc. v. Simpson Timber Co.*, 92 Wash.App. 275, 966 P.2d 355, 358 (1998) (holding that dictionary definition of the word "structure" as "something constructed or built" governs in applying UCC § 2-107(1)).

For these reasons, I find that this action is barred by the Virginia statute of frauds relating to the sale of real estate.

Even if the UCC statute of frauds applied as the plaintiff contends, the result would not be different. The plaintiff contends that his action falls within the so-called "judicial admission" exception to the UCC statute of frauds providing that an oral contract is enforceable "if the party against whom enforcement is sought admits in his pleading, testimony or otherwise in court that a contract for sale was made." Va.Code Ann. § 8.2-201(3)(b). However, the plaintiff has not shown that there has been any such admission. In fact, the employees of the defendant who dealt with the plaintiff both expressly deny the existence of a contract in affidavits filed with the court in support of summary judgment. (Bass Aff. ¶¶ 6, 7; Meadows Aff. ¶¶ 8, 9, 14.) The affidavits of witnesses for the plaintiff who claim that these employees made out-of-court admissions do not constitute judicial admissions.

A separate judgment will be entered.

Because of the basis of my ruling, it is unnecessary for me to rule on the defendant's Motion to Strike as to one of the plaintiff's affidavits, or the plaintiff's Motion for Leave to Answer Request for Admission Number Four.

Source: Westlaw Ron BAKER, Plaintiff, v. JIM WALTER HOMES, INC., Defendant. No. 2:05CV00059. Reprinted with permission form Westlaw.

Chapter 8

Deeds

CHAPTER OBJECTIVES

Upon completion of this chapter, you will be able to:

- Identify the types of deeds.
- Explain the requirements necessary for a valid deed.
- Discuss delivery and acceptance of a deed.
- Understand how to prepare a deed.

One of the critical components of a real estate transaction that transfers title involves a legal document known as a deed. A deed is essential to evidencing conveyance of real property. Since a deed is a formal legal document, there are certain requisite elements that must be present in the deed in order for it to validly convey title. This chapter will examine the types, elements, and delivery of deeds.

TYPES OF DEEDS

deed
The written document transferring title, or an ownership interest in real property, to another person.

doctrine of merger
The proposition that the contract for the conveyance of property merges into the deed of conveyance; therefore, any guarantees made in the contract that are not reflected in the deed are extinguished when the deed is conveyed to the buyer of the property.

indenture
A written agreement in which bonds and debentures are issued.

A **deed** is the document that is used to transfer title to real property. In order for a deed to be considered valid, it must

- Be in writing;
- Be signed by the grantor;
- Identify the parties; and
- Describe the land that is the subject of the transaction.

A deed is not a contract, so no consideration is necessary when it is conveyed. However, once a contract for land sale is completed and the deed is conveyed, the seller's obligations are measured by the warranties contained in the deed and not by the terms of the contract. In this way, the contract and the deed merge. This is known as the **doctrine of merger**.

There is more than one type of deed. The three most common types are (1) the quitclaim deed, (2) the limited warranty deed, and (3) the general warranty deed. Once a deed has been prepared, executed, and delivered properly, it must be recorded in the county recorder's office in the county in which the property is located. Once the deed is recorded, it provides public notice of ownership and title to a particular parcel of property. Additionally, an **indenture** is a formal written instrument made between parties with different interests. It traditionally has the edges serrated, or indented, in a way intended to distinguish it from a **deed poll**. A deed poll is a deed made by and binding on only one party, or on two or more parties having similar interests. It is so named because the parchment was traditionally "polled," or shaved.

Quitclaim Deed

A **quitclaim deed** will convey only the interest in the property that the **grantor** possesses and not the property itself. For example, if the grantor possesses complete ownership of the property at the time of the conveyance, then the **grantee** will receive complete ownership of the property. A quitclaim deed has no warranties or covenants of title. Therefore, if the grantor quitclaims to the grantee some interest that is encumbered, or less than full ownership, the grantee will not have a claim against the grantor. No representations with respect to the nature of title or interest in the land are made with a quitclaim deed.

For example, Patricia is interested in purchasing the gas station that is on the corner of her street. She speaks to the gas station attendant, Louie, who states that he owns the gas station. Louie executes a quitclaim for his interest in the gas station to Patricia in exchange for $300,000. Louie leaves the area, and Patricia finds out that Louie had no ownership interest in the gas station, but merely worked there. Patricia has no claim against Louie because the quitclaim deed makes no warranties as to title.

Quitclaim deeds transfer or "quit" any interest in real property that a grantor may have. However, the grantor may not be in the title at all, so a grantee cannot assume that the grantor has any real interest in the property to convey.

Quitclaim deeds are the least desirable of the deeds because of the fact that no covenants or warranties exist as to title. Quitclaim deeds can be found in actions that involve foreclosures and probates.

Limited Warranty Deed

A **limited warranty deed** provides greater protection to the grantee than a quitclaim deed. These types of deeds are usually associated with foreclosures, probates, and trust actions. With a limited warranty deed, the grantor warrants only against his own acts or omissions and agrees to defend the grantee against any claims or actions by any other parties claiming by, through, or under the grantor that they have superior title to what was conveyed to the grantee. A limited warranty deed protects the grantee only against any defects in title that were created by the grantor; it does not protect the grantee from any claims brought by parties who came before the grantor.

For example, Joe owns a parcel of property. He sells the property to Jennifer. Joe transfers the property via a limited warranty deed. Jennifer discovers that there is an easement on the property. The easement was placed on the property by a predecessor of Joe's. Since Joe conveyed the property via a limited warranty deed, Jennifer cannot bring a claim against Joe, because he only warranted the property for any actions that he might have taken on the property, not those of his predecessor.

General Warranty Deed

The **general warranty deed** offers a grantee the most protection against title defects of all of the deeds (see Figure 8.1). These **covenants of title** ensure that specific warranties of title are contained in the deed. They are usually found in a general warranty deed.

deed Poll
A deed binding on one party.

quitclaim deed
A deed transferring only the interest in property of the grantor, without guarantees.

grantor
The person who is the transferor of the property by deed.

grantee
The person to whom the property is to be transferred by deed.

limited warranty deed
Deed wherein the grantor covenants and warrants only against the lawful claims of parties claiming by, through, and under the grantor.

general warranty deed
Type of deed in which the grantor guarantees that he holds clear title to a piece of real estate and has a right to sell it; it contains covenants concerning the quality of title, including warranties of seisin, quiet enjoyment, right to convey, freedom from encumbrances, and defense of title against all claims.

covenants of title
Promises that bind the grantor to ensure the completeness, security, and continuance of the title transferred.

 SPOT THE ISSUE

A grantor has given a buyer a limited warranty deed to a parcel of land. During the time the grantor owned the land, another party got title to the land through adverse possession. Does the buyer have title to the land?

FIGURE 8.1
General Warranty Deed

General Warranty Deed

I, _____, grant to _____ and her heirs and assigns forever, for $1000 and other good and valuable consideration the following real estate situated in _____ County, State of _____, described as follows:

[Description of Land]

To have and to hold the premises, with all the privileges and appurtenances belonging thereunto, to the use of the grantee and her heirs and assigns forever.

The grantor, for himself and his heirs and assigns, covenants (1) that the grantor is lawfully seized in fee simple of the premises, (2) that he has a good right to convey in fee simple, (3) that the premises are free from all encumbrances, (4) that the grantor and his heirs and assigns will forever warrant and defend the grantee and her heirs and assigns against every person lawfully claiming the premises or any part of the premises, (5) that the grantor and his heirs and assigns will guarantee the quiet enjoyment of the premises to the grantee and her heirs and assigns, and (6) that the grantor and his heirs and assigns will execute any instrument reasonably required to provide further assurance of the title to the premises.

Dated this _____ day of _____, 20_____.

_____
Signature of Grantor

Covenants contained in a deed only warrant against the rights of third parties to the granted property and encumbrances outstanding at the time of the delivery of the deed. Covenants do not warrant against any right asserted or encumbrances that arise subsequent to the granting of the deed to the grantee. A general warranty deed contains both present covenants and future covenants. Three are present covenants. Present covenants have to be breached at the time that the deed is delivered in order to be actionable. The statute of limitations for an action on a present covenant begins to run at the time that the deed is delivered. Two of the covenants are future covenants. Future covenants can be breached in the future, when the grantor fails to live up to her promise. The statute of limitations does not begin to run until an actual breach has occurred. These covenants are discussed below (see Figure 8.2).

Covenant of Seisin

seisin
The condition of having both possession and title to property.

Seisin means the right to possession of the property. The grantor has possession of the property being transferred, or has a right to the possession of the property. The covenant of seisin also warrants that the grantor has ownership or title to the property that he purports to convey. The covenant is satisfied if the grantor has possession of the title and not the title to the property. The covenant of seisin is a present covenant and must be breached at the time of delivery of the deed.

Covenant of Right to Convey

The covenant of the right to convey is a promise made on behalf of the grantor that she owns the property and has the right to transfer the ownership of the property.

FIGURE 8.2
The Six Express Warranties

The Six Express Warranties

Covenant of Seisin
Covenant of Right to Convey
Covenant against Encumbrances
Covenant of General Warranty
Covenant of Quiet Enjoyment
Covenant of Further Assurances

An interest in the property that is held by a person other than the grantor would cause a breach of this covenant. The covenant of the right to convey exists together with the covenant of seisin. If the grantor possesses a lesser interest in the property or no interest at the time of conveyance, then both the covenant of seisin and the covenant of the right to convey are breached. The covenant of the right to convey is a present covenant and is breached at the time of delivery of the deed.

Covenant against Encumbrances

The **covenant against encumbrances** is a warranty by the grantor that the property is unencumbered and is free and clear of all mortgages, liens, taxes, leases, and easements, and any other restrictions or debts. This covenant warranties that the title to the property is not subject to those lesser property interests and does not breach the covenant of seisin. The covenant against encumbrances is also a present covenant and must be breached at the time of the delivery of the deed if it is going to be breached at all.

covenant against encumbrances
A grantor's promise that the property has no visible or invisible claims, liabilities, or other rights attached to it that may lessen its value.

Covenant of Further Assurance

The **covenant of further assurance** is a warranty by a grantor that in the future, the grantor will make any conveyance necessary to vest in the grantee of the deed the title intended to be conveyed. This covenant is limited in scope and is different from the other covenants, because the remedy for this cause of action is specific performance based on the grantor's failing to convey the title to the property. The remedy for breach of the other covenants is in money damages. The covenant of further assurance requires that the grantor will execute any additional documents or take any other actions necessary to perfect the grantee's interest in the property. This covenant is a future covenant, which means that it can be breached in the future, sometime after the deed is delivered.

covenant of further assurance
A promise to do whatever is reasonably necessary to perfect the title conveyed if it turns out to be imperfect

Covenants of Quiet Enjoyment and Warranty

The **covenant of quiet enjoyment** is often seen as being synonymous with the **covenant of warranty**. These two covenants are virtually the same, and typically involve a warranty that the grantee of the deed will be able to quietly enjoy the property without the apprehension of being evicted and without the apprehension that any third party will assert any adverse claims. In order for breach of these covenants to occur, a third party must assert his interest in the property. If a third party does not assert an interest in the property, then no breach will occur. These covenants are future covenants, and cannot be breached until the third-party assertion has occurred.

covenant for quiet enjoyment
A promise insuring against the consequences of a defective title; a promise ensuring a tenant will not be evicted by the grantor or a person having lien or superior title.

covenant of warranty
A promise by which the grantor agrees to defend the grantee against any lawful or reasonable claims of superior title by a third party and to indemnify the grantee for any loss sustained due to the claim.

BASIC REQUIREMENTS OF A VALID DEED

Deeds, when properly prepared, executed, delivered, and accepted, transfer title to real property from one person to another. There are several requirements in order for a deed to be valid. Those requirements are discussed below.

Written Instrument

A deed must be in writing in order to be effective. The Statute of Frauds requires all deeds to be written, and every American state has also created a similar requirement. However, there is no prescribed form in order for a deed to be valid. American courts tend to be quite liberal with regard to the placement of the writing. Some states require that the grantor's signature be under **seal**. Others require attestation by one or more witnesses. Almost all states require an acknowledgement by a notary public for recording purposes.

seal
An impression or sign that has legal consequence when applied to an instrument.

LEGAL RESEARCH MAXIM

If the grantee is deceased, the deed is void. Other examples in which a deed is void may include: a deceased grantor, deceased heirs of a living person, or a corporation not in existence. However, there are times when a court will reform a deed that would otherwise be void in order to carry out the grantor's intent. See *Haney's Chapel United Methodist Church v. United Methodist Church*, 716 So. 2d 1156 (Ala.1998).

voidable
Legally valid until annulled; capable of being affirmed or rejected at the option of one of the parties.

void
Describing a transaction that is impossible to enforce because it is invalid.

Competent Grantor

The deed must clearly state and be signed by the grantor. Like contracts, deeds executed by minors are **voidable**, and deeds executed by persons who are mentally incompetent can be void. The grantor must be the owner or have an ownership interest in the property that is being conveyed.

Identity of the Grantee

A deed must identify the grantee with reasonable certainty. If the grantee does not exist or her identity is vague, the deed will be **void**.

Words of Conveyance

A deed must contain words that manifest the intent to transfer title or convey, or it is ineffective. Typically, no specific words of conveyance are required, just words that indicate the grantor's intent to make a present conveyance of the property by way of the deed. Common words of conveyance include, but are not limited to, "sell and convey," "grant, bargain, sell and convey" or "convey and warrant."

Description of the Property

A deed is not valid unless it legally describes the property to be conveyed. A platted description, a government rectangular survey description, or a metes and bounds description based on a registered land surveyor's survey are all acceptable descriptions. However, if the same legal description is used that has been used in prior conveyances of the same property, discrepancies can be avoided. The deed conveys only the property that is described in the deed. The deed will convey all improvements, buildings, air rights, mineral rights, and other appurtenances that belong to the owner of the property unless expressly excluded by reference. A metes and bounds description is one which individually describes every line which is part of the land's boundaries. The government survey system is based on Principal Meridians, which run north-south, and Base Lines, which run east-west. Land is divided into squares about six miles on each side. The squares are called townships. A plat is a map legally approved by a government agency and filed as a permanent record in the local recording office. For example, to describe a lot, a plat would refer to the number, such as "lot 3, block A, Southfield Subdivision as shown in plat book 22, page 77, official records of Hall County."

Recital of Consideration

A deed is valid in most states without consideration, but it should at least contain a recital of consideration. Consideration is something of value given for the deed.

Signature

The grantor is the only person required to sign the deed. Deeds are not signed by the grantee. If the grantor does not sign the deed, then the deed is not valid. A few states require a seal for a deed to be valid. Additionally, most states require that a married grantor add his or her spouse's signature on the deed, even if the property is titled in only one name, because of the possibility of forced share inheritance issues.

Acknowledgment or Witnessing of Deeds

The requirement for the witnessing, attestation, or acknowledgment of the grantor's signature on a deed varies from state to state. Each jurisdiction should be checked to ensure that the execution of the deed is in compliance with state law.

DELIVERY AND ACCEPTANCE

The deed does not transfer title to property until the deed is delivered to the grantee or someone on the grantee's behalf and is accepted by the grantee. The intent of the grantor determines delivery. A deed is delivered when the grantor places the deed in the possession of the grantee with the intention that the deed should pass present title of the property to the grantee. At that time, the grantee accepts the delivery of the deed. Presenting the deed to the grantee merely for examination does not constitute delivery. The grantor must deliver possession of the deed with the intent to pass title to the grantee. The critical issue is whether the grantor does some act with intent to make the deed presently operative. For example, if a grantor has the deed recorded, nearly all courts will apply a strong presumption that delivery has taken place.

PREPARATION OF A DEED

The law of the state in which the property is located controls the deed preparation and conveyance. More often than not, state bar associations, title companies, or law firms will have deed forms that can be used in order to follow the appropriate format for the particular jurisdiction in which the deed is going to be filed. Use of these types of deed forms will simplify the process. Most deeds have the following components:

Caption

The **caption** of a deed provides a place to demonstrate where the deed was executed. The caption indicates the county and state in which the deed was signed by the grantor. The caption does not refer to the county and state where the property is located.

caption
The heading of the deed, which indicates the location at which the grantor signed the deed.

Preamble

The **preamble** is the section that states the identities of the parties that are transferring interest via the deed. The preamble also states the date of the deed. A deed can still be valid without a date, but most deeds contain a date. The date should be the day that the deed is signed by the grantor.

preamble
The section of the deed that identifies the parties to the deed.

Granting Clause

The granting clause contains the language that uses the words of conveyance that property is being granted or conveyed. The granting clause identifies the document as a deed that is transferring interest in real property.

Description

The description section of the deed is where the description of the property that is being conveyed is located. As discussed previously, it is best to use consistent descriptions for the same property in order to alleviate discrepancies.

Habendum Clause

The **habendum clause** is a clause stated on deeds used to transfer ownership rights on property. The clause defines the nature of the estate granted to a person, the extent of the interest transferred, and the rights and obligations on the property. The clause is usually written in language such as this: "To have and to hold the property herein granted to the party of the second part, the heirs and successors and assigns of the party of the second part, forever." The statement implies that the owner of real property in the deed is transferring the property to the grantee. The clause is included in the deed in order to clarify that the grantor has transferred absolute title or ownership rights on the property to the grantee. This implies that the grantee receives title that is free of any lien or judgment.

habendum clause
A clause found in a deed that indicates what estate in real property is being transferred by the deed.

Warranty Clause

The warranty clause usually contains words of warranty. If the deed is a quitclaim deed, no words of warranty will be found.

Testimonium

testimonium
The portion of a deed that the grantor signs and that is usually witnessed or notarized.

The **testimonium** is the spot where the grantor signs the deed. Most deeds are signed under hand and witnessed. Some are sealed and notarized, depending on state law.

DEFECTS IN DEEDS

A deed may be defective if it contains an unintentional error which does not reflect the parties' intentions, or because some required formality is absent. The customary method for correcting an error contained in a deed is for the grantor to execute and deliver to the grantee a revised deed. A revised deed is valid without any additional consideration. Acceptance by the grantee is admission of the error contained in the original deed, as well as the correction of the error in the revised deed.

law of equity
The body of principles constituting what is fair and right; natural law.

If a mutual mistake of fact is involved in the preparation, execution, and delivery of the deed, the **law of equity** will reform the deed in order to correct its condition. If there is some unilateral mistake of fact or fraud involved in the execution and delivery of the deed, the deed can be rescinded by the party who is mistaken or on whom the fraud was perpetrated. Destruction of a deed does not return legal title to the grantor. Legal title does not return if the grantee delivers the deed back to the grantor. If it is desired for some reason that the grantee return title to the property back to the grantor, the proper method to accomplish this is for the grantee to prepare, sign, and deliver a new deed to the grantor, who will then accept the new deed. In other words, there must be a reconveyance of the property back to the grantor. If a deed is defective in its formalities, the defect may make the deed void or voidable. The difference is that a void deed will be set aside even as against a bona fide purchaser, while a voidable deed will not.

YOU BE THE JUDGE

Stuart, an art dealer, decided to defraud Joe of his flourishing apple orchard. Stuart promised Joe that in return for the deed to the orchard, he would deliver to Joe a priceless painting on display at Stuart's art gallery. In fact, Stuart had no title to the painting; he held it strictly on consignment. Joe gave Stuart the deed to the orchard. Stuart immediately transferred the land to James, who was a bona fide purchaser. When Joe realized he would not get the painting, he sued Stuart for cancellation of the deed and return of the land. What will the court hold?

CASE FACT PATTERN

Jane is selling a vacant lot in another town for $75,000. Paula decides that she likes the area and wants to build a house on the lot. Jane and Paula agree to terms of the sale of the property. Jane executes a general warranty deed to Paula. At the time of the conveyance, Jane did not have possession or title to the property, as she had lost it through adverse possession to Alberto. Alberto had been living in a trailer on the property for over ten years and had brought an adverse possession action and claimed title to the property the year before Jane conveyed title to Paula. Paula sues Jane. Because Jane executed a general warranty deed that included the covenants of seisin and the right to convey, Paula will prevail, as Jane's warranties were breached at the time that she conveyed the property to Paula.

THE RECORDING SYSTEM

All American states operate recording systems designed to help people determine who has title to a given parcel of land. These recording systems are essentially collections of documents which have been executed and entered into the system by their parties. Each system takes one of three approaches. About half of all states have "notice" statutes requiring that a given party must take without notice of a subsequent claim and give value. A few states are considered "race" jurisdictions and require that a purchaser must record a deed first to take. The remaining states are "race–notice" and combine the features of both "race" and "notice" jurisdictions. The various recording systems are discussed further in Chapter 11.

RESEARCH THIS

Real property law is regulated by the state. Research the laws in your state and determine what elements are required for a valid deed and whether or not a deed needs to be sealed, witnessed, or notarized in order to be valid.

PRACTICE TIP

Ten states provide an alternative to the conventional recording system. It is referred to as the "Torrens" or title registration system. The Torrens system, named after Sir Robert Torrens, a nineteenth-century Australian who reformed land laws, has been adopted by several heavily populated counties in the United States. It is a system for establishing title to real estate in which a claimant first requires an abstract of title and then applies to a court for the issuance of a title certificate, which serves as conclusive proof of ownership. The certificate shows the names of the parties holding the fee title as well as "memorials" identifying all liens or encumbrances against the title. Claims not shown on the certificate are extinguished.

EYE ON ETHICS

The requirements of a deed are very specific. It is very important to be familiar with all of the legal requirements for a deed in a particular jurisdiction. Failure to abide by these requirements can make a deed invalid. The validity of a deed can be corrected if the parties are still alive. However, if the validity of a deed is questioned after the death of one of the parties, a beneficiary could sustain a great loss as a result of the deed's being declared invalid for failing to comply with deed requirements.

SURF'S UP

Most counties have Web sites that will set forth the requirements for a deed. Check out some of the following:
  http://www.broward.org/records/cri00500.htm
  http://www.wycokck.org/gen/wyco_generated_pages/
http://www.co.utah.ut.us/Dept/Record/Policiesand Procedures/Reference.asp.
http://www.nhdeeds.com

Summary

The most commonly used document used to transfer title to real property in the United States is a deed. In order for a deed to be considered valid, it must (1) be in writing; (2) be signed by the grantor; (3) identify the parties; and (4) describe the land that is the subject of the transaction. There are many different types of deeds; three commonly used forms are the quitclaim deed, the limited warranty deed, and the general warranty deed.

A quitclaim deed will convey only the interest in the property that the grantor possesses, and not the property itself. For example, if the grantor possesses complete ownership of the property at the time of the conveyance, then the grantee will receive complete ownership of the property. A quitclaim deed has no warranties or covenants of title.

A limited warranty deed provides greater protection to the grantee than a quitclaim deed. These types of deeds are usually associated with foreclosures, probates, and trust actions. With a limited warranty deed, the grantor warrants against only her own acts or omissions, and agrees to defend the grantee against any claims or actions by any other party claiming by, through, or under the grantor that they have superior title to what was conveyed to the grantee.

The general warranty deed offers a grantee the greatest protection against title defects of all of the deeds. A purchaser always wants to ensure that specific warranties of title, known as covenants, are contained in the deed before purchasing the property. These covenants are usually found in a general warranty deed. Covenants contained in a deed warrant against only the rights of third parties to the granted property and encumbrances outstanding at the time of the delivery of the deed. Covenants do not warrant against any rights asserted or encumbrances that arise subsequent to the granting of the deed to the grantee. A general warranty deed contains both present covenants and future covenants.

The deed does not transfer title to property until the deed is delivered to the grantee or someone on the grantee's behalf and accepted by the grantee. The intent of the grantor determines delivery. A deed is delivered when the grantor places the deed in the possession of the grantee with the intention that the deed should pass present title of the property to the grantee. At that time, the grantee accepts the delivery of the deed. Presenting the deed to the grantee merely for examination does not constitute delivery. The grantor must deliver possession of the deed with the intent to pass title to the grantee.

The law of the state in which the property is located controls the deed preparation and conveyance. More often than not, state bar associations, title companies, or law firms will have deed forms that can be used in order to follow the appropriate format for the particular jurisdiction where the deed is going to be filed.

The customary method for correcting an error contained in a deed is for the grantor to execute and deliver to the grantee a revised deed. A revised deed is valid without any additional consideration. Acceptance by the grantee is admission of the error contained in the original deed as well as the correction of the error in the revised deed.

If a mutual mistake of fact is involved in the preparation, execution, and delivery of the deed, the law of equity will reform the deed in order to correct its condition. If there is some unilateral mistake of fact or fraud involved in the execution and delivery of the deed, the deed can be rescinded by the party who is mistaken or on whom the fraud was perpetrated. Destruction of a deed does not return legal title to the grantor. Legal title does not return if the grantee delivers the deed back to the grantor. If it is desired for some reason that the grantee return title to the property to the grantor, the proper method to accomplish this is for the grantee to prepare, sign, and deliver a new deed to the grantor, who will then accept the new deed. In other words, there must be a reconveyance of the property back to the grantor.

Review Questions

1. What is a quitclaim deed?
2. What is the difference between a general warranty deed and a limited warranty deed?
3. List the elements required for a valid deed.
4. Why is a preamble important?
5. What purpose does the testimonium serve?
6. Describe the doctrine of merger.
7. What is the purpose of the caption of a deed?
8. Does a deed have to be dated to be valid?
9. Why is the covenant of seisin important?
10. What is the difference between a present and a future covenant?
11. Why is the covenant of further assurance different from the other covenants?
12. Why does a deed have to be reconveyed back to the grantor in order to return title to the grantor?
13. How do you correct a deed?
14. How does the property have to be described in a deed?
15. What is delivery?

Exercises

1. Locate a warranty deed form for your jurisdiction. With yourself as the grantor and your teacher as the grantee, convey your school. Be sure to incorporate all features that would make the conveyance a valid transaction and valid deed if the deal were real.
2. Sherry conveyed a house and lot to Bert under a general warranty deed. The deed did not list any encumbrances or encroachments. At the time Bert received the deed, he was aware that a garage built and belonging to Sherry's eastern neighbor, Melissa, was located half on Melissa's property and half on Sherry's property. Bert went ahead with the transaction anyway, as he thought the property was a steal. Several years later, Bert decided that he could not tolerate the situation any longer. He sued Sherry. Under which covenant should Bert sue, and what will be the result?
3. Lois is selling her townhome to Nancy. Who is required to sign the deed in connection with the ownership transfer?

4. Identify and explain the warranties included in a general warranty deed.

5. Archibald Andrews, who was old and feeble, wrote out a deed on his farm to Nancy, his favorite niece, and placed it in his desk drawer. He later called Nancy to his bedside and told her that he wanted her to have the farm and that the deed was in the drawer. At her uncle's urging, Nancy took the deed and recorded it. After Archibald's death, his estranged son sued Nancy for quiet title to the farm, claiming that delivery had never occurred. Was there valid delivery? Why or why not?

6. Identify which covenant of title offers protection to a grantee against a lien on property which impairs the grantor's title to the property.

7. Explain the distinction between *void* and *voidable*. Give a specific example of each.

8. Using the sample warranty deed provided, identify and explain each of the six express warranties included.

 PORTFOLIO ASSIGNMENT

Many local jurisdictions have recorded documents available online. Visit your local jurisdictions' Web sites and find copies of recorded documents to include in your portfolio.

Vocabulary Builders

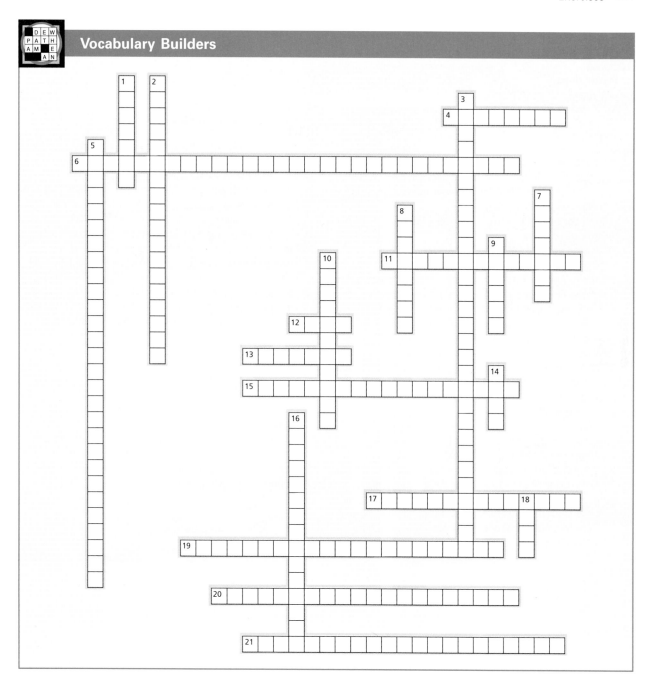

Vocabulary Builders

Instructions
Use the key terms from this chapter to fill in the answers to the crossword puzzle.
NOTE: When the answer is more than one word, leave a blank space between words.

ACROSS

4. legally valid until annulled; capable of being affirmed or rejected at the option of one of the parties.
6. a grantor's promise that the property has no visible or invisible claims, liabilities, or other rights attached to it that may lessen its value.
11. the body of principles constituting what is fair and right; natural law.
12. having no legal effect; an absolute nullity.
13. the person who is the transferor of the property by deed.
15. the proposition that the contract for the conveyance of property merges into the deed of conveyance; therefore, any guarantees made in the contract that are not reflected in the deed are extinguished when the deed is conveyed to the buyer of the property.
17. a deed that contains no warranties of title.
19. deed wherein the grantor convenants and warrants only against the lawful claims of parties claiming by, through, and under the grantor.
20. a promise by which the grantor agrees to defend the grantee against any lawful or reasonable claims of superior title by a third party and to indemnify the grantee for any loss sustained by the claim.
21. type of deed in which the grantor guarantees that he holds clear title to a piece of real estate and has a right to sell it; it contains convenants concerning the quality of title, including warranties of seisin, quiet enjoyment, right to convey, freedom from encumbrances, and defense of title against all claims

DOWN

1. the person to whom the property is to be transferred by deed.
2. promises that bind the grantor to ensure the completeness, security, and continuance of the title transferred.
3. a promise to do whatever is reasonably necessary to perfect the title conveyed if it turns out to be imperfect.
5. a promise insuring against the consequences of a defective title; a promise ensuring a tenant will not be evicted by the grantor or a person having lien or superior title.
7. the heading of the deed, which indicates the location at which the grantor signed the deed.
8. the section of the deed that identifies the parties to the deed.
9. the condition of having both possession and title to property.
10. the portion of a deed that the grantor signs and that is usually witnessed or notarized.
14. an impression or sign that has legal consequence when applied to an instrument.
16. a clause found in a deed that indicates what estate in real property is being transferred by the deed.
18. a written document that transfers ownership of real property from one person to another.

U.S. v. Kubalak
365 F.Supp.2d 677
W.D.N.C.,2005.

I. DISCUSSION

The parties have agreed that Plaintiff's chain of title is correctly set forth in its Exhibits 3-A through 3-L and that Defendant's chain of title is correctly set forth in Plaintiff's Exhibits 4-A through 4-S. These instruments reflect that both parties rely on titles originating in a common source known as the James R. Love lands.

A standard and acceptable method of proving superior title to real estate in North Carolina is accomplished by a plaintiff "connect[ing] the defendant with a common source of title, and show[ing] in himself a better title from that source." Brothers v. Howard, 57 N.C.App. 689, 691, 292 S.E.2d 139, 141 (1982).

A description of both Plaintiff's and Defendant's lands first appears in the March 1890 decree recorded in Haywood County, North Carolina, Register of Deeds, in Deed Book 1 page 1, known as the Scottish Timber Reserve. This decree conveys "a tract of forty five hundred acres of land" to the Scottish Carolina Timber & Land Co., Ltd. It excepts from this conveyance "a tract of fifty acres known as the Messer tract. . .

The Plaintiff's chain of title continues by successive deeds recorded in the Haywood County Register of Deeds.

Up to this point in Plaintiff's chain of title, the Defendant's land was simply referred to as the Messer Tract exception. Neither of the aforementioned deeds sought to convey the Messer Tract, nor did any deed describe the Messer exception by metes and bounds or other reference to a specific description. However, in this last deed the Messer Tract exception is described by metes and bounds as follows:

> to Corner 12, a point at intersection of Carolina Power and Light Company line with W.D. Messer line.

Thence with four lines of W.D. Messer, N. 50 04' W. 7.60 chains FN1 to corner 13, a 3" chestnut (dead) growing from a 48" chestnut stump on south slope of spur ridge, 1.00 chain Northeast of branch. Bearing tree: a 12" black gum S. 27 W. 0.18 chain.

Chain is defined as a unit of length used in surveying that measures 66 feet.

S. 37 58' W. 24.40 chains to Corner 14, a stake on west slope of spur ridge. Bearing tree: a 5" chestnut N. 24 E. 0.20 chain, a 3" locust S. 36 E. 0.09 chain and a 3" sourwood S. 78 E. 0.10 chain.

S. 51 50' E. 18.55 chains to Corner 15, a planted stone on south slope of spur ridge. Bearing trees: an 8" chestnut N. 44 E. 0.25 chain, a 16" chestnut S. 14 E. 0.25 chain and an 8" black gum S. 66 W. 0.40 chain.

N. 38 34' E. 17.54 chains to Corner 16, a point at intersection of W.D. Messer's line with line of Carolina Power and Light Company. Corner 5 of Tract # 31a bears N. 38 34' E. 3.57 chains.

Defendant Messer's first deed of conveyance appearing in his chain of title is found at Deed Book 48, Page 395, recorded February 17, 1917, in the Haywood County Register of Deeds, from W.J. Hannah, Trustee for the Estate of James R. Love, to W.D. Messer. The deed recites that in 1861, J.R. Love executed a bond for title to the disputed tract to Benjamin Garner and took Garner's note for $100 for the purchase money. The bond was then assigned to W.O. Messer, then to W.D. Messer, then to W.W. Stringfield, then to W.J.G.B. Boyd. W.O. Messer then paid part of the purchase price to Boyd and assigned his part of the bond to W.D. Messer who in turn paid the remainder of the purchase price to Boyd. As a result of the payment, the duly authorized representative of the James R. Love Estate conveyed the following described land by deed dated March 31, 1915:

[L]ying and being on the long arm of Mount Sterling at the Poplar Gap in the County of Haywood, N.C. and adjoining the lands of Haddock France Lumber Co. and others, and bounded as follows:

Beginning on a stake on the South East side of the Mountain runs North 38 East 100 poles to a blackoak; then runs North 52 West 80 poles to a chestnut; Thence South 38. W. 100 poles to a stake; thence South 52. E. 80 poles to the beginning, containing Fifty (50) acres more or less.

The bond for title does not appear of record, but its existence is not disputed even though the parties do not agree as to its effect.

In this case, there is no showing of any prior possession by Defendant or full compliance with the terms of the bond prior to the execution of the conveyance by W.J. Hannah, Trustee. Nor does a prior metes and bounds description of the tract appear of record before this deed. The bond for title creates an equitable interest in the purchaser in the land described in the bond. Fortune v. Watkins, 94 N.C. 304, 1886 WL 901 (N.C.1886). It is also a sufficient claim of title under the common source to preserve his claims under his contract. Ryan v. Martin, 91 N.C. 464, 1884 WL 2015 (N.C.1884). However, where a land owner gives to another a bond for title to a tract of land, legal title remains in him until conveyed out by proper deed of conveyance. He does not become the beneficial owner until payment of the purchase money is made. Morrison v. Chambers, 122 N.C. 689, 30 S.E. 141 (1898). Thus, full record title does not ripen in W.D. Messer until February 17, 1917.

By judgment in the action entitled Carolina Power & Light Co. v. W.D. Messer and wife, E.M. Messer, entered February 7, 1927, and recorded by the Haywood County Register of Deeds on April 30, 1927, in Deed Book 73, Page 599, Carolina Power & Light Company ("CP & L") obtained title to 3.28 acres of the W.D. Messer Tract and a right-of-way described as follows:

First: Beginning at a black oak the northeast corner of the W.D. Messer tract, and being also the corner of the Haywood Land and Timber Company lands, and running thence with the line of the Haywood Land and Timber Company N. 46 14' W. with a marked line 785 feet to a stake; thence S. 21 45' E. 865 feet along other land of W.D. Messer to a stake in the line of the land of the Haywood Land and Timber Company; thence with said last mentioned line N. 43 E. 365 feet to the point or place of Beginning, containing 3.28 acres, be the same, more or less.

Second: A right of way over such part or parts of a trail that lies on the W.D. Messer Tract, which trail leads from the Cotton Patch on the Pigeon River over the long arm of Mount Sterling Ridge to Hickory Gap on the Mount Sterling-Catalooche Highway, crossing W.D. Messer's fifty acre tract, approximately 600 feet northwest from the northeast corner thereof, and running through an old pasture on said tract, approximately 1,500 feet to midway of the south side of said tract.

This Judgment does not purport to convey any right-of-way to Messer.

By deed recorded in the Haywood County Register of Deeds at Deed Book 99, Page 24, on May 13, 1937, W.D. Messer conveyed his tract to Irving Messer. This deed contains the same description as that set forth in the March 1915 deed and includes the new lines described in the CP & L Judgment. The acreage is described as "containing 46.72 acres, more or less."

On October 7, 1946, Irving Messer and wife, Dollie Messer, conveyed the property to Rankin Ferguson using the same description as the deed from W.D. Messer to Irving Messer and excepts a right-of-way across the land for CP & L. This deed was recorded on October 10, 1946, in the Haywood County Register of Deeds in Deed Book 130, Page 414.

Using the same description as the two previous deeds, the property was conveyed to Hardy W. Phillips and wife, Martha Phillips, by Rankin Ferguson and wife, Celestine Ferguson, by deed dated October 14, 1955, and recorded in the Haywood County Register of Deeds at Deed Book 164, Page 486, on October 26, 1955.

On November 24, 1997, Leon W. Killian, III, court appointed guardian for the Estate of Martha E. Phillips, conveyed the subject property to Defendant Herbert E. Kubalak by a new description which, for the first time, referenced corner monuments installed by the Forest Service:

EXHIBIT "A"

BEGINNING at a U.S. Forest Service Monument (found), a corner between the United States of America Forest Service Tract 31-B (Pisgah National Forest), known as Corner # 16, in the western margin of a Carolina Power & Light Company right of way (Deed Book 73, Page 599), and running thence with the said right of way, N. 20 deg. 56 min. 14 sec. W. 858.18 feet to a USFS Monument (found), for Tract 31-B, known as Corner # 12; thence leaving the Carolina Power & Light Company right of way line and running with the United States of America Forest Service Tract 31-B (Pisgah National Forest) lines, four calls as follows: N. 50 deg. 08 min. 32 sec. W. 499.20 feet to USFS Monument (found) for Tract 31-B, known as Corner # 13; S. 38 deg. 00 min. 00 sec. W. 1609.84 feet to a USFS Monument (found) for Tract 31-B, known as Corner # 14; S. 51 deg. 44 min. 56 sec. E. 1229.36 feet to a USFS Monument (found) for Tract 31-B, known as Corner # 15; and N. 38 deg. 14 min. 00 sec. E. 1156.25 feet to the BEGINNING, containing 41.519 acres, according to the plat of survey entitled "Plat Prepared for Herbert E. Kubalak," by J. Randy Herron, R.L.S. dated September 2, 1997.

BEING the same property described in a deed dated October 14, 1955 from Rankin Ferguson and wife, Celestine Ferguson to Hardy W. Phillips and wife, Martha Phillips, of record in Deed Book 164, Page 486, Haywood County Registry.

This deed was recorded on November 24, 1997, in the Haywood County Register of Deeds at Deed Book 462, Page 1588. Id.FN2

[T]he rule is that where there is a particular and a general description in a deed, the particular description prevails over the general. It is only when the specific description is ambiguous, or insufficient, or the reference is to a fuller and more accurate description, that the general clause is allowed to control or is given significance in determining the boundaries. Applying this principle to description in the deeds under consideration, the particular description is clear and specific, and, when considered in connection with the admitted plat, leaves no room to doubt that it covers the land in controversy.

Whiteheart v. Grubbs, 232 N.C. 236, 242, 60 S.E.2d 101, 104-05 (1950)

The description above indicates it ties to marked Forest Service corners and "run[s] with the United States of America Forest Service Tract 31-B (Pisgah National Forest) lines, four calls as follows[.]" This clearly shows the intent of the grantor to convey that tract of land bounded by Plaintiff's monuments and lines. As observed by the Defendants, North Carolina law supports this conclusion. The plat prepared by Defendant J. Randy Herron on December 17, 1997, is consistent with this idea of intent that there does not appear to have been any challenge to the location of the Messer tract boundaries from the time James R. Love executed his bond for title in 1861 until the Kubalak deed was recorded in 1997. This lack of challenge was despite the fact that there had been several transfers of title to the Messer tract, a condemnation of a portion of the tract, and Forest Service surveys with marked lines and monumentation in 1935 and 1978. There were also timber cuttings in and around the disputed area from 1982 to 1987 by Powell Wholesale Lumber Company under Forest Service contract. Forest Service Road # 287, constructed in 1980–82, undisputedly runs well inside the land claimed by Defendant Messer. Marked corners, blazed and painted trees, metal Forest Service markers, are all indicia of claimed ownership and may not be ignored by a "prudent owner." Fulcher v. United States, 696 F.2d 1073, 1077 (4th Cir.1982). It is very unlikely that one or more of the owners over the years would have failed to challenge a true encroachment or trespass by one of the surrounding timber companies or the Forest Service. Parrish v. Hayworth, 138 N.C.App. 637, 642, 532 S.E.2d 202, 206 (2000).

On November 26, 1997, Kubalak conveyed the identically described property to Herbert E. Kubalak, Trustee, by deed recorded in the Haywood County Register of Deeds at Deed Book 462, Page 1717. Defendant Messer became owner of the entire Messer Tract minus the CP & L acquisition.

It is noted that the two deeds recorded at Deed Book 477, Page 1918, and at Deed *685 Book 477, Page 1920, each purport to convey one half of the Messer Tract (23.04 acres for a total of 46.08 acres); however, both deeds refer to new boundaries beyond the Forest Service markers referred to in the deeds recorded at Deed Book 462, Page 1588 and at Deed Book 462, Page 1717). These deeds also note "that a dispute exists with the Forest Service as to the exact location of boundaries of both tracts." These deeds also seek to convey a 20-foot right-of-way over adjoining lands owned by the United States.

As the source for the new boundaries claimed easement, Defendants refer to the plat of a survey by Defendant Herron recorded in Cabinet E, Slot 2323 of the Haywood County Registry. Herron testified at his deposition that his survey reference to a 20-foot right-of-way was to a right-of-way granted for the sole use of CP & L and that it did not grant a right-of-way to owners of the former Messer tract across the surrounding lands owned by the United States.

By deed recorded in the Haywood County Register of Deeds at Deed Book 571, Page 1934, Defendant Messer conveyed a three-acre tract of land and purported 20-foot right-of-way to Norman Doyle Green, Jr., on September 2, 2003.

By deed recorded in the Haywood County Register of Deeds at Deed Book 576, Page 929, Defendant Messer conveyed a one-acre tract of land and purported 20-foot right-of-way to Thurman A. Evans, Jr., and wife, Brenda Evans, on October 9, 2003.

By contract for deed recorded in the Haywood County Register of Deeds at Deed Book 586, Page 1915, Defendant Messer agreed to convey a one-acre tract of land and purported 20-foot right-of-way to Rickey Ogle and wife, Crystal D. Ogle, on January 30, 2004.

By deed recorded in the Haywood County Register of Deeds at Deed Book 594, Page 2205, Thurman and Brenda Evans conveyed their one-acre tract of land and purported 20-foot right-of-way to Rickey Ogle and wife, Crystal D. Ogle, on April 19, 2004.

The Plaintiff contends that each of these deeds, identified as Plaintiff's Exhibits 4-N, 4-P, 4-Q, and 4-R, attempts to convey title to lands and rights-of-way owned at least in part by the United States.

In November and December 1997, Defendant Messer contacted Forest Service personnel asking for information on how to obtain a permit to widen and improve Forest Service Road # 3537, but no such permit was ever issued.

In depositions, both Defendants Kubalak and Messer admitted to placing fencing in the disputed area., Deposition of Troy Steven Messer, at 44-45; Deposition of Herbert E. Kubalak, at 34, 38. Defendant Herron testified that during his employment by Defendants Messer and Kubalak, he placed boundary markers in the disputed area and along Forest Service Road # 3537. Messer also testified to building a new road from the southeast corner of the Messer tract to Forest Service Road # 287.

Herron testified that he actually located on the ground each of the corners referenced in the deed from Leon Killian, guardian for the Estate of Martha Phillips, to Kubalak and accurately shown on Drawing Number 2965-2126-B prepared by him and recorded in the public registry of Haywood County. Herron Deposition, at 53-57. It was after this deed and plat were recorded that Kubalak and Messer requested Herron to prepare new plats showing new boundary and corner locations, as well as a 20-foot right-of-way.

Defendants do not dispute the amounts claimed, i.e., $6,011.71 for illegal widening of Forest Service Road # 3537; $950.00 for fence and marker removal; and $2,002.00 for removal of new road connecting Forest Service Road # 287.

After full review of his work in this case and his resume, the Court concludes that by education, training, and experience, Gary I. Seiler is an expert in the field of forestry and land surveying with prior experience testifying before the Superior Court of Buncombe County, North Carolina.

In Seiler's report submitted in connection with this action, he explains the variations in the Messer metes description and the bounds markings as follows:

Variances exist between the W.D. Messer metes description versus the bounds markings found on the ground in 1999, 1978 [and] 1935. . . .

First, magnetic north bearings in the locality in 1915 did not differ much from true north bearings (18.5' east declination). The lines surveyed by the U.S.F.S. in 1935 and as resurveyed in 1999 approximate the 1915 W.D. Messer bearings when allowance is made for the usual survey techniques practiced in this region in 1915.

Second, though the distances surveyed by the U.S.F.S. in 1935 are shorter than the 1915 W.D. Messer deed, there is a significant and well known possible reason for this. Distance measurements of woodland in mountainous terrain in 1915, made prior to North Carolina's requirement for the use of horizontal distances in land surveys, frequently relied on surface measurements (a.k.a. slant or slope distances). These measurements were quicker and easier to make because no vertical angle needed to be measured and no trigonometric calculation of reduction of surface measurement to horizontal measurement needed to be made. Surveyor's Report, attached to Second Affidavit of Gary Seiler.

With this in mind, the Court next looks to the North Carolina law as set forth in the seminal case cited to and quoted from by the parties in their briefs.

[W]henever a natural boundary is called for in a patent or deed, the line is to terminate at it, however wide of the course called for it may be, or however short or beyond the distance specified. A natural monument is fixed and permanent, and its being called for in the deed or patent, marks, beyond controversy, the intention of the party to select that land from the inappropriate mass.

Cherry v. Slade's Administrator, 3 Mur. 82, 7 N.C. 82, 1819 WL 293, *3 (N.C.1819). The parties also agree that in interpreting deed descriptions, references to natural monuments control references to artificial monuments, artificial monuments control courses, courses control distances, and recitals of quantity are the least reliable forms of description. Webster's Real Estate Law in N.C., § 10-38, at 422 (5th ed.1999). Thus, the conclusion in the first Messer deed of record and carried through Defendant Messer's chain of title to Irving Messer, that the tract of land being conveyed contains "fifty (50) acres more or less" is entitled to little weight under North Carolina real property law. It is also clear that under North Carolina law that the two natural monuments mentioned in the original deed, i.e., the black oak and the chestnut trees, overrule the calls to courses and distances, as do the artificial monuments, the Forest Service monuments, referenced in the Killian to Kubalak deed of 1997.

The field notes generated by the 1935-36 survey of the Messer Tract are compelling. At their corner marked 13, the surveyors found a four foot chestnut stump. Subsequent surveys located the same corner stump, samples of which were confirmed as chestnut by an expert in wood and paper science analysis. See, Report of Elisabeth Field Wheeler, Ph.D. Nearby, a black gum was found with old marks and paint as a witness tree. This note also references a "3" chestnut sapling (dead) that had been growing out of the chestnut stump. *Id.* At corner 14, the surveyors found an old boundary corner stake on the west slope of the spur ridge. They also found the black oak referenced in the Messer deed and market it as corner 16. The notes further indicate remaining corners were marked and lines painted. These marks would indicate the Messer Tract had, in fact, been previously surveyed and marked at the time or before execution of the deed to W.D. Messer from Hannah, Trustee.

In 1978, Plaintiff again surveyed the Messer Tract exception. The old corners were found, lines were painted and blazed and new corner monuments consisting of 30″ × 3″ capped aluminum pipes. Metal Forest Service signs were placed at various corners.

In 1997 when Defendant Herron surveyed the Messer Tract in order to prepare a plat and deed description for the Killian to Kubalak deed, he found and used the Forest Service capped aluminum monuments from the 1978 survey to describe the land being conveyed.

In 1999, Seiler performed another re-survey. This survey confirms and supports the work done in the 1978 survey. It also supports the conclusion that known and visible bounds of the Forest Service lands were clearly established and recognized by the owners of the Messer Tract. This conclusion is further verified by Herron's original survey and plat prepared by him after personally going on the lands involved. This original 1997 Herron plat correctly shows the Troy Steven Messer Tract, formerly the W.D. Messer Tract, as it is bounded by Forest Service and CP & L lands. "[N]othing greater than the tract graphically depicted on the 1997 Herron Plat and specifically verbally described in the first paragraph of Exhibit A to the Kubalak Deed is vested in the grantees. . . ." Goldstein Report.

The Court finds Steven L. Goldstein to be a board certified specialist in North Carolina real property law and qualified by training and experience to testify as an expert in this field.

The Defendants' claim of a 20-foot right-of-way over any of Plaintiff's surrounding lands is void of any supporting instrument of record that would serve to vest title in Defendants to such a right-of-way. Thus, Defendants' claim of a right to a 20-foot right-of-way across Plaintiff's adjoining lands as shown in the February 8, 1999, plat prepared by Defendant Herron is determined by the Court to be void.

Likewise, the Defendants' claim that Plaintiff's right to bring a trespass action is barred by the three year statute of limitations under N.C. Gen.Stat. § 1-52 is without merit. The United States may bring an action in trespass within a six year period. Such a provision, of course, preempts the North Carolina statute of limitations. "[I]n pursuing a viable claim, a federal agency is bound by the terms of the federal statute of limitations, which may not be lengthened or shortened by a state enactment." *F.D.I.C. v. Hinkson*, 848 F.2d 432 (3d Cir.1988). Therefore, the amount of Plaintiff's claims for damages being undisputed, they will be awarded in the full amount requested.

II. CONCLUSION

For the reasons stated infra, and based on consideration of the deeds, maps, affidavits of the parties, and the corner and boundary indicia located upon the ground, the Court concludes that Plaintiff has superior title to the lands disputed by the Defendants. The Court further concludes that the Defendants, having "failed to bring forth facts showing that reasonable minds could differ on [the] material point" of the proper location of the Messer Tract boundaries, summary judgment is appropriate and will be entered. *Bouchat*, 346 F.3d at 522.

Source: *United States v. Kubalak* 365 F.Supp.2d 677 W.D.N.C., 2005.

Chapter 9

Mortgages

CHAPTER OBJECTIVES

Upon completion of this chapter, you will be able to:

- Understand the provisions of a promissory note.
- Discuss how a mortgage operates.
- Explain the rights and remedies under a default.
- Identify the different types of foreclosures.

Most people who purchase real property do not have enough cash on hand to be able to pay for the property in full. Therefore, it is necessary to obtain money from some other source in order to pay the entire price of the property. The purchaser borrows funds from a lender and then pays the lender back over time. These lenders want assurances that they will get their money out of the property and that they are experiencing a minimal amount of risk by lending money for the purchase. This chapter examines the relationships among the borrower, the lender, and the property in a mortgage situation.

PROMISSORY NOTE

A **promissory note** is a written instrument that documents a transaction in which money is lent from one party to another. It is a promise by one party to pay money to another party. The person who promises to pay the money is known as the **payor**, and the person whom the payor promises to repay is known as the **payee**. Typically, a promissory note is in writing and signed by the payor. The promissory note contains the terms of the loan, the repayment schedule, and the interest rate, as well as the lending institution's place of address where payments are to be made. It contains a promise to pay an amount of money within a period of time, by a deadline or on demand. The note is then kept by the payee as evidence of the loan and the repayment agreement.

Notes can be **negotiable**; this means that they can be transferred by the payee to another party. The person who receives the note in a transfer is known as the holder of the note. Most holders take the note in due course, which enables them to be able to collect on the note that has been transferred to them. A non-negotiable note cannot be transferred, but it can still be collected on by the holder.

Many lending institutions make it a common practice to buy and sell notes. Notes are transferred and sold by **endorsement**. An endorsement is a direction stating that the money is to be paid to the holder of the note. Endorsements are usually printed on the back of or attached to the note.

promissory note
A promise or engagement, in writing, to pay a specified sum at a time therein stated, or on demand, or at sight, to a person therein named, or to his order, or bearer.

payor
The person by whom a bill or note has been or should have been paid.

payee
The person in whose favor a bill of exchange, promissory note, or check is made or drawn.

negotiable
Legally capable of being transferred by endorsement or delivery.

endorsement
The act of a payee of a negotiable instrument, in writing her name upon the back of the instrument, with or without further or qualifying words, whereby the property in the same is assigned and transferred to another.

A payor makes an unconditional promise to pay when she signs a promissory note. In addition, the payor is not released from paying on the note even if the real property that has been used to secure the note is sold. If the property is sold, the proceeds need to go to pay off the promissory note, or the payor will still be liable to pay. If more than one payor is listed on the note, then each of the co-payors is responsible for the payment of the note, and the payee can collect from either or all of the payors. This is known as being **jointly and severally liable**.

joint and several liability
Shared responsibility, apportioned between all of the defendants, but in no case can the plaintiff recover more than 100 percent of the damages awarded.

A note cannot be prepaid before the date established in the note for payment, unless it is specifically stated in the promissory note that prepayment is acceptable. Sometimes, a lender will provide a condition for prepayment on the note so long as the payor pays an additional premium or penalty for the privilege of being able to prepay.

Most states have statutes that indicate the maximum rate of interest that can be charged on a note. Penalties vary from state to state for charging interest rates that exceed the maximum rate determined by law.

The promissory note is signed by the payor, but the signature does not usually need to be witnessed or notarized. The promissory note is not typically recorded with the county recorder; however, a copy can be attached to a deed of trust when real property is being used to secure the note.

GUARANTY

Sometimes, a lender may require that a person other than the payor be held responsible for paying the debt should the payor fail to pay. The mortgage lender may require a person other than the debtor to guarantee the payment of the debtor's note. This is known as a **guaranty**. The guaranty gives the lender the right to sue the person guaranteeing the loan, called the **guarantor** as well as the payor, if payment is not made on the note. The lender has the right to recover the debt from the personal assets of the guarantor as well as those of the payor.

guaranty
A promise to answer for the payment of some debt or perform some duty, in case of the failure of another who is liable.

guarantor
One who makes a guaranty.

A guaranty of a note must be in writing. There are typically two types of guaranty: a "payment guaranty" and a "collection guaranty." The guarantor who signs a payment guaranty unconditionally guarantees to pay the debt on the note when it is due without the lender's looking to any other party for payment, including the original payor. If the guaranty is a collection guaranty, then the lender must first look to the original payor for payment of the debt when it is due. If the original payor cannot pay, then the lender must sue the original payor, obtain a judgment, and try to enforce the judgment against the payor. If the payor is insolvent or lacks funds to pay the judgment, then the lender can turn to the guarantor for payment on the debt.

Under the terms of both the payment guaranty and the collection guaranty, if a change in the terms of the note that is being guaranteed is made without the guarantor's consent, the guarantor will be released from payment. If a note is modified or amended, it is necessary that all guarantors consent to the modification or amendment. If they do not consent, then they will be released from being liable for payment.

MORTGAGES

mortgage
An interest in land created by a written instrument, providing security for the performance of a duty or the payment of a debt.

collateral
Property that is pledged as security for the satisfaction of a debt.

Typically, when a promissory note is made on real property, it is secured by an instrument that connects the promissory note to the real property. Requirements vary among states, but typical security instruments are a **mortgage**, a deed of trust, and a security deed. The main purpose of the security instrument is to convey real property as **collateral** for the repayment of the debt, as stated in the note.

A mortgage is a security interest given to the lender by the payor to guarantee the repayment of a loan. In other words, the payor is purchasing the property and requires financing from the lender in order to do so. To secure the promissory note, the lender will require the payor to execute another document, called a mortgage, that gives the lender the right to attach the property and sell it should the payor **default** on the loan. A mortgage creates an encumbrance on the property. However, a mortgage does not affect legal title to the property. Legal title remains with the owner.

A **deed of trust** is a document by which the owner of the property conveys title to another person, known as a **trustee**. The trustee holds the title in trust for the benefit of the lender. If the debt is not paid, the trustee, at the request of the beneficiary, can conduct a public foreclosure sale and use the proceeds from the sale to pay the debt owed to the lender. In many jurisdictions the deed of trust is the most often used mortgage instrument. Although the parties are referred to differently when a deed of trust is used, it still is essentially a mortgage, and traditional mortgagor protections apply. Deeds of trust are generally used to make the foreclosure process less difficult, and not to avoid basic principles of mortgage laws. Deeds of trust are considered mortgage variants. Mortgage substitutes are often seen when a party is trying to avoid the right to redemption and pro-mortgagor principles.

A **security deed** is a security instrument by which the owner of the property conveys legal title straight to the lender, instead of to a third party, as security for the repayment of the debt. The lender can sell the property to satisfy the debt if the debt is not paid.

A mortgage is an interest in land, and as such, it needs to be in writing in order to satisfy the Statute of Frauds and be enforceable. A mortgage must have the following requirements:

- The names of the parties
- Words of conveyance or grant
- Valid description of the property being pledged
- Proper execution and attestation
- Effective delivery to the lender

A mortgage is entered into by the **mortgagor** and the **mortgagee**. The mortgagor is the owner of the property and the debtor. The mortgagee is the lender. A mortgage is given by the mortgagor to the mortgagee.

The mortgage must describe in words and figures the nature of the debt that is being secured by the real property. The date that the mortgage is due must also be specified in the mortgage. Any land or interest in land that can usually be conveyed by a deed can also be conveyed by way of a mortgage. The real property described in a mortgage must be described with the same precision as it would be in a deed.

When a person or entity acquires title in a piece of property for the purpose of evidencing a security interest rather than with the intention of transferring title, this type of mortgage is known as an **equitable mortgage**. Some jurisdictions require other documents to evidence an equitable mortgage. Also, an equitable mortgage, if proved, may be enforceable without a writing.

default
The omission of or failure to perform a legal or contractual duty.

deed of trust
An instrument in use in some states, taking the place of and serving the uses of a mortgage, by which the legal title to real property is placed in one or more trustees until the grantor repays a loan, to secure the payment of a sum of money or the performance of other conditions.

trustee
Person holding property in trust.

security deed
A legal document that conveys title to the lender in order to secure a debt.

mortgagor
One who, having all or some part of title to property, by written instrument pledges that property for some particular purpose, such as security for a debt.

mortgagee
A person that takes, holds, or receives a mortgage.

equitable mortgage
An agreement to post certain property as security before the security agreement is formalized.

 LEGAL RESEARCH MAXIM

Our culture repeats a common, widely used misnomer among most homeowners by stating that, "they," the homeowners have a mortgage. This is incorrect. The homeowner has a loan and the lending institution has the mortgage.

assignable
Legally capable of being transferred or negotiated.

Mortgages are **assignable**. A person who is assigned the mortgage may exercise any and all of the rights and powers that are contained in the mortgage. A transfer of the mortgage will convey both the real property and the secured debt that is evidenced by the note. Most mortgages are assignable by language of assignment that is included in the mortgage, or by a separate document that is signed by the lender who is allowing for the assignment. Once it is signed, the document is recorded with the county recorder where the property is located.

Some mortgages include a phrase called the "due on sale" provision. A "due on sale" provision bars the sale of the real property without first obtaining the mortgagee's consent. A sale of the property that violates this provision is considered to be a default of the mortgage. The mortgagee can then seek legal remedies against the mortgagor as a result of this violation.

If a mortgagor wishes to transfer the property, he may do so even if the property is encumbered by a mortgage. The person to whom the property is transferred acquires the property either subject to the mortgage or by assuming the mortgage that exists on the property. A person who acquires the real property subject to a mortgage does not have personal liability for repayment of the debt. The person who acquires the property will make the loan payments in order to protect the property from any legal remedies as a result of default; however, the new owner cannot be sued to recover on the debt. The transferor remains liable for the debt. If the transferor fails to pay or otherwise causes the debt to be in default, the transferee could lose the property. A sale of the real property does not release the original mortgagor from liability, nor does it cause the new owner to be liable for the debt.

When a person acquires real property and assumes the mortgage, the transferee now becomes personally liable for the debt. If the loan is in default, the lender can seek legal remedies against the new owner of the real property, who has assumed the debt, and sue the original mortgagor. In order to effectuate a transfer of property that assumes the mortgage, there must be a writing stating that the transferee intends to assume the mortgage, and there must be another document evidencing the assumption of the mortgage.

A mortgage debt is released by full payment of the debt. However, full payment of the debt does not release the mortgage of record. In order to release the mortgage of record, the mortgagee has to file a cancellation or satisfaction of mortgage with the office of the county recorder where the mortgage was been recorded. Once the cancellation or satisfaction of the mortgage has been recorded, then the mortgage of record has been released.

YOU BE THE JUDGE

Mary and Brad are a young couple who want to buy a house. They locate a small house in Anytown. The house is perfect, and they believe that it will be good place for them to start their lives together. They go to USA Bank to borrow money to finance the purchase of the house. Mary and Brad have 10 percent of the $100,000 purchase price of the house for a down payment. They need to finance the remaining 90 percent in order to complete the purchase. USA Bank agrees to finance the purchase. To ensure that USA Bank will not lose the money in the process for the purchase, the bank insists that Mary and Brad give the bank a $90,000 mortgage on the house. Mary and Brad agree. The couple lives in the house for three years, and now Mary is expecting their first child. They realize that the house will now be too small for a family. They want to purchase a larger home. Mary's mother, Margaret, is a widow and wants a smaller home. Mary and Brad sell their home to Margaret. Margaret agrees to assume the mortgage so that she can buy the property for a lower purchase price. Margaret fails to make the payments on the house, and the loan defaults. Whom can the lender sue to recover the money still outstanding on the debt?

SECOND MORTGAGE LOANS

It is possible to obtain more than one mortgage on real property. Unless expressly prohibited by the terms of the mortgage, a borrower can obtain two or more mortgages on the same piece of real property. A borrower can mortgage the property as many times as a lender is willing to take a security interest in the property. However, a lender who makes a second mortgage loan on the property is exposed to some risk. If the first mortgage goes into default and is foreclosed, the second mortgage will be terminated at the foreclosure sale. However, in an attempt to protect its interest in the property, the second mortgage lender will oftentimes receive an **estoppel certificate** from the first mortgage lender. An estoppel certificate states that the lender of the first mortgage will not foreclose on the loan without first giving notice of default to the holder of the second mortgage. The notice enables the second mortgage lender to have time to try to have the default cured. If the default is cured, then the second mortgage lender's interest in the property will remain protected.

For further protection, the second mortgage lender will also want to state in the mortgage that any default under any prior mortgage shall constitute a default under the terms of the second mortgage. The second mortgage lender protects its interest in the property by curing any defaults under a prior mortgage and adding the cost of curing to the debt secured by the second mortgage. The lender of a second mortgage will take any excess proceeds that may be generated from the foreclosure and sale of a prior mortgage in order to pay off or pay down what is due on the second mortgage. A second mortgage lender can also seek legal remedies should its loan be in default, without waiting for the first mortgage lender to bring such actions.

estoppel certificate
A signed statement by a party, such as a tenant or a mortgagee, certifying for the benefit of another party that a certain statement of facts is correct as of the date of the statement.

THE ACCELERATION CLAUSE

Nearly all modern mortgages include acceleration clauses. An **acceleration clause** gives the mortgagee, in case of a default by the mortgagor, the right to declare the entire mortgage debt due and payable. Acceleration can occur not only after a failure to make timely payments, but also because of failure to comply with other covenants included within the mortgage. There is no general legal requirement of notice of default before acceleration can take place; however, most mortgagees will give a mortgagor in default a notice of intent to accelerate. If a mortgagee fails to accelerate a

acceleration clause
A loan agreement provision that requires the debtor to pay off the balance sooner than the due date if some specified event occurs.

PRACTICE TIP

The Fannie Mae–Freddie Mac residential mortgage form limits the acceleration process. It requires both a detailed mailed notice and a thirty-day grace period as a condition precedent to acceleration. It also gives the mortgagee the right to defeat acceleration, up until five days before the foreclosure, by payment. Because most lenders like to keep the option of selling their mortgages to secondary entities, they are likely to use the Fannie Mae–Freddie Mac form. Fannie Mae is a private, shareholder-owned company that works to make money available for Americans trying to buy homes. It does not lend money directly to home buyers, but works with lenders to ensure that mortgage funds are available for prospective homebuyers. Fannie Mae was created by Congress in 1938 to assist the struggling housing market during the Depression. Like Fannie Mae, Freddie Mac is a stockholder-owned corporation created by Congress in 1970 to create an uninterrupted flow of money to mortgage lenders in support of both home ownership and rental housing. Freddie Mac purchases mortgages from lenders and packages them into securities before selling them to investors. The ultimate goal of Freddie Mac is to provide both homeowners and renters with lower housing costs and better opportunities for home financing.

mortgage debt upon the first default, it does not serve as a waiver of a right to fore-close because of a later default. However, the right to accelerate may be defeated when late payments have been routinely accepted by the mortgagee. Failure to provide an acceleration clause in the mortgage can have disastrous consequences for the mort-gagee. The mortgagee will have to either wait for all installments to come due and then foreclose for the entire amount or foreclose based on the mortgagor's default on one or more installments.

FORECLOSURE

foreclosure
A legal proceeding to terminate a mortgagor's interest in property, instituted by the lender either to gain title or to force a sale to satisfy the unpaid debt secured by the property.

Foreclosure is a process by which the real property conveyed in the mortgage may be sold and the sale proceeds used to pay the debt. Foreclosure is instituted when the borrower fails to pay the loan on the note or fails to perform some other obligation on the mortgage that is secured by the property, so that the mortgage goes into default. Some of the ways that a borrower can default on a mortgage other than failing to pay the debt are failure to pay taxes, failure to insure the property, selling the property without the permission of the mortgagee, and failure to keep the property in good repair. Any of these events could lead a mortgage lender to foreclose on the property, as they jeopardize the security interest that the lender has on the property.

Strict Foreclosure

Strict foreclosure is a rarely used procedure that gives the mortgagee title to the mort-gaged property. Title is passed without a sale occurring first. It passes automatically when a defaulting mortgagor does not pay the mortgage debt within a period of time set out by the court.

Judicial Foreclosure

A judicial foreclosure is a legal proceeding. The mortgage lender can request a court to order a foreclosure sale of the property. The mortgagee will file a complaint against the debtor alleging that there is a debt owed and that the debt is in default. The mortgagee will have to demonstrate that the debt is secured by the real property stated in a mortgage. The lender will ask the court to grant relief by ordering that the prop-erty be sold in order to pay the debt. The debtor is given an opportunity to answer or respond to the complaint filed by the creditor. A hearing is held to decide if suf-ficient evidence exists to determine if the foreclosure should occur. If the court grants the creditor the right to foreclose, the court will then order the property be sold. The sale is typically conducted by a public official and often occurs on the courthouse steps at a date after the court order. The sale is a public sale. Notice of the sale must be given to the public, usually via newspaper advertisement. After the sale has been held and a buyer established, the sale will then be reported back to the court for approval. If the court approves the sale, it will be final. If the foreclosure sale does not yield the full amount of the debt due, a deficiency judgment may be entered against the debtor for the unpaid balance of the debt.

 SPOT THE ISSUE

After Andy defaults on his mortgage, judicial foreclosure takes place. After notice of the sale is given to the public, a public sale takes place. The property sells for $50,000. Andy still owes $57,000 on the mortgage. What happens next?

Foreclosure by Advertisement

A foreclosure by advertisement is a nonjudicial foreclosure right that is given to the mortgage holder in the mortgage. In a foreclosure by advertisement, the mortgage lender is given the right to sell the property without a court order, provided that the mortgage lender places a notice of the foreclosure sale for a period of time that is dictated by state statute. After the proper notice period, the mortgage lender will conduct a nonjudicial, but public, sale of the real property similar to the one conducted for a judicial foreclosure.

Effect of a Foreclosure Sale

A foreclosure sale has the effect of terminating all ownership rights of the debtor in the real property. It also terminates any claims that any subsequent encumbrances have in or on the property. Any encumbrance, mortgage, easement, etc., that has been created after the date of the mortgage that is being foreclosed will be terminated at the foreclosure sale.

The money received as a result of a foreclosure sale is used to pay the debt as well as to cover the expenses of the sale. If there is any excess money after the foreclosed debt and expenses are paid, then this money will first go to any junior mortgage holders. If there is any excess money after the junior mortgage holders have been paid, then this money will go to the debtor.

RESEARCH THIS

Foreclosure sales are governed by state law. It is important to know the processes involved in a foreclosure sale when you are working in real property law. Certain statutory waiting periods, notice requirements, and documentation requirements must be fulfilled in order to effectuate a valid foreclosure sale. Research your state laws in order to determine how a foreclosure proceeding works in your jurisdiction.

REDEMPTION

Starting in seventeenth-century England, mortgagors who failed to satisfy a mortgage debt were frequently given the opportunity to redeem the land by payment of the mortgage debt if they produced both the principal and the interest owed within a reasonable time. The right to **redemption** was then adopted by American courts. Many American states also have statutory redemption legislation in place. Such legislation allows a mortgagor to redeem property after a foreclosure sale within various lengths of time. The difference between equity redemption and statutory redemption is that equity redemption

redemption
The act or instance of reclaiming or regaining possession by paying a specific price; the payment of a defaulted mortgage debt by a borrower who does not want to lose the property.

CASE FACT PATTERN

Susie had missed her monthly mortgage payments for six months in a row. The bank gave her numerous chances to pay the amount owed. After the six months of nonpayment, the bank made moves to foreclose on the property A date had been set by the courts for a foreclosure sale in two weeks, to be held on April 1st.

On March 27th of that year, Susie won the lottery and received $500,000. She met with the court, paid the amount owed to her bank, and was able to keep her home. Generally, banks do not like foreclosures, as banks are in the business of money, not real property. Banks and lending institutions will foreclose on a homeowner, but usually try to give the mortgagor a number of chances to pay the amount owed before the date of the foreclosure sale.

allows the mortgagor to redeem until the foreclosure sale occurs, while statutory redemption will generally only take place after a valid foreclosure.

OTHER MORTGAGE REMEDIES

Mortgagee in Possession

If the debt goes into default, most mortgages allow the mortgage lender the right to take possession of the property. The right to take possession of the property can prevent the property from being destroyed or damaged, or it may enable the mortgage holder to obtain payment on the debt if the real property is income-producing, such as an apartment building from which rents can be collected.

Receivership

receiver
A third party that is appointed by the court to take possession of the real property and take care of the real property in the event of a default on the mortgage.

A **receiver** is a third party that is appointed by the court in order to take possession of the property. A receiver is responsible for taking care of the property, collecting rents and income generated from the property, and ensuring that any money collected from the property is applied to the debt or to the expense associated with taking care of the property.

Waiver

Once the mortgagees receive notice that a default has occurred on the mortgage, they must take action. If the mortgagees do not act promptly to exercise any remedies available to them or if the mortgagees act in a way that would lead the debtors to believe that being in default is acceptable, the mortgagees may waive their rights to seek remedies against the debtors. By way of their actions, the mortgagees can waive their right to seek legal redress as a result of the debtors' being in default.

DEFENSE TO FORECLOSURE

Injunction

A debtor has a right to go to court and seek an injunction if the debtor has knowledge or belief that the foreclosure is not justified. An injunction will stop any foreclosure proceedings until such time as the matter can be heard in court and a final determination made.

Conversion

conversion
An overt act to deprive the owner of possession of personal property with no intention of returning the property, thereby causing injury or harm.

If a person or entity forecloses on real property without the legal right to do so, then she may have committed **conversion**. A debtor can sue for conversion and recover not only actual damages that he incurred, but also **punitive damages** from the foreclosing lender as a result of her actions.

Bankruptcy

punitive damages
An amount of money awarded to a nonbreaching party that is not based on the actual losses incurred by that party, but as a punishment to the breaching party for the commission of an intentional wrong.

A debtor can seek relief from a foreclosure sale by instituting bankruptcy proceedings. Once a bankruptcy petition is filed with the court, an automatic stay of all litigation against the debtor occurs, by operation of bankruptcy laws. Any efforts to collect debts or enforce liens against the debtor's property, including foreclosure sales, is stopped until the bankruptcy proceeding can be concluded. The bankruptcy proceeding may enable a debtor to reorganize and pay off debt, may allow her to reaffirm the mortgage and retain the property, or it may just buy the debtor time to make plans for her future.

EYE ON ETHICS

In real estate transactions, legal assistants are exposed to very personal and confidential information concerning a client. Such information can include their financial status, marital status, or legal status. Since the legal assistant works under the supervision of an attorney, all ethical and professional codes concerning confidentiality of client information are also applicable to the legal assistant. It is very important to remember to keep client information confidential and to guard against any unauthorized releases of such information.

SURF'S UP

The Internet provides many resources on mortgages. Some of the following Web sites offer information on mortgages:
www.mortgage101.com
www.mortgage.com
www.fanniemae.com
www.mbaa.org
www.mortgageit.com
www.hrblockcom

Summary

A promissory note is a written instrument that documents a transaction in which a loan of money is made from one party to another. It is a promise by one party to pay money to another party. The person who promises to pay the money is known as the payor, and the person to whom the payor promises to repay the loan is known as the payee. Typically, a promissory note is in writing and signed by the payor. The promissory note contains the terms of the loan, the repayment schedule, the interest rate, and the lending institution's place of address where the payments are to be made. It contains a promise to pay an amount of money within a period of time, by a deadline, or on demand. The note is then kept by the payee as evidence of the loan and the repayment agreement.

Sometimes, a lender may require that a person other than the payor be held responsible for paying the debt should the payor fail to pay. The mortgage lender may require a person other than the debtor to guarantee the payment of the debtor's note. This is known as a guaranty. The guaranty gives the lender the right to sue the person guaranteeing the loan (the guarantor) as well as the payor if payment is not made on the note. The lender has the right to recover the debt from the guarantor.

Typically, when a promissory note is made on real property, it is secured by an instrument that connects the promissory note to the real property. Requirements vary among states, but security instruments are typically a mortgage, a deed of trust, or a security deed. The main purpose of the security instrument is to convey real property as collateral for the repayment of the debt as stated in the note.

A mortgage is a security interest given to the lender by the payor to guarantee the repayment of a loan. In other words, the payor is purchasing the property and requires financing from the lender in order to do so. To secure the promissory note, the lender will require the payor to execute another document, called a mortgage, that gives the lender the right to attach the property and sell it should the payor default on the loan. A mortgage creates an encumbrance on the property. However, a mortgage does not affect legal title to the property. Legal title remains with the owner.

Mortgages are assignable. A person who is assigned the mortgage may exercise any and all of the rights and powers that are contained in the mortgage. A transfer of the mortgage will convey both the real property and the secured debt that is evidenced by the note. Most mortgages are assignable by the inclusion of language of assignment in the mortgage, or by a separate document that is signed by the lender who is allowing for the assignment. Once it is signed, the document is recorded with the county recorder where the property is located.

A mortgage debt is released by full payment of the debt. However, full payment of the debt does not release the mortgage of record. In order to release the mortgage of record, the mortgagee has to file a cancellation or satisfaction of mortgage with the office of the county recorder where the mortgage has been recorded. Once the cancellation or satisfaction of the mortgage has been recorded, then the mortgage of record has been released.

Foreclosure is a process by which the real property conveyed in the mortgage may be sold and the sale proceeds used to pay the debt. Foreclosure is instituted when the borrower fails to pay the loan on the note or fails to perform some other obligation on the mortgage that is secured by the property, so that the mortgage goes into default. Some of the ways that a borrower can default on a mortgage other than failing to pay the debt are failure to pay taxes, failure to insure the property, selling the property without the permission of the mortgagee, and failure to keep the property in good repair. Any of these events could lead a mortgage lender to foreclose on the property, as each of them jeopardizes the security interest that the lender has on the property.

A foreclosure sale has the effect of terminating all ownership rights of the debtor in the real property. It also terminates any claims that any subsequent encumbrances have in or on the property. Any encumbrance, mortgage, easement, etc., that has been created after the date of the mortgage that is being foreclosed will be terminated at the foreclosure sale.

Key Terms

Acceleration clause	Mortgage
Assignable	Mortgagee
Collateral	Mortgagor
Conversion	Negotiable
Deed of trust	Payee
Default	Payor
Endorsement	Promissory note
Equitable mortgage	Punitive damages
Estoppel certificate	Receiver
Foreclosure	Redemption
Guarantor	Security deed
Guaranty	Trustee
Joint and several liability	

Review Questions

1. A promissory note is negotiable; what is the importance of the negotiability?
2. What is an endorsement?
3. How many mortgages can be obtained on a parcel of real property?
4. What is the difference between acquiring real property subject to a mortgage and assuming a mortgage?
5. What risk does a second mortgagor face?
6. What is an estoppel certificate, and why is it important?
7. How does bankruptcy affect the foreclosure process?

8. What is the difference between a judicial foreclosure and a foreclosure by advertisement?

9. Why is a waiver important in a default action?

10. What is a trustee?

11. List the requirements for a mortgage.

12. What is conversion, and how is it applicable to a foreclosure?

13. What does it mean that a mortgage is assignable, and how is that different from assuming the mortgage?

14. What is an injunction?

15. What duty does a guarantor have under a guaranty?

Exercises

1. Locate a deed that can be used in your jurisdiction. Prepare the deed for Mary and Brad who are referenced in the section of this chapter titled "You Be the Judge." The deed should be between USA Bank and Mary and Brad Everett. The amount of the mortgage is $150,000. The property address is 193 Elm Street, Anytown, USA 12345. Using the knowledge that you have gained, make sure that every element of the deed is complete, so that it is a valid deed.

2. You are working for a law firm that specializes in real property law. The law firm has as a client a lender that specializes in second mortgages. As you are working on the client's matters, you discover that the first mortgage lender on one of your client's properties is foreclosing on the first mortgage. Should your firm's client be concerned if the first mortgage lender forecloses on the property? If your answer is yes, what steps should your firm's client take in order to protect their interest in the property?

3. As a legal assistant working for a firm that handles real property law, you assist clients in a variety of ways. One of those ways is to prepare documentation for the clients concerning their real property transactions. For example, your supervising attorney has a client known as The Land Company. A lending institution holds a promissory note from The Land Company that is personally guaranteed by the principal shareholder of The Land Company, Mr. Arthur Goodfellow. The note is to be modified to extend the period of time for repayment for five more years. Is there documentation to extend the promissory note that you should prepare for The Land Company?

4. You work for the in-house general counsel of Marvelous Mortgage. Marvelous Mortgage gave Jeremy and Jane Richards a $30,000 second mortgage on their home. Two years later Jeremy and Jane defaulted on both of their mortgages. The mortgage company holding the first mortgage is still owed $62,000. Marvelous Mortgage is still owed $27,000. The foreclosure sale results in the property's being sold for $75,000. Will Marvelous Mortgage recover the $27,000 it is owed? Why or why not?

5. Create a chart that distinguishes a mortgage from a deed of trust.

PORTFOLIO ASSIGNMENT

Visit www.mortgage-investments.com/Real_estate_and_mortgage_Forms/ and download sample forms for your portfolio.

Vocabulary Builders

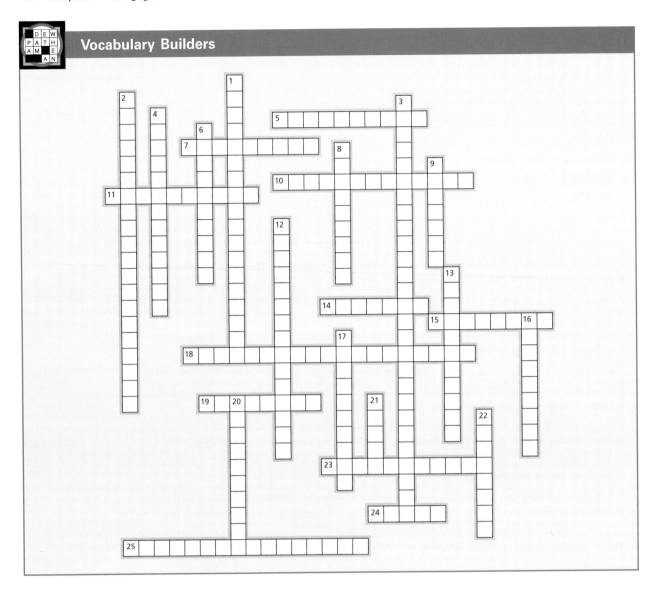

Vocabulary Builders

Instructions

Use the key terms from this chapter to fill in the answers to the crossword puzzle.

NOTE: When the answer is more than one word, leave a blank space between words.

ACROSS

4. the act or instance of reclaiming or regaining possession by paying a specific price; the payment of a defaulted mortgage debt by a borrower who does not want to lose the property.
7. a person that takes, holds, or receives a mortgage.
10. a legal document that conveys title to the lender in order to secure a debt.
11. legally capable of being transferred by endorsement or delivery.
14. person holding property in trust.
15. an interest in land created by a written instrument providing security for the performance of a duty or the payment of a debt.
18. a loan agreement provision that requires the debtor to pay off the balance sooner than the due date if some specified event occurs.
19. a promise to answer for the payment of some debt or perform some duty, in case of the failure of another who is liable.
23. a legal proceeding to terminate a mortgagor's interest in property, instituted by the lender either to gain title or to force a sale to satisfy the unpaid debt secured by the property.
24. the person by whom a bill or note has been or should have been paid.
25. damages that are levied in an effort to punish the wrongdoer for his conduct.

DOWN

1. an agreement to post certain property as security before the security agreement is formalized.
2. a signed statement by a party, such as a tenant or a mortgagee, certifying for the benefit of another party that a certain statement of facts is correct as of the date of the statement.
3. responsibility together and individually.
4. an instrument in use in some states, taking the place of and serving the uses of a mortgage, by which the legal title to real property is placed in one or more trustees until the grantor repays a loan, to secure the payment of a sum of money or the performance of other conditions.
6. property that is pledged as security for the satisfaction of a debt.
8. one who, having all or some part of title to property, by written instrument pledges that property for some particular purpose, such as security for a debt.
9. the omission of or failure to perform a legal or contractual duty.
12. a promise or engagement, in writing, to pay a specified sum at a time therein stated, or on demand, or at sight, to a person therein named, or to his order, or bearer.
13. the act of a payee of a negotiable instrument, in writing her name upon the back of the instrument, with or without further or qualifying words, whereby the property in the same is assigned and transferred to another.
16. one who makes a guaranty.
17. an unauthorized assumption and exercise of the right of ownership over goods or personal chattels belonging to another, to the alteration of their condition or the exclusion of the owner's rights.
20. legally capable of being transferred or negotiated.
21. the person in whose favor a bill of exchange, promissory note, or check is made or dawn.
22. a third party who is appointed by the court to take possession of the real property and take care of the real property in the event of a default on the mortgage.

United States District Court,

D. Hawaii.

Samuel Laureano VIERNES and Imelda Legaspi Viernes, Plaintiffs,

v.

EXECUTIVE MORTGAGE, INC; Argent Mortgage Company, LLC; Ameriquest

Mortgage Company; and Lydia Pascual, as an individual, Defendants.

372 F.Supp.2d 576

No. CIV. 04-00212ACKLEK.

Oct. 13, 2004.

BACKGROUND

Mortgagors brought action against mortgage broker, broker's officer, and other defendants, alleging violation of the federal Consumer Credit Protection Act, fraud, intentional infliction of emotional distress, deceptive and unfair trade practices, and breach of fiduciary duty. Mortgage broker defendants moved for summary judgment on federal claim and for **dismissal of state law claims.**

Holdings: The District Court, Kay, J., held that:

(1) mortgage broker and officer were not "creditors" under Truth-in-Lending Act (TILA) and Regulation Z, and

(2) values of economy, convenience, and fairness all favored court's retention of jurisdiction over state law claims against mortgage broker defendants.

Summary judgment motion granted; **dismissal motion denied.**

KAY, District Judge

BACKGROUND

In 2003, Plaintiffs Samuel Laureano Viernes and Imelda Legaspi Viernes sought to refinance the mortgage(s) on their home in Waipahu, Hawaii. Plaintiffs used the services of Defendant Executive Mortgage, Inc. ("Executive Mortgage").

Defendant Argent Mortgage Company, LLC ("Argent-Mortgage") approved Plaintiffs' mortgage application; Plaintiffs signed mortgage papers to that effect, naming Argent Mortgage as the lender. Plaintiffs allege that Executive Mortgage made misrepresentations regarding the mortgage Plaintiffs were receiving from Argent Mortgage, and allege that required loan disclosures were not properly made to Plaintiffs. Plaintiffs subsequently sought to cancel the mortgage with Argent Mortgage but apparently their request was disallowed.

On April 2, 2004, Plaintiffs filed a Complaint against Executive Mortgage, Argent Mortgage, and Ameriquest Mortgage Company, alleging (1) violation of the federal Consumer Credit Protection Act, (2) fraud, (3) intentional infliction of emotional distress, (4) deceptive and unfair trade practices, (5) breach of fiduciary duty, and (6) punitive damages.

On August 6, 2004, Defendants filed a Motion for Summary Judgment and to Dismiss, seeking summary judgment on the federal Consumer Credit Protection Act claim and dismissal of all remaining claims. On September 20, 2004,

Plaintiffs filed an Opposition. On October 1, 2004, Defendants filed a Reply to the Opposition. Plaintiffs and Defendants also filed concise statements of fact. On September 24, 2004, Defendants Argent Mortgage and Ameriquest Mortgage filed a statement of no position as to the Motion. A hearing was held on October 12, 2004.

Defendants Argent Mortgage and Ameriquest Mortgage take "no position" on the motion for summary judgment and dismissal. Argent Mortgage and Ameriquest Mortgage stated at the hearing on October 12, 2004 that they have reached a settlement with Plaintiffs but that Plaintiffs have attempted to repudiate the agreement. These Defendants also stated that they intend to file a motion to enforce the settlement agreement. Should it be determined that there is no settlement, these Defendants have indicated that they will move to assert cross-claims for indemnity and contribution against Executive Mortgage.

[Text omitted]

DISCUSSION

I. Motion for Summary Judgment on TILA Issues

The Truth-in-Lending Act ("TILA"), which is contained in Title I of the Consumer Credit Protection Act, as amended (15 U.S.C. § 1601, et seq.), is intended to assure a meaningful disclosure of credit terms so that consumers can compare more readily various available terms and avoid the uninformed use of credit. 15 U.S.C. § 1601(a). TILA requires that creditors disclose to borrowers specific information, including finance charges, annual percentage rate, and the right to rescind a transaction. See, e.g., 15 U.S.C. §§ 1635, 1638. Regulation Z, 12 C.F.R. Part 226, is issued by the Board of Governors of the Federal Reserve System to implement TILA. See 12 C.F.R. § 226.1(a).

Defendants seek summary judgment on the federal claim made under TILA on following grounds: (1) Executive Mortgage and Ms. Pascual are not "creditors" within the meaning of TILA; (2) Executive Mortgage and Ms. Pascual did not violate TILA; and (3) Executive Mortgage and Ms. Pascual did not wrongfully dishonor Plaintiffs' attempted rescission.

A. Definition of "Creditor"

The parties agree that the disclosure and other requirements of TILA apply only to "creditors:

The term "creditor" refers only to a person who both (1) regularly extends, whether in connection with loans, sales of property or services, or otherwise, consumer credit which is payable by agreement in more than four installments or for which the payment of a finance charge is or may be required, and (2) is the person to whom the debt arising from the consumer credit transaction is initially payable on the face of the evidence of indebtedness or, if there is no such evidence of indebtedness, by agreement. . . .

Regulation Z, which implements TILA, defines "creditor" as:

A person (A) who regularly extends consumer credit that is subject to a finance charge or is payable by written agreement in more than 4 installments (not including a downpayment), and (B) to whom the obligation is initially payable, either on the face of the note or contract, or by agreement when there is no note or contract.

The parties agree that Defendants Executive Mortgage (which is a mortgage broker) and Ms. Pascual (who is an officer and shareholder of Executive Mortgage) do not qualify as creditors under this two part definition.

However, Plaintiffs argue that an independent definition of "creditor" is contained in the last sentence of the statutory provision defining the term, 15 U.S.C. § 1602(f). Defendants argue that sentence does not create an independent definition of "creditor" separate from the two-part definition described above.

The last sentence of 15 U.S.C. § 1602(f) states:

Any person who originates 2 or more mortgages referred to in subsection (aa) of this section in any 12-month period or any person who originates 1 or more such mortgages through a mortgage broker shall be considered to be a creditor for purposes of this subchapter.

15 U.S.C. § 1602(aa)(1) states:

A mortgage referred to in this subsection means a consumer credit transaction that is secured by the consumer's principal dwelling, other than a residential mortgage transaction, a reverse mortgage transaction, or a transaction under an open end credit plan, if (A) the annual percentage rate at consummation of the transaction will exceed by more than 10 percentage points the yield on Treasury securities having comparable periods of maturity . . . . or (B) the total points and fees payable by the consumer at or before closing will exceed the greater of: (i) 8 percent of the total loan amount; or (ii) $400.

Regulation Z, discussed above and issued by the Board of Governors of the Federal Reserve System to implement TILA, explains this sentence in a footnote to the definition of "creditor":

A person regularly extends consumer credit only if it extended credit (other than credit subject to the requirements of § 226.32) more than 25 times (or more than 5 times for transactions secured by a dwelling) in the preceding calendar year. If a person did not meet these numerical standards in the preceding calendar year, the numerical standards shall be applied to the current calendar year. A person regularly extends consumer credit if, in any 12-month period, the person originates more than one credit extension that is subject to the requirements of § 226.32 or one or more such credit extensions through a mortgage broker.

On its face, Regulation Z makes clear that the language contained in the last sentence of § 1602(f) does not create an independent definition of a "creditor." Rather, as explained in footnote 3 of the regulation, the last sentence of § 1602(f) modifies the two part definition contained in § 1602(f), so that to be a "creditor," one must meet the two part test of (1) regularly extending consumer credit and (2) being the person to whom the obligation is initially payable; but a person can be considered to "regularly extend consumer credit" under part 1 of the two-part test "if" it does the things described in the last sentence of § 1602(f). 12 C.F.R. § 226.2(a)(17)(i) Other courts have implicitly reached this same conclusion that the last sentence of § 1602(f) does not create an independent basis for meeting the definition of "creditor." See, e.g., *Robey-Harcourt v. Bencorp Financial Co., Inc.*, 326 F.3d 1140, 1142 (10th Cir.2003) (applying the 2-part definition to determine that a mortgage broker is not a "creditor" under TILA and Regulation Z); *Noel v. Fleet Finance, Inc.*, 971 F.Supp. 1102, 1109 (E.D.Mich.1997) (applying the 2-part definition to determine that two parties were creditors but third party was mortgage broker and therefore not a creditor under the 2-part definition); see also A.S. Pratt & Sons, Truth-in-Lending Manual ¶ 1.04[23] at 19, Author's Note (2004) ("The last sentence of the statute quite clearly was not intended to create another category of creditors."). But see *Anderson v. Wells Fargo Home Mortgage, Inc.*, 259 F.Supp.2d 1143, 1149 (W.D.Wash.2003) (finding that last sentence of § 1602(f) is a stand-alone definition, but that its meaning is not clear from the statutory language; leaving for trial the question of applicability of the provision).

This Court does not consider subsections (ii), (iii), or (iv) of the definition of creditor contained in Regulation Z, 12 C.F.R. § 226.2(a)(17). This Court does not reach the issue of whether those subsections or any additional sentences contained in 15 U.S.C. § 1602(f) (that are not discussed in this decision) may contain additional independent tests for a "creditor," because those provisions were not raised by the parties and are inapplicable to the instant case.

The Federal Reserve Board Official Staff Interpretations of Regulation Z support this conclusion by making clear that both parts of the two-part test must be met before reaching footnote 3 of Section 226.2(a)(17): the test for a "creditor" under § 226.2(a)(17)(i) "is composed of 2 requirements, both of which must be met in order for a particular credit extension to be subject to the regulation and for the credit extension to count towards satisfaction of the numerical tests mentioned in footnote 3 to § 226.2(a)(17)." See Official Staff Interpretations, 12 C.F.R. Pt. 226, Supp. I, at § 226.2(a)(17). The Supreme Court has stated that such Federal Reserve Board staff opinions construing TILA and Regulation Z should be treated as dispositive unless demonstrably irrational. See *Ford Motor Credit Co. v. Milhollin*, 444 U.S. 555, 565-568, 100 S.Ct. 790, 63 L.Ed.2d 22 (1980).

Accordingly, the Court finds that the last sentence of 15 U.S.C. § 1602(f) does not create an independent definition of "creditor" under TILA. The Court finds that Defendants Executive Mortgage and Ms. Pascual are not "creditors" under TILA and Regulation Z. Plaintiffs do not contest that Defendants do not meet the two-part test to be "creditors." Moreover, the affidavits and other evidence do not present an issue of material fact as to whether the Defendants are creditors: Ms. Pascual's declaration states that neither Executive Mortgage nor Ms. Pascual extend credit and neither are the person to whom Plaintiffs' obligation is payable; Plaintiffs' declarations do not allege that Defendants extended them credit or are the persons to whom the loan obligation is payable; and the exhibits provided by Defendants name Argent Mortgage, not Defendants Executive

Mortgage or Ms. Pascual, as the lender to whom Plaintiff's obligation is payable.

B. Alleged Violation of TILA

Since the Court has determined that Defendants Executive Mortgage and Ms. Pascual are not "creditors" for purposes of TILA, and the parties agree that the disclosure and other requirements of TILA are only applicable to creditors, FN11 the disclosure and other requirements of TILA are not applicable to Defendants Executive Mortgage and Ms. Pascual. Therefore, the Court need not address the other arguments raised regarding whether these Defendants violated the disclosure or other requirements of TILA. Accordingly, Defendants Executive Mortgage and Ms. Pascual's Motion for Summary Judgment on the federal TILA claim is GRANTED.

II. Motion to Dismiss Remaining Claims

The remaining claims against Defendants Executive Mortgage and Ms. Pascual are state law claims for fraud, intention infliction of emotional distress, deceptive and unfair trade practices, breach of fiduciary duty, and punitive damages. Defendants Executive Mortgage and Ms. Pascual ask the Court to decline to exercise supplemental jurisdiction over the remaining state law claims. A district court may decline to exercise supplemental jurisdiction over a claim where it has dismissed all claims over which it has original jurisdiction. 28 U.S.C. § 1367(c). The original subject matter jurisdiction in this case is based on the federal TILA claims.

Although there are no remaining federal claims against Defendants Executive Mortgage and Ms. Pascual, there are remaining federal TILA claims against Defendants Argent Mortgage and Ameriquest Mortgage. Defendants Argent Mortgage and Ameriquest Mortgage have indicated that while they believe they have reached a settlement agreement with Plaintiffs, Plaintiffs have attempted to repudiate that settlement and a motion to enforce the settlement will be filed by these Defendants. Defendants Argent Mortgage and Ameriquest Mortgage also indicate that, should it be determined that there is no settlement, they will move to assert cross-claims for indemnity and contribution against Defendants Executive Mortgage and Ms. Pascual. Argent Mortgage and Ameriquest Mortgage's Statement of Position at ¶

At this time, the federal TILA claims against Defendants Argent Mortgage and Ameriquest Mortgage have not been dismissed, and no motion or stipulation to dismiss has been filed with the Court. Because this Court has original jurisdiction over a remaining federal claim that involves the same nucleus of facts and case or controversy, this Court will exercise its supplemental jurisdiction over the remaining state law claims at this time. The values of economy, convenience, and fairness all favor this Court's retention of jurisdiction in this circumstance. See *Executive Software N. Am. Inc. v. United States Dist. Ct.*, 24 F.3d 1545, 1557 (9th Cir.1994); see also Matsuda v. Wada, 128 F.Supp.2d 659, 671 (D.Haw.2000).

Accordingly, the Court DENIES Defendants Executive Mortgage and Ms. Pascual's motion to dismiss the remaining state law claims at this time. Should the federal cause of action against Defendants Argent Mortgage and Ameriquest Mortgage be dismissed before trial, whether through settlement or otherwise, the Court will permit Defendants Executive Mortgage and Ms. Pascual to bring a renewed the motion to dismiss the remaining state law claims under 28 U.S.C. § 1367.

CONCLUSION

In summary, the Court finds that the last sentence of 15 U.S.C. § 1602(f) does not create an independent definition of "creditor" under TILA. Under the two-part definition of "creditor" contained in § 1602(f) and Regulation Z, Defendants Executive Mortgage and Ms. Pascual are not creditors for purposes of the TILA. Moreover, Plaintiffs have not raised a material question of fact on this issue. Accordingly, the Court GRANTS summary judgment for Defendants Executive Mortgage and Ms. Pascual on the TILA claim.

At this time, the Court DENIES Defendants Executive Mortgage and Ms. Pascual's motion to dismiss the remaining state law claims. Because there is a remaining federal TILA claim against Defendants Argent Mortgage and Ameriquest Mortgage in this case, involving the same facts and case or controversy as the remaining state law claims, this Court will exercise supplemental jurisdiction over the remaining state law claims. However, should the federal cause of action against Defendants Argent Mortgage and Ameriquest Mortgage be dismissed before trial, the Court will permit Defendants Executive Mortgage and Ms. Pascual to bring a renewed motion to dismiss the remaining state law claims.

IT IS SO ORDERED.

[Footnotes omitted]

Source: Reprinted with permission from Westlaw. VIERNES v. EXECUTIVE MORTGAGE, INC 372 F.Supp.2d 576.

Chapter 10

Real Estate Finance

CHAPTER OBJECTIVES

Upon completion of this chapter, you will be able to:

- Identify mortgage loan resources.

- Explain the types of loans.

- Discuss the secondary loan market.

- Understand permanent and construction loans.

The real estate industry operates almost entirely on various methods of financing. The real estate financing industry is big business. Mortgage loans are offered to consumers from a variety of sources. As a legal assistant working in real estate law, it is important that you understand the basics of the mortgage loan.

MORTGAGE RESOURCES

On rare occasions, mortgage loans can be made by private individuals or companies. For the most part, however, mortgage loans are made by lending institutions. The following is a discussion on the various types of lending institutions that are resources for mortgage loans.

Savings and Loan Associations

A **savings and loan association** is a financial institution that specializes in accepting savings deposits and making mortgage loans. In the early history of the savings and loan association, the objective of the association was to encourage savings deposits and investments by ordinary people. In addition to encouraging savings and investment, the savings and loan association also provided loans for big-ticket items such as homes to people who proved to be responsible.

Savings and loan associations lend money for home purchases that are secured by real property. They usually lend money for purchases of real property that are located in the vicinity of the savings and loan association. Since 1933 the federal government has chartered savings and loan associations, although they have not generally been required to be federally chartered. These institutions can also be chartered by a state government. In 1932, the **Federal Home Loan Bank** System (FHLB) was created to oversee the savings and loan associations, with deposits to be insured by the Federal Savings and Loan Insurance Corporation (FSLIC). The FHLB establishes mandatory guidelines for the associations to follow.

savings and loan association
A financial institution—often organized and chartered like a bank—that primarily makes home mortgage loans but also usually maintains checking accounts and provides other banking services; often shortened to S & L.

Federal Home Loan Bank
Government agency, consisting of twelve regional banks owned by savings and homestead associations, that issues bonds and notes to finance the home building and mortgage loans of their member associations.

YOU BE THE JUDGE

Harry and Debbie found a home that they loved and wanted to purchase. They had saved $75,000 at a savings and loan bank and were going to use part of that for a down payment to purchase the home. A day before the down payment was to be made, a major economic crash occurred, leaving Harry and Debbie without their $75,000 and without a solvent bank. Both knew the money was insured, so not all was lost. Harry said that it would take forever to get their money, as it was the government, *as its own insurer*, that would handle these matters. Debbie said that wasn't true, as she thought their savings was insured by a private entity. You be the judge. Who is correct?

deposit insurance
Insurance, created by the Deposit Insurance Act, in which the federal government insures deposits made by consumers in qualifying banking institutions.

The savings and loan institution went through many changes in recent years, primarily due to deregulatory measures instituted in the 1980s by the federal government of the United States. This deregulation enabled the savings and loan associates to offer a wider variety of services than they ever had previously. These services included, but were not limited to, commercial lending, trust services, and non-mortgage consumer lending. The Depository Institutions Deregulation and Monetary Control Act of 1980 began these changes. One of the significant changes was that **deposit insurance** was raised from $40,000 to $100,000. It is believed by many experts that the increase in the deposit insurance coverage encouraged the savings and loan associations to take part in riskier loans than they had offered previously.

In 1982, the Depository Institutions Act gave savings and loan institutions the right to make secured and unsecured loans to a wide range of markets. A secured loan is one that is secured by property or securities, while an unsecured loan is not. The act also allowed developers to own savings and loan associations; in addition, it enabled owners of these institutions to make loans to themselves. Under the Depository Institutions Act, the Federal Home Loan Bank Board (FHLBB) allowed savings and loan associations to print their own money and escape charges of insolvency through the use of "goodwill," whereby customer loyalty and market share were counted as an asset of the institution. As a result, an institution that was technically bankrupt could stave off government seizure.

Federal Deposit Insurance Corporation
An independent governmental agency that insures bank deposits up to a statutory amount per depositor at each participating bank.

As a result of the above, savings and loan associations began to engage in large-scale speculation in real estate. Many of them made bad investments. Financial failure of the institutions became excessive, and over five hundred of them were forced to close their doors during the 1980s. In 1989, the FSLIC went bankrupt. The **Federal Deposit Insurance Corporation**, often called the the FDIC, took over the insurance obligations of the FSLIC. The Resolution Trust Corporation was created to purchase and sell defaulted savings and loan associations. The Office of Thrift Supervision was also established in order to identify savings and loan associations that are having financial difficulties before it is too late.

RESEARCH THIS

The savings and loan problems of the 1980s caused many people to lose their money and rocked the economy. Deregulation of the industry caused many companies to stretch themselves beyond their means. Research the Depository Institutions Act of 1982. What was the purpose of the act? What was it trying to promote? How did it go so wrong?

Mutual Savings Banks

Mutual savings banks are financial institutions that are owned by the depositors. Each depositor has a right to receive net earnings from the bank in proportion to her deposits. Mutual savings banks are located primarily in the northeastern United

States. As stated above, the depositors in a mutual savings bank are the owners, and the "interest" they receive is the result of the bank's success or failure in its lending decisions. Mutual savings banks offer accounts similar to those offered by saving and loan associations. In order to protect depositors, the laws require mutual savings banks to place deposits in high-quality investments. Real estate loans account for two out of every three loan dollars at mutual savings banks. Mutual savings banks are chartered and controlled by state regulatory agencies. Membership in the FDIC is available and optional to these institutions.

Mortgage Banking Companies

A mortgage bank is a state-licensed banking entity that originates and services mortgages. Mortgage banks make loans to consumers. Mortgage companies then typically sell these loans to other lenders and investors. Some mortgage companies may be subsidiaries of depository institutions or their holding companies, but they do not receive money from individual depositors. A mortgage bank uses funds from the **secondary mortgage market** such as Fannie Mae, Freddie Mac, or other large mortgage servicing companies. Mortgage banks require secondary market funds because a mortgage bank is a nondepository institution; that means mortgage banks do not receive income from deposits, as do savings banks. The secondary mortgage market is discussed in greater detail later in the chapter.

secondary mortgage market
Condition that exists as to demand for purchase of second mortgages, generally by financial institutions that use mortgages as part of their investment portfolio.

A mortgage bank can vary in size. Some mortgage banking companies are nationwide. Some may originate a large loan volume exceeding that of a nationwide commercial bank. Unlike a savings bank, a mortgage bank generally specializes only in making mortgage loans. It does not take deposits from customers. A mortgage bank generally operates under the specific banking laws applicable to the state in which it does business.

Commercial Banks

Commercial banks are institutions that accept deposits, make business loans, and offer other similar types of services. Commercial banks have a variety of deposit accounts, such as checking and savings accounts. Commercial banks are primarily concerned with receiving deposits and lending money to businesses. They become members of the Federal Reserve System. Commercial banks earn revenue from a variety of sources, some of which include, but are not limited to, check writing, trust account management fees, investments, loans, and mortgages. Although commercial banks do not generally focus on mortgage lending, commercial banks hold nearly a quarter of all mortgage debts.

commercial bank
A bank that is authorized to receive both demand and time deposits, to take part in trust services, to issue letters of credit, to rent time-deposit boxes, and to provide other related services.

Commercial banks principally make loans for construction and short-term loans for property acquisition. These types of short-term loans are referred to as **bridge loans**. A bridge loan is typically for one or two years. During this time, the borrower will try to secure long-term financing on the property in order to repay the bridge loan. Commercial banks will also make second mortgage loans on the equity of a property.

bridge loan
A one- to two-year loan that enables a borrower to acquire property.

Life Insurance Companies

Life insurance companies administer individual and group annuities. The companies' major nonfinancial source of funds is premium receipts paid by their policyholders. These companies receive substantial investment income from their holdings of tangible and financial assets, primarily corporate and government agency bonds, such as federally backed mortgage loans and corporate equities.

Life insurance companies also engage in mortgage loans. They invest in long-term loans used to finance the acquisition or construction of both commercial and industrial real estate projects.

Credit Unions

credit union
A nonprofit financial institution owned and operated by its members, who operate a cooperative that provides members with financial services, including savings and lending.

A **credit union** is a nonprofit financial institution that is owned and operated entirely by its members. Bringing their money together as savings and by making low-cost loans to each other, they establish a cooperative that provides its members with other services and added benefits. At the heart of a credit union are goals of placing service and members' needs above all else. Credit unions provide financial services for their members, including savings and lending. Large organizations and companies may organize credit unions for their members and employees. To join a credit union, a person ordinarily must belong to a participating organization, such as a college alumni association or labor union. When a person deposits money in a credit union, he becomes a member of the union, because the deposit is considered partial ownership in the credit union.

Pension Funds

The private pension funds sector encompasses all private pension plans, in accordance with Title I of the Employee Retirement Security Act of 1974 (ERISA). It also includes the Federal Employees Retirement System (FERS) Thrift Savings Plan, a supplementary retirement option available to federal employees since 1984. The sector covers both defined benefit plans and defined contribution plans and includes both the retirement funds of nonprofit organizations and the single-employer and multi-employer plans of for-profit firms that are qualified for tax preferences.

Pension funds are funds established by an employer to facilitate and organize the investment of retirement funds contributed by the employer and employees. The pension fund is a common asset pool meant to generate stable growth over the long term and provide pensions for employees when they reach the end of their working years and commence retirement. Pension fund administrators are required by law to make reasonable and prudent investments. These prudent investments include residential and commercial mortgage loans. A portion of pension funds may be allocated to promissory notes or deeds of trust as a way of generating returns for the funds.

Issuers of Mortgage-Backed Bonds

Issuers of mortgage-backed securities are entities established by contractual arrangement to hold assets and to issue debt obligations backed by the assets. The issuers of mortgage-backed bonds are similar to federally related mortgage pools in that they are not actual institutions, but are created for bookkeeping purposes.

The financial assets of the sector are federally related mortgage pool securities and various types of loans, including student and business loans, mortgages, consumer credit (such as automobile loans and credit card receivables), and trade credit. These assets are often referred to as *securitized assets*.

TYPES OF LOANS

Mortgage loans can be divided into two different categories. The first category is conventional and governmental loans. The second category is mortgage loan programs that may be classified as fixed-rate loans, adjustable-rate loans, and any combination of the two.

Conventional Loans

conventional loan
Mortgage loans in which the risk of payment depends on the borrower's ability to pay and the value of the property being used to secure the loan.

Conventional loans are loans in which the risk of payment of the debt on the loan depends on the ability of the borrower to pay the debt. When considering a conventional loan, the lending institution will require an appraisal of the value of the real property that is being used as collateral to secure the loan. In order to determine if the potential borrower is a good risk, the lender will review the potential borrower's credit report, financial statements, and income information.

Typically, a lender of a conventional loan will require that the **loan-to-value ratio** of the real property be lower than might be required by lenders of other types of loans. The lower the loan-to-value or "LTV" ratio, the better the possibility that the loan will be repaid.

Conventional loans are usually divided into two types: conforming and nonconforming. Conforming loans have conditions attached to them that are established by governmental agencies. For example, the maximum amount that could be borrowed for a first mortgage on a conforming loan during 2006 for a one-family home was $417,000. The maximum amount for a second mortgage conforming loan for 2006 was $208,500. The total of the two loans could not exceed the $417,000 cap.

Any loan that exceeds the $417,000 amount is considered a nonconforming loan, also known as a jumbo loan. Because jumbo loans are bought and sold on a much smaller scale, they often have a slightly higher interest rate than conforming loans.

Insured Loans

An **insured loan** is a loan in which a governmental agency or private mortgage insurance company will guarantee the lender that a portion of the loan will be repaid by the agency or company. Governmental agency guarantees usually cover repayment of 60 to 90 percent of the loan, depending on the governmental program under which the loan was originally issued. Insured loans include, but are not limited to, **FHA**, **VA**, **RHS**, and **SBA loans**.

There are many types of mortgage loans. The **fixed-rate mortgage** loan provides that the *interest* rate paid on the monthly mortgage payments remains fixed for the period of the loan. Fixed rate mortgages are available for 40, 30, 25, 20, 15, and 10 years. Typically, the smaller the time period, the lower the interest rate that is assessed on the loan. The most common loan terms are 30 and 15 years. The monthly mortgage payments for the 30-year term would be lower than that of the 15-year term; however, the borrower would be in debt for a longer period of time.

Adjustable-rate mortgages, sometimes called variable-rate mortgages, are loans whose interest rate as well as monthly payments vary over the period of the loan. With this type of mortgage loan, periodic adjustments are made to the interest rate based on changes in a specifically defined index. The particular index used for the

loan-to-value ratio
Ratio of the amount borrowed on a mortgage loan to the value of the real property being used to secure the loan.

insured loan
A loan in which a governmental agency or private mortgage insurance company will guarantee the lender that a portion of the loan will be repaid by the agency or company.

FHA loans
Loans that have been insured in whole or in part by the Federal Housing Administration.

VA loans
Home mortgage loans provided to veterans and their spouses that are guaranteed by the Veterans Administration.

RHS loans
Loans that are guaranteed by the Rural Housing Service.

SBA loans
Loans made by the Small Business Administration to small businesses.

Fixed-rate mortgage
A mortgage that specifies an interest rate that remains fixed for the life of the mortgage, regardless of market conditions.

PRACTICE TIP

Both the Federal Housing Administration (FHA) and the Department of Veterans Affairs (VA) have released guidelines for any loans which they insure or guarantee. These guidelines extend the time that must pass between a default and a foreclosure and also require that the mortgagee allow reinstatement by payment of arrearages.

interest
A charge by a lender to a borrower for the use of money.

adjustable-rate mortgage
A mortgage in which the interest rate is not fixed, but is tied to an index and is periodically adjusted as the rate index moves up or down.

subprime lending
A type of lending in which higher interest rates and higher loan fees are extended to higher-risk borrowers.

equity stripping
A practice that involves providing a loan based on the equity of a property rather than the borrower's ability to repay.

primary market
Lenders who lend money directly to borrowers.

servicing the loan
The collecting of loan payments by one entity for another entity for a fee.

SPOT THE ISSUE

Bob and Bonnie are tired of living in their small cramped apartment and really want to buy a new home. One day they are driving down the street and see that a house they have always admired is for sale. They quickly call the realtor and find out that the sellers are asking $200,000 for the property. The mortgage company reviews Bob and Bonnie's finances and concludes that their small annual income will make it extremely difficult for them to make payments on a $200,000 mortgage. Despite concluding that Bob and Bonnie will likely default, the mortgage company extends the loan, because the house appraises for $250,000.

loan is determined and specified at the time that the loan is originated. Types of indexes that might be used for an adjustable rate mortgage are

- Constant Maturity Treasury
- Treasury Bill
- 12-month Treasury Average
- Certificate of Deposit Index
- 11th District Cost of Funds Index
- Cost of Savings Index
- London Interbank Offering Rates
- Bank Prime Loan
- Fannie Mae's Required Net Yield
- National Average Contract Mortgage Rate

Many other types of mortgage loans and combinations of terms are available to the consumer. The fixed-rate mortgage and the adjustable-rate mortgage are the most common.

There has been enormous growth in **subprime lending** within the mortgage industry in recent years. Subprime lending occurs when higher-risk borrowers are extended credit at higher interest rates or with higher fees. Subprime lending does allow some people who would otherwise not be able to buy a home the opportunity to do so. However, it has also created controversy. The Federal Trade Commission has been involved in investigating claims of abuse by mortgage companies. One type of abuse that may occur in subprime lending situations is **equity stripping**. Equity stripping occurs when a loan is made strictly on the equity of a property rather than on the borrower's ability to repay. This practice often results in the mortgage company's acquiring both the borrower's home and all the equity the borrower had in the home.

SECONDARY MORTGAGE MARKET

The lender who makes a mortgage loan directly to the borrower is known as a primary lender. The **primary market** is made up of lenders who lend money directly to borrowers and lenders who originate loans in order to sell them to investors. Once the mortgage loan is completed in the primary market, it can be bought and sold on the secondary mortgage market.

The secondary mortgage market exists because mortgage loans bear interest. Entities that purchase these loans are entitled to receive the interest the loans generate. Primary lenders will sell mortgage loans in order to generate revenue. After a loan has been sold on the secondary mortgage market, the original lender may continue to collect the payments on the loan from the borrower. The original lender then relays the payments to the investor who purchased the loans. In essence, the original lender acts as a collector for the secondary mortgage purchaser. The original lender will charge the secondary mortgage purchaser a fee for such a service. This relationship is known as **servicing the loan**.

A number of agencies actively participate in the secondary mortgage market by purchasing numerous mortgage loans and packaging them for resale to investors. Some of these agencies are the Federal National Mortgage Association, the Government National Mortgage Association, and the Federal Home Loan Mortgage Corporation.

Federal National Mortgage Association

The Federal National Mortgage Association (FNMA) is a privately owned corporation that is organized for the purpose of providing loans to the secondary mortgage market. The FNMA is also known as **Fannie Mae** and invests primarily in FHA and VA loans. FHA loans have lower down payment requirements and are usually easier to qualify for than conventional mortgage loans. VA loans enable veterans and servicepersons to obtain home loans with favorable loan terms and do not usually require a down payment. It is typically easier to qualify for a VA loan than for a conventional loan.

The FNMA raises money to buy loans by selling government-backed bonds at market interest rates. These bonds are secured in pools of mortgages acquired through FNMA programs.

Fannie Mae
Federal National Mortgage Association, organized for the purpose of investing in FHA and VA loans.

Government National Mortgage Association

The Government National Mortgage Association (GNMA), also known as **Ginnie Mae**, was designed to administer special assistance programs, as well as to work with the FNMA in the secondary mortgage market. Sometimes, when the economy is tight and interest rates are going higher, the FNMA and the GNMA work together in the secondary mortgage market. The FNMA will buy high-risk loans that have a low yield at full market value, and GNMA will guarantee the payments as well as take up the difference between the low yield and current market prices.

Ginnie Mae
Governmental National Mortgage Association, a government corporation organized to administer special assistance programs and to work with the FNMA in the secondary mortgage market.

Federal Home Loan Mortgage Corporation

The Federal Home Loan Mortgage Corporation is also known as **Freddie Mac** As discussed previously, FNMA provides the secondary market for conventional mortgage loans. FNMA is authorized to purchase mortgages, to pool them, and to sell them in the open market. These mortgages operate as securities. Freddie Mac raises most of its capital by selling mortgage-backed securities.

Freddie Mac
Federal Home Loan Mortgage Corporation, designed to purchase and invest in mortgages.

PERMANENT AND CONSTRUCTION LOANS

Most **permanent loans** are long-term loans that finance the acquisition of real property or refinance construction loans on improvements. The payments on a permanent loan are **amortized** over the life of the loan. At the end of the specified loan period, the loan will be paid in full. For example, the last loan payment of a 30-year mortgage will pay off the loan.

A **construction loan** is issued in order to finance construction on improvements on a piece of real property. Construction loans are typically short-term loans that have a term of one year or less. The monthly payments required on a construction loan are interest-only payments. At the end of the term, the entire amount of principal borrowed as well as the agreed-upon interest must be paid in full. Typically, a construction loan is paid off with the proceeds received by securing a permanent loan to pay it off.

permanent loan
A long-term loan that finances the acquisition of real property or refinances a construction loan on improvements.

amortize
To extinguish a debt gradually through incremental payments.

construction loan
A mortgage loan made for the purpose of providing money to construct improvements on real property.

EYE ON ETHICS

Many lending institutions advertise throughout various regions and jurisdictions. It is important to make sure that a lending institution that is conducting business in the jurisdiction is properly licensed to conduct business in that jurisdiction.

SURF'S UP

To learn more about real estate financing, the following Web sites are helpful:

http://www.lendny.com/nymortgagebanker.htm

http://mortgage-x.com.

http://www.fanniemae.com

http://www.ginniemae.gov

http://www.freddiemac.com

LEGAL RESEARCH MAXIM

Paralegals looking for resources pertaining to mortgages and the mortgage industry will find an excellent source at http://www.mortgage101.com.

Usually, a lender will not approve a construction loan unless the borrower has secured a commitment for a permanent loan. Construction loans are characteristically disbursed in installments as phases of the construction improvements are completed. Construction loans are made for the estimated cost of the construction. The lender will inspect the property each time a portion of the construction has been completed. The lender will frequently disburse 90 percent of the loan during construction and keep 10 percent of the loan in case the project manager has underestimated costs.

Summary

A savings and loan association is a financial institution that specializes in accepting savings deposits and making mortgage loans. In the early history of the savings and loan association, the objective of the association was to encourage savings deposits and investments by ordinary people. In addition to encouraging savings and investment, the savings and loan association also provided loans for big-ticket items such as homes to people who proved to be responsible.

Savings and loan associations lend money for home purchases that are secured by real property. They usually lend money for purchases of real property that are located in the vicinity of the savings and loan association. Since 1933 the federal government has chartered savings and loan associations, although they have not generally been required to be federally chartered. These institutions can also be chartered by a state government. In 1932, the Federal Home Loan Bank system (FHLB) was created to oversee the savings and loan associations, with deposits to be insured by the Federal Savings and Loan Insurance Corporation (FSLIC).

Mutual savings banks are financial institutions that are owned by the depositors. Each depositor has a right to receive net earnings from the bank in proportion to his deposits. Mutual savings banks are located primarily in the northeastern United States. As stated above, the depositors in a mutual savings bank are the owners, and the "interest" they receive is the result of the bank's success or failure in its lending decisions. Mutual savings banks offer accounts similar to those offered by saving and loan associations. In order to protect depositors, the laws require mutual savings banks to place deposits in high-quality investments. Real estate loans account for two out of every three loan dollars at mutual savings banks. Mutual savings banks are chartered and controlled by state regulatory agencies. Membership in the FDIC is available and optional to these institutions.

A mortgage bank is a state-licensed banking entity that originates and services mortgages. Mortgage banks make loans to consumers. Mortgage companies then typically sell these loans to other lenders and investors. Some mortgage companies may be subsidiaries of depository institutions or their holding companies, but they do not receive money from individual depositors. A mortgage bank uses funds from the secondary mortgage market, such as Fannie Mae, Freddie Mac, or other large mortgage servicing companies. They require secondary market funds because a mortgage bank is a nondepository institution; that means mortgage banks do not receive income from deposits, as do savings banks.

Commercial banks are institutions that accept deposits, make business loans, and offer other similar types of services. Commercial banks have a variety of deposit accounts, such as checking and savings accounts. Commercial banks are primarily concerned with receiving deposits and lending money to businesses. They become members of the Federal Reserve System. Commercial banks earn revenue from a variety of sources, some of which include, but are not limited to, check writing, trust account management fees, investments, loans, and mortgages.

Conventional loans are loans in which the risk of payment of the debt on the loan depends on the ability of the borrower to pay the debt. When considering a conventional loan, the lending institution will require an appraisal of the value of the real property that is being used as collateral to secure the loan. In order to determine if the potential borrower is a good risk, the lender will review her credit report, financial statements, and income information.

An insured loan is a loan for which a governmental agency or private mortgage insurance company will guarantee the lender that a portion of the loan will be repaid by that agency or company. Governmental agency guarantees usually cover repayment of 60 to 90 percent of the loan, depending on the governmental program under which the loan was originally issued. Insured loans include, but are not limited to, FHA, VA, RHS, and SBA loans.

The fixed-rate mortgage loan provides that the interest rate paid on the monthly mortgage payments remains fixed for the period of the loan. Fixed-rate mortgages are available for 40, 30, 25, 20, 15, and 10 years. Typically, the smaller the time period, the lower the interest rate that is assessed on the loan. The most common loan terms are 30 and 15 years. The monthly mortgage payments for the 30-year term would be lower than those for the 15-year term; however, the borrower would be in debt for a longer period of time.

Adjustable-rate mortgages, sometimes called variable-rate mortgages, are loans whose interest rates as well as monthly payments vary over the period of the loan. With this type of mortgage loan, periodic adjustments are made to the interest rate based on changes in a specifically defined index. The particular index used for the loan is determined and specified at the time that the loan is originated.

The lender who makes a mortgage loan directly to the borrower is known as a primary lender. The primary market is made up of lenders who lend money directly to borrowers and lenders who originate loans in order to sell them to investors. Once the mortgage loan is completed in the primary market, it can be bought and sold on the secondary mortgage market.

Key Terms

Adjustable-rate mortgage
Amortize
Bridge loan
Commercial bank
Construction loan
Conventional loan
Credit union
Deposit insurance
Equity stripping
Fannie Mae
Federal Deposit Insurance Corporation
Federal Home Loan Bank
FHA loans
Fixed-rate mortgage

Freddie Mac
Ginnie Mae
Insured loan
Interest
Loan-to-value ratio
Permanent loan
Primary market
RHS loans
Savings and loan association
SBA loans
Secondary mortgage market
Servicing the loan
Subprime lending
VA loans

Review Questions

1. What is the difference between a conventional loan and an insured loan?
2. What is a loan-to-value ratio, and why is it important?
3. What is a VA loan?
4. List six indexes upon which an adjustable-rate mortgage might be based.
5. What is a fixed-rate mortgage?
6. How do a fixed-rate mortgage and an adjustable-rate mortgage differ?
7. What is a construction loan?
8. What is a permanent loan?
9. What is the secondary mortgage market?
10. What is a primary lender?

Exercises

1. If you have a mortgage loan with an outstanding principal balance of $75,000 and an interest rate of 10.25 percent, calculate what portion of the $710 monthly payment will be interest and what portion will be paid to the principal.
2. Looking in the resource of your choice, find one example of each of the following types of entities. In each case, give the name of the company, the rate charged, and whether or not it is insured.
   a. Savings and loan association
   b. Commercial bank
   c. Life insurance company
   d. Pension plan
3. Look up the requirements for being eligible to acquire a Fannie Mae loan.
4. Where does Freddie Mac raise the capital that allows it to purchase mortgages on the secondary market?
5. Howard and Holly are searching for a bigger house for their growing family. They find a house they believe to be perfect, but their loan application is denied. The mortgage company tells Howard and Holly that the LTV ratio was too high to approve financing. Explain why this ratio is important, and why a high LTV ratio caused Howard and Holly's mortgage application to be denied.
6. If Howard and Holly are subsequently approved for financing, what benefit would a 15-year fixed-rate mortgage have over a 30-year fixed- rate mortgage?
7. Tom and Joan have owned a small home for the past ten years and have considerable equity in it. They now wish to purchase a bigger home for their growing family. They find the perfect new home, but can't secure long-term financing until they sell the smaller home in which they currently reside. Identify and explain a type of loan that would enable Tom and Joan to purchase the bigger home before they sell the one in which they currently reside.

 PORTFOLIO ASSIGNMENT

Research the case cited below and list the issues found, the rules used, the analysis, and the conclusion (IRAC).
Warren v. Government National Mortgage Association 611 F.2d 1229 (8th Cir. 1980).

Vocabulary Builders

Vocabulary Builders

Instructions

Use the key terms from this chapter to fill in the answers to the crossword puzzle.

NOTE: When the answer is more than one word, leave a blank space between words.

ACROSS

3. federal National Mortgage Association, organized for the purpose of investing in FHA and VA loans.
4. a one- to two-year loan that enables a borrower to acquire property.
5. a loan in which a governmental agency or private mortgage insurance company will guarantee the lender that a portion of the loan will be repaid by the agency or company.
12. insurance created by the Deposit Insurance Act where the federal government insures deposits made by consumers in qualifying banking institutions.
13. conditions that exist as to demand for purchase of second mortgages generally by financial institutions that use mortgages as part of their investment portfolio.
14. to extinguish a debt gradually through incremental payments.
15. a charge by a lender to a borrower for the use of money.
16. government agency, consisting of twelve regional banks owned by savings and homestead associations, that issues bonds and notes to finance the home building and mortgage loans of their member associations.

DOWN

1. an independent governmental agency that insures bank deposits up to a statutory amount per depositor at each participating bank.
2. mortgage loans in which the risk of payment depends on the borrower's ability to pay and the value of the property being used to secure the loan.
6. a financial institution often organized and chartered like a bank that primarily makes home mortgage loans. It maintains checking accounts and provides other banking services.
7. one in which the loan that has been insured in whole or in part by the Federal Housing Administration.
8. a type of lending in which higher interest rates and higher loan fees are extended to higher risk borrowers.
9. ratio of the amount borrowed on a mortgage loan to the value of the real property being used to secure the loan.
10. a bank that is authorized to receive both demand and time deposits, to take part in trust services, to issue letters of credit, to rent time-deposit boxes, and to provide other related services.
11. a nonprofit financial institution owned and operated by its members, who operate a cooperative that provides members with financial services, including savings and lending.

Gina ALFEO

v.

Mark T. DINSMORE & another. Andrea J. Kozol.

861 N.E.2d 491

Appeals Court of Massachusetts, Middlesex.

No. 05-P-1678.

Argued Oct. 16, 2006.

Decided Feb. 16, 2007.

BACKGROUND

Failed purchaser brought action against vendors to recover deposit after residential real estate purchase failed to close, and vendors filed counterclaims for fraud and breach of the covenant of good faith and fair dealing. The Superior Court, Middlesex County, Wendie I. Gershengorn, J., granted purchaser's motion for summary judgment, and vendors appealed.

Holdings: The Appeals Court, Katzmann, J., held that:

(1) failed purchaser applied "for a conventional bank or other institutional mortgage loan" as required by agreement, and

(2) purchaser's failure to disclose to vendors that she was simultaneously purchasing another home and seeking mortgage financing for that purchase did not constitute fraud or a breach of the covenant of good faith and fair dealing.

Affirmed.

KATZMANN, J.

BACKGROUND

In late 2002, the plaintiff, Gina Alfeo, and her fiancé were looking to purchase a home in Sudbury. On November 22, 2002, the plaintiff entered into a purchase and sale agreement with third parties respecting a home located on Hudson Road in Sudbury (Hudson Road property), with the closing scheduled for January 15, 2003. To finance the purchase, the plaintiff applied for mortgage financing from Drew Mortgage Associates, Inc. (Drew). Drew is licensed in Massachusetts as a mortgage lender and as a mortgage broker, and is also an approved FHA (Federal Housing Administration) loan correspondent. Drew does its business as follows. Drew closes more than 2,000 residential mortgage loans per year, utilizing a mechanism known as "table funding," which is common in the residential mortgage lending industry. Drew takes loan applications from customers, underwrites loans based on Federal National Mortgage Association and mortgage investor guidelines, and makes credit determinations. At the time of a mortgage closing, Drew sells the mortgage note and mortgage instrument securing the note to the participating mortgage servicer, simultaneously with the provision of the loan amount by the mortgage servicer.

The plaintiff alone was acting as buyer because she had better credit than her fiancé, a self-employed contractor who had credit issues.

By way of background, we note that table funding has been defined as "a settlement at which a loan is funded by a contemporaneous advance of loan funds and an assignment of the loan to the person advancing the funds." 24 C.F.R. § 3500.2(b) (1997). . . .

On December 12, 2002, three weeks after entering the agreement on the Hudson Road property, the plaintiff submitted an offer to purchase a second property, owned by the defendant sellers, located on Horsepond Road in Sudbury (Horsepond Road property). The plaintiff and her fiancé had decided to purchase both homes, apparently intending to improve and sell the Hudson Road property while living in the Horsepond Road property, but they did not inform the defendant sellers of their intent to purchase or apply for financing for two homes. On December 16, 2002, the plaintiff applied for mortgage financing from Drew for the Horsepond Road property, and Drew issued a preapproval letter for the loan, which was provided to the defendant sellers. The preapproval letter, signed by a Drew vice-president, stated that "we have pre-approved you for a mortgage loan . . . based on a purchase price of $365,000." On December 23, 2002, the plaintiff entered into a purchase and sale agreement with the defendant sellers for the Horsepond Road property for $364,500, paying $18,250 as a total deposit held by the sellers' broker, and setting the closing for January 16, 2003 (one day after the scheduled closing on the Hudson Road property). Paragraph 26 of the purchase and sale agreement contained a mortgage contingency clause, which provides as follows:

A Drew employee had informed the plaintiff and her fiancé that she was likely to obtain financing for both properties.

"In order to help finance the acquisition of said premises, the BUYER shall *apply for a conventional bank or other institutional mortgage loan* of $328,500.00 at prevailing rates, terms and conditions. If despite the BUYER's diligent efforts a commitment for such loan cannot be obtained on or before December 31, 2002 the BUYER may terminate this agreement by written notice to the SELLER and/or the Broker(s), as agent(s) for the SELLER, prior to the expiration of such time whereupon any payments made under this agreement shall be forthwith refunded and all obligations of the parties hereto shall cease and this agreement shall be void without recourse by the parties hereto. In no event will the BUYER be deemed to have used diligent efforts to obtain a commitment unless the BUYER submitted a complete mortgage loan application conforming to the foregoing provisions on or before December 23, 2002. *Application to one institutional lender shall satisfy Buyer's diligent efforts under this agreement.*"

The purchase and sale agreement was executed using the "Standard Form Purchase and Sale Agreement" (standard form) developed by the Greater Boston Real Estate Board. The language of the mortgage contingency clause quoted above follows that of the standard form in all material respects except that the final sentence was an addition made by the parties.

On December 30, 2002, the defendant sellers were informed that the plaintiff had submitted an application for financing but that more time was needed for it to be processed. The purchase and sale agreement was extended in writing several times to accommodate the plaintiff while her loan application was pending. On January 15, 2003, the plaintiff closed on and took title to the Hudson Road property, for which she paid $285,000, having obtained a mortgage through Drew that was funded by Ohio Savings Bank. The next day, the parties executed a fifth and final extension of the Horsepond Road agreement, extending the time for giving notice of termination for failure to obtain mortgage financing to January 22, 2003, and postponing the closing date to February 4, 2003. On January 22, 2003, after learning that Drew had denied the plaintiff's application for financing, plaintiff's counsel sent a letter timely notifying the defendant sellers that the plaintiff had been unable to obtain financing, and requesting the return of the deposit. The sellers responded by requesting proof of the plaintiff's diligent efforts to obtain financing under paragraph 26. The plaintiff provided the defendants' attorney with a copy of a rejection letter dated January 24, 2003, from Drew's operations manager to the plaintiff, stating that her "loan request . . . was not approved by the Loan Committee of our company" for the reason that the "[r]atio of housing expense to verified income [was] too high." The sellers refused to return the deposit and this action ensued.

[Text omitted]

Discussion. a. Mortgage contingency clause. . . . Our decisions remind us that it is the buyer who is the usual proponent and primary beneficiary of a mortgage contingency clause, which serves as a safety valve when she is unable to obtain financing. See *Tremouliaris v. Pina*, 23 Mass.App.Ct. 722, 726, 505 N.E.2d 225 (1987); *Churgin v. Hobbie*, 39 Mass.App.Ct. 302, 305, 655 N.E.2d 1280 (1995). The clause incidentally benefits the seller by setting a certain date by which the deal may fail or after which the seller knows the buyer is bound to perform.

The typical clause also protects the seller by requiring that the buyer direct her borrowing efforts toward an appropriate entity engaged in the business of mortgage lending (as opposed to, for example, the proverbial rich uncle or aunt). The clause here thus imposes as its basic requirement that the plaintiff "apply for a conventional bank or other institutional mortgage loan . . . at prevailing rates, terms and conditions" and use "diligent efforts [to obtain] a commitment for such loan." Additionally, in language tacked on to the standard form clause, the parties specified that "[a]pplication to one institutional lender shall satisfy Buyer's diligent efforts." The evident purpose of this language is to protect the plaintiff from the possibility that "diligent efforts" require multiple applications for financing. The reasonable reading of the language in its context and in conjunction with the basic requirement above is simply that the plaintiff need only once "apply for a conventional bank or other institutional mortgage loan . . . at prevailing rates, terms and conditions."

[Text omitted]

The question before us distills to whether, in submitting her application to Drew, the plaintiff in fact "appl[ied] for a conven-

tional bank or other institutional mortgage loan." The defendants argue that Drew is not an "institutional mortgage [lender]" because it does not use its own funds to finance mortgages, but rather table funds them using outside lenders, and that Drew does nothing more than act as a "broker" who brings borrowers and lenders together. We disagree.

The defendant sellers offer two affidavits, of principals of another lender and of a real estate management company, containing their respective opinions that Drew is not an "institutional lender." Even if this were the controlling point, the interpretation of the purchase and sale agreement is a matter of law, not a question of fact. See *Sarvis v. Cooper,* 40 Mass.App. Ct. 471, 475, 665 N.E.2d 119 (1996). The defendants cannot create an issue of fact by submission of the affidavits containing opinion evidence. To the extent that affidavit evidence offered by the plaintiff similarly contains opinion, we disregard it in our analysis.

First, the very fact that Drew is a licensed mortgage lender under G.L. c. 255E in the Commonwealth, and subject to examination and regulation by the Commissioner of Banks, is supportive of Drew's status as an institutional mortgage lender. Moreover, many conventional banks, which indisputably are institutional lenders, also use funds from outside sources to fund borrowers' mortgages-for example, those of their depositors. The instantaneous nature of the mechanism by which Drew provides funding should make it no less eligible to be considered an institutional mortgage lender than a conventional bank which engages in an effectively similar financing practice. Finally, because Drew processes mortgage applications, underwrites loans, and makes credit determinations in accordance with industry standards, it behaves as a conventional mortgage lender in its decisional processes, and is far more than a simple mortgage broker as the defendants claim.

. . . We also note that the closing failed to occur because the plaintiff did not qualify for the requested loan, not because Drew could not procure funding. And, as the judge noted, the sellers were informed that the plaintiff was preapproved for the loan and did not complain about the nature of the lender until the loan fell through. Although seller Andrea J. Kozol averred that "[a]t all times prior to my receipt of . . . notice [of termination on January 22], it was represented to me, by the Plaintiff, that she was actively pursuing a commitment for financing from a conventional bank or institutional mortgage lender," Kozol did not contradict expressly the plaintiff's averment that the plaintiff provided notice of Drew's preapproval of the loan. All of the formal extensions are signed on the plaintiff's behalf by her counsel, and not the plaintiff herself. Even assuming that there is enough to create a factual issue whether the plaintiff ever stated that she was applying for bank financing (notwithstanding widespread colloquial acceptance of the term "bank" to refer to the lender, whatever its nature), any such factual issue is still irrelevant if the plaintiff complied with the requirement of diligent efforts in any event, as the judge concluded.

However, we need not decide specifically that Drew is itself an "institutional mortgage [lender]" for the plaintiff to have met her obligation. Even if Drew is not, it is nonetheless not in dispute that so far as a buyer and seller are concerned, a successful application to Drew is designed to yield, instantaneously at the time of closing when table funding and mortgage transfer to the mortgage servicer occurs, a "conventional bank or other institutional mortgage loan." The application to Drew was therefore an application for precisely such a loan. We cannot reasonably conclude, as the defendants would have us do, that the parties by their contract meant for the plaintiff to forfeit her $18,250 deposit despite having timely sought financing in a manner that, through application to a single entity, effectively involved multiple potential lenders of an otherwise suitable nature. See *Haverhill v. George Brox, Inc.,* 47 Mass.App.Ct. 717, 720, 716 N.E.2d 138 (1999) ("Justice, common sense and the probable *256 intention of the parties are guides to construction of a written instrument"), quoting from *Stop & Shop, Inc. v. Ganem,* 347 Mass. 697, 701, 200 N.E.2d 248 (1964). The motion judge was therefore correct in concluding that the plaintiff satisfied her obligations under the mortgage contingency clause.

[Text omitted]

b. *Counterclaims for fraud and breach of the covenant of good faith and fair dealing.* Quite apart from the institutional lender argument, on the issues of good faith and fair dealing and fraud, the defendant sellers assert that "it was concealed from the [defendants] that [the plaintiff] simultaneously had an agreement to purchase another residence and was actively seeking mortgage financing for that purchase. . . . At no time did [the plaintiff,] or anyone acting on [her] behalf, disclose that she had another home in Sudbury under agreement, or that she was purchasing another home." The contention is that the plaintiff was not acting in good faith because she had no reasonable expectation of obtaining two mortgage loans (and that she could and would have obtained financing for the Horsepond Road property had she not purchased the other property), and that the sellers were harmed by being induced to take their property off the market. On this summary judgment record, however, where the plaintiff applied for one mortgage from Drew, was later preapproved by Drew for the other mortgage, and was informed by Drew that she was likely to qualify for the mortgages for both homes, the sellers could not demonstrate that the plaintiff was acting unreasonably or in bad faith. We also agree with the judge that in the circumstances, the sellers failed to show that the plaintiff had any affirmative duty to disclose her pending mortgage on the Hudson Road property. The defendants therefore cannot prevail on their counterclaims of fraud and breach of the covenant of good faith and fair dealing.

Judgment affirmed.

[Footnotes omitted]

Source: Reprinted with permission from Westlaw ALFEO v. Mark T. DINSMORE 861 N.E.2d 491.

Chapter 11

Recording Statutes and Title Examinations

CHAPTER OBJECTIVES

Upon completion of this chapter, you will be able to:

- Understand the bona fide purchaser for value.

- Identify the different types of recording statutes.

- Explain the methods of examining title.

- Discuss the title report.

One of the most important aspects of real property ownership is to make sure that you have good title to the property. Before purchasing property, it is important to have the title to the property examined to make sure that no unforeseen problems arise with title and ownership after the purchase. This chapter will discuss the various aspects of ensuring good title to real property.

BONA FIDE PURCHASER FOR VALUE

bona fide purchaser for value A person who purchases real property in good faith for valuable consideration without notice of any claim to or interest in the real property by any other party.

Generally, a seller cannot convey better title to property than he holds himself. However, there are times when a seller can convey title that is not good, and it can turn into better title than he held. The common law rule of a **bona fide purchaser for value** was created to protect the innocent buyer. The rule states that a person who purchases real property for consideration or value and without notice that any claim or interest exists on the property by anyone else is considered a bona fide purchaser for value. The bona fide purchaser for value will then take the property free and clear of any other claims or interests by any other parties on the property. The bona fide purchaser for value is allowed to receive the full benefit of his purchase, including the right to transfer title of the real property to any subsequent purchaser.

 SPOT THE ISSUE

Wilma and Martha have entered into a contract for the sale of a house owned by Martha. Before closing, Martha refuses to honor the contract with Wilma and decides to sell the property to Robert. Wilma files a lawsuit against Martha for breach of contract. What else should Wilma do to protect her rights against Martha and in the property?

RECORDING STATUTES

No one is required to record any deed or other document, and unrecorded conveyances are still valid. However, strong reasons to record do exist. The purpose of recording statutes is to give a prospective purchaser a way in which to check title to a property and to determine if an earlier transaction has occurred on the property that might take priority over her interest. For example, assume a landowner deeds land to Buyer A. Then the same landowner deeds the same piece of land to Buyer B. If A has failed to record, A may lose priority to B. The recording acts exist in some manner or form in every jurisdiction and govern the transfer of property. They were enacted to protect people who acted in good faith when purchasing a parcel of real property. All American states use recording systems to help interested parties determine who has title to a particular piece of land. Anyone may examine the records to make such a determination.

Recording statutes provide for the following:

- They give the community notice of any changes in ownership that have occurred in the property interests;
- They protect subsequent purchasers of property conveyed by the same common grantor by giving the subsequent purchasers notice of information contained in the recorded documents that concern the property; and
- They determine priority of conflicting claims to the same real property.

The Statute of Frauds and the recording statutes operate hand in hand. The Statute of Frauds states that all transfers of any interest in real property must be in writing. The recording statutes state that the writing concerning the transfer of interest in the property must be recorded, or it will not be valid.

There are three types of notice statutes:

- Race statutes
- Notice statutes
- Race-notice statutes

A **race statute** is just what it states: a race. The person who records her interest in a particular piece of real property first at the county recorder's office or other proper recording authority is protected. Only three states (Delaware, North Carolina, and Louisiana) use "race" statutes. When there are conflicting claims on the same property, the priority of one claim over another is determined by who wins the race to the recording office. For example, if Bob buys a piece of property from Chuck, and, later, Peter buys the same property from Chuck, and Peter records his interest in the property before Bob, then Peter's interest will take priority over Bob's interest. In a race statute, the first to record the title documentation has priority of title, and it does not matter in what order they purchased the property.

A **notice statute** provides that an unrecorded instrument that transfers property is invalid against any subsequent purchaser without notice. About half of all states have "notice" statutes. It does not matter whether or not the subsequent purchaser recorded his documentation prior to the first purchaser. Notice can be given by the recording of the transfer documents, or through constructive notice obtained through means other than recording. Under this statute, the grantee of a deed is not required to record the deed in order to obtain priority in title over some subsequent purchaser of the same property. An unrecorded transfer instrument is valid against a subsequent purchaser when the purchaser paid value with a notice of the unrecorded instrument. The transfer documentation is invalid if the subsequent purchaser paid value without notice of the unrecorded instrument. States that use notice statutes include Alabama,

race statute
Recording act providing that the person who records first, regardless of notice, has priority.

notice statute
A recording act providing that the person with the most recent valid claim, and who purchased without notice of an earlier, unrecorded claim, has priority.

YOU BE THE JUDGE

Yvette owned land in fee simple. She gave a mortgage on the land to Laura, but Laura did not record it. One year later, Yvette gave another mortgage on the same land to Oliver, who also did not record. Oliver had no knowledge of Laura's mortgage. A few months later, Oliver inherited a large sum of money. He then gave Yvette a loan giving value for the land. Soon after, Laura recorded her mortgage. Oliver recorded his a few days after Laura. When Yvette defaulted on both mortgages, Laura and Oliver sought a declaration as to which mortgage had priority. Whose mortgage would have priority in a notice jurisdiction? a race jurisdiction? a race-notice jurisdiction?

Additionally, an important point to remember is that all recording acts (except those in the three "race" states)

protect subsequent transferees only if value has been paid. Thus, those who receive gifts of land are not protected by the recording acts. Also, it is generally held that a judgment creditor has not paid value and therefore is not protected against a prior unrecorded conveyance by the judgment debtor. The value given must also be contemporaneous with the receipt of the interest in the land in question. Value given subsequent to receipt of the interest does not count. For example, when a creditor takes a mortgage or other interest in land to secure what was previously an unsecured debt, most courts hold that the lender has given no value unless it has also given some type of additional consideration.

Arizona, Connecticut, Florida, Illinois, Iowa, Kansas, Kentucky, Maine, Massachusetts, Missouri, New Hampshire, New Mexico, Oklahoma, Rhode Island, South Carolina, Tennessee, Vermont, and West Virginia.

race notice statute
Recording act providing that the person who is first to record in the chain of title without notice of a prior unrecorded deed or mortgage has priority.

A **race-notice statute** protects the subsequent purchaser if she records prior to the first purchaser and she takes the property without actual notice of the earlier conveyance. About half of the states use race-notice statutes which combine the features of race-type statutes and notice-type statutes. These states include Alaska, Arkansas, California, Colorado, the District of Columbia, Georgia, Hawaii, Idaho, Indiana, Maryland, Michigan, Minnesota, Mississippi, Montana, Nebraska, Nevada, New Jersey, New York, North Dakota, Ohio, Oregon, Pennsylvania, South Dakota, Texas, Utah, Washington, Wisconsin, and Wyoming.

If a jurisdiction is either race or race-notice, the subsequent purchaser will be protected if he records first. However, the documentation must be eligible to be recorded. If the documentation is not the proper documentation for recording, the subsequent purchaser's interest will not be protected. Notice plays an important part in determining a subsequent purchaser's interest. There are three types of notice: actual, record, and inquiry.

actual notice
Notice given directly to or received personally by a party.

Actual notice means that the subsequent purchaser has knowledge of the existence of a prior unrecorded interest. If he does have actual knowledge, the subsequent purchaser will not have protection under the recording statutes in a notice or race-notice jurisdiction. A purchaser may acquire knowledge of title defects from statements by the seller or by third parties such as neighbors. Actual notice can also result from an actual examination of the public records.

record notice
Constructive notice of the contents of an instrument, such as a deed or mortgage, that has been properly recorded.

Record notice will protect a holder of an interest in real property if he records it. The recorded interest holder will not be vulnerable against any subsequent interest. If an instrument is recorded, it will constitute notice to any people making subsequent claims against the property. However, one must be careful to make sure that the documentation is eligible for recording. If the documentation is recorded mistakenly and is not eligible for recording, then the holder of the recorded interest will not be protected.

LEGAL RESEARCH MAXIM

When a party purchases real property, it is expected that she will gain knowledge of title defects from statements of the seller, third parties, or other sources, such as a visit to the property, or by personally examining public records. A wise purchaser will make use of all sources available to ensure the quality of title.

If a document is not entitled to be recorded, some jurisdictions hold that if a subsequent purchaser actually sees the recorded document, even though it should not have been recorded, the subsequent purchaser is placed on inquiry notice. **Inquiry notice** means that because the subsequent purchaser now has knowledge that a document exists, she must inquire as to its validity, or she will not be protected by the recording statutes. However, some courts hold that any document that is not eligible for recording does not place subsequent purchasers on inquiry notice. Inquiry notice exists when a purchaser has knowledge of facts that would lead a reasonable person in the same situation to make a further investigation that would give her knowledge of the existence of a prior unrecorded right.

inquiry notice
Notice attributed to a person when the information would lead an ordinary prudent person to investigate the matter further.

RESEARCH THIS

Each jurisdiction has its own recording statutes. It is important to know what recording statute applies to the jurisdiction that governs your client's case. Research your jurisdiction to see if inquiry notice applies.

INDEXES TO THE RECORD

A typical recording office generally contains many volumes which contain the multitude of individual recorded documents pertaining to land transactions. Because of the enormous number of records, an index is necessary to allow a searcher to find documents pertaining to the land in which he is interested. Generally, two types of indexes are used. Names indexes are maintained in all states. Names indexes consist of two sets of books; one lists the last names of grantors alphabetically and the other lists the last names of grantees alphabetically. A few states also maintain tract indexes. Such an index has a page or a group of pages that lists all documents affecting a certain piece of land. Keep in mind that index books do not contain full replicas of documents. Instead, they list the names of the parties, the date of the instrument and its recording, and the book and page numbers in the deed book where the full replica of the document can be found.

When using a tract index to search, the searcher needs merely to glance down the proper column on the correct page in the book and note all documents which pertain to the land. Then the searcher can find and read those relevant documents. The name index system is a little more complicated for the legal researcher. When searching the grantee index, the searcher must begin with the present owner and find his or her name in the index. The index entry will give the searcher the name of the grantor who granted the land to the present grantee, and that person's name is then searched for in the grantee index. This process continues, and the chain of title can be searched as far back as needed. Each individual identified in the chain of title by using the grantee index is then checked in the grantor index to trace any possible conveyances made that are adverse to the established chain of title. The final step in establishing a complete chain of title is finding and reading the actual copy of each relevant document.

The recording system is not a perfect system. There are reasons why title searches may produce incorrect results. Recorded documents are not always valid and enforceable. For example, such documents may be forged or undelivered. There are also several events and claims which are outside the coverage of the recording system. Adverse possession title would be one example of a claim outside the coverage. Additionally, title searches are often limited to a certain period of time, even though a complete search would require tracing title back over two hundred years. Title searchers generally limit their searches to a shorter period of time, and that creates a risk that there is a defect in title that was not discovered. Finally, there is always the possibility that an error or a mistake of judgment may be made causing a title searcher to reach an incorrect result.

TITLE EXAMINATION

title examination
An investigation of the title made by a person who intends to purchase real estate or to ascertain the history and present condition of the title to such land.

PRACTICE TIP

The Real Estate Settlement Procedures Act, RESPA, which was enacted by Congress to stop questionable behavior by lenders during real estate closings, contains two provisions affecting title insurers. Section 2607 prohibits kickbacks or fee splitting involving federally regulated mortgage loans. Section 2608 prohibits the seller of property, purchased with a federally regulated mortgage loan, from requiring that the buyer purchase title insurance from a particular company.

chain of title
The ownership history of a piece of land, from its first owner to the present one.

grantee index
An index, usually kept in the county recorder's office, alphabetically listing by grantee the volume and page number of grantees' recorded property transactions.

A **title examination** is very important. A title examination makes sure that a seller has the ability to convey good title to a purchaser at the time of the closing of a real estate transaction. The title examination ensures that a borrower has good title to the property before it is used as collateral and security for a loan. Proper recording of property interests places all subsequent purchasers on notice. Courts will attribute knowledge to a subsequent purchase if a recorded document exists. A recorded document imputes the knowledge to a subsequent purchaser as if the subsequent purchaser had actual knowledge of the recorded document through a diligent title search. A title examination is most often performed by a title insurance company, but some jurisdictions use attorney opinions rather than title insurance. Although an attorney's opinion is produced by a licensed attorney rather than a title insurance company, it fulfills the same function, and the same exclusions apply.

In order to conduct a title examination, certain documentation must be available. Such information includes the legal description of the property and the name of the owner as well as copies of any pertinent deeds, insurance policies, or other documentation concerning the property.

In order to conduct a title search, a person typically goes to the local county recorder's office or courthouse that contains the information recorded for the property located in that jurisdiction. A title examination will search the owner's **chain of title** by starting with the current owner and working backward to some determined point in time. The purpose of the examination is to establish evidence of title for each owner in the chain of title for that piece of real property. Most title searches will search backward for approximately fifty years. To accurately construct a chain of title, one needs to look at the documents affecting the property, including deeds, mortgages, contracts, covenants, easements, judgments, leases, and liens. (See Appendix B: Abstract Of Title.) Technology now allows many title searches to be performed electronically via the Internet.

A title examination involves searching the two aforementioned indices. The first is the grantee index of the owner's chain of title. A **grantee index** is an alphabetical index organized by last name of all of the people who are grantees of any property interests of property located in a given county during a given year. The examiner will search backward in the grantee index to some point in time in order to establish evidence of title for each owner in the chain of title. A grantee index shows every grantee who took title by a conveyance. However, it will not show grantees who took title by will or intestacy. In order to determine if any grantees exist by will or intestacy, the examiner will have to search the local probate records. An examiner will probably look in the probate records if she discovers a break in the chain of title while searching the grantee index.

After searching the grantee index, the examiner will search forward for each grantor in the chain of title in the grantor index from the date the grantor acquired title to the next grantor in the chain, until she establishes evidence of title for each grantor. The grantor index contains an annual alphabetical index organized by the last name of all of the people who are grantors of real property located within the county.

An examiner will also examine a plat index. A plat is a map which meets set standards and is legally enforced by the local government. A plat may show a single lot or a number of lots. If there are many lots, they are typically lettered or numbered. The legal description of the lot boundaries is noted on the plat. An example would be "lot 2, block 4, Westridge Subdivision." Most modern housing subdivisions use plat descriptions. In order to search a plat index, one needs the following information:

- The lot and district in which the property is located
- The name of the owner
- The subdivision designation

Once the grantee, grantor, and plat indices have been examined for evidence of the chain of title, the examiner will then search other indices to determine whether there are any other recorded claims against the property. During a title examination, sources such as the bankruptcy court, local trial court dockets, tax and assessment liens records, and other local government offices may be checked. Types of recorded claims which may be discovered include, but are not limited to, judgment liens, mechanic's liens, and tax liens.

Judgments

A **judgment** is a money debt resulting from a lawsuit. A judgment may have been entered against an owner in the chain of title as a result of a lawsuit. Once a judgment has been recorded in the public records, in effect it becomes a lien on the property of the judgment debtor. Usually an index for judgments exists in the local county in which the real property is located. The majority of cases hold that the judgment creditor has not paid value, and will not be protected against a prior unrecorded conveyance by a judgment debtor.

judgment
A court's final determination of the rights and obligations of the parties in a lawsuit.

Tax Lien

The federal and state governments have the right to file a **tax lien** against the property of any taxpayer who is delinquent in payment of his taxes. Once a federal tax lien is filed, it becomes a lien on the property owned by the taxpayer at the time the lien was filed. The federal tax lien affects not only property currently owned by the delinquent taxpayer, but also any future property that may be acquired by the taxpayer. The lien will stay in effect until the lien has been paid in full by the taxpayer.

tax lien
A legal right or interest that the government has in a delinquent taxpayer's property.

In addition to federal and state tax liens, all property is taxed by county or city governments where the property is located. Liens against property located in the jurisdiction may be assessed for sanitation, sewer, or other local services. Liens for local taxes and assessments may be found in a tax assessor's or tax collector's office for the particular local jurisdiction.

Lis Pendens

A **lis pendens**, a Latin term meaning "suit pending," is filed when there is an issue affecting title to real estate that has not been resolved and is still pending in the judicial system. A lis pendens is filed in the county recorder's office where the property is located and gives notice to third parties that a legal action is pending against the property. If the third party were to acquire the property or acquire a loan on the property, she would be bound by any judgment rendered in the lawsuit. A lis pendens can make a piece of land unmarketable. The lis pendens doctrine is applicable only in an action that directly affects the real property. It is based on the notion that nothing should be changed during the pendency of a legal action.

lis pendens
Jurisdiction, power, or control that courts acquire over property in litigation pending action and until final judgment.

Mechanic's Lien

A **mechanic's lien** may have been filed against the property for work done on the property. A mechanic's lien is located either in the grantor's index or in a separate index for such liens. These indices are located in the county recorder's office in the county in which the property is located. For example, if a plumber did several thousand dollars' worth of work on a home and was never paid, he could then file a mechanic's lien. If the property owner decided to sell the property, the mechanic's lien would show up during the title search, as the plumber would have a legal interest in the property.

mechanic's lien
A legal right or interest that a tradesperson or another has in the property of another for work done on the property.

THE TITLE REPORT

Once a title examination is completed, a title report is issued by the examiner. The title report states the conclusion of the examiner after examining the title of the property. The examiner will certify the title of the real property to a title insurance company if title insurance is being taken out on the transaction. After the certification has been issued by the examiner, an insurance commitment, or binder, is issued by the title insurance company prior to the closing of the transaction. The title report should include the following:

- The name of the current record title holder
- The legal description of the property
- Any existing loans or mortgages on the property
- Any other liens
- Any taxes
- A list of all easements, covenants, and other restrictions on the property
- Any objections to marketability of title

TITLE INSURANCE

title insurance
A policy issued by a title company after searching the title, representing the state of that title and insuring the accuracy of its search against claims of title defects.

indemnify
To restore the victim of a loss, in whole or in part, by payment, repair, or replacement.

Title insurance insures a person against the risk that the title to the property may be different from the title described in the insurance policy. It is a contract to **indemnify** the insured against loss associated with any defects in the title, or against liens or encumbrances that may affect the title at the time that the policy was issued on the property.

There are two types of title insurance policies: the owner's policy and the loan policy. An owner's policy indemnifies the owner of property against title defects. A loan policy insures a lender that holds a mortgage, deed of trust, or other loan against loss caused by a title defect not listed on the policy. Nearly all lenders in the United States require loan policies. Owner policies are somewhat less common. Title insurance protects against loss or damage incurred from any defect in title or from any lien or encumbrance that may be on the title to the property that is the subject of the title insurance. The property is insured only against defects, liens, or encumbrances that have attached to the title as of the date of the issuance of the policy of title insurance. The title company is not liable for any event taking place after the issuance date that impairs the title. The company's total liability is additionally limited to the face value of the policy; this is true even when the land later increases in value to such an extent that the policy's face value provides inadequate coverage.

A policy insures against four types of defects. These defects are

- The lack of access to and from the land
- Unmarketable title
- Any defect or lien or encumbrance on the title
- Title to the estate being vested in a manner other than that which is stated on the title

CASE FACT PATTERN

Bert is buying a piece of property in Anytown, USA. The property is located at the base of the mountains, right near a river, and fronts the highway. The area has been growing rapidly, and Bert wants to build a shopping center on the property. During the transaction, Bert has a title examination conducted on the property. Bert takes out title insurance on the property in order to protect himself against any future claims against title by third parties once the transaction is finalized. The transaction closes, and Bert begins the process of obtaining permits to build his shopping center. During the permit process, Bert discovers that the property is encumbered by a governmental regulation protecting endangered species. Bert sues the title company, claiming losses as a result of the governmental restriction. The title company prevails in the lawsuit, because the title insurance policy excludes coverage for zoning and governmental regulations that exist on the property.

EYE ON ETHICS

Protecting a client's interest in property is very important. It is always important to have a thorough examination of the title to any property involved in a real estate transaction. Make sure that all of the indices are checked thoroughly. If possible, hire a reputable title company to conduct the search for you, so that if any mistakes in the search occur, your client will have recourse.

SURF'S UP

To learn more about real estate closings and processes, search the Internet. Many sites are very helpful. You can get an overview of the real estate closing process from the following Web sites:
    www.ziprealty.com
    www.public.findlaw.com
www.hg.org/realest.html.
homebuying.about.com
www.realtor.com
realtytimes.com

Some items are excluded from being covered under a title insurance policy. Zoning and other governmental regulations are typically excluded from title insurance coverage. This exclusion states that the property is not insured against matters of zoning and other restrictions or regulations placed upon the real property by a governmental entity. In addition, a title insurance company will not insure against the threat of eminent domain by a governmental body. Remember, **eminent domain** is the right of a governmental entity to take the land for public good. Title insurance companies will not insure against defects, liens, encumbrances, adverse claims, or other matters created, suffered, assumed, or agreed to by the insured should they make a claim on those types of matters. Also, if an insured cannot prove that he suffered a loss, the title insurance company will not indemnify him without damages. (See Appendix B: Title Insurance Policy.)

The title insurance company will not insure against title defects that were not known to the insurance company and were not recorded, but were known to the insured, who failed to tell the title insurance company at the time of the issuance of the policy.

Recent cases have explored whether titled insurers can be held liable for negligently searching title in tort. A majority opinion has not been reached thus far, but a tort theory would offer the insured some unique advantages over a contract theory. First, it would allow the insured to bring an action even if she did not do so within the time limits set out in the policy. Second, it would allow the insured to claim consequential or punitive damages. Additionally, it would allow for an opportunity for the insured to get damages for emotional distress.

Title insurance does not guarantee that the title to real property will be perfect. Instead, title insurance pays damages sustained as a result of any defect to title that the title company should have discovered but did not.

eminent domain
The inherent power of a governmental entity to take privately owned property, especially land, and convert it to public use, subject to reasonable compensation for the taking.

Summary

The common law rule of a bona fide purchaser for value states that a person who purchases real property for consideration or value and without notice that any claim or interest exists on the property by anyone else is considered a bona fide purchaser for value. The bona fide purchaser for value will then take the property free and clear of any other claims or interests by any other parties on the property. The bona fide purchaser for value is allowed to receive the full benefit of his purchase, including the right to transfer title to the real property to any subsequent purchaser.

The purpose of recording statutes is to give a prospective purchaser a way in which to check title to a property and to determine if an earlier transaction has occurred on the property that might take priority over her interest. The recording acts exist in some manner or form in every jurisdiction and govern the transfer of property. They were enacted to protect people who acted in good faith when purchasing a parcel of real property. Recording statutes provide for the following: they give the community notice of any changes in ownership that have occurred in the property interests; they protect subsequent purchasers of property conveyed by the same common grantor by giving the subsequent purchasers notice of information contained in the recorded documents that concern the property; and they determine priority of conflicting claims to the same real property.

A race statute is just what it states: a race. The person who records his interest in a particular piece of real property first at the county recorder's office or other proper recording authority is protected. When there are conflicting claims on the same property, priority is determined by who wins the race to the recording office.

A notice statute provides that an unrecorded instrument that transfers property is invalid against any subsequent purchaser without notice. It does not matter whether or not the subsequent purchaser recorded her documentation prior to the first purchaser.

A race-notice statute protects the subsequent purchaser if he records prior to the purchaser and he takes the property without actual notice of the earlier conveyance.

Title examinations make sure that a seller has the ability to convey good title to a purchaser at the time of the closing of a real estate transaction. Title examinations ensure that a borrower has good title to the property before placing it as collateral as security for a loan. Proper recording of property interests places all subsequent purchasers on notice. Courts will attribute knowledge to a subsequent purchaser if a recorded document exists. A recorded document imputes the knowledge to a subsequent purchaser as if the subsequent purchaser had actual knowledge of the recorded document through a diligent title search.

Title insurance insures a person against the risk that the title to the property may be different from the title described in the insurance policy. It is a contract to indemnify the insured against loss associated with any defects in the title or against liens or encumbrances that may affect the title at the time that the policy was issued on the property.

Key Terms

Actual notice	Mechanic's lien
Bona fide purchaser for value	Notice statute
Chain of title	Race-notice statute
Eminent domain	Race statute
Grantee index	Record notice
Indemnify	Tax lien
Inquiry notice	Title examination
Judgment	Title insurance
Lis pendens	

Review Questions

1. Why is it important to examine title to a property during a real estate transaction?
2. What is a judgment lien?
3. What is inquiry notice?
4. What are the three different recording statutes, and how do they differ?
5. What is actual notice?
6. What is record notice?
7. Explain the bona fide purchaser for value.

8. What is a lis pendens?

9. Why is title insurance important?

10. What does it mean to indemnify?

11. What is the difference between the grantee and the grantor indices?

12. What information is required for a title examination?

13. List three items that are not covered by title insurance.

14. What do title insurance policies cover?

15. Why are recording statutes important?

Exercises

1. Derek conveyed his ranch to Akin in 1999. Akin did not record his interest at the time. Derek then conveyed the same ranch to Bret in 2002. Bret did not know about the deed to Akin at the time that he took interest in the property. In 2003, Akin recorded his interest, without knowledge of the conveyance by Derek to Bret. In 2004, Bret discovered the conveyance to Akin by doing a title search. Bret immediately recorded his interest. If the jurisdiction has a "race-notice" statute, who has title, Akin or Bret? Why?

2. If you are conducting a title examination of a house at 123 Elm Street in Anytown, USA, would it be easier to find a recorded mortgage on the property by Nancy Owner to Sally Seller by looking under Nancy Owner's name in the grantor index, or by looking under Sally Seller's name in the grantee index?

3. A bank gave Sam a loan of $25,000, taking Sarah's unsecured promissory note. Sam owned a valuable piece of real property which he then deeded to Sarah; Sarah did not record the deed. When Sam's note was due, the bank demanded payment. Sam did not have the money, so he offered the bank a mortgage on the same land he had deeded to Sarah. The bank assumed he still owned the land and took the mortgage. Soon afterwards, Sam disappeared. The bank then sued to foreclose the mortgage, and Sarah argued she owned the land free of the mortgage, because her deed was delivered prior to its execution. Will Sarah prevail? Why or why not?

4. Monica owns land in fee simple absolute. She deeds it to Chloe, who is a bona fide purchaser for value. Chloe fails to record. Monica then places a mortgage on the land to State Bank, which makes a contemporaneous loan to Monica and records the mortgage. The bank has no notice of Monica's rights. Under which type(s) of the recording acts would State Bank have a valid mortgage?

5. Marci buys real property, including a small residence, on North Road in the community of Riverdale. Marci has a title examination performed that reveals no defects, liens, or encumbrances. Three years later, because of population growth and increased traffic, the city of Riverdale decides it needs to widen North Road. This results in Marci's losing a sizeable piece of her lot under the principle of eminent domain. Is Marci protected by her title insurance? Why or why not?

6. Visit the county recorder's office and view the grantor/grantee indices.

7. Several recent real property cases have held title insurers liable for negligently searching title under tort law principles. Read and brief *Bank of California v. First American Title Insurance Co.*, 826 P.2d 1126 (Alaska 1992).

 PORTFOLIO ASSIGNMENT

The first title insurance company was chartered in 1876. Read and brief *Watson v. Muirhead*, 57 Pa. 161 (1868), the case largely responsible for the development of title insurance.

Vocabulary Builders

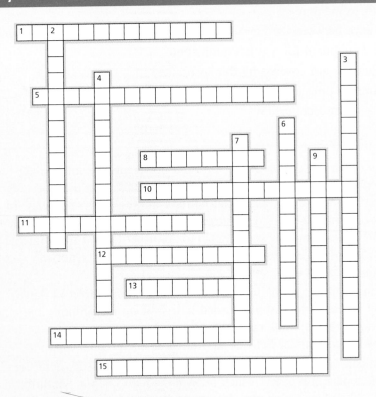

Instructions

Use the key terms from this chapter to fill in the answers to the crossword puzzle.

NOTE: When the answer is more than one word, leave a blank space between words.

ACROSS

1. the inherent power of a governmental entity to take privately owned property, especially land, and convert it to public use, subject to reasonable compensation for the taking.
5. an investigation of the title made by a person who intends to purchase real estate or to ascertain the history and present condition of the title to such land.
8. a legal right or interest that the government has in a delinquent taxpayer's property.
10. the ownership history of a piece of land, from its first owner to the present one.
11. a recording act providing that the person who records first, regardless of notice, has priority.
12. jurisdiction, power, or control that courts acquire over property in litigation pending action and until final judgment.
13. a court's final determination of the rights and obligations of the parties in a lawsuit.
14. notice given directly to or received personally by a party.
15. a policy issued by a title company after searching the title, representing the state of that title, and insuring the accuracy of its search against claims of title defects.

DOWN

2. notice attributed to a person when the information would lead an ordinary prudent person to investigate the matter further.
3. a person who purchases real property in good faith for valuable consideration without notice of any claim to or interest in the real property by any other party.
4. a legal right or interest that a tradesman or another has in the property of another for work done on the property.
6. an index, usually kept in the country recorder's office, alphabetically listing by grantee the volume and page number of each grantee's recorded property transactions.
7. constructive notice of the contents of an instrument, such as a deed or mortgage, that has been properly recorded.
9. a recording act providing that the person with the most recent valid claim, and who purchased without notice of an earlier, unrecorded claim, has priority.

Petitioner: Lexie-Leigh SHEPLER and Scott Thornock,

v.

Respondent: Michael WHALEN

119 P.3d 1084

Supreme Court of Colorado,

No. 04SC553.

Sept. 12, 2005.

Background: Junior judgment lienholder moved for writ of execution on judgment creditor's real property occupied by creditor and his wife, alleging that creditor's transfer of funds to pay off wife's mortgage on the property held in her name, was fraudulent. The District Court, City and County of Denver, Robert L. McGahey, Jr., J., found that transfer was fraudulent, granted senior judgment lienholders' motions to intervene, imposed constructive trust on property and established equitable lien in favor of junior lienholder, but included other lienholders and gave priority to senior lienholders. Junior lienholder appealed. The Court of Appeals, 104 P.3d 243, reversed. Junior lienholder petitioned for review.

Holding: The Supreme Court granted certiorari, and in an opinion by Mullarkey, C.J., held that junior lienholder who exposed fraudulent transfer had priority.

Affirmed.

I. Introduction

In this dispute among judgment creditors, we examine the creditors' priority to real property that was never titled in the name of the judgment debtor. We determine that the state's race-notice statute does not control the priority among creditors under the facts of this case. Where the judgment debtor had neither a legal nor an equitable interest in the property, recording a judgment does not create a lien on the property because there is no interest on which the lien could attach. Where it is alleged that property titled in the name of another has been fraudulently conveyed by the judgment debtor, the creditor must file an action to uncover the fraud. Such an action, along with a notice of lis pendens, does establish the creditor's lien on the fraudulently conveyed property. Accordingly, a junior creditor who successfully exposes a fraudulent transfer by filing suit takes priority over senior creditors holding judgments recorded prior to the junior creditor uncovering the fraud. The court of appeals' judgment is affirmed. See *Whalen v. Shepler*, 104 P.3d 243 (Colo.App.2004).

II. Facts and Prior Proceedings

Both the petitioners, Lexie-Leigh Shepler and Scott Thornock, and the respondent, Michael Whalen, are creditors of Sanford Altberger and Orovi, Inc. The creditors recorded judgments against Altberger and Orovi in the following order: Rodney Lamb, Shepler, Thornock and Whalen. The earliest judgment was recorded on November 27, 2000.

Through discovery, Whalen learned that the townhouse where Altberger and his wife, Judith Altberger, lived had been purchased with a loan from P.C. Financial. From the time of its purchase, the townhouse had always been titled solely in Judith Altberger's name. In 1998, before any of the judgments were recorded, Altberger transferred $353,000 from Orovi to P.C. Financial, to pay off the mortgage. At the time Altberger made the transfer, he and Orovi owed money to numerous creditors, including the parties to this action.

After learning of the transactions, Whalen filed a "motion for declaration of equitable lien or constructive trust and for the issuance of a writ of execution on the "Judith Altberger residence'" as well as a notice of lis pendens concerning the property. In his motion, Whalen asserted that Altberger had fraudulently caused Orovi to pay off the townhouse mortgage in order to defraud their creditors. Upon learning of Whalen's action, Shepler, Thornock and Lamb made a joint motion to intervene, which was granted.

Following a hearing, the trial court found that the transfer of funds from Orovi to P.C. Financial was "fraudulent and done with the intent to hinder, delay or defraud creditors of the debtor, Sanford Altberger and/or Orovi, Inc." Subsequently, the court imposed a constructive trust on the residence and established an equitable lien in favor of Altberger's creditors. Although the written order stated that the lien was established in favor of Whalen, the court clarified at the hearing that it was naming Whalen because he was the party making the motion, and the trust was created for the benefit of all creditors. The trial court expressly reserved the issue of priority for later determination.

After a hearing on priority, the trial court was persuaded that Altberger "had 'an interest' in the subject residence at the time the Intervenors' [Shepler, Thornock and Lamb's] judgment liens were filed," and the imposition of the constructive trust "only identified or exposed an already existing interest." The court provided no explanation as to the nature of that interest. Because all of the creditors had recorded judgments, the court concluded that liens against the Altberger residence "shall be established as set forth in C.R.S.1973 § 13-52-102 and statutory scheme for enforcement of such liens." The court's ruling set priority of the liens in the order that the judgments were recorded, making Whalen's judgment the last to be satisfied. Whalen appealed.

The court of appeals reversed the trial court, finding that Whalen should be given priority over Shepler, Thornock and Lamb. Discerning "no basis on which intervenors' judgment liens could attach to the townhouse," the court rejected the argument that Colorado's race-notice statute should be applied to establish priority in the order the judgments were recorded. *Whalen v. Shepler*, 104 P.3d at 246. Rather, the court determined that "when a junior judgment creditor obtains the debtor's equitable interest in real property, through an equitable action in the nature of a creditor's bill, senior judgment liens do not attach," and the creditor who brought the action has priority.

Shepler, Thornock and Lamb petitioned this court for certiorari review of the court of appeals' opinion. Lamb was subsequently dismissed from the action. We uphold the decision of the court of appeals for reasons similar to those that court espoused.

We granted certiorari on the following questions:

1. Whether a judgment debtor that fraudulently pays off a promissory note encumbering real property titled in the debtor's spouse holds an equitable interest to which creditor's recorded transcripts of judgment may attach.

2. Whether a junior judgment creditor is entitled to priority over senior judgment creditors where the junior judgment creditor first obtained an equitable lien against real property titled in a third person but tainted by a judgment debtor's fraud.

III. Analysis
[Text omitted]

Colorado is a race-notice jurisdiction, meaning that, once a debtor's real property has been sold, creditors' judgments are satisfied out of the proceeds of the sale in the order that their judgments were recorded in the county clerk and recorder's office. § 38-35-109, C.R.S. (2004). The race-notice statute describes the types of instruments that may be recorded and states:

No such unrecorded instrument or document shall be valid against any person with any kind of rights in or to such real property who first records and those holding rights under such person, except between the parties thereto and against those having notice thereof prior to the acquisition of such rights.

This provision guarantees that the creditor who first recorded a judgment against a debtor is the first to have his or her debt satisfied. The race-notice statute can come into operation only when the debtor has an interest in a particular property to which the creditor's judgment can attach.

Shepler and Thornock contend that the race-notice statute should control the order in which the creditors share the proceeds of the sale of the townhouse, respectively giving them second and third priority. We reject this contention as contrary to the race-notice statute. Because the judgment debtor Altberger did not have any recognizable interest in the townhouse prior to the trial court's imposition of a constructive trust, the race-notice statute does not give priority to judgment creditors Shepler and Thornock. . . .

The fraudulent transfer at issue in this case is not the purchase or conveyance of the townhouse. Rather, it is the fraudulent transfer of funds to pay off the mortgage on the house, thereby giving Judith Altberger an unencumbered interest in the property. Because the townhouse was always solely titled in Judith Alberger's name, Altberger never had any legal interest in the property. Nor did he have an equitable interest. The only "interest" Altberger could be said to have in the townhouse arose through the fraudulent payment of the mortgage balance. An equitable interest in the townhouse cannot arise solely from Altberger's perpetration of fraud.

Furthermore, although section 38-10-117, C.R.S. (2004), provides that conveyances made with the intent to hinder, delay, or defraud creditors "shall be void," the statute has been interpreted to mean that the conveyance is voidable rather than void. *Sec. Serv., Ltd. v. Equity Mgmt.*, Inc., 851 P.2d 921, 924 (Colo.App.1993). As between the grantor and the grantee, a fraudulent conveyance is valid "until some action is taken to uncover the fatal flaw in the transaction." *Sec. Serv.*, 851 P.2d at 924. Consequently, the fraudulent transfer of funds from

Altberger to the lender on behalf of his wife, the borrower, was presumptively valid until Whalen brought the action to uncover the fraud. At the time Shepler and Thornock recorded their judgments, the transfer was considered complete, leaving Judith Altberger with an unencumbered interest in the property and Altberger without any interest. Because the debtor retains no interest, "a recorded transcript of judgment does not automatically create a lien upon property which a judgment debtor has allegedly fraudulently conveyed to a third party." Before the judgment can attach, the "creditor must successfully prosecute a fraudulent conveyance lawsuit." Accordingly, the judgments initially recorded by Shepler, Thornock, Whalen and Lamb did not attach to the townhouse. Because none of the creditors who is a party to this action had a recorded judgment capable of establishing a lien on the townhouse, those judgments and the race-notice statute do not apply to the issue of priority in this instance.

[Text omitted]

Shepler and Thornock, however, argue that Altberger essentially purchased and paid for the townhouse, but caused title to be conveyed to his wife, and Altberger therefore can be considered the equitable and beneficial owner of the townhouse. Based on their version of the facts, Shepler and Thornock argue that a trust results in Altberger's favor. They contend that "the trial court found that Altberger retained beneficial use of the property transferred by granting Whalen's motion." As we will demonstrate, Shepler and Thornock's argument, that Altberger had an equitable interest in the property to which their judgments could attach, is premised upon a misunderstanding of the difference between resulting trusts and constructive trusts, as well as a misinterpretation of the facts of the case. Both resulting and constructive trusts are implied trusts, where the intent of the parties to form a trust is not apparent. . . .

By contrast, constructive trusts are "fraud-rectifying" trusts in which the court does not "infer or presume that any such intent [to have a trust] existed, but the court uses trust terminology as the most convenient method for working out justice and preventing one party from unjustly enriching himself at the expense of the other." *Id.* Bogert notes that errors are sometimes made "classifying some trusts which are founded on positive wrongdoing as 'resulting.'"

We examined the differences between a resulting and constructive trust in *Page v. Clark, 197 Colo. 306,* 592 P.2d 792 (1979). We summarized three situations where a resulting trust is properly found:

"(1) where an express trust fails in whole or in part; (2) where an express trust is fully performed without exhausting the trust estate; (3) where property is purchased and the purchase price is paid by one person and at his direction the vendor conveys the property to another person." . . .

A resulting trust could not have been created here. As Bogert notes in his treatise:

If one pays off a mortgage on land already owned by another . . . he has not paid the purchase price of the land in the sense of the resulting trust rule. He has merely removed a lien or encumbrance from another's realty. If he desires a trust interest in that realty . . . he should expressly stipulate for it and get a written declaration of trust. The law does not imply such a security interest by way of resulting trust for him.

Bogert, supra, § 455 at 282–83. Moreover, a trust was imposed in the present case because of the fraudulent transfer, not because Altberger and his wife intended Altberger to retain an interest in the townhouse. The transfer at issue is unlike the classic resulting trust situation where one person pays for property while directing title in another. See *Valley State Bank v. Dean,* 97 Colo. 151, 154, 47 P.2d 924, 926 (1935). Here, Judith Altberger initially purchased the property, and subsequently, Altberger paid off the mortgage interest using money he owed to creditors, with the intention of defrauding those creditors. Imposition of a constructive trust on the property was proper because " 'though acquired originally without fraud, it is against equity that it should be retained by him who holds it.' "

Having concluded that the race-notice statute cannot be used to determine the priority of creditors in this instance because Altberger did not have a legal or equitable interest in the townhouse, we must now decide the proper way to set priority. We hold that Whalen takes first priority because he first established a lien that attached to the property by bringing the action to uncover the fraud and impose the constructive trust.

Long ago, in *Shuck v. Quackenbush,* 75 Colo. 592, 601, 227 P. 1041, 1045 (1924), we held that where a creditor had filed a complaint or service of summons in a civil action, "[b]y filing at the same time notice of lis pendens, there was created a lien which attached [to the property] at the time the notice was filed." The Colorado Court of Appeals applied this principle decades later to conclude that a fraudulent conveyance claim and notice of lis pendens established an equitable interest in property that took first priority in the proceeds of the sale of the property. *Emarine v. Haley,* 892 P.2d 343, 348–49 (Colo. App.1994). As previously noted, "the judgment creditor must successfully prosecute a fraudulent conveyance lawsuit before [his or her] recorded transcript of judgment attaches as a valid lien against the property." *Sec. Serv.,* 851 P.2d at 923.

Whalen was the only creditor to file suit pertaining to the townhouse property, and the lien established by Whalen's suit dates back to the filing of his complaint and lis pendens. Shepler, Thornock and Lamb did not intervene until after the initial filing, and consequently they did not become lienholders until after *Whalen.* The principle that the creditor who first brings suit to uncover fraud takes priority has long been recognized by commentators in this area. Freeman observed that "the creditor who first proceeds in equity to reach property fraudulently transferred thereby obtains a right to priority to which the claims of other judgment creditors, whether prior or subsequent, must yield precedence."

We find this rule to work the most just result because it rewards the creditor who put forth the most effort. Granting first priority to the creditor bringing suit is consistent with the maxim that "the law favors diligent creditors." To hold to the contrary would allow creditors to "lie idle until others have by their superior diligence discovered the fraud and commenced proceedings in equity to thwart it by obtaining the cancellation of the conveyance, and then step forward and reap the first fruits of their diligence."

As the creditor who brought suit, Whalen may first satisfy his judgment from the proceeds of the sale of the townhouse. The remaining creditors, Shepler, Thornock and Lamb all intervened in Whalen's action at the same time. Consequently, they each established a lien capable of attachment to the townhouse at the same time. Liens established at the same time are accorded equivalent priority, and Shepler, Thornock and Lamb must share equally after Whalen has satisfied his judgment. See *Id.* § 975, at 2054 ("[T]hose [liens] taking effect simultaneously would have no priority over each other except such as might be gained by prior diligence in subjecting property by appropriate proceedings.").

IV. Conclusion

Because neither Altberger nor Orovi, Inc., had an interest in the townhouse, none of the creditors' liens attached to the townhouse as a result of recording their judgments against the debtors. Consequently, the race-notice statute does not apply. A lien on the property was not established until Whalen filed his lis pendens and prevailed in his action for imposition of a constructive trust. Having established the fraud and obtained the first lien on the property, Whalen holds first priority. Accordingly, we affirm the judgment of the court of appeals.

[Text omitted]

[Footnotes omitted]

Source: Reprinted with permission from Westlaw.

Chapter 12

Real Estate Closing

CHAPTER OBJECTIVES

Upon completion of this chapter, you will be able to:

- Understand the Real Estate Settlement Procedures Act.

- Explain the Truth-in-Lending Act.

- Discuss interest rate disclosures.

- Identify the documents associated with a real estate closing.

The real estate closing represents the ending and wrapping up of a purchase and sale of real property, as well as all the documentation that goes with that process. The location of the real property will dictate the process of the real estate closing. In some areas, attorneys may close the transaction. In other areas, escrow and real estate agents conduct the closing. This chapter discusses government regulations associated with real estate closings, along with an overview of many of the forms that are used in real estate closings.

REAL ESTATE SETTLEMENT PROCEDURES ACT

Real Estate Settlement Procedures Act (RESPA)
Federal statute governing real estate closings for all federally guaranteed mortgage loans.

The **Real Estate Procedures Act (RESPA)** is a federal statute that governs all federally guaranteed mortgage loans. RESPA was passed in order to redesign the real estate closing process and to protect consumers from high closing and settlement costs associated with the purchase of property. It is applicable to transactions that involve a federally regulated mortgage loan. This includes the majority of loans involving a lien on residential property. Specifically, it applies to home purchase loans, home refinancing, home improvement loans, reverse mortgages, and many equity lines of credit. Types of transactions not typically covered would include case sales and rental property transactions. According to RESPA, all settlement or closing costs must be disclosed to the consumer in advance of the closing. In addition, RESPA eliminates kickbacks and referral fees that occurred in the real estate closing process in the past. RESPA also dictates the maximum amount of funds that may be required to be placed into escrow accounts in order to pay for recurring charges or assessments.

LEGAL RESEARCH MAXIM

Under RESPA, the monthly payment into the escrow account is limited to one-twelfth of the estimated annual charges for these items. Also, when a loan is made and an escrow account is created, the lender cannot require more than one-sixth of the annual charges to be paid in as a "cushion" over and above the amount estimated to be needed. Keep in mind, however, that RESPA does not require that the borrower maintain an escrow account. This decision is left to the lender. RESPA only sets the maximum amount that a lender can require a borrower to maintain in the account.

Federally related mortgage loans secured by a first lien on a residential property are subject to RESPA. Federally related mortgage loans include the following:

* Loans made by a lender regulated by a federal agency or whose deposits into the institution are insured by a federal agency such as the Federal Deposit Insurance Corporation (FDIC);

* Loans that are made, insured, guaranteed, supplemented, or assisted by a federal agency such as the **Federal Housing Administration** (FHA);

* Loans that are intended to be sold to the Federal National Mortgage Association, Government National Mortgage Association, or Federal Home Loan Mortgage Corporation;

* Loans made by a lender who makes or invests more than one million dollars per year in residential real estate loans.

Certain federally regulated mortgage loans are exempted from RESPA. These loans are the following:

* A loan that finances a purchase or transfer of twenty-five or more acres;

* Loans that do not involve a transfer of title, such as home equity loans and refinance loans;

* Loans to purchase vacant land where none of the funds will go to constructing a residential dwelling;

* Transactions that involve loans that are to be assumed;

* Construction loans, except when those loans are used or converted to a permanent loan to finance the purchase by a first user.

RESPA dictates that certain activities need to be disclosed and other activities are prohibited. Some of the activities that need to be disclosed are discussed below.

* Information Booklet. An informational booklet written by United States Department of Housing and Urban Development has to be distributed by lenders to each loan applicant at least three business days after the applicant has turned in an application for credit. The purpose of the informational booklet is to explain to the applicant the costs and expenses associated with the real estate closing process.

* Good Faith Estimates. Each lender is required to give good faith estimates of the costs and types of expenses that the applicant may incur as a result of completing a loan and closing a purchase or transfer of real property. These estimates must be given to the applicant within three business days after the application for credit has been submitted.

* Uniform Settlement Statement. A uniform settlement statement known as **HUD-1** must be used for all transactions that involve a federally related mortgage loan. All required charges on the borrowers and sellers must be clearly stated. See Figure 12.1 for an example of a HUD statement.

* One-Day Advance Inspection. The borrower has the right to inspect the closing costs during the day immediately preceding the closing date. The closing agent or agency must present the closing documentation in as complete a form as possible for the inspection.

* Escrow Limitations. An escrow account is permitted to be established under RESPA in order to deposit a sum of money in advance of the closing so that recurring charges may be paid. Such charges can include, but are not limited to, taxes and insurance.

Federal Housing Administration
A division of the U.S. Department of Housing and Urban Development (HUD) which insures mortgage loans made by private lenders on residential real estate.

HUD-1
A uniform settlement statement required by the Real Estate Settlement Procedures Act for all real estate transactions that involve a federally related mortgage loan.

FIGURE 12.1 HUD Settlement Statement

A. **Settlement Statement**	U.S. Department of Housing and Urban Development	OMB Approval No. 2502-0265 (expires 9/30/2006)

B. Type of Loan

1. ☐ FHA 2. ☐ FmHA 3. ☐ Conv. Unins.	6. File Number:	7. Loan Number:	8. Mortgage Insurance Case Number:
4. ☐ VA 5. ☐ Conv. Ins.			

C. Note: This form is furnished to give you a statement of actual settlement costs. Amounts paid to and by the settlement agent are shown. Items marked "(p.o.c.)" were paid outside the closing; they are shown here for informational purposes and are not included in the totals.

D. Name & Address of Borrower:	E. Name & Address of Seller:	F. Name & Address of Lender:

G. Property Location:	H. Settlement Agent:	
	Place of Settlement:	I. Settlement Date:

J. Summary of Borrower's Transaction		**K. Summary of Seller's Transaction**	
100. Gross Amount Due From Borrower		**400. Gross Amount Due To Seller**	
101. Contract sales price		401. Contract sales price	
102. Personal property		402. Personal property	
103. Settlement charges to borrower (line 1400)		403.	
104.		404.	
105.		405.	
Adjustments for items paid by seller in advance		**Adjustments for items paid by seller in advance**	
106. City/town taxes to		406. City/town taxes to	
107. County taxes to		407. County taxes to	
108. Assessments to		408. Assessments to	
109.		409.	
110.		410.	
111.		411.	
112.		412.	
120. Gross Amount Due From Borrower		**420. Gross Amount Due To Seller**	
200. Amounts Paid By Or In Behalf Of Borrower		**500. Reductions In Amount Due To Seller**	
201. Deposit or earnest money		501. Excess deposit (see instructions)	
202. Principal amount of new loan(s)		502. Settlement charges to seller (line 1400)	
203. Existing loan(s) taken subject to		503. Existing loan(s) taken subject to	
204.		504. Payoff of first mortgage loan	
205.		505. Payoff of second mortgage loan	
206.		506.	
207.		507.	
208.		508.	
209.		509.	
Adjustments for items unpaid by seller		**Adjustments for items unpaid by seller**	
210. City/town taxes to		510. City/town taxes to	
211. County taxes to		511. County taxes to	
212. Assessments to		512. Assessments to	
213.		513.	
214.		514.	
215.		515.	
216.		516.	
217.		517.	
218.		518.	
219.		519.	
220. Total Paid By/For Borrower		**520. Total Reduction Amount Due Seller**	
300. Cash At Settlement From/To Borrower		**600. Cash At Settlement To/From Seller**	
301. Gross Amount due from borrower (line 120)		601. Gross amount due to seller (line 420)	
302. Less amounts paid by/for borrower (line 220)	( )	602. Less reductions in amt. due seller (line 520)	( )
303. **Cash** ☐ From ☐ To Borrower		603. **Cash** ☐ To ☐ From Seller	

Section 5 of the Real Estate Settlement Procedures Act (RESPA) requires the following: • HUD must develop a Special Information Booklet to help persons borrowing money to finance the purchase of residential real estate to better understand the nature and costs of real estate settlement services; • Each lender must provide the booklet to all applicants from whom it receives or for whom it prepares a written application to borrow money to finance the purchase of residential real estate; • Lenders must prepare and distribute with the Booklet a Good Faith Estimate of the settlement costs that the borrower is likely to incur in connection with the settlement. These disclosures are mandatory.

Section 4(a) of RESPA mandates that HUD develop and prescribe this standard form to be used at the time of loan settlement to provide full disclosure of all charges imposed upon the borrower and seller. These are third party disclosures that are designed to provide the borrower with pertinent information during the settlement process in order to be a better shopper.

The Public Reporting Burden for this collection of information is estimated to average one hour per response, including the time for reviewing instructions, searching existing data sources, gathering and maintaining the data needed, and completing and reviewing the collection of information.

This agency may not collect this information, and you are not required to complete this form, unless it displays a currently valid OMB control number.

The information requested does not lend itself to confidentiality.

Cont'd...

FIGURE 12.1 HUD Settlement Statement *Cont'd...*

L. Settlement Charges

		Paid From Borrower's Funds at Settlement	Paid From Seller's Funds at Settlement
700. Total Sales/Broker's Commission based on price $ @ % =			
Division of Commission (line 700) as follows:			
701. $ to			
702. $ to			
703. Commission paid at Settlement			
704.			
800. Items Payable In Connection With Loan			
801. Loan Origination Fee %			
802. Loan Discount %			
803. Appraisal Fee to			
804. Credit Report to			
805. Lender's Inspection Fee			
806. Mortgage Insurance Application Fee to			
807. Assumption Fee			
808.			
809.			
810.			
811.			
900. Items Required By Lender To Be Paid In Advance			
901. Interest from to @$ /day			
902. Mortgage Insurance Premium for months to			
903. Hazard Insurance Premium for years to			
904. years to			
905.			
1000. Reserves Deposited With Lender			
1001. Hazard insurance months@$ per month			
1002. Mortgage insurance months@$ per month			
1003. City property taxes months@$ per month			
1004. County property taxes months@$ per month			
1005. Annual assessments months@$ per month			
1006. months@$ per month			
1007. months@$ per month			
1008. months@$ per month			
1100. Title Charges			
1101. Settlement or closing fee to			
1102. Abstract or title search to			
1103. Title examination to			
1104. Title insurance binder to			
1105. Document preparation to			
1106. Notary fees to			
1107. Attorney's fees to			
(includes above items numbers:)			
1108. Title insurance to			
(includes above items numbers:)			
1109. Lender's coverage $			
1110. Owner's coverage $			
1111.			
1112.			
1113.			
1200. Government Recording and Transfer Charges			
1201. Recording fees: Deed $; Mortgage $; Releases $			
1202. City/county tax/stamps: Deed $; Mortgage $			
1203. State tax/stamps: Deed $; Mortgage $			
1204.			
1205.			
1300. Additional Settlement Charges			
1301. Survey to			
1302. Pest inspection to			
1303.			
1304.			
1305.			
1400. Total Settlement Charges (enter on lines 103, Section J and 502, Section K)			

SPOT THE ISSUE

Donna and Dave want to buy a new home and apply for financing at a local mortgage company. They find a house they like and the mortgage company agrees to give them the requested loan. What important right does the Truth in Lending Act provide Donna and Dave as borrowers? Why might this right be so important?

Certain activities are prohibited by RESPA. Some of those activities are as follows:

kickback
A payment of money or something of value to a person for the purpose of obtaining business from that person.

- Title Insurance. A seller of property is prohibited from requiring the buyer to purchase title insurance from any particular company. The buyer is allowed to purchase from any title insurance company he wishes. If a seller violates this provision, the seller can be liable for up to three times the amount of the title insurance charges that the buyer paid.

- **Kickbacks**. In the past, kickbacks were problematic during real estate transactions. RESPA prohibits kickbacks. No person is permitted to give and no person can accept any fee or thing of value pursuant to any agreement or understanding that entails the referral of a real estate transaction that involves a federally related loan.

- Unearned Fee. RESPA prohibits anyone from giving or accepting any portion, split, or percentage of any charge made or received for rendering services for a real estate closing that involves a federally related loan. However, if more than one person performs an actual service on the real estate closing, then those individuals are permitted to split the payment for the portion of the service that they rendered.

Although kickbacks and unearned fees are prohibited by RESPA, certain types of payments are still allowed. These include payments made to lawyers, title companies, lenders, and others for any services actually rendered, and payments to employees and others for services rendered or goods or facilities provided. Additionally, real estate agents are allowed to split commissions and controlled business arrangements are permitted, as long as the relationship is disclosed to the customer when the referral is made; the person making the referral provides the customer with an estimate of the range of charges usually made by the provider to whom the referral is made; the customer is not required to use the provider; and the referrer receives nothing for the referral except a return on its ownership interest. Finally, settlement service providers may mark up the cost of services they purchase from other parties and then sell to borrowers.

If anyone violates the RESPA provisions, the violators may be fined up to $10,000 and could face up to a year in prison. In addition, the violator may be liable for civil penalties up to three times the amount of the fees that were wrongfully charged as well as court costs and attorney's fees. If an individual believes that RESPA has been violated, she should send a written complaint describing the act in question. The complaint should include names, addresses, and phone numbers of the alleged violators and sent to this address:

U.S. Department of Housing and Urban Development
Office of RESPA and Interstate Land Sales
451 7th Street SW, Room 9154
Washington, D.C., 20410

RESEARCH THIS

Research RESPA to ascertain in more detail what types of transactions are subject to RESPA, as well as who is obligated to perform certain types of duties. How does RESPA protect a consumer financially?

YOU BE THE JUDGE

Home Federal Mortgage Company provides many services to its clients. One of these services is the providing of credit reports. Home Federal purchases credit reports for $15. It then charges clients $50 for the same credit report. Does RESPA allow this?

TRUTH IN LENDING

The **Truth-in-Lending Act** is another act that was passed by the United States Congress with the intent of protecting the consumer. The act, passed in 1969, is contained within the Consumer Credit Protection Act. The Truth-in-Lending Act protects consumers from inaccurate and unfair billing practices. Initially it was basically a disclosure statute, but in 1980 it was amended to provide many more consumer protections. Then, in 1994, it was amended to include the Homeowner's Equity Protection Act. This was a deliberate effort to improve lending practices within the mortgage industry. Today, the Truth-in-Lending Act promotes informed decision-making by consumers, including potential home buyers, by requiring disclosures about terms and costs of loan offers. In addition, the act also provides for the disclosure of credit terms that can be easily read by consumers, so that they can compare the rates from different lenders for a variety of terms. Specifically, the lender must disclose to the borrower the annual percentage rate. To simplify, the Truth-in-Lending Act requires that the lender make all details about the mortgage readily available and accessible so that the consumer understands the agreement into which he is entering. Then the consumer can make an informed decision regarding whether or not the loan offer is in his best interest.

The Truth-in-Lending Act provides for creditors to make certain disclosures. The disclosure must be made to the consumer, or borrower. The Truth-in-Lending Act affects real estate transactions that are not subject to RESPA. Under the Truth-in-Lending Act, all disclosures must be made prior to the time that the borrower becomes contractually obligated to make payments on the loan.

The disclosure must be in writing and clear and conspicuous. It must be provided to the consumer in such a form that the consumer may be able to keep possession of it. The disclosure information is to be kept separate and apart from all nondisclosure information and should be placed on a separate form.

The disclosure is usually based on the terms of the legal obligation that has been reached between the borrower and the lender. The following information must be contained in the disclosure:

- The name of the creditor, or lender, as well as the creditor's address and telephone number
- The amount of money to be financed, along with prepaid finance charges
- The amount of the **finance charges**.
- The number, amount, and timing of the payments that must be made. This is known as the payment schedule and includes the repayment of not only the principal amount borrowed, but any finance charges and interest that have been imposed. The total number of payments that must be paid must also be stated.
- A demand statement that states why the debt may become due prior to the normal **amortization** of the loan.
- Any prepayment provisions such as prepayment penalties that may be assessed should the borrower pay the loan earlier than scheduled.

Truth-in-Lending Act
A federal regulation passed to protect consumers from unfair billing practices, as well as provide them with information for an informed credit use.

finance charge
The consideration for the privilege of deferring payments of a purchase price.

amortization
The allocation of the cost or other basis of an intangible asset over its estimated useful life.

- Any charges that may be assessed should the borrower make late payments on the loan.
- The security interest and insurance charges that might be assessed.

rescission
A party's unilateral unmaking of a contract for a legally sufficient reason.

The Truth-in-Lending Act also provides consumers with the right of **rescission**. Usually, the right of rescission gives a consumer anywhere from three to five days to change her mind about having contracted for the loan, and allows the borrower to void the transaction without incurring any penalties. The rescission provision typically states that if the borrower wishes to rescind the transaction, she must provide a notice, in writing, to the creditor within the rescission period. For example, when there is a three-day right of rescission on a mortgage and the mortgage closes on Tuesday, the three-day rescission period includes Wednesday, Thursday, and Friday, and the loan is disbursed on Saturday. Keep in mind that Saturday is considered a business day, but Sundays and federal holidays are not. If the right of rescission is exercised, a lender must return any fees already received.

A rescission notice must be provided from the creditor to the borrower. The creditor is required to provide two copies of the notice to each person who is a borrower. For example, if John and Paul seek to secure a loan, the creditor must provide two copies of the rescission notice to John and two copies of the notice to Paul, for a total of four copies. The notice will include the following information:

- The date of the transaction
- The security interest that is being taken in the borrower's dwelling
- The borrower's right to rescind
- The terms that dictate how the rescission must be implemented
- The effects of a rescission
- The expiration date indicating the end of the rescission period

A borrower may also waive his right to rescind the transaction and permit performance on the deal.

PRACTICE TIP

Mortgage brokers often help borrowers get loans. The borrower may then pay an interest rate higher than the lender's market rate, and the lender may pay the present value of the difference; this is referred to as a yield spread premium. Borrowers have argued that such payments are actually illegal referral fees under RESPA, but HUD has issued policy statements approving the practice, if the compensation of the broker is for services rendered and is reasonably related to the actual value of such services.

INTEREST RATES

Creditors are required to disclose their interest rates on any loan transaction, so that consumers can make informed transactions. The **annual percentage rate** being assessed on the loan must be disclosed. On some loans the interest rate is set and fixed, and does not vary for the life of the loan. For other loans, the interest rate will fluctuate up or down, depending on a predetermined variable to which the interest rate is tied.

CASE FACT PATTERN

Marta and Manny are purchasing a single-family home. They have secured a mortgage from a mortgage loan company. Marta and Manny want to have a low monthly payment initially on the loan, because Manny started a new job approximately four months ago and they do not want their cash flow during the first year to be too tight. Their loan is an adjustable rate mortgage. The loan is for $250,000 and has an initial interest rate of 3 percent. The interest rate is tied to the six-month treasury bill. If the rate on the six-month treasury bill rises, so will Marta and Manny's mortgage payment. The adjustable rate mortgage provides for a cap on the interest rate that can be charged on the loan. The cap is 9 percent. That means that the interest rate on the loan can rise up to 9 percent, but can never be higher than 9 percent for the life of the loan. The interest rate can also be lower, but can never be lower than the initial 3 percent rate that was assessed at the time the loan was originated. In addition, the interest on the loan can be raised or lowered every year. Marta and Manny are sure that they will be making more money in the future, so they are willing to gamble on what the interest rates will do on their ARM.

EYE ON ETHICS

Disclosure information is an important part of the loan process. A legal assistant who is working with real estate transactions needs to be very familiar with all of the information and elements that are required in a proper disclosure. This information must be meticulously checked so that the client is fully informed of all aspects of the loan. Only with the proper and accurate information can a client make an informed decision and can all rights and interests of the client be protected.

SURF'S UP

If you are interested in finding out the interest rates that are being charged for adjustable rate mortgages in your state, you only have to check rates on the Internet to get a good idea. Some of the following Web sites offer information on mortgages:

www.wellsfargo.com
www.bankamerica.com
www.mortgagenewsdaily.com
www.legalclosing.com

Variable interest rates are known as adjustable interest rates and are tied to a particular interest rate index. These rates are usually known as **adjustable rate mortgages** (ARM). The interest rate index to which these types of loans are tied can be a treasury bill or a prime lending rate. As the index increases or decreases, the interest rate on the mortgage will increase or decrease as well. As the interest rates increase and decrease, the borrower's mortgage payment will increase or decrease accordingly.

The Competitive Equality Banking Act of 1987 placed a cap on adjustable rate mortgages. What that means is that any adjustable rate mortgage that is secured by a family dwelling where the loan originates from a national bank must have a maximum amount of interest that can be charged on the loan. The cap must be stated in the documentation so that it is easily discernable by the consumer.

DOCUMENTS ASSOCIATED WITH A REAL ESTATE CLOSING

Affidavit

An **affidavit** is a written statement of fact that is sworn to by the person who is attesting to the truth of the statement of facts contained in the document. The person's signature on the affidavit is usually attested to by a notary public. The notary's signature will appear on the affidavit, along with a notary seal. Should a person lie or falsify statements in an affidavit, he has committed the criminal act of **perjury**. If someone is found liable for having committed an act of perjury, that person may face both civil and criminal penalties.

A particular type of affidavit usually found in real estate transactions is the title affidavit. The title affidavit usually assists in removing standard exceptions from title insurance policies. A title affidavit is a statement of facts that attests to the following:

- The person signing the affidavit owns the real property that is being described in the affidavit.
- The boundary lines of the real property are certain and not in dispute.
- The person signing the affidavit has a right to possession of the real property.

annual percentage rate
The actual cost of borrowing money, expressed in the form of annual interest rate to make it easy for one to compare the cost of borrowing money among several lenders.

adjustable rate mortgage
A mortgage format under which the lender is permitted to adjust the mortgage interest rate from time to time in accordance with fluctuations in some external index.

affidavit
Any written document in which the signer swears under oath that the statements in the document are true.

perjury
A false statement knowingly made concerning a matter wherein an affiant is required by law to be sworn as to some matter material to the issue or point in question.

FIGURE 12.2 **Affidavit of Title**

AFFIDAVIT OF TITLE

State of New York, Country of   ss.:   Title No. _____

being duly sworn, says:

*If owner is a corporation, fill in office held by deponent and name of corporation

I reside at No.
I am the *
owner in fee simple of premises
and   the grantee described in a certain deed of said premises recorded in the Register's
Office of   Country in (Liber) (Record Liber) (Reel)   of Conveyances,
page

Said premises have been in $^{my}_{its}$ possession since   ; that $^{my}_{its}$ possession thereof has been peaceable and undisturbed, and the title thereto has never been disputed, questioned, or rejected, nor insurance thereof refused, as far as I know. I know of no facts by reason of which said possession or title might be called in question, or by reason of which any claim to any part of said premises or any interest therein adverse to $^{me}_{it}$ me might be set up. There are no Federal tax claims or liens assessed or filed against $^{me}_{it}$. There are no judgments against $^{me}_{it}$ unpaid or unsatisfied or record entered in any court of this state, or of the United States, and said premises are, as far as I know, free from all leases, mortgages, taxes, assessments, water charges, sewer rents and other liens and encumbrances, except

Said premises are now occupied by

No proceedings in bankruptcy have ever been instituted by or against $^{me}_{it}$ in any court or before any officer of any state, or of the United States, nor $^{have~I}_{has~it}$ at any time made an assignment for the benefit of creditors, nor an assignment, now in effect, of the rents of said premises or any part thereof.

*I am a citizen of the United States, and am more than 18 years old. I am by occupation

I am married to

who is over the age of 18 years and is competent to convey or mortgage real estate. I was married to her on the

day of   I have never been married

*This paragraph to be omitted if owner is a corporation

to any other person now living. I have not been known by any other name during the past ten years.

* That the charter of said corporation is in full force and effect and no proceeding is pending for its dissolution or annulment. That all license and franchise taxes due and payable by said corporation have been paid in full.

There are no actions pending affecting said premises. That no repairs, alterations or improvements have been made to said premises which have not been completed more than four months prior to the date hereof; nor have any obligations been incurred which have become or will become liens on the above premises.

*This paragraph to be omitted if owner is not a corporation.

There are no facts known to me relating to the title to said premises which have not been set forth in this affidavit.

This affidavit is made to induce
to accept a $^{of}_{on}$ said premises,
and to induce Chicago Title Insurance Company hereinafter called "The Company" to issue its policy of title insurance covering said premises knowing that they will rely on the statements hrein made.

Sworn to before me this

day of   ,20   _____

- No liens, encumbrances, easements, or leases exist on the real property unless they are expressly identified in the affidavit.
- There are no judgments, bankruptcies, or other restrictions against the person who is signing the affidavit and who owns the real property.
- The affidavit is being made by the person signing the affidavit with knowledge that it will be relied on by purchasers, lenders, and title insurance companies.

See Figure 12.2 for an example of an affidavit of title.

Most transactions involving real property require the transfer of a deed or bill of sale or assignment of warranties, to name a few of the many documents that might be found. Remember that a deed is a legal document that transfers ownership of real property from one person to another.

Bill of Sale

If the real estate transaction involves both real and personal property, then a separate legal document is required for the transfer of the personal property. This legal document is called a **bill of sale**. The bill of sale can contain warranties of title or it can be a quitclaim bill of sale without warranties. A general warranty bill of sale warranties that the seller lawfully owns and is in possession of the personal property that is being sold, that the seller has a right to sell or transfer the property, and that the personal property is free and clear of any and all encumbrances or security interests. The seller will further warrant and defend the title of the personal property against claims from any third persons that may be asserted after the transfer. See Figure 12.3 for an example of a bill of sale.

> **bill of sale**
> A written agreement by which one person assigns or transfers his right to or interest in goods and personal chattels to another.

Assignment of Leases

If any leases exist on the real property, they may be transferred with the real property. Usually this is found with commercial real property that has tenants. All leases are usually assigned to the purchaser, along with any security deposits that may need to be returned to the tenants upon the expiration of the leases. An assignment of leases usually is signed by both the purchaser and the seller, and their signatures are witnessed and notarized.

1099-B Report Form

The Internal Revenue Service requires real estate agents or others involved in real estate closings to report the sales of real estate transactions, because the transaction of real property is taxable. The Internal Revenue Service provides form 1099-B to be used to accomplish this reporting.

FIGURE 12.3
Sample Bill of Sale

Bill of Sale

_____ (Seller) hereby sells, transfers, assigns and conveys unto _____ (Purchaser) and its successors and assigns forever with quitclaim covenants only, the following described property:

Seller hereby sells and transfers only such right, title and interest as it may hold and that said chattels sold herein are sold subject to such prior liens, encumbrances and adverse claims, if any, that may exist, and Seller disclaims any and all warranties thereto.

Said assets are further sold in "as is" condition and where presently located.

Signed this _____ day of _____, 20__.

_____
Seller

FIGURE 12.4 **Sample Closing Statement**

FIDELITY TITLE COMPANY
A Title Insurance Agency • Est. 1987

SAMPLE CLOSING STATEMENT

FTC No: T0-0110

Seller: Thomas and Sandra Seller   Purchaser: Steven and Debra Buyer

Closing Date: 2 /   7 2000
Adjustment Date: 2 /   7 2000   Prorations based on 365
Property Address: 1234 Seller Street

PURCHASER'S STATEMENT:

Sale Price			$ 200,000.00
1999 Winter Taxes 2 / 7 to 11/30	$ 293.47		
0.80 /day x 297 days		$	238.80
1999 Summer Taxes 2 / 7 to 6/30	$ 2,604.16		
7.13 /day x 144 days		$	1,027.39
RECORD WARRANTY DEED		$	17.00
		$	
TOTAL CHARGES		**$**	**201,283.19**

CREDITS: Deposit Paid		$ 1,500.00	
		$	
TOTAL CREDITS		**$**	**1,500.00**
Balance Due from Purchaser		$	199,783.19
LESS: NEW MORTGAGE		$	190,000.00
Net Balance Due from Purchaser		$	9,783.19

I / We consider the foregoing to be a correct accounting:

Purchaser ....   Purchaser ....
Steven Buyer   Debra Buyer

SELLER'S STATEMENT:

Balance due from Purchaser to Seller	$	199,783.19
	$	
Deposit previously paid broker/seller	$	
TOTAL FUNDS	**$**	**199,783.19**

DISBURSEMENTS:

PAYOFF	$	81,000.00
Title Policy Premium	$	850.00
Revenue Stamps	$	1,720.00
RECORD WARRANTY DEED	$	17.00
SELLER RECORDING/DISCHARGE	$	14.00
DOC PREP FEE	$	250.00
OCCUPANCY ESCROW (30 DAYS @ 44.86 PER DAY)	$	1,345.60
WATER ESCROW	$	200.00
	$	
TOTAL DISBURSEMENTS	**$**	**85,396.60**
NET BALANCE DUE TO SELLER	**$**	**114,386.59** *

I / We consider the foregoing to be a correct accounting:

Seller ....   Seller ....
Thomas Seller   Sandra Seller

THE PARTIES SHALL PAY ANY SUMS NECESSARY TO   Furnished   by FIDELITY TITLE CO.
CORRECT ANY DISCOVERED ERRORS IN COMPUTATIONS
AT ANY TIME.

Commission on Sale .... $ * If deposit is paid to Seller
LISTING BROKER:
Percentage:
SELLING BROKER:
Percentage: Less Deposit:

32100 Telegraph Rd., Suite 115 • Bingham Farms, MI 48025
Phone: 248-642-1115 • Fax: 248-642-0935

Closing Costs

Closing costs are not part of the purchase price, but are those costs associated with obtaining a mortgage loan. These costs typically include attorney fees, brokerage commissions, loan fees, an appraisal fee, credit fees, inspection fees, and insurance fees. For example, lawyers and brokers are compensated for their assistance to both buyer and seller during the closing process. Remember, RESPA provides some protection by requiring that a lender provide the buyer with a good faith estimate of what those costs may be. After closing costs are paid, the home loan becomes official.

Closing Statement

The **closing statement** is provided in a real estate transaction and sets forth the financial terms of a sale or loan closing. The statement indicates all the money involved and to whom the funds have been disbursed. See Figure 12.4 for an example of a closing statement.

closing statement
A written breakdown of the costs involved in a particular real estate transaction; usually prepared by a lender or escrow agent.

Summary

The Real Estate Procedures Act (RESPA) is a federal statute that governs all federally guaranteed mortgage loans. RESPA was passed in order to redesign the real estate closing process and protect consumers from the high closing and settlement costs associated with the purchase of property. According to RESPA, all settlement or closing costs must be disclosed to the consumer in advance of the closing. In addition, RESPA eliminates the kickbacks and referral fees that previously plagued the unsuspecting purchasers of real property. RESPA also dictates the maximum amount of funds that may be required to be placed into escrow accounts in order to pay for recurring charges or assessments.

The Truth-in-Lending Act is another act passed by the United States Congress with the intent of protecting the consumer. It protects consumers from inaccurate and unfair billing practices. It also provides for the disclosure of credit terms in a form that is easily read by consumers, so that they can compare the rates from different lenders for a variety of terms.

The Truth-in-Lending Act provides for creditors to make certain disclosures to the consumer or borrower. It affects real estate transactions that are not subject to RESPA. Under the Truth-in-Lending Act, all disclosures must be made prior to the time that the borrower becomes contractually obligated to make payments on the loan.

The Truth-in-Lending Act also provides consumers with the right of rescission. Usually, the right of rescission gives a consumer anywhere from three to five days to change her mind about having contracted for the loan, and allows the borrower to void the transaction without incurring any penalties.

Creditors are required to disclose their interest rates on any loan transaction so that consumers can make informed transactions. The annual percentagerate being assessed on the loan must be disclosed. On some loans the interest rate is set and fixed and does not vary for the life of the loan. For other loans, the interest rate will fluctuate up or down, depending on a predetermined variable to which the interest rate is tied.

Variable interest rates are known as adjustable interest rates and are tied to a particular interest rate index. These rates are usually known as adjustable rate mortgages (ARM). The interest rate index to which these types of loans are tied can be a treasury bill or a prime lending rate. As the index increases or decreases, the interest rate on the mortgage will increase or decrease as well. As the interest rates increase and decrease, the borrower's mortgage payment will increase or decrease accordingly.

An affidavit is a written statement of fact that is sworn to by the person who is attesting to the truth of the statement of facts contained in the document. The person's signature on the affidavit is usually attested to by a notary public. The notary's signature will appear on the affidavit along with a notary seal. Should a person lie or falsify statements in an affidavit, he has committed the criminal act of perjury.

If the real estate transaction involves both real and personal property, then a separate legal document is required for the transfer of the personal property. This document is called a bill of sale. The bill of sale can contain warranties of title, or it can be a quitclaim bill of sale without warranties. A general warranty bill of sale warranties that the seller lawfully owns and is in possession of the personal property that is being sold, that the seller has a right to sell or transfer the property, and that the personal property is free and clear of any and all encumbrances or security interests. The seller will further warrant and defend the title of the personal property against claims from any third persons that may be asserted after the transfer.

Key Terms

Adjustable rate mortgage
Affidavit
Amortization
Annual percentage rate
Bill of sale
Closing statement
Federal Housing Administration

Finance charge
HUD-1
Kickback
Perjury
Real Estate Settlement Procedures Act
Rescission
Truth-in-Lending Act

Review Questions

1. What is the purpose of RESPA?
2. What is a kickback?
3. What is an affidavit?
4. What types of transactions are subject to RESPA, and what types of transactions are exempt from RESPA?
5. What is the purpose of the Truth-in-Lending Act?
6. What is perjury?
7. List the types of disclosures that need to be made under the Truth-in-Lending Act.
8. What is an annual percentage rate?
9. What is an ARM?
10. What is the difference between an annual percentage rate and an ARM?

Exercises

1. Using the scenario in the Case Fact Pattern, create a disclosure for a loan for Marta and Manny. Make sure that the disclosure has all the required provisions and language required by the Truth-in-Lending Act. You will need to research and read the Truth-in-Lending Act in order to complete this assignment. You may want to locate a form on the Internet or from some other source to provide you with the appropriate format for the disclosure.
2. Create a bill of sale for Marta and Manny in order to purchase all of the furniture that is located in the house that they are purchasing. They are purchasing a model home from Kirby Development, and they are to purchase all of the furnishings in the home for the sum of $75,000.

3. Marta and Manny wish to rescind their transaction. Prepare the proper rescission notification for the couple. When must the rescission be sent?

4. Homestead Title Company regularly charges borrowers $60 to record a mortgage, when the county recorder's fee is only $39. Is this allowed by RESPA? Why or why not?

5. Look up the following case: *Washington Mut. Sav. Bank v. Superior Court*, 89 Cal. Rptr.2d 560 (Cal.App.1999). What does this case demonstrate?

6. What does RESPA require a lender to do to prepare buyers for the paying of closing costs?

7. Visit www.hud.gov and find specific information on real estate closings for your home state.

PORTFOLIO ASSIGNMENT

Research real estate closing software on the Internet. Create a list of such software programs for your portfolio.

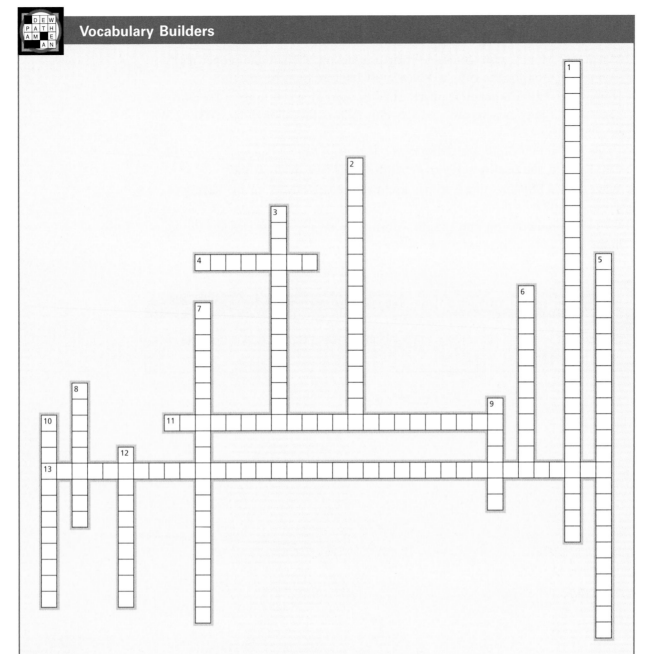

Instructions

Use the key terms from this chapter to fill in the answers to the crossword puzzle.

NOTE: When the answer is more than one word, leave a blank space between words.

ACROSS

4. a payment of money or something of value to a person for the purpose of obtaining business from that person.

11. the actual cost of borrowing money, expressed in the form of annual interest rate to make it easy for one to compare the cost of borrowing money among several lenders.

13. federal statute governing real estate closings for all federally guaranteed mortgage loans.

DOWN

1. a component of the U.S. Department of Housing and Urban Development (HUD) which insures mortgage loans made by private lenders on residential real estate.

2. a written breakdown of the costs involved in a particular real estate transaction; usually prepared by a lender or escrow agent.

3. the consideration for privilege of deferring payments of purchase price.

5. a mortgage format under which the lender is permitted to adjust the mortgage interest rate from time to time in accordance with fluctuations in some external index.

6. a written agreement by which one person assigns or transfers his right to or interest in goods and personal chattels to another.

7. a federal regulation passed to protect consumers from unfair billing practices as well as provide them with information for an informed credit use.

8. any written document in which the signer swears under oath that the statements in the document are true.

9. a false statement knowingly made concerning a matter wherein an affiant is required by law to be sworn as to some matter material to the issue or point in question.

10. the allocation of the cost or other basis of an intangible asset over its estimated useful life.

12. a party's unilateral unmaking of a contract for a legally sufficient reason.

COUNTRYWIDE HOME LOANS, INC. and LandSafe Services, Inc., Appellants,

v.

KENTUCKY BAR ASSOCIATION, Appellee.

Kentucky Land Title Association, Appellant,

113 S.W.3d 105

Supreme Court of Kentucky.

Aug. 21, 2003.

I. INTRODUCTION

On March 1, 2000, Movants, Countrywide Home Loans, Inc. ("Countrywide") and LandSafe Services, Inc. ("LandSafe"), Kentucky Land Title Association ("KLTA"), and Kentucky Association of Realtors, Inc. ("KAR") and Home Builders Association of Kentucky, Inc. ("HBAK"), moved under SCR 3.530(5) for this Court to review Advisory Opinion U-58, adopted by the Kentucky Bar Association ("KBA") Board of Governors in November 1999 and published in the January 2000 issue of Kentucky Bench & Bar. U-58 declares that performance of a real estate closing by a lay closing agent is the unauthorized practice of law. Movants request that the Court vacate U-58, and, in support of that request, argue that U-58 is contradictory to both public policy and U-31, a previous advisory opinion that had allowed laypersons to conduct real estate closings subject to certain limitations. On March 2, 2000, Movant, Kentucky Bankers Association ("Bankers"), filed a similar motion and requested that this Court clarify that U-58 does not change U-31 to the extent that the earlier opinion permitted banks and other lending institutions to close real estate transactions when they provide lender services. We granted the motions to review U-58, allowed the parties to take evidence, and heard oral argument on the issues. We now vacate U-58 and hold that U-31 accurately states the law regarding lay closing agents' ability to perform real estate closings in Kentucky.

II. BACKGROUND

The Unauthorized Practice Committee of the KBA may submit to the KBA Board of Governors recommendations for advisory opinions delineating what activities constitute the unauthorized practice of law. If the recommended opinion is approved by three-fourths of the Board of Governors, it carries the weight of an advisory opinion. This Court, however, is not bound by its terms. On proper request by an aggrieved party, we have the authority to evaluate the opinion and determine whether it accurately states the law. Movants made such a request in this case as to U-58, and we therefore decide whether the conduct of a real estate closing by a lay closing agent is the unauthorized practice of law. . . .

Does a real estate mortgage lender, or a title insurance company on behalf of a real estate mortgage lender, commit the unauthorized practice of law by performing the ministerial acts necessary in the closing of a real estate loan?

The Board of Governors answered with a "qualified no." Essentially, U-31 permitted laypersons to conduct real estate closings so long as they avoided giving legal advice. . . . In reaching this conclusion, the Board of Governors recognized that

"[a] 'real estate closing' is at best ministerial in nature. Some lawyers will allow secretaries and paralegals to participate in closings. . . . The Board did, however, offer a warning that "[f]ederal loans involve significant knowledge of the law, and questions as to what is meant in the documents would certainly involve the unauthorized practice of law."

The Unauthorized Practice Committee thus continued its work on the issue, and, in 1999, the Committee submitted a revised opinion to the Board of Governors. The opinion was adopted by the Board in November 1999, and it was published as U-58 in the January 2000 issue of Kentucky Bench & Bar.

After the opinion was published, petitioners moved this Court, under the authority of SCR 3.530(5), to evaluate U-58. They urge us to review and vacate U-58 and reinstate U-31 as the law on layperson-conducted real estate closings in Kentucky. We begin our evaluation of U-58 with the text of the opinion.

U-58

Question: May real estate closings be conducted by persons who are not real parties in interest without direct supervision of a licensed attorney?

Answer: No.

Question: May title agencies or title insurance companies conduct real estate closings?

Answer: No.

Unauthorized Practice of Law

Only licensed attorneys may practice law in Kentucky. The compelling reason for such regulation is to protect the public against rendition of legal services by unqualified persons. Kentucky Rule of Professional Conduct (RPC) 5.5. . . .

The "unauthorized" practice of law is the performance by those services contained in the definition by "non-lawyers" for "others."

Real Estate Closings

Real estate closings typically have either two or three real parties in interest: seller and buyer, borrower and lender, or seller, buyer-borrower, and lender. Of these three, the least complex are the two-party closings of single sale or loan transactions involving the transfer of an interest in real estate, by deed or mortgage, for purchase money or loan proceeds. The sale of real estate financed by a third party lender is the more complex because it involves separate sale and secured loan transactions in a simultaneous closing.

The "conduct" of a closing is the culmination of such transactions. . . . The preparation and presentation of closing documents is an implied representation that the documents fulfill the requirements of the parties' contractual commitments and the law, and that the documents have been reviewed and found to be legally sufficient. Real estate closings should be conducted only under the supervision of an attorney because questions of legal rights and duties are always involved, and there is no way of assuring that lay settlement agents would raise, or would not attempt to answer, the legal questions. *State v. Buyer's Service Co.,* [292 S.C. 426] 357 S.E.2d 15 (S.C.1987). . . .

[Text omitted]

Closing Supervision by Attorney

An attorney need not be physically present at the closing, so long as it is in fact conducted under his supervision and control, but the responsible attorney must be familiar with the documentation and be available at the time of closing for consultation. He bears ultimate responsibility for the closing and is subject to disciplinary action for any act or omission which otherwise would be misconduct by him or his closing employees, as well as being legally accountable under the duty imposed by *Seigle v. Jasper,* 867 S.W.2d 476 (Ky.App.1993). . . .

Closing by Institutional Lender

When an institutional lender is a real party in interest to a real estate transaction as mortgagee, its lay employee or in-house attorney may preside over the mortgage closing with a customer not represented by an attorney. . . . The lender's employee may attend to the ministerial issues of financial matters, payments, and insurance related to the loan, as these are commonly non-legal functions. KBA U-31.

[Text omitted]

Closing by Title Companies

A distinction must be made as to lay settlement agencies such as title companies and title insurance companies which are not real parties in interest to the real estate or loan transactions. Their only interest is the payment of settlement fees. They act only as a conduit to exchange funds and documents. A lay settlement agency may compile and report factual information from the public records, including abstracts of title, but may not render title opinions. They may act as an agent or broker in connection with the issuance of title insurance commitments and policies and may provide clerical services for a closing. KBA U-21; U-31. . . .

[Text omitted]

III. ARGUMENTS AND EVIDENCE

U-58 has a potential impact on nearly all of the regular participants in real estate transactions. The parties to this motion are representative of most of the affected individuals, although in addressing the issue before us, we must balance the concerns of these parties with the interests and largely-unvoiced concerns of real estate consumers across this state.

[Text omitted]

In support of their motion, Countrywide and Landsafe assert that "the KBA's Unauthorized Practice of Law Committee suffered from a lack of input from interested parties and informed sources outside the members of the state bar." They contend that the evidence produced by the KBA suffers from the same lack of perspective, and maintain that the evidence produced by Movants, which is summarized in Part IV(A), provides the needed insight. . . . Countrywide and Landsafe also emphasize that the presence of lay closing agents contributes to a more competitive market for real estate consumer services, and maintain that U-58 is merely an attempt by the real estate bar to thwart competition. Accordingly, they urge us to

follow the majority of other jurisdictions by clarifying that lay-persons may conduct real estate closings in Kentucky without engaging in the unauthorized practice of law.

KLTA is an association of title companies and agents that attempts to: (1) promote the general welfare of the abstract and title insurance industry; (2) promote professional standards and ethics; (3) promote the safe and efficient transfer of ownership of and interests in real property within the free enterprise system; (4) provide information and education to consumers, to those who regulate, supervise, or enact legislation affecting the land title industry, and to its members; and (5) maintain liaison with governmental agencies and users of the products and services provided by its members. KLTA also petitions this Court to vacate U-58, and similarly argues that there is no evidence of any changes in the real estate market that would warrant a change from U-31. Specifically, KLTA argues that a real estate closing is ministerial or administrative in nature—particularly since the transaction has become so standardized—and suggests that the closing rarely, if ever, engenders the types of legal questions hypothesized by U-58. . . . Finally, KLTA urges that even if this Court were to find the conduct of a real estate closing to be the practice of law, it should authorize the practice. Essentially, KLTA argues that barring lay closing agents from the closing room will harm the public unnecessarily because: (1) title companies produce high quality work; (2) closings remain affordable because of the competition created by title companies; and (3) title companies are substantially regulated by both insurers and lenders. . . .

KAR and HBAK have joined in the request for review of U-58 on behalf of realtors and home builders across Kentucky. . . .

Bankers is a non-profit trade association, consisting of 284 member banks and thrifts having offices in Kentucky, that is concerned primarily with whether U-58 changes U-31, i.e., whether the performance of ministerial tasks of completing promissory notes, mortgages or other documents integral to the closing without the supervision of an attorney, which were permissible under U-31, constitutes the unauthorized practice of law. . . . Thus, they urge us to affirm their authority to conduct closings.

The United States of America, Department of Justice ("Department") has filed an amicus curiae brief in support of Movants. The Department states:

KBA U-58 likely will cause costs for all Kentucky consumers to rise while providing them no more protection than they currently receive. On the other hand, there is no demonstrated harm from the lay closings that have taken place in Kentucky since the KBA sanctioned the practice in 1981, and less drastic measures than banning lay settlements are available if additional consumer protections are required.

Essentially, the Department argues that the interests of the public are best served by keeping open the option of selecting a lay closing agent. . . . Thus, it urges us to vacate U-58.

[Text omitted]

IV. ANALYSIS

A. REVIEW OF THE EVIDENTIARY RECORD

From the evidence, we have identified six major issues relating to: (1) the origination of U-58; (2) the nature of a real estate closing; (3) the types of changes, if any, that the advent of the secondary mortgage market has had upon real estate transactions; (4) the types of questions that arise at closings; (5) closing fees; and (6) professional accountability.

[Text omitted]

The day for closing arrives and everyone meets, . . . each without an attorney; the broker is there, and the title officer is there. The funds are there. And the critical legal documents are also on hand usually prepared by the title company, indicating how much is owed, what deductions should be made for taxes and other costs and what credits are due; and the final marked-up title binder, which evidences the obligation of the title company to issue a title policy to the buyer, and which at that point is probably practically meaningless to the buyer. All are executed and delivered, along with other documents, and the funds are delivered or held in escrow until the title company arranges to pay off prior mortgages and liens.

. . . The witnesses dispute, the effect that technological changes have had on real estate closings. All agree that the pile of documents required at the closing has grown significantly as a result of the stringent requirements for resale of mortgages on the secondary market. . . .

[Text omitted]

Before '75, there was no uniform settlement statement, and a lot of the certifications and mortgage credit related documentation that tends to get executed at a settlement table, was not needed—either not needed or was unique to each individual lender, and whatever they decided was required. Now you have a Fannie Mae or Freddie Mac sellers or guide that dictates most of these forms or the response to them.

[Text omitted]

From the evidence, we agree with Movants that few, if any, significant legal questions arise at most residential closings. It is true that several of the KBA witnesses testified that they anticipate these types of questions and therefore, undertake to avoid them by thoroughly explaining all of the documents presented at the closing. This evidence, however, does not demonstrate that these types of questions arise regularly at closings, and the depositions provided widespread evidence of closings where the parties ask no questions. Moreover, the evidence has convinced us that in those few instances where legal questions do arise, lay closing agents are properly trained to answer only if they can do so by reading from the document itself without providing any additional explanation. If they cannot do so, they are trained to halt the closing so that the parties may seek legal counsel. Thus, the evidence demonstrates that, by and large, lay closers have been following the mandates of U-31.

[Text omitted]

Many witnesses testified that the majority of title companies in this state are owned and operated by attorneys.

B. LAY CLOSINGS AND UNAUTHORIZED PRACTICE OF LAW

We are asked today to decide an issue of first impression in this state. It is an issue of much less breadth than the evidence adduced by the parties would suggest: Is conducting a real estate closing the unauthorized practice of law? Based on our review of the evidence and arguments presented to us, we hold that it is not the unauthorized practice of law for a layperson to conduct a real estate closing for another party. Therefore, we vacate U-58 and adopt the reasoning of U-31.

Our Supreme Court rules define the practice of law as "any service rendered involving legal knowledge or legal advice, whether of representation, counsel or advocacy in or out of court rendered in respect to the rights, duties, obligations, liabilities, or business relations of one requiring the services." The General Assembly has criminalized the unauthorized practice of law and our disciplinary rules prohibit attorneys from "[a]ssist[ing] a person who is not a member of the bar in the performance of an activity that constitutes the unauthorized practice of law." The rationale for such restrictions is that "limiting the practice of law to members of the bar protects the public against rendition of legal services by unqualified persons."

Accordingly, the conduct of a closing is the practice of law if (1) it requires legal knowledge or legal advice, (2) involves representation, counsel or advocacy on behalf of another party, and (3) involves the rights, duties, obligations, liabilities, or business relations of that other party . . . The question now before us, however, concerns the events at a real estate closing, which we earlier characterized as the "final event" of the real estate transaction where the parties execute documents and funds transfer hands.

The KBA recognized in U-31 and in U-58 that there are many ministerial acts that transpire at a real estate closing, including handling financial matters, payments, and loan insurance. Clearly none of these "ministerial" acts requires legal knowledge or advice and, therefore, cannot be termed the practice of law. . . . The dispute arises with regard to one issue—the potential for legal questions and issues to arise at the closing. The KBA argues that this potential renders any conduct at the real estate closing by a person not a party to the transaction the unauthorized practice of law. We disagree.

In our view, U-58 rests on several faulty assumptions. The first is that "it is unrealistic and naive to assume that . . . the settlement agent can present important legal documents to the seller, buyer, borrower, and/or lender at a closing without legal questions being asked and without giving legal advice." This statement is a broad overgeneralization, and the evidence described above has exposed its inaccuracy by illustrating that many closings occur without even one question being asked. . . . Further, the undisputed evidence was that title companies train their employees that, if a question cannot be answered by reading the face of the document or by offering a black letter description, the closing agent is to: (1) explain to the questioning party that he or she should seek legal counsel for an answer to their question; and (2) stop the closing until the party has had an opportunity to seek legal advice and is ready to continue.

[Text omitted]

In a similar statement, U-58 provides that "[t]he legal questions present at a closing, whether asked or should be asked, are endless. . . ." This statement implies that attorneys must conduct or at least supervise closings because there are questions that should be asked at real estate closings that are not asked and having an attorney present will somehow ensure that these questions are asked and answered. Again we fail to see how requiring attorneys to conduct or supervise real estate closings will meet this perceived need. . . . Because lay closing agents conduct closings in a nearly identical fashion, the supervision or even presence of an attorney at the closing offers no more protection to the parties with regard to their unasked questions.

U-58 also states that "questions of legal rights and duties are always involved [in real estate closings], and there is no way of assuring that lay settlement agents would raise, or would not attempt to answer, the legal questions." . . . We do not agree with the KBA's efforts to paint title agents in such a negative light, especially since the evidence has revealed that their services are comparable to those provided by attorneys.

[Text omitted]

Finally, the KBA insists that U-31 and U-58 can coexist without conflict. We fail to see any logic in this argument. In its very first line, U-31 recognizes that it is concerned with the activities of real estate mortgage lenders and title insurance companies. Quickly its text goes on to permit lay real estate closings by these groups. The opinion provides:

A "real estate closing" is at best ministerial in nature. Some lawyers allow secretaries and paralegals to participate in closings. The closing, which consists mainly of financial matters, payments, schedules of payment, and insurance, is basically a nonlegal function.

[Text omitted]

U-58, however, explicitly denies that title companies can perform real estate closings without engaging in the unauthorized practice of law when it states that "[a] title agency may not conduct real estate closings or mask legal fees for closing services under the guise of a 'settlement fee' or other charge. Their conduct of a closing absent independent legal counsel constitutes the unauthorized practice of law." . . . The KBA has not shown any changes or injuries to consumers that would warrant such wholesale change from U-31.

[Text omitted]

We do not deny that there are some portions of the residential real estate transaction that do constitute the practice of law, i.e., the title commitment letter and the preparation of deeds and mortgages, but this case has not asked us to deal with those matters attendant to the real estate closing itself. What we have been concerned with today is merely the thin slice at the end of the real estate transaction that we refer to as the closing. . . .

Thus, we vacate U-58. In doing so, we recognize that U-31 properly states the law on real estate closings in Kentucky: laypersons may conduct real estate closings on behalf of other parties, but they may not answer legal questions that arise at the closing or offer any legal advice to the parties. If they do answer such questions, they are then engaged in the unauthorized practice of law.

V. CONCLUSION

For the above reasons, we hereby vacate U-58 and hold that U-31 accurately describes the unauthorized practice of law parameters for real estate closings conducted by non-lawyers.

All concur.

[footnotes omitted]

Source: Reprinted with permission from Westlaw. Countrywide Home Loans, Inc. v. Kentucky Bar Association, Appellee. 113 S.W.3d 105.

Appendix A

ABSTRACT OF TITLE

to

Lot 1, Block 28, Chase's Addition to Vermillion, Clay County, South Dakota.

----------1----------

GRANT

United States   Approved May 15, 1890

      to

State of South Dakota

----------2----------

PATENT

State of South Dakota   Dated July 5, 1892

      to   Filed July 7, 1892

Vermillion Rail Road Company   Land Record "H," Page 25

CONVEYS: The West ½ of Section 15, Township 89, Range 47.

----------3----------

PLAT

Jack and Terri Bauer,   Dated May 7, 1901
Husband and Wife,

                                Filed May 10, 1901

      to

                                Plat Book 8, Page 19

Whom It May Concern

Plat of Chase's Addition, an Addition to Vermillion, Clay County, South Dakota, comprising the whole of the West ½ of Section 15, Township 89, Range 47.

(Copy of said plat available for inspection at the office of the Clay County Register of Deeds.)

----------4----------

DEED

Jack and Terri Bauer,
Husband and Wife

    To

Tony Almeida and Michele Dessler,
Husband and Wife as Joint Tenants

Consideration: $1.00

Dated April 28, 1902

Book 12, Page 55

CONVEYS: *CAPTION DESCRIPTION*

----------5----------

CONTRACT

Tony Almeida and Michele Dessler,
Husband and Wife

    to

Peter and Lois Griffin,
Husband and Wife

Consideration: $15,500

Dated August 1, 1908

Book 25, Page 250

CONVEYS: *CAPTION DESCRIPTION*

Provides for monthly contract payments or principal and interest with the last payment being due and payable on August 1, 1913.

----------6----------

IN THE CIRCUIT COURT FOR CLAY COUNTY, SOUTH DAKOTA

In the Matter of the Estate

    of

Tony Almeida

Case No. PR009-5

Docket 10, Page 220

(1) INVENTORY filed July 19, 1909, Lists *CAPTION DESCRIPTION*, subject to a Contract for Deed to Peter and Lois Griffin (surviving joint tenant is Michele Dessler).
(2) No federal estate tax return will be filed in this case.
(3) No state inheritance tax is due.

---------7----------

DEED

Michele Dessler,   Consideration: $1.00
A Single Person
                                                          Dated February 25, 1910

to   Filed February 26, 1910

Peter and Lois Griffin,
Husband and Wife   Book 29, Page 3

CONVEYS: *CAPTION DESCRIPTION*

Deed given in fulfillment of one certain Contract for Deed (See Entry No. 5)

---------8----------

EASEMENT
Recorded in Book 50, Page 367

This Easement, executed this 1st day of April, 1917, by PETER and LOIS GRIFFIN, Husband and Wife, and GLEN QUAGMIRE, a Single Man.

1. PETER and LOIS GRIFFIN are the owners in fee of *CAPTION DESCRIPTION*, hereinafter called Parcel A.
2. GLEN QUAGMIRE is the owner in fee of Lot 2, Block 28, Chase's Addition to Vermillion, Clay County, South Dakota, hereinafter called Parcel B.
3. For the purposes of creating perpetual easements for joint driveway purposes as described below, PETER and LOIS GRIFFIN and GLEN QUAGMIRE grand such reciprocal easements, which shall run with the respective grantors' land and title thereto and be binding on the grantors and their heirs and any person who shall hereafter acquire title to Parcels A and B.
4. Easement No. 1: The West 5.0 feet of Parcel A.
5. Easement No. 2: The East 5.0 feet of Parcel B.
6. Attached hereto is a survey of Cleveland Brown, Land Surveyor, dated March 2, 1916, depicting the above-described easements. (Note of Abstractor: Said survey available for inspection in the office of the Clay County Register of Deeds.

Dated April 1, 1916.

----------9----------

JUDGMENT

Against: Peter Griffin

In Favor of: State of South Dakota

Case No. CR20-355

Dated: August 15, 1920

Amount: $100 plus costs

----------10----------

MORTGAGE

Peter and Lois Griffin,
Husband and Wife

to

Quahog Savings and Loan

Consideration: $15,000

Dated July 29, 1923

Filed July 30, 1923

Book 102, Page 12

ENCUMBERS: *CAPTION DESCRIPTION*

Secures one note of even date herewith, providing for monthly installments of principal and interest, with the balance of the indebtedness, if not sooner paid, due and payable on September 1, 1938.

***

17.   Transfer of the Property or a Beneficial Interest in Borrower. If all or any part of the Property or any interest in it is sold or transferred (or if a beneficial interest in Borrower is sold or transferred and Borrower is not a natural person) without Lender's prior written consent, Lender may, at its option, require immediate payment in full of all sums secured by this Security Instrument. However, this option shall not be exercised by Lender if exercise is prohibited by federal law as of the date of this Security Instrument.

18.   WAIVER OF HOMESTEAD EXEMPTION: I understand that homestead property is in many cases protected by claims of creditors and exempt from judicial sale; and that by signing this mortgage, I voluntarily give up my right to this protection for this mortgaged property with respect to claims based upon this mortgage.

***

----------11----------

SATISFACTION

The records of the Clay County Clerk of Court shows the judgment entered in Case No. CR20-355 is paid in full (See Entry No. 9).

----------12----------

JUDGMENT

Against: Peter Griffin   Case No. SMC29-53

In Favor of: Bunyan's   Dated: December 11, 1928

                                                     Amount: $53.20 plus costs

----------13----------

IN THE CIRCUIT COURT OF CLAY COUNTY, SOUTH DAKOTA

Quahog Savings and Loan,
        Plaintiff,

                                                     Case No. CIV29-102

        vs.

Peter and Lois Griffin,
Husband and Wife,
and Bunyan's,
        Defendants.

COMPLAINT

Filed November 19, 1930, seeking foreclosure of one certain mortgage (See Entry No. 10)

----------12(a)----------
RETURN OF SERVICE
Service of Summons and Complaint upon Peter Griffin by personal service on November 22, 1930, by Clay County Sheriff's Deputy Joe Swanson.

----------12(b)----------
RETURN OF SERVICE

Service upon Summons and Complaint upon Lois Griffin by personal service on November 22, 1930, by Clay County Sheriff's Deputy Joe Swanson.

----------12(c)----------
RETURN OF SERVICE

Service upon Summons and Complaint upon Bunyan's by personal service upon Horace Bunyan, Registered Agent of Bunyan's, on November 24, 1930, by Clay County Sheriff's Deputy Joe Swanson.

----------12(d)----------
DEFAULT JUDGMENT
Dated December 31, 1930

Judgment is hereby entered in favor of Quahog Savings and Loan and against Peter Griffin and Lois Griffin, foreclosing the mortgage encumbering *CAPTION DESCRIPTION*. The liens of any and all junior lien holders are hereby extinguished.

----------12(e)----------
NOTICE OF SHERIFF'S SALE

Posted and published according to law. Sheriff's sale to take place on the steps of the Clay County Courthouse at 9:00 a.m. on February 1, 1931.

----------13----------

SHERIFF'S DEED

Sheriff of Clay County   Consideration: $10,200

        To   Dated: February 1, 1931

Ward and June Cleaver,   Book 200, Page 311
Husband and Wife

CONVEYS: *CAPTION DESCRIPTION*

Subject to easements of record, if any.

----------14----------

CONTRACT

Ward and June Cleaver,
Husband and Wife

to

Stewart Gilligan Griffin,
A Single Man

Consideration: $25,000

Dated June 1, 1938

Filed June 4, 1938

Book 225, Page 506

CONVEYS: *CAPTION DESCRIPTION*

Provides for monthly contract payments or principal and interest with the last payment being due and payable on June 1, 1948.

----------15----------

WARRANTY DEED

Ward and June Cleaver,
Husband and Wife

to

Stewart Gilligan Griffin,
A Single Man

Consideration: $1.00

Dated June 1, 1948

Filed June 1, 1948

Book 452, Page 6

CONVEYS: *CAPTION DESCRIPTION*

Deed given in fulfillment of one certain Contract for Deed (See Entry No. 14)

----------16----------

MORTGAGE

Stewart Gilligan Griffin,
A Single Person

to

First National Bank

Consideration: $35,000

Dated December 1, 1949

Filed December 10, 1949

Book 501, Page 125

ENCUMBERS: *CAPTION DESCRIPTION*

Secures one note of even date herewith, providing for monthly installments of principal and interest, with the balance of the indebtedness, if not sooner paid, due and payable on December 1, 1979.

***

19.   Transfer of the Property or a Beneficial Interest in Borrower. If all or any part of the Property or any interest in it is sold or transferred (or if a beneficial interest in Borrower is sold or transferred and Borrower is not a natural person) without Lender's prior written consent, Lender may, at its option, require immediate payment in full of all sums secured by this Security Instrument. However, this option shall not be exercised by Lender if exercise is prohibited by federal law as of the date of this Security Instrument.

20.   WAIVER OF HOMESTEAD EXEMPTION: I understand that homestead property is in many cases protected by claims of creditors and exempt from judicial sale; and that by signing this mortgage, I voluntarily give up my right to this protection for this mortgaged property with respect to claims based upon this mortgage.

***

----------17----------

ASSIGNMENT OF MORTGAGE

First National Bank
By: John B. Dagle,
    Vice President
By: William M. Carlson,
    Loan Officer
(Corporate Seal Affixed)

Dated January 15, 1950

Filed January 27, 1950

Book 505, Page 242

to

Countrywide Advantage Mortgage
Corporation

Assigns Mortgage recorded in Book 501, Page 125.
(See Entry No. 16)

----------18----------

WARRANTY DEED

Stewart Gilligan Griffin,
A Single Person

Consideration: $1.00

Dated: March 17, 1961

to

Filed: March 22, 1961

William J. Jankhigh,
A Single Person.

Book 615, Page 422

CONVEYS: *CAPTION DESCRIPTION*

----------19----------

SATISFACTION

Countrywide Advantage Mortgage
Corporation by Edward Hightower,
President, and Michael Sanzere,
Vice President, (Corporate Seal
Affixed),

Dated March 17, 1961

Filed: March 22, 1961

Book 615, page 421

to

Stewart Gilligan Griffin,
A Single Person.

Releases Mortgage recorded in Book 501, Page 125.

(See Entry No. 16)

----------20----------

MORTGAGE

William J. Jankhigh,
A Single Person

Consideration: $50,000

Dated March 16, 1961

Filed: March 22, 1961

to

First National Bank

Book 615, Page 422

ENCUMBERS: *CAPTION DESCRIPTION*

Secures one note of even date herewith, providing for monthly installments of principal and interest, with the balance of the indebtedness, if not sooner paid, due and payable on April 1, 1991.

***

21.   Transfer of the Property or a Beneficial Interest in Borrower. If all or any part of the Property or any interest in it is sold or transferred (or if a beneficial interest in Borrower is sold or transferred and Borrower is not a natural person) without Lender's prior written consent, Lender may, at its option, require immediate payment in full of all sums secured by this Security Instrument. However, this option shall not be exercised by Lender if exercise is prohibited by federal law as of the date of this Security Instrument.

22. WAIVER OF HOMESTEAD EXEMPTION: I understand that homestead property is in many cases protected by claims of creditors and exempt from judicial sale; and that by signing this mortgage, I voluntarily give up my right to this protection for this mortgaged property with respect to claims based upon this mortgage.

***

----------21----------

JUDGMENT

Against: William J. Jankhigh   Case No. CR61-100

In favor of: The City of Vermillion   Dated: March 31, 1961

                                                                  Amount: $5.00 plus costs

----------22----------

JUDGMENT

Against: William J. Jankhigh   Case No. CR61-146

In favor of: The City of Vermillion   Dated: July 4, 1961

                                                                  Amount: $5.00 plus costs

----------23----------

JUDGMENT

Against: William J. Jankhigh   Case No. CR61-189

In favor of: The State of South Dakota   Dated: August 31, 1961

                                                                  Amount: $5.00 plus costs

----------24----------

JUDGMENT

Against: William J. Jankhigh

In favor of: The City of Vermillion

Case No. CR61-205

Dated: September 15, 1961

Amount: $5.00 plus costs

----------25----------

JUDGMENT

Against: William J. Jankhigh

In favor of: The City of Vermillion

Case No. CR61-276

Dated: November 30, 1961

Amount: $5.00 plus costs

----------26----------

JUDGMENT

Against: William J. Jankhigh

In favor of: The City of Vermillion

Case No. CR62-1

Dated: January 1, 1962

Amount: $7.50 plus costs

----------27----------

JUDGMENT

Against: William J. Jankhigh

In favor of: The City of Vermillion

Case No. CR62-19

Dated: January 21, 1962

Amount: $7.50 plus costs

----------28----------

JUDGMENT

Against: William J. Jankhigh

In favor of: The State of South Dakota

Case No. CR62-79

Dated: March 11, 1962

Amount: $7.50 plus costs

----------29----------

JUDGMENT

Against: William J. Jankhigh

In favor of: The City of Vermillion

Case No. CR62-125

Dated: May 3, 1962

Amount: $7.50 plus costs

----------30----------

SATISFACTION

First National Bank
by E. Allan Farnsworth,
President, and Laurence Tribe,
Vice President, (Corporate Seal
Affixed),

Dated March 17, 1961

Filed: March 22, 1961

Book 615, page 421

to

William J. Jankhigh,
A Single Person.

Releases Mortgage recorded in Book 615, Page 422.

(See Entry No. 20)

----------31----------

WARRANTY DEED

William J. Jankhigh and Carrie M. Jankhigh,
Husband and Wife

to

Timothy J. Powell and Kathleen A. Powell,
Husband and Wife

CONVEYS: *CAPTION DESCRIPTION*

Consideration: $1.00

Dated: November 21, 1963

Filed: November 26, 1963

Roll 2, Image 415

----------32----------

SATISFACTION

Judgment entered against William J. Jankhigh in Case No. CR61-100 is paid in full.

----------33----------

SATISFACTION

Judgment entered against William J. Jankhigh in Case No. CR61-146 is paid in full.

----------34----------

SATISFACTION

Judgment entered against William J. Jankhigh in Case No. CR61-189 is paid in full.

----------35----------

SATISFACTION

Judgment entered against William J. Jankhigh in Case No. CR61-205 is paid in full.

----------36----------

SATISFACTION

Judgment entered against William J. Jankhigh in Case No. CR61-276 is paid in full.

----------37----------

SATISFACTION

Judgment entered against William J. Jankhigh in Case No. CR62-1 is paid in full.

----------38----------

SATISFACTION

Judgment entered against William J. Jankhigh in Case No. CR62-14 is paid in full.

----------39----------

SATISFACTION

Judgment entered against William J. Jankhigh in Case No. CR62-79 is paid in full.

----------40----------

SATISFACTION

Judgment entered against William J. Jankhigh in Case No. CR62-125 is paid in full.

----------41----------

MORTGAGE

Timothy J. Powell and
Kathleen A. Powell,
Husband and Wife

to

Bank of America

Consideration: $75,000

Dated: November 21, 1963

Filed November 26, 1963

Roll 2, Image 416

ENCUMBERS: *CAPTION DESCRIPTION*

Secures one note of even date herewith, providing for monthly installments of principal and interest, with the balance of the indebtedness, if not sooner paid, due and payable on December 1, 1993.

***

23. Transfer of the Property or a Beneficial Interest in Borrower. If all or any part of the Property or any interest in it is sold or transferred (or if a beneficial interest in Borrower is sold or transferred and Borrower is not a natural person) without Lender's prior written consent, Lender may, at its option, require immediate payment in full of all sums secured by this Security Instrument. However, this option shall not be exercised by Lender if exercise is prohibited by federal law as of the date of this Security Instrument.

24. WAIVER OF HOMESTEAD EXEMPTION: I understand that homestead property is in many cases protected by claims of creditors and exempt from judicial sale; and that by signing this mortgage, I voluntarily give up my right to this protection for this mortgaged property with respect to claims based upon this mortgage.

***

----------42----------

ASSIGNMENT OF MORTGAGE

Bank of America
By: Lilly M. Rush,
    Vice President
By: Scott Valens,
    Loan Officer
(Corporate Seal Affixed)

Dated December 23, 1963

Filed January 27, 1963

Roll 3, Page 21

        to

Nationwide Home Mortgage Company

    Assigns Mortgage recorded in Roll 2, Image 416.

    (See Entry No. 41)

----------43----------

IN THE CIRCUIT COURT OF CLAY COUNTY, SOUTH DAKOTA

Timothy J. Powell,

                   Case No. DIV72-54

  Plaintiff

vs.

Kathleen A. Powell,

  Defendant.

JUDGMENT
August 4, 1972

Against: Timothy J. Powell

In favor of: Kathleen A. Powell

Amount: $25,000 property settlement

The marriage between the parties is dissolved. Plaintiff is awarded all right, title, and interest in the real estate legally described as *CAPTION DESCRIPTION*. Defendant shall execute a quit claim deed to Plaintiff.

----------44----------

QUIT CLAIM DEED

Kathleen A. Powell n/k/a   Dated August 10, 1972
Kathleen A. Lumpkin,
A Single Person   Filed August 10, 1972

    To   Roll 67, Image 702

Timothy J. Powell,
A Single Person

  Quitclaims all right, title, and interest in *CAPTION DESCRIPTION*.

  Deed given pursuant to a divorce decree entered in Case No. DIV72-54 on August 4, 1972.

----------45----------

MORTGAGE

Timothy J. Powell,
A Single Person

Consideration: $75,000

Dated: August 10, 1972

to

Filed: August 10, 1972

Bank of America

Roll 67, Image 704

ENCUMBERS: *CAPTION DESCRIPTION*

Secures one note of even date herewith, providing for monthly installments of principal and interest, with the balance of the indebtedness, if not sooner paid, due and payable on September 1, 2002.

***

25.   Transfer of the Property or a Beneficial Interest in Borrower. If all or any part of the Property or any interest in it is sold or transferred (or if a beneficial interest in Borrower is sold or transferred and Borrower is not a natural person) without Lender's prior written consent, Lender may, at its option, require immediate payment in full of all sums secured by this Security Instrument. However, this option shall not be exercised by Lender if exercise is prohibited by federal law as of the date of this Security Instrument.

26.   WAIVER OF HOMESTEAD EXEMPTION: I understand that homestead property is in many cases protected by claims of creditors and exempt from judicial sale; and that by signing this mortgage, I voluntarily give up my right to this protection for this mortgaged property with respect to claims based upon this mortgage.

***

----------46----------

IN THE CIRCUIT COURT OF CLAY COUNTY, SOUTH DAKOTA

Timothy J. Powell,

Case No. DIV72-54

     Plaintiff

vs.

SATISFACTION

Kathleen A. Powell
n/k/a Kathleen A. Lumpkin,

     Defendant.

     COMES NOW the Defendant and hereby satisfies in full the property settlement judgment previously entered herein.

     Dated August 10, 1972.

----------47----------

ASSIGNMENT OF MORTGAGE

Bank of America
By: Lilly M. Rush,
     Vice President
By: Scott Valens,
     Loan Officer
(Corporate Seal Affixed)

Dated September 10, 1972

Filed September 17, 1972

Roll 68, Page 120

     to

Nationwide Home Mortgage Company

     Assigns Mortgage recorded in Roll 67, Image 704.

     (See Entry No. 45)

----------48----------

SATISFACTION

Nationwide Home Mortgage Company
by E. Allan Farnsworth,
President, and Laurence Tribe,
Vice President, (Corporate Seal
Affixed),

Dated June 16, 1995

Filed: June 21, 1995

Roll 312, Image 401

to

Timothy J. Powell,
A Single Person.

Releases Mortgage recorded in Roll 67, Image 704.

(See Entry No. 45)

----------49----------

REAL ESTATE TAX STATEMENT

Taxes of 2004/2005 paid in full.

No search is made for zoning ordinances.

WE HEREBY CERTIFY that we have carefully searched the public records of Clay County, South Dakota, and find no unsatisfied judgments, no conveyances, mortgages, instruments filed under the provisions of the Uniform Commercial Code which describe or identify all or a portion of the property described in the caption hereof, or other instruments, Federal Liens, State Tax Liens, mechanics' liens, suits pending, attachments, unpaid real estate taxes against other persons or corporations named in this Abstract, and no unredeemed tax sales, or unpaid special assessments except as shown upon this Abstract of Title, which are or have been become a lien against property described in Caption since March 17, 2006 at 5:00 p.m.

We have examined the records of the United States District Court for the District of South Dakota, for the ten years prior to this Certificate, and find no bankruptcy proceedings involving title to the property described in caption prior to October 1,1979, and no suits pending and no unpaid judgments except as shown upon this Abstract of Title.

Witness our hand and Seal at Vermillion, South Dakota

This 17th day of March, 2006, at 5:00 p.m.

COYOTE TITLE COMPANY

By:_____
          WYLE E. COYOTE, President

Appendix B

OWNER POLICY OF TITLE INSURANCE

Dakota Homestead Title Insurance Company furnishes to its agents, upon request, Owner Policies of Title Insurance drafted by the American Land Title Association (ALTA), the national trade association of the title industry. These policies are accepted throughout the country.

The Owner Policy insures the interest of an owner in real property. The most common insurable interest is fee simple ownership; however, leasehold interests can be insured. The insurance coverage is normally the purchase price of the real estate but may be an amount in excess of the purchase price to include the cost of contemplated improvements. The coverage amount for a leasehold interest should be either the aggregate amount of rent for the primary term or the fair market value of the real property, whichever is less.

The 1970 ALTA Owner Policy was completely revised in 1987 to clarify coverage, expand coverage in some areas and to define coverage in other areas. The Owner Policy was revised again in 1990 and 1992. The 1992 version revised the creditors rights language in the conditions and stipulations. Fannie Mae now requires that the 1992 ALTA Owner Policy be used.

INSURING PROVISIONS OF ALTA OWNER POLICY

The ALTA owner's title insurance policy contains four insuring provisions. These provisions are standard and will appear in any title insurance policy issued by any title insurance agent writing title policies on behalf of any title insurance underwriter issuing ACT approved forms. The four insuring provisions are:

1. Title to the estate or interest described in Schedule A being vested otherwise than as stated therein:

    A. This provision of the policy provides coverage against loss incurred as a consequence of the fact that any party other than the named insured actually owning the interest insured under the policy.

    B. This provision is straight forward and comes into the play typically only when there has been a forgery in the chain or, alternatively, when a document has been signed by someone without legal capacity.

2. Any defect in or lien or encumbrance on such title.

    A. This is the broadest of the four insuring provisions and has been the subject of considerable litigation between title insurers and their insured.

    B. It is important to note that this insuring provision provides protection only against such defects, liens and encumbrances as are not excepted under Schedule B of the policy.

3. Unmarketability of such title. Prior to the 1987 draft of the ALTA owner's and mortgagee's policy the meaning of this term was unclear. The ALTA tried to partially remedy this inherent ambiguity by defining the term in Paragraph 1 (g) of the Conditions and Stipulations of the policy. This definition reads as follows:

    ". . . an alleged or apparent matter affecting the title to the land, not excluded or excepted from coverage, which would entitle a purchaser of the estate or interest . . . to be released from the obligation to purchase . . ."

    This definition, in practical terms, states that if the policy does not except a matter affecting the title in so as to create a doubt in a reasonable person that title is good, the title is unmarketable.

4. Lack of a right of access to and from the land.

    A. This is an important insuring provision and a frequent source of claims for title insurers. This insuring provision insures a legally enforceable right of access to and from the land. It is not enough that there be a physical means of ingress and egress to the property. The insured must have the right to enforce its legal right to go to and from the insured land or this insuring provision of the policy is triggered.

    B. When examining title in conjunction with issuing a title insurance policy, one must be particularly cautious when a larger parcel which has legal access is subdivided into smaller parcels. If the parcels, after subdivision, are not physically contiguous to a public right-of-way, an exception for lack of a right of access must be inserted unless the property owners of the remaining parcel(s) which retain(ed) legal access, grant(s) access easements in favor of the landlocked parcels.

    C. Courts are split as to the liability of the title insurer when a property has legal access, in some manner, but its owners, their guests and invitees utilize a different means of ingress and egress for which they have no legal right, and this is known to the insurer. Some courts have imposed liability in these instances while others have not as long as any legal access exists.

Dakota Homestead
Title Insurance Company

OWNER POLICY OF TITLE INSURANCE

SUBJECT TO THE EXCLUSIONS FROM COVERAGE, THE EXCEPTIONS FROM COVERAGE CONTAINED IN SCHEDULE B AND THE CONDITIONS AND STIPULATIONS, DAKOTA HOMESTEAD TITLE INSURANCE COMPANY, a South Dakota corporation, herein called the Company, insures, as of Date of Policy shown in Schedule A, against loss or damage, not exceeding the Amount of Insurance stated in Schedule A, sustained or incurred by the insured by reason of:

1. Title to the estate or interest described in Schedule A being vested other than as stated therein;

2. Any defect in or lien or encumbrance on the title;

3. Unmarketability of the title;

4. Lack of a right of access to and from the land.

The Company will also pay the costs, attorneys' fees and expenses incurred in defense of the title, as insured, but only to the extent provided in the Conditions and Stipulations.

IN WITNESS WHEREOF, DAKOTA HOMESTEAD TITLE INSURANCE COMPANY has caused its corporate name and seal to be hereunto affixed by its duly authorized officers, the Policy to become valid when countersigned by an authorized officer or agent of the Company.

Issued by:

_____
Authorized Signature

Dakota Homestead
Title Insurance Company

By: _____
PRESIDENT

By: _____
SECRETARY

EXCLUSIONS FROM COVERAGE

The following matters are expressly excluded from the coverage of this policy and the Company will not pay loss or damage, costs, attorneys' fees or expenses which arise by reason of:

1. (a) Any law, ordinance or governmental regulation (including but not limited to building and zoning laws, ordinances, or regulations) restricting, regulating, prohibiting or relating to (i) the occupancy, use, or enjoyment of the land; (ii) the character, dimensions or location of any improvement now or hereafter erected on the land; (iii) a separation in ownership or a change in the dimensions or area of the land or any parcel of which the land is or was a part; or (iv) environmental protection, or the effect of any violation of these laws, ordinances or governmental regulations, except to the extent that a notice of the enforcement thereof or a notice of a defect, lien or encumbrance resulting from a violation or alleged violation affecting the land has been recorded in the public records at Date of Policy.

    (b) Any governmental police power not excluded by (a) above, except to the extent that a notice of the exercise thereof or a notice of a defect, lien or encumbrance resulting from a violation or alleged violation affecting the land has been recorded in the public records at Date of Policy.

2. Rights of eminent domain unless notice of the exercise thereof has been recorded in the public records at Date of Policy, but not excluding from coverage any taking which has occurred prior to Date of Policy which would be binding on the rights of a purchaser for value without knowledge.

3. Defects, liens, encumbrances, adverse claims or other matters:

    (a) created, suffered, assumed or agreed to by the insured claimant;

    (b) not known to the Company, not recorded in the public records at Date of Policy, but known to the insured claimant and not disclosed in writing to the Company by the insured claimant prior to the date the insured claimant became an insured under this policy;

    (c) resulting in no loss or damage to the insured claimant;

    (d) attaching or created subsequent to Date of Policy; or

    (e) resulting in loss or damage which would not have been sustained if the insured claimant had paid value for the estate or interest insured by this policy.

4. Any claim which arises out of the transaction vesting in the insured the estate or interest insured by this policy, by reason of the operation of federal bankruptcy, state insolvency, or similar creditors' rights laws that is based on:

    (a) the transaction creating the estate or interest insured by this policy being deemed a fraudulent conveyance or fraudulent transfer; or

    (b) the transaction creating the estate or interest insured by this policy being deemed a preferential transfer except where the preferential transfer results from the failure: (i) to timely record the instrument of transfer; or (ii) of such recordation to impart notice to a purchaser for value or a judgment or lien creditor.

1992 OWNER POLICY OF TITLE INSURANCE

INSTRUCTIONS FOR SCHEDULE A.

Policy Number: Policy covers are numbered and assigned to the issuing agent by the Company. The number on the Owner's Policy cover assigned to this transaction is typed in this space.

File No: Designed for the agent's own file numbering system.

Date and Time of Policy: The date and time when the instrument which created the interest of the insured was recorded.

Amount of Insurance: Must be the full value of the insured's interest in the property and would include mortgages assumed or other consideration. A leasehold interest must be insured for the aggregate of the rentals payable under the primary term of the lease or full value of the land, whichever is less.

Premium Amount: The amount charged for issuing the policy.

1.   **Name of Insured:** The full name of the insured as it appears on the recorded instrument.

2.   **The estate or interest . . . covered by this policy is:** The insured estate or interest of the insured, such as Fee Simple, Leasehold, Land Contract Vendee, Life Estate or other insured interest.

3.   **The estate or interest ... vested in:** The name of the insured as the same appears on the instrument of record which creates the insured interest.

4.   **The land ... is described as follows:** A full, complete and accurate legal description of the real estate to be insured must appear here. A copy of the legal description may be attached to the policy as Exhibit A and incorporated by reference if the space on Schedule A at item Number 5 is inadequate.

AGENT	PREMIUM AMOUNT	SIMULTANEOUS ISSUE (other policy number)	ENDORSEMENTS	REISSUE DISCOUNT AMOUNT
	$			$

	FOR INTERNAL USE ONLY			
PROPERTY TYPE	SPECIAL CHARGE	SPECIAL SPLIT $/%	REINSURANCE EXPENSE	PREMIUM TAX
	$		$	$

OWNER POLICY

SCHEDULE A

Policy Number: _____

OFFICE FILE NUMBER	DATE & TIME OF POLICY	AMOUNT OF INSURANCE
		$

1.   Name of Insured:

2.   The estate or interest in the land which is covered by this policy is:

3.   Title to the estate or interest in the land is vested in:

4.   The land referred to in this policy is described as follows:

This Policy is valid only if Schedule B is attached.   Schedule A of this Policy consists of _____ page (s).

Dakota Homestead
Title Insurance Company

Schedule A
ALTA Owner Policy
Revised 10/17/92

1992 OWNER POLICY OF TITLE INSURANCE

INSTRUCTIONS FOR SCHEDULE B

Policy No: Policy covers are numbered and the number on the Owner's Policy assigned to this transaction which appears on Schedule A must also appear in this space.

Exceptions: Nos. 1, 2, 3, 4, 5 and 6 appear as preprinted exceptions in all commitments and policies. The paragraphs will not appear on extended coverage policies, except as to such parts thereof which may be typed as a Special Exception.

OWNER POLICY

SCHEDULE B

Policy Number: _____

EXCEPTIONS FROM COVERAGE

This policy does not insure against loss or damage (and the Company will not pay costs, attorneys' fees or expenses) which arise by reason of:

1. Rights or claims of parties in possession not shown by the public records.
2. Encroachments, overlaps, boundary line disputes, and any other matters which would be disclosed by an accurate survey or inspection of the premises including, but not limited to, insufficient or impaired access or matters contradictory to any survey plat shown by the public records.
3. Easements, or claims of easements, not shown by the public records.
4. Any lien, or right to a lien, for services, labor, or material heretofore or hereafter furnished, imposed by law and not shown by the public records.
5. (a) Unpatented mining claims; (b) reservations or exceptions in patents or in Acts authorizing the issuance thereof; (c) water rights, claims or title to water, whether or not the matters excepted under (a), (b), or (c) are shown by the public records.
6. Taxes or special assessments which are not shown as existing liens by the records of any taxing authority that levies taxes or assessments on real property or by the public records. Proceedings by a public agency which may result in taxes or assessments, or notices of such proceedings, whether or not shown by the records of such agency or by the public records.
7. Any Service, installation or connection charge for sewer, water or electricity.*
8. Any right, title, or interest in any minerals, mineral rights, or related matters, including but not limited to oil, gas, coal, and other hydrocarbons.*

Examples of Additional Exceptions

9. Mortgage from John P. Doe and Mary E. Doe, Husband and Wife to Hometown Savings & Loan Association in the face amount of $60,000.00 dated January 2, 1992 and recorded on January 3, 1992 at 4:42 p.m. in Volume 10900, Page F-02, _____ County Records.

10. Restrictions in deed recorded in Volume 220, Page 41, _____ County Records.

11. Easement over the West (side) five (5) feet for the purpose of storm sewers, according to instrument recorded in Book 218, Page 87.

    NOTE: No examination has been made under the estate created under the above instrument.

12. Easement over the South (rear) five (5) feet for the purpose of installation and maintenance of public utilities, according to plat of said subdivisions recorded in Plat Book 21, Page 96.

13. Restrictions in instrument recorded in Volume 21, Page 96, _____ County Records contain a North (front) building setback line of twenty-five (25) feet.

This Policy is valid only if Schedule A is attached.

Schedule B of this Policy consists of _____ page(s).

Schedule B
ALTA Owner Policy
Revised 10/17/92

Dakota Homestead
Title Insurance Company

CONDITIONS AND STIPULATIONS

1. Definition of Terms

The following terms when used in this policy mean:

(a) "insured": the insured name in Schedule A, and, subject to any rights or defenses the Company would have had against the named insured, those who succeed to the interest of the named insured by operation of law as distinguished from purchase including, but not limited to, heirs, distributees, devisees, survivors, personal representatives, next of kin, or corporate or fiduciary successors.

(b) "insured claimant": an insured claiming loss or damage.

(c) "knowledge" or "known": actual knowledge, not constructive knowledge or notice which may be imputed to an insured by reason of the public records as defined in this policy or any other records which impart constructive notice of matters affecting the land.

(d) "land": the land described or referred to in Schedule A, and improvements affixed thereto which by law constitute real property. The term "land" does not include any property beyond the lines of the area described or referred to in Schedule A, nor any right, title, interest, estate or easement in abutting streets, roads, avenues, alleys, lanes, ways or waterways, but nothing herein shall modify or limit the extent to which a right of access to and from the land is insured by this policy.

(e) "mortgage": mortgage, deed of trust, trust deed, or other security instrument.

(f) "public records": records established under state statutes at Date of Policy for the purpose of imparting constructive notice of matters relating to real property to purchasers for value and without knowledge. With respect to Section 1(a)(iv) of the Exclusions from Coverage, "public records" shall also include environmental protection liens filed in the records of the clerk of the United States district court for the district in which the land is located.

(g) "unmarketability of the title": an alleged or apparent matter affecting the title to the land, not excluded or excepted from coverage, which would entitle a purchaser of the estate or interest described in Schedule A to be released from the obligation to purchase by virtue of a contractual condition requiring the delivery of marketable title.

2. Continuation of Insurance After Conveyance of Title

The coverage of this policy shall continue in force as of Date of Policy in favor of an insured only so long as the insured retains an estate or interest in the land, or holds an indebtedness secured by a purchase money mortgage given by a purchaser from the insured, or only so long as the insured shall have liability by reason of covenants of warranty made by the insured in any transfer or conveyance of the estate or interest. This policy shall not continue in force in favor of any purchaser from the insured of either (i) an estate or interest in the land, or (ii) an indebtedness secured by a purchase money mortgage given to the insured.

3. Notice of Claim to be Given by Insured Claimant

The insured shall notify the Company promptly in writing (i) in case of any litigation as set forth in Section 4(a) below, (ii) in case knowledge shall come to an insured hereunder of any claim of title or interest which is adverse to the title to the estate or interest, as insured, and which might cause loss or damage for which the Company may be liable by virtue of this policy, or (iii) if title to the estate or interest, as insured, is rejected as unmarketable. If prompt notice shall not be given to the Company, then as to the insured all liability of the Company shall terminate with regard to the matter or matters for which prompt notice is required; provided, however, that failure to notify the Company shall in no case prejudice the rights of any insured under this policy unless the Company shall be prejudiced by the failure and then only to the extent of the prejudice.

4. Defense and Prosecution of Actions; Duty of Insured Claimant to Cooperate

(a) Upon written request by the insured and subject to the options contained in Section 6 of these Conditions and Stipulations, the Company, at its own cost and without unreasonable delay, shall provide for the defense of an insured in litigation in which any third party asserts a claim adverse to the title or interest as insured, but only as to those stated causes of action alleging a defect, lien or encumbrance or other matter insured against by this policy. The Company shall have the right to select counsel of its choice (subject to the right of the insured to object for reasonable cause) to represent the insured as to those stated causes of action and shall not be liable for and will not pay the fees of any other counsel. The Company will not pay any fees, costs or expenses incurred by the insured in the defense of those causes of action which allege matters not insured against by this policy.

(b) The Company shall have the right, at its own cost, to institute and prosecute any action or proceeding or to do any other act which in its opinion may be necessary or desirable to establish the title to the estate or interest, as insured, or to prevent or reduce loss or damage to the insured. The Company may take any appropriate action under the terms of this policy, whether or not it shall be liable hereunder, and shall not thereby concede liability or waive any provision of this policy. If the Company shall exercise its rights under this paragraph, it shall do so diligently.

(c) Whenever the Company shall have brought an action or interposed a defense as required or permitted by the provisions of this policy, the Company may pursue any litigation to final determination by a court of competent jurisdiction and expressly reserves the right, in its sole discretion, to appeal from any adverse judgment or order.

(d) In all cases where this policy permits or requires the Company to prosecute or provide for the defense of any action or proceeding, the insured shall secure to the Company the right to so prosecute or provide defense in the action or proceeding, and all appeals therein, and permit the Company to use, at its option, the name of the insured for this purpose. Whenever requested by the Company, the insured, at the Company's expense, shall give the Company all reasonable aid (i) in any action or proceeding, securing evidence, obtaining witnesses, prosecuting or defending the action or proceeding, or effecting settlement, and (ii) in any other lawful act which in the opinion of the Company may be necessary or desirable to establish the title to the estate or interest as insured. If the Company is prejudiced by the failure of the insured to furnish the required cooperation, the Company's obligations to the insured under the policy shall terminate, including any liability or obligation to defend, prosecute, or continue any litigation, with regard to the matter or matters requiring such cooperation.

5. Proof of Loss or Damage

In addition to and after the notices required under Section 3 of these Conditions and Stipulations have been provided the Company, a proof of loss or damage signed and sworn to by the insured claimant shall be furnished to the Company within 90 days after the insured claimant shall ascertain the facts giving rise to the loss or damage. The proof of loss or damage shall describe the defect in, or lien or encumbrance on the title, or other matter insured against by this policy which constitutes the basis of loss or damage and shall state, to the extent possible, the basis of calculating the amount of the loss or damage. If the Company is prejudiced by the failure of the insured claimant to provide the required proof of loss or damage, the Company's obligations to the insured under the policy shall terminate, including any liability or obligation to defend, prosecute, or continue any litigation, with regard to the matter or matters requiring such proof of loss or damage.

In addition, the insured claimant may reasonably be required to submit to examination under oath by any authorized representative of the Company and shall produce for examination, inspection and copying, at such reasonable times and places as may be designated by any authorized representative of the Company, all records, books, ledgers, checks, correspondence and memoranda, whether bearing a date before or after Date of Policy, which reasonably pertain to the loss or damage. Further, if requested by any authorized representative of the Company, the insured claimant shall grant its permission, in writing, for any authorized representative of the Company to examine, inspect and copy all records, books, ledgers, checks, correspondence and memoranda in the custody or control of a third party, which reasonably pertain to the loss or damage. All information designated as confidential by the insured claimant provided to the Company pursuant to this Section shall not be disclosed to others unless, in the reasonable judgment of the Company, it is necessary in the administration of the claim. Failure of the insured claimant to submit for examination under oath, produce other reasonably requested information or grant permission to secure reasonably necessary information from third parties as required in this paragraph shall terminate any liability of the Company under this policy as to that claim.

6. Options to Pay or Otherwise Settle Claims; Termination of Liability

In case of a claim under this policy, the Company shall have the following additional options:

(a) **To Pay or Tender Payment of the Amount of Insurance**

(i) To pay or tender payment of the amount of insurance under this policy together with any costs, attorneys' fees and expenses incurred by the insured claimant, which were authorized by the Company, up to the time of payment or tender of payment and which the Company is obligated to pay.

(ii) Upon the exercise by the Company of this option, all liability and obligations to the insured under this policy, other than to make the payment required, shall terminate, including any liability or obligation to defend, prosecute, or continue any litigation, and the policy shall be surrendered to the Company for cancellation.

(b) **To Pay or Otherwise Settle With Parties Other Than the Insured or With the Insured Claimant**

(i) to pay or otherwise settle with other parties for or in the name of an insured claimant any claim insured against under this policy, together with any costs, attorneys' fees and expenses incurred by the insured claimant which were authorized by the Company up to the time of payment and which the Company is obligated to pay; or

(ii) to pay or otherwise settle with the insured claimant the loss or damage provided for under this policy, together with any costs, attorneys' fees and expenses incurred by the insured claimant which were authorized by the Company up to the time of payment and which the Company is obligated to pay.

Upon the exercise by the Company of either of the options provided for in paragraphs (b)(i) or (ii), the Company's obligations to the insured under this policy for the claimed loss or damage, other than the payments required to be made, shall terminate, including any liability or obligation to defend, prosecute, or continue any litigation.

7. Determination, Extent of Liability and Coinsurance

This policy is a contract of indemnity against actual monetary loss or damage sustained or incurred by the insured claimant who has suffered loss or damage by reason of matters insured against by this policy and only to the extent herein described.

(a) The liability of the Company under this policy shall not exceed the least of:

(i) the Amount of Insurance stated in Schedule A; or,

(ii) the difference between the value of the insured estate or interest as insured and the value of the insured estate or interest subject to the defect, lien or encumbrance insured against by this policy.

(b) In the event the Amount of Insurance stated in Schedule A at the Date of Policy is less than 80 percent of the value of the insured estate or interest or the full consideration paid for the land, whichever is less, or if the subsequent to the Date of Policy an improvement is erected on the land which increases the value of the insured estate or interest by at least 20 percent over the Amount of Insurance stated in Schedule A, then this Policy is subject to the following:

(i) where no subsequent improvement has been made, as to any partial loss, the Company shall only pay the loss pro rata in the proportion that the amount of insurance at Date of Policy bears to the total value of the insured estate or interest at Date of Policy; or

(ii) where a subsequent improvement has been made, as to any partial loss, the Company shall only pay the loss pro rata in the proportion that 120 percent of the Amount of Insurance stated in Schedule A bears to the sum of the Amount of Insurance stated in Schedule A and the amount expended for the improvement.

The provisions of this paragraph shall not apply to costs, attorneys' fees and expenses for which the Company is liable under this policy, and shall only apply to that portion of any loss which exceeds, in the aggregate, 10 percent of the Amount of Insurance stated in Schedule A.

(c) The Company will pay only those costs, attorneys' fees and expenses incurred in accordance with Section 4 of these Conditions and Stipulations.

8.   Apportionment

If the land described in Schedule A consists of two or more parcels which are not used as single site, and a loss is established affecting one or more of the parcels but not all, the loss shall be computed and settled on a pro rata basis as if the amount of insurance under this policy was divided pro rata as to the value on Date of Policy of each separate parcel to the whole, exclusive of any improvements made subsequent to Date of Policy, unless a liability or value has otherwise been agreed upon as to each parcel by the Company and the insured at the time of the issuance of this policy and shown by an express statement or by an endorsement attached to this policy.

9.   Limitation of Liability

(a) If the Company establishes the title, or removes the alleged defect, lien or encumbrance, or cures the lack of a right of access to or from the land, or cures the claim of unmarketability of title, all as insured, in a reasonably diligent manner by any method, including litigation and the completion of any appeals therefrom, it shall have fully performed its obligations with respect to that matter and shall not be liable for any loss or damage caused thereby.

(b) In the event of any litigation, including litigation by the Company or with the Company's consent, the Company shall have no liability for loss or damage until there has been a final determination by a court of competent jurisdiction, and disposition of all appeals therefrom, adverse to the title as insured.

(c) The Company shall not be liable for loss or damage to any insured for liability voluntarily assumed by the insured in settling any claim or suit without the prior written consent of the Company.

10.   Reduction of Insurance; Reduction or
         Termination of Liability

All payments under this policy, except payments made for costs, attorneys' fees and expenses, shall reduce the amount of the insurance pro tanto.

11.   Liability Noncumulative

It is expressly understood that the amount of insurance under this policy shall be reduced by any amount the Company may pay under any policy insuring a mortgage to which exception is taken in Schedule B or to which the insured has agreed, assumed, or taken subject, or which is hereafter executed by an insured and which is a charge or lien on the estate or interest described or referred to in Schedule A, and the amount so paid shall be deemed a payment under this policy to the insured owner.

12.   Payment of Loss

(a) No payment shall be made without producing this policy for endorsement of the payment unless the policy has been lost or destroyed, in which case proof of loss or destruction shall be furnished to the satisfaction of the Company.

(b) When liability and the extent of loss or damage has been definitely fixed in accordance with these Conditions and Stipulations, the loss or damage shall be payable within 30 days thereafter.

13.   Subrogation Upon Payment or Settlement
(a) The Company's Right of Subrogation

Whenever the Company shall have settled and paid a claim under this policy, all right of subrogation shall vest in the Company unaffected by any act of the insured claimant.

The Company shall be subrogated to and be entitled to all rights and remedies which the insured claimant would have had against any person or property in respect to the claim had this policy not been issued. If requested by the Company, the insured claimant shall transfer to the Company all rights and remedies against any person or property necessary in order to perfect this right of subrogation. The insured claimant shall permit the Company to sue, compromise or settle in the name of the insured claimant and to use the name of the insured claimant in any transaction or litigation involving these rights or remedies.

If a payment on account of a claim does not fully cover the loss of the insured claimant, the Company shall be subrogated to these rights and remedies in the proportion which the Company's payment bears to the whole amount of the loss.

If loss should result from any act of the insured claimant, as stated above, that act shall not void this policy, but the Company, in that event, shall be required to pay only that part of any losses insured against by this policy which shall exceed the amount, if any, lost to the Company by reason of the impairment by the insured claimant of the Company's right of subrogation.

(b) The Company's Rights Against Non-insured
      Obligors

The Company's right of subrogation against non-insured obligors shall exist and shall include, without limitation, the rights of the insured to indemnities, guaranties, other policies of insurance or bonds, notwithstanding any terms or conditions contained in those instruments which provide for subrogation rights by reason of this policy.

14.   Arbitration

Unless prohibited by applicable law, either the Company or the insured may demand arbitration pursuant to the Title Insurance Arbitration Rules of the American Arbitration Association. Arbitrable matters may include, but are not limited to, any controversy or claim between the Company and the insured arising out of or relating to this policy, any service of the Company in connection with its issuance or the breach of a policy provision or other obligation. All arbitrable matters when the Amount of Insurance is $1,000,000 or less shall be arbitrated at the option of either the Company or the insured. All arbitrable matters when the Amount of Insurance is in excess of $1,000,000 shall be arbitrated only when agreed to by both the Company and the insured. Arbitration pursuant to this policy and under the Rules in effect on the date the demand for arbitration is made or, at the option of the insured, the Rules in effect at Date of Policy shall be binding upon the parties. The award may include attorneys' fees only if the laws of the state in which the land is located permit a court to award attorneys' fees to a prevailing party. Judgment upon the award rendered by the Arbitrator(s) may be entered in any court having jurisdiction thereof.

The law of the situs of the land shall apply to an arbitration under the Title Insurance Arbitration Rules.

A copy of the Rules may be obtained from the Company upon request.

15.   Liability Limited to this Policy; Policy Entire Contract

(a) This policy together with all endorsements, if any, attached hereto by the Company is the entire policy and contract between the insured and the Company. In interpreting any provision of this policy, this policy shall be construed as a whole.

(b) Any claim of loss or damage, whether or not based on negligence, and which arises out of the status of the title to the estate or interest covered hereby or by any action asserting such claim, shall be restricted to this policy.

(c) No amendment of or endorsement to this policy can be made except by a writing endorsed hereon or attached hereto signed by either the President, a Vice President, the Secretary, an Assistant Secretary, or validating officer or authorized signatory of the Company.

16.   Severability

In the event any provision of the policy is held invalid or unenforceable under applicable law, the policy shall be deemed not to include that provision and all other provisions shall remain in full force and effect.

17.   Notices, Where Sent

All notices required to be given the Company and any statement in writing required to be furnished the Company shall include the number of this policy and shall be addressed to the Company at:

Dakota Homestead Title Insurance Company
315 South Phillips Avenue
Sioux Falls, South Dakota, 57104.

Glossary

12(b)(6) motion A motion under the provisions of Rule 12 of the Rules of Civil Procedure that challenges the basis of the complaint for failure to state a claim upon which relief can be granted.

A

abandoned property Personal property that the owner has intentionally discarded and to which the owner has relinquished ownership rights.

abandonment Quitting the use by the adverse user, which terminates the tolling of time.

abatement Doctrine in which will bequests may fail due to insufficient estate funds at the time of testator's death.

ability to cure A breaching party may be able to fix the defective performance.

absolute sale The title transfers upon delivery and payment.

abuse of discretion Standard of review on appeal that judge's decision is unreasonable and not logically based upon the facts.

abuse of process Using the threat of resorting to the legal system to extract agreement to terms against the other party's will.

acceleration clause A loan agreement provision that requires the debtor to pay off the balance sooner than the due date if some specified event occurs.

acceptance The act of a person to whom a thing is offered or tendered by another, whereby he receives the thing with the intention of retaining it, such intention being evidenced by a sufficient act.

acceptance of services or goods Where an offeree has taken possession of the goods or received the benefit of the conferred services, he has been deemed to have accepted the offer.

accord Agreement, but it must be agreement to substitute.

accord and satisfaction An agreement to accept the imperfectly proffered performance as a fulfillment of the contractual obligations.

actions inconsistent with rejection A buyer must not do anything that is contrary to her previous refusal of the goods.

active concealment Knowingly hiding a situation that another party has the right to know and, being hidden from them, assumes that it does not exist.

active voice A verb form in which the subject of the sentence performs the action.

actual notice Notice given directly to or received personally by a party.

actus reus The guilty act.

ad valorem tax A tax imposed on the value of the property.

ademption Failed bequest in a will because the property no longer exists.

adequacy of consideration Sufficient under the circumstances to support the contract.

adequacy of performance An obligation meets the minimum or completeness test.

adequate assurances Either party may request the other to provide further guarantees that performance will be forthcoming if the requesting party has reasonable suspicion that the other may default. Under the UCC, merchants may request of each other further promises that performance will be tendered.

adequate compensation A party denied the benefit of his bargain may be paid or otherwise put in a position equivalent to where he would have been had performance been in compliance with the contractual terms.

adequate consideration Exchanges that are fair and reasonable as a result of equal bargaining for things of relatively equal value.

adjustable rate mortgage A mortgage in which the interest rate is not fixed, but is tied to an index and is periodically adjusted as the rate index moves up or down.

administrative agency regulations and rules (administrative codes) Processes and guidelines established under the particular administrative section that describe acceptable conduct for persons and situations under the control of the respective agency.

Administrative Law The body of law governing administrative agencies, that is, those agencies created by Congress or state legislatures, such as the Social Security Administration.

admissibility A ruling on whether the jury will be allowed to view proffered evidence.

admission Acknowledgement of the facts as true.

admit To agree or stipulate to the allegations presented in a complaint.

adoption The taking of a child into the family, creating a parent-child relationship where the biological relationship did not exist.

advance sheets Softcover pamphlets containing the most recent cases.

adversarial documents Documents that are argumentative, drafted to emphasize the strong points of your client's position and the weaknesses of the opposing party's.

adverse possession The legal taking of another's property by meeting the requirements of the state statute, typically open and continuous use for a period of five years.

advisory letter A formal letter that offers legal opinions or demands.

advisory opinion Statement of potential interpretation of law in a future opinion made without real case facts at issue.

affidavit A sworn statement.

affirm(ed) Disposition in which the appellate court agrees with the trial court.

affirmative acts Knowing and conscious efforts by a party to the contract that are inconsistent with the terms of the agreement and that make contractual obligations impossible to perform.

affirmative defense An "excuse" by the opposing party that does not just simply negate the allegation, but puts forth a legal reason to avoid enforcement. These defenses are waived if not pleaded.

affirmative duty The law requires that certain parties positively act in a circumstance and not have to wait until they are asked to do that which they are required to do.

against the drafter Imprecise terms and/or ambiguous wording is held against the party who wrote the document as he was the party most able to avoid the problem.

agency adoption Using an agency, either government or private, but government-regulated, to facilitate the process.

aggravating Enhancing.

Alert The case-clipping system used by Lexis to monitor legal developments.

alimony Court-ordered money paid to support a former spouse after termination of a marriage.

alimony pendente lite Temporary order for payments of a set amount monthly while the litigation continues.

allegations Facts forming the basis of a party's complaint.

alter ego doctrine A business set up to cover or be a shield for the person actually controlling the corporation, and thus the court may treat the owners as if they were partners or a sole proprietor.

alternative dispute resolution (ADR) Method of settling a dispute before trial in order to conserve the court's time.

ALWD Citation Manual A legal citation resource, published by the Association of Legal Writing Directors, that contains local and state sources that may not be found in *The Bluebook.*

ambiguity Lack of precision and clarity.

amended pleading A pleading that changes, corrects, revises, or deletes information from a prior pleading.

American Bar Association (ABA) A national organization of lawyers, providing support and continuing legal education to the profession.

American Jurisprudence (Am. Jur. and Am. Jur. 2d) Legal encyclopedia organized by topics and subheadings presenting law and scholarly discussion from multiple jurisdictions.

American Law Institute A nongovernmental organization composed of distinguished judges and lawyers in the United States.

American rule of attorney fees and costs Expenses incurred by the parties to maintain or defend an action for the breach of contract are generally not recoverable as damages.

amicus brief Brief filed by a nonparty to an appeal who has an interest, whether political, social, or otherwise, in the outcome of the case.

amicus curiae Brief filed by a nonparty known as a "friend of the court."

amortization The allocation of the cost or other basis of an intangible asset over its estimated useful life.

amortize To extinguish a debt gradually through incremental payments.

analysis Applied after finding the law and interpreting the application to the facts to formulate a persuasive argument supporting your position.

annotated code A code that provides, in addition to the text of the codified statutes, such information as cases that have construed the statute; law review articles that have discussed it; the procedural history of the statute (amendments or antecedents); cross-references to superseded codifications; cross-references to related statutes; and other information.

annotated version Presents the law as enacted or case opinion as stated, along with discussion and commentary.

annotation An in-depth analysis of a specific and important legal issue raised in the accompanying decision, together with an extensive survey of the way the issue is treated in various jurisdictions.

annulment Court procedure dissolving a marriage, treating it as if it never happened.

annual percentage rate The actual cost of borrowing money, expressed in the form of annual interest rate to make it easy for one to compare the cost of borrowing money among several lenders.

answer The defendant's response to the plaintiff's complaint.

anticipation An expectation of things to come that has reasonable basis for the conclusion.

anticipatory breach Party provides notice, or otherwise it becomes known, that the anticipated performance will not be completed.

anticipatory repudiation Words or acts from a party to the contract that clearly and unquestionably state the intent not to honor his contractual obligations before the time for performance has arrived.

apostrophe A form of punctuation used to create a contraction or a possessive noun.

appeal Tests the sufficiency of the verdict under the legal parameters or rules.

appellant The party filing the appeal; that is, bringing the case to the appeals court.

appellant's brief Brief of the party filing the appeal.

appellate brief Brief filed in an appeals court.

appellate court The court of appeals that reviews a trial court's record for errors.

appellate rules Procedures set forth by the appeals court in processing an appeal.

appellee The prevailing party in the lower court, who will respond to the appellant's argument.

appellee's brief Brief of the party responding to the appeal.

appendix Contains the supplementary collection of the sources from the trial court.

appraisal The evaluation by an expert of the cash value of a contested item.

appropriation The capture or diversion of water from its natural course or channel and its application to some beneficial use by the appropriator to the exclusion of all other persons.

arbitration Alternative dispute resolution method mediated or supervised by a neutral third party who imposes a recommendation for resolution, after hearing evidence from both parties and the parties participated in reaching, that is fully enforceable and treated in the courts the same as a judicial order.

arbitrator Individual who imposes a solution on the parties based on the evidence from both parties.

argument Section of the brief where the issues are analyzed through citation of legal authorities.

arraignment A court hearing where the information contained in an indictment is read to the defendant.

arrest The formal taking of a person, usually by a police officer, to answer criminal charges.

articles of incorporation The basic charter of an organization, written and filed in accordance with state laws.

articles of partnership Written agreement to form a partnership.

Articles of the Constitution Establish government form and function.

assault Intentional voluntary movement that creates fear or apprehension of an immediate unwanted touching; the threat or attempt to cause a touching, whether successful or not, provided the victim is aware of the danger.

assertion of defenses Either the original parties or a third-party beneficiary has the right to claim any legal defenses or excuses that they may have as against each other. They are not extinguished by a third party.

assessment The process of ascertaining and adjusting the shares respectively to be contributed by several persons toward common beneficial object according to the benefit received.

assignable Legally capable of being transferred or negotiated.

assignee The party to whom the right to receive contractual performance is transferred.

assignment The transfer of the rights to receive the benefit of contractual performance under the contract.

assignor The party who assigns his rights away and relinquishes his rights to collect the benefit of contractual performance.

associate attorney An attorney who is an employee of an attorney partnership.

assumption of the risk The doctrine that releases another person from liability for the person who chooses to assume a known risk of harm.

attempt To actually try to commit a crime and have the actual ability to do so.

attestation clause The section of the will where the witnesses observe the act of the testator signing the will.

attorney/client privilege The legal relationship established between attorney and client allowing for free exchange of information without fear of disclosure.

attractive nuisance doctrine The doctrine that holds a landowner to a higher duty of care even when the children are trespassers, because the potentially harmful condition is so inviting to a child.

audience The person or persons to whom a legal document is directed, such as a client or the court.

authentication Proof by an officer, witness or certifying document that evidence is what it is claimed to be.

authorization letter A letter the client provides the attorney granting permission to contact employers, doctors, or other individuals who have records that relate to a case.

avoid The power of a minor to stop performance under a contract.

avoid the contract Legally sufficient excuse for failure to complete performance under the contract.

B

bad faith Intentional misrepresentation, wanton disregard for truth, fraudulent activity that can be the basis for an additional award of damages to the party that can establish such activity occurred.

bail Court-mandated surety or guarantee that the defendant will appear at a future date if released from custody prior to trial.

bailee The recipient of the property, temporarily taking possession.

bailment The delivery of personal property from one person to another to be held temporarily.

bailor The owner of the property transferring possession.

bar examination A test administered to graduates from approved law schools that determines the applicant's knowledge of the law and suitability to practice in the state.

battery An intentional and unwanted harmful or offensive contact with the person of another; the actual intentional touching of someone with intent to cause harm, no matter how slight the harm.

battle of the forms An evaluation of commercial writings whose terms conflict with each other in order to determine what terms actually control the performances due from the parties.

bcc Blind copy.

bench trial A case heard and decided by a judge.

beneficiaries The persons named in a will to receive the testator's assets.

benefit conferred The exchange that bestows value upon the other party to the contract.

benefit Gain acquired by a party or parties to a contract.

bequest Gift by will of personal property.

best interest of the child Premier concern in every family law matter.

beyond a reasonable doubt The requirement for the level of proof in a criminal matter in order to convict or find the defendant guilty. It is a substantially higher and more-difficult-to-prove criminal matter standard.

bifurcated Separated from other issues.

bigamy One spouse knowingly enters a second marriage while the first remains valid.

bilateral contract A contract in which the parties exchange a promise for a promise.

Bill of Rights Sets forth the fundamental individual rights that government and law function to preserve and protect; the first ten amendments to the Constitution of the United States.

bill of sale A written agreement by which one person assigns or transfers his right to or interest in goods and personal chattels to another.

billing Record keeping of time and tasks performed by a paralegal for each client and the legal task performed on behalf of the client.

binding authority (mandatory authority) A source of law that a court must follow in deciding a case, such as a statute or federal regulations.

black letter law The strict meaning of the law as it is written without concern or interpretation of the reasoning behind its creation.

Black's Law Dictionary Dictionary of legal terminology and word usage.

blackmail The extortion of payment based on a threat of exposing the victim's secrets.

block quote A quotation over 50 words that is single-spaced and indented.

board of directors Policy managers of a corporation, elected by the shareholders, who in turn choose the officers of the corporation.

body (writing) The portion of a paragraph that contains the material that you claim supports the contention raised in the topic sentence; the text that contains the information you wish to communicate in a letter.

body Main text of the argument section of the appellate brief.

boilerplate Standard language in a form.

bona fide purchaser for value A person who purchases real property in good faith for valuable consideration without notice of any claim to or interest in the real property by any other party.

brackets A form of punctuation that indicates changes or additions.

breach A violation or infraction of a law or an obligation.

breach of contract A party's performance that deviates from the required performance obligations under the contract; a violation of an obligation under a contract for which a party may seek recourse to the court.

breach of duty The failure to maintain a reasonable degree of care toward another person to whom a duty is owed.

brevity Strong, tight writing.

bridge loan A one- to two-year loan that enables a borrower to acquire property.

brief A formal written argument presented to the court.

brief bank A document depository of briefs prepared by a law firm in previous matters.

briefing a case Summarizing a court opinion.

briefing schedule Timetable for various required filings by both parties throughout the appeal process.

bright line rules A legal standard resolves issues in a simple, formulaic manner that is easy in application although it may not always be equitable.

building codes Laws, ordinances, or governmental regulations concerning fitness for habitation, setting forth standards and requirements for the construction, maintenance, operation, occupancy, use, or appearance of buildings, premises, and dwelling units.

bulk sale Agreement to transfer all or substantially all the goods to the buyer.

bundle of rights The concept of ownership that embraces certain rights of ownership, such as possession, control, use, enjoyment, and disposition.

burden of proof Standard for assessing the weight of the evidence.

burglary Breaking and entering into a structure for the purpose of committing a crime.

business judgment rule The rule that protects corporate officers and directors from liability for bad business decisions.

business organization A form of conducting business.

"but for" test If the complained-of act had not occurred, no injury would have resulted.

bylaws Corporate provisions detailing management structure and operating rules.

C

calendar call A mandatory court hearing in which the judge inquires about the readiness of the parties to go to trial; also known as a docket call.

calendaring System of tracking dates, appointments, filing deadlines for documents, and events throughout the case file for both the attorney and the paralegal.

cancel the contract The aggrieved party has the right to terminate the contractual relationship with no repercussions.

cap on damages Limit established by statutes.

capacity The ability to understand the nature and significance of a contract; to understand or comprehend specific acts or reasoning.

caption The full name of the case, together with the docket number, court, and date of the decision.

Cardozo test Zone of foreseeability and proximate cause analysis as a test of the scope of damages.

case (common) law Published court opinions of federal and state appellate courts; judge-created law in deciding cases, set forth in court opinions.

case brief An objective summary of the important points of a single case; a summary of a court opinion.

case evaluation The process of investigating the facts, issues, and legal implications of a proposed lawsuit before it is ever filed.

case holding The statement of law the case opinion supports.

case law Published court opinions of federal and state appellate courts; judge-created law in deciding cases, set forth in court opinions.

case management Keeping track of the progress or status of the file and proactively organizing the work of both the attorney and the paralegal.

case of first impression A case in which no previous court decision with similar facts or legal issue has arisen before; a case with a legal issue that has not been heard by the court before in a specific jurisdiction.

case on all fours A case in which facts, issues, parties, and remedies are analogous to the present case.

case on point A case involving similar facts and issues to the present case.

case opinions Explanations of how and why the court interpreted the law as it did under the specific facts and applicable law of the individual case.

case reporters Sets of books that contain copies of appellate court opinions from every case heard and published within the relevant jurisdiction.

causation Intentional act resulting in harm or injury to the complaining plaintiff.

cause of action A personal, financial, or other injury for which the law gives a person the right to receive compensation.

cc Copy.

certainty The ability for a term to be determined and evaluated by a party outside of the contract; the ability to rely on objective assurances to make a determination without doubt.

certificate of compliance Attorney certification at the end of an appellate brief attesting to compliance with the page limitations set forth by that court's rules.

certificate of interested parties Statement in a brief identifying parties who have an interest in the outcome and financial affiliations.

certificate of marriage Completed when the official completes the ceremony confirming the ceremony took place and is recognized by the state.

certificate of service Verification by attorney that pleadings or court documents were sent to the opposing counsel in a case.

certification The recognition of the attainment of a degree of academic and practical knowledge by a professional.

Certified Legal Assistant (CLA) Standardized test based primarily on general concepts and federal law administered in connection with paralegal certification.

certiorari (Cert) (Latin) "To make sure." An appellate court's authority to decide which cases it will hear on appeal.

chain of title Record of successive conveyances, or other forms of alienation, affecting a particular parcel of land, arranged consecutively, from the government or original source of title down to the present holder.

challenge An attorney's objection, during voir dire, to the inclusion of a specific person on the jury.

chattel Tangible personal property or goods.

checks and balances Mechanism designed into the Constitution that prevents one branch from overreaching and abusing its power.

child custody Arrangement between the parties for residential and custodial care of the minor children.

child support The right of a child to financial support and the obligation of a parent to provide it.

Chinese wall The shielding, or walling off, of a new employee from a client in the new firm with whom there may be a conflict of interest.

circuit One of several courts in a specific jurisdiction.

circumstantial evidence Evidence that suggests a conclusion.

citation Information about a legal source directing you to the volume and page in which the legal source appears.

civil cause of action A claim for damages that is based on the relevant substantive area of law and has facts that support a judicial resolution.

civil law The legal rules regarding offenses committed against the person.

civil liability Finding that the defendant acted or failed to act, resulting in damages or harm. It cannot be punished by incarceration.

civil verdict Finds liability.

claimant One who claims or asserts a right, demand, or claim.

clarity The ability to accurately convey the intended message to the reader in a clear, precise manner.

class action A lawsuit involving a large group of plaintiffs who have been certified by a court as having mutual interests, common claims, and a representative plaintiff who will pursue the action on the basis of the entire group.

clean hands doctrine A plaintiff at fault is barred from seeking redress from the courts.

clear and convincing evidence Having a high probability of truthfulness, a higher standard being preponderance of the evidence.

clerk A government official responsible for maintaining public records.

clerk of the court An individual who manages the administrative functions of the court.

clichés Overused figures of speech.

client intake Basic demographic and case-specific information developed in the first meeting with the client following the formal engagement.

closely held corporation A business that is incorporated with limited members, typically related family members.

closing sentence A sentence at the end of a paragraph that summarizes the topic; the concluding message in a letter.

closing statement In real estate law, written breakdown of the costs involved in a particular real estate transaction; usually prepared by a lender or escrow agent. In trial law (also called closing argument), a statement by a party's attorney that summarizes that party's case and reviews what that party promised to prove during trial.

Code of Federal Regulations (C.F.R.) Federal statutory law collection.

Code of Hammurabi First formalized legal system (1792–1750 B.C.).

codes Set of volumes that groups statutes by subject matter and is well indexed, in order to make the statutes more accessible for research purposes.

codicil A provision that amends or modifies an existing will.

cohabitation agreement A contract setting forth the rights of two people who live together without the benefit of marriage.

collateral Property that is pledged as security for the satisfaction of a debt.

collateral source rule A rule of evidence that allows the jury to be informed about the plaintiff's other sources of compensation, such as insurance, worker's compensation, and so forth.

collection letter A letter that demands payment of an amount claimed to be owed to a client.

colloquialisms Informal language used in everyday conversation.

collusion Illegally created agreement of the parties.

colon A form of punctuation that joins together phrases or explanatory clauses or introduces a block quote.

comity Federal government respect for state government power and authority results in federal refusal to intervene in matters clearly within the sole jurisdiction of the state government.

comma Punctuation used to re-create verbal pauses.

commencement of action The formal document filed in the court describing the plaintiff, the party bringing the action, and the wrongdoing alleged by the plaintiff against the defendant, or the party against whom the claim is made.

Commerce Clause Statement in the Constitution that the federal government has absolute authority in matters affecting citizens of all states.

commercial bank A bank that is authorized to receive both demand and time deposits, to take part in trust services, to issue letters of credit, to rent time-deposit boxes, and to provide other related services.

commercial impracticability Impossibility of performance in a commercial context and contracts governed by UCC Article 2.

commercial unit A batch of goods packaged or sold together in the normal course of the relevant industry.

commingle To combine funds or properties into a common fund or stock.

commingling A term for mixing a client's funds with the attorney's personal funds without permission; an ethical violation.

common areas Those portions of the condominium property that are owned in common by all of the owners of units in the condominium.

common law Judge-made law, the ruling in a judicial opinion.

common law marriage A form of marriage that is legally recognized in certain states, if the two people have been living together for a long period of time, have represented themselves as being married, and have the intent to be married.

community property All property acquired during marriage in a community property state, owned in equal shares.

comparative negligence Applies when the evidence shows that both the plaintiff and the defendant acted negligently.

compensatory damages A payment to make up for a wrong committed and return the nonbreaching party to a position where the effect or the breach has been neutralized.

competence The ability and possession of expertise and skill in a field that is necessary to do the job.

competent jurisdiction The power of a court to determine the outcome of the dispute presented.

complaint Document that states the allegations and the legal basis of the plaintiff's claims.

complete defense The individual entered the relationship knowingly with legal capacity.

complete integration A document that contains all the terms of the agreement and the parties have agreed that there are no other terms outside the contract.

complex sentence A sentence that contains a subordinate clause or clauses in addition to the main clause.

compound sentence A sentence in which the clauses could stand separately, each ending with a period.

compulsory counterclaim A counterclaim that is required to be pleaded because the facts relate to the same transaction as that set forth in the original complaint.

computer-assisted legal research (CALR) Research method using electronically retrieved source materials.

conclusion Summation of your analysis in a memorandum, or relief requested in a brief.

concur To agree with the majority opinion.

concurrence Another view or analysis written by a member of the same reviewing panel.

concurrent condition An event that happens at the same time as the parties' performance obligations.

concurrent jurisdiction Jurisdiction over the subject matter exists in both state and federal court, unless statutorily prohibited.

concurrent ownership More than one individual shares the rights of ownership.

concurring opinion An opinion in which a judge who agrees with the ultimate result wishes to apply different reasoning from that in the majority opinion.

condemnation The determination and declaration that certain property is assigned to public use, subject to reasonable compensation.

condemnation proceedings The process by which state or federal government obtains property.

condition An event that may or may not happen upon which the rest of the performance of the contract rests.

condition precedent An event that happens beforehand and gives rise to the parties' performance obligations. If the condition is not satisfied, the parties do not have a duty to perform.

condition subsequent An event that, if it happens after the parties' performance obligations, negates the duty to perform. If the condition is satisfied, the parties can "undo" their actions.

conditional acceptance A refusal to accept the stated terms of an offer by adding restrictions or requirements to the terms of the offer by the offeree.

conditional sale Terms other than delivery and payment must be met to transfer title of the goods.

conditional transfer Conditions stated at the time of the conveyance; the original owner, despite the conveyance, retains an interest.

condominium Form of property ownership in which the owner owns an individual unit in a multi-unit building and is a tenant in common with other individual unit owners in the common areas.

condominium declaration A legal document required by state condominium acts to create a condominium.

confidentiality Lawyer's duty not to disclose information concerning a client.

confirmation letter A letter designed to create a record or restate the content of the original oral communication.

conflict check A procedure to verify potential adverse interests before accepting a new client.

conflict of interest Clash between private and professional interests or competing professional interests that makes impartiality difficult and creates an unfair advantage.

conflict letter A letter sent by an attorney to the judge explaining that the attorney has several different appearances scheduled for the same date and detailing which courts the attorney will go to first.

Confrontation Clause Sixth Amendment guarantee that the accused has the absolute right to confront his or her accusers and all evidence.

consanguinity The relationship between blood relatives, such as brothers and sisters.

consent All parties to a novation must knowingly assent to the substitution of either the obligations or the parties to the agreement.

consequential damages Damages resulting from the breach that are natural and foreseeable results of the breaching party's actions.

consideration Something of value received by a promisor from a promisee.

conspicuous limitation or exclusion of warranties A seller may specifically deny any warranties as long as the limitation or exclusion of the warranties is set forth in language that is understandable and noticeable by the buyer.

conspiracy By agreement, parties work together to create an illegal result, to achieve an unlawful end.

constitutional law Based on the federal Constitution and arising from interpretations of the intent and scope of constitutional provisions.

construction loan A mortgage loan made for the purpose of providing money to construct improvements on real property.

constructive eviction Option of a tenant to leave and surrender premises without penalty, because while not depriving tenant of possession, the landlord has made the premises untenantable through disrepair or some act rendering the premises unlivable.

consular marriage Conducted by a diplomat of the U.S. government.

contingency fee The attorney's fee calculated as a percentage of the final award in a civil case.

continuing consideration Extends over time.

continuing legal education (CLE) Continued legal competence and skills training required of practicing professionals.

contraband Commodity that cannot be legally possessed.

contract A legally binding agreement between two or more parties.

contract of adhesion An agreement wherein one party has total control over the bargaining process and therefore the other party has no power to negotiate and no choice but to enter into the contract.

contract for the sale of land A contract that calls for conveyance of interest in real estate and requires a writing signed by party sought to be charged as being within the Statute of Frauds.

contractual capacity Legal capability to enter a contract.

contractual good faith See *good faith.*

contradictory Evidence which is in conflict with the terms of the contract and inadmissible under the parol evidence rule.

contribution The right of one who has discharged a common liability to recover of another also liable.

contributory negligence The plaintiff played a large part in causing the injury, thus, fundamental fairness precludes assigning liability to the defendant.

conventional loan Mortgage loan in which the risk of payment depends on the borrower's ability to pay and the value of the property being used to secure the loan.

conversion An overt act to deprive the owner of possession of personal property with no intention of returning the property, thereby causing injury or harm.

conveyance A transfer.

conviction Results from a guilty finding by the jury in a criminal trial.

cooperative A form of ownership of real property in which a corporation owns a multi-unit building and leases living space in the building to the shareholders of the corporation.

corporation An organization formed with state government approval to act as an artificial person to carry on business and issue stock.

Corpus Juris Secundum (Cor. Jur. 2d) Legal encyclopedia organized by topics and subheadings presenting law and scholarly discussion from multiple jurisdictions.

count The cause of action in the complaint.

counterclaim A claim made by the defendant against the plaintiff—not a defense, but a new claim for damages, as if the defendant were the plaintiff in a separate suit; a countersuit brought by the defendant against the plaintiff.

counteroffer A refusal to accept the stated terms of an offer by proposing alternate terms.

course of dealing The parties' actions taken in similar previous transactions.

course of performance The parties' actions taken in reliance on the particular transaction in question.

Court of International Trade Part of the federal lower-court level authorized to hear matters related to international trade agreements and disputes.

court reporter Individual who transcribes the court proceedings and certifies their authenticity.

covenant The promise upon which the contract rests. In real estate law, a promise of two or more parties written into a conveyance of land, usually a deed, binding either party to the other that something be done or not be done.

covenant against encumbrances A grantor's promise that the property has no visible or invisible claims, liabilities, or other rights attached to it that may lessen its value.

covenant for quiet enjoyment A promise insuring against the consequences of a defective title; a promise ensuring a tenant will not be evicted by the grantor or a person having lien or superior title.

covenant marriage The couples make an affirmative undertaking to get counseling prior to the marriage and to seek counseling if contemplating divorce.

covenant of further assurance A promise to do whatever is reasonably necessary to perfect the title conveyed if it turns out to be imperfect.

covenant of warranty A promise by which the grantor agrees to defend the grantee against any lawful or reasonable claims of superior title by a third party and to indemnify the grantee for any loss sustained by the claim.

covenant not to compete An employment clause that prohibits an employee from leaving his job and going to work for a competitor for a specified period of time in a particular area.

covenant not to sue An agreement by the parties to relinquish their right to commence a lawsuit based on the original and currently existing cause of action under the contract.

covenants of title Promises that bind the grantor to ensure the completeness, security, and continuance of the title transferred.

cover letter A standard form letter identifying information such as document filings.

cover The buyer can mitigate her losses from the seller's breach by purchasing substitute goods on the open market; the nonbreaching party's attempt to mitigate damages may require that he purchase alternate goods on the open market to replace those never delivered by the breaching party.

credit union A nonprofit financial institution owned and operated by its members, who operate a cooperative that provides members with financial services, including savings and lending.

creditor A party to whom a debt is owed.

criminal law The legal rules regarding wrongs committed against society.

criminal verdict Finds the defendant guilty or not guilty of the criminal offense charged and tried.

criticism An opinion.

critique A position that is presented with supporting evidence.

cross examination Occurs when the opposing attorney asks the witness questions.

cross-claim lawsuit A lawsuit against a party of the same side; plaintiffs or defendants suing each other (defendant versus defendant or plaintiff versus plaintiff).

cumulative sentence A sentence that conveys the information in a comprehensive manner.

cure The seller is given a reasonable opportunity to fix the defects in the goods found by the buyer.

curtesy A life estate by which in common law a man held property of his deceased wife if children were born during the marriage.

custodial parent Parent with whom the child(ren) resides primarily following dissolution of the marriage.

custody The legal authority to make decisions concerning a child's interests.

D

damage Detriment, harm, or injury.

damages Money paid to compensate for loss or injury.

dash A punctuation mark longer than a hyphen, which is used for limited purposes, such as separating the segments of a two-part sentence.

database A collection of information used in computer systems to provide access to related fields of interest.

de novo Standard appellate review where the appellate court reviews the facts and law independent of the trial court's decision.

deadline date A certain date by which a request or demand should be fulfilled.

deadly force Defense available in cases involving the defense of persons, oneself or another.

death or incapacity of a party An excuse for performance on a contract due to the inability of the party to fulfill his obligation.

decedent The person who has died.

Declaration of Independence Statement, preceding the U.S. Constitution, giving the intention to form a new government in the colonies and including general principles guiding the form of that new government.

declaratory judgment The court's determination of the rights and responsibilities of a party with respect to the subject matter of the controversy.

decree nisi The divorce and all related issues are finalized pending passage of the statutorily prescribed period.

deed The written document transferring title, or an ownership interest in real property, to another person.

deed of trust An instrument in use in some states, taking the place of and serving the uses of a mortgage, by which the legal title to real property is placed in one or more trustees until the grantor repays a loan, to secure the payment of a sum of money or the performance of other conditions.

deed poll A deed binding on one party.

defamation An act of communication involving a false and unprivileged statement about another person, causing harm.

default The omission of or failure to perform a legal or contractual duty.

default judgment A judgment entered by the court against the defendant for failure to respond to the plaintiff's complaint.

defects in formation Errors or omissions made during the negotiations that function as a bar to creating a valid contract.

defendant The party against whom a lawsuit is brought.

defendant/plaintiff table List of the cases alphabetically by the defendant first or a table of cases listing the name of the case both ways.

defense Legally sufficient reason to excuse the complained-of behavior.

defense of arrest In situations involving police officers or, rarely, private citizens with evidence that the arrest was in furtherance of the reasonable duties of the officer.

defense of consent The plaintiff consented fully, knowingly, and willingly to the act or acts.

defense of discipline Requires the discipline be reasonable under the circumstances.

defense of necessity Available with invasion of property when such occurs in an emergency.

delegant/delegator The party who transfers his obligation to perform his contractual obligations.

delegate/delegatee The party to whom the obligation to perform the contractual obligations is transferred.

delegation The transfer of the duties/obligations to perform under the contract.

delivery In commercial contracts, delivery may be accomplished by transferring actual possession of the goods, or putting the goods at the disposal of the buyer, or by a negotiable instrument giving the buyer the right to the goods.

demand letter A letter requesting action on a legal matter.

democracy Government form characterized by rule of and by the people or, if more practical, by elected representatives of the people.

demonstrative evidence Any object, visual aid, model, scale drawing, or other exhibit designed to help clarify points in the trial.

deny (denial) To disagree with or contest the allegations presented in a complaint

deponent The party or witness who is questioned in a deposition.

deposit insurance Insurance, created by the Deposit Insurance Act, in which the federal government insures deposits made by consumers in qualifying banking institutions.

deposition A discovery tool in a question-and-answer format in which the attorney verbally questions a party or a witness under oath.

deposition digest A summary of deposition testimony of a witness.

deposition on written questions A deposition based on written questions submitted in advance to a party; only those questions are answered, with no follow-up questions allowed.

deprived of expected benefit A party can reasonably expect to receive that for which he bargained; if he does not receive it, the breach is considered material.

descriptive word index A subject index that provides a researcher with a quick survey of specific key numbers, often from several topics, which apply to a given subject area.

destruction or loss of subject matter The nonexistence of the subject matter of the contract, which renders it legally valueless and unable to be exchanged according to the terms of the contract; excuse of performance is based on the unforeseeable and unavoidable loss of the subject matter.

deterrent effect The authority to assess excessive fines on a breaching party often can dissuade a party from committing an act that would subject him to these punitive damages.

detriment A loss or burden incurred because of contract formation.

detriment incurred The exchange that burdens the party in giving the consideration to the other party to the contract.

detrimental effect A party's worsening of his position due to his dependence on the terms of the contract.

detrimental reliance An offeree has depended upon the assertions of the offeror and made a change for the worse in his position depending on those assertions.

devise A disposition of real property by will.

dictum (plural: dicta) A statement made by the court in a case that is beyond what is necessary to reach the final decision.

digest A collection of all the headnotes from an associated series of volumes, arranged alphabetically by topic and by key number or summary of testimony with indexed references of a deposition.

direct evidence Evidence that establishes a particular fact without resort to other testimony or evidence.

direct examination Occurs when the attorney questions his or her own witness.

disaffirm Renounce, as in a contract.

disavowal A step taken by a formerly incapacitated person that denies and cancels the voidable contract and thereby makes it unenforceable.

disbarment Temporary suspension or permanent revocation of an individual's license to practice law.

discharge of duties Recognition by both parties that contract obligations are completed whether by performance or by agreement of the parties.

discharged Contract completion as to every requirement; that is, completed and terminated.

disclaimer A term which limits claim or denial.

disclosure Act of disclosing; revelation.

discovery The pretrial investigation process authorized and governed by the rules of civil procedure; the process of investigation and collection of evidence by litigants; process in which the opposing parties obtain information about the case from each other; the process of investigation and collection of evidence by litigants.

discussion and analysis The heart of the memorandum, which presents the legal analysis with supporting citations.

disposition Appears at the end of the opinion and tells the reader how the court handled the lower court decision.

dispositive motion A motion that terminates some or all of the pending issues in a case.

dissent (dissenting opinion) Opinion in which a judge disagrees with the result reached by the majority; an opinion outlining the reasons for the dissent, which often critiques the majority and any concurring opinions.

dissipating Wasting the marital estate.

dissolution of marriage Process resulting in termination of the marital union.

distinguishing Explaining why the factual differences call for a decision differing from established law.

distinguishing facts Facts that establish the different analysis and application of settled law.

diversity jurisdiction Authority of the federal court to hear a case if the parties are citizens of different states and the amount at issue is over $75,000.

diversity of citizenship Federal jurisdiction conferred when the case involves citizens of different states.

dividends Portion of profits, usually based on the number of shares owned.

divisibility/severability A contract may be able to be compartmentalized into separate parts and seen as a series of independent transactions between the parties.

divorce/dissolution The legal termination of a marriage.

docket number The number assigned by the court to the case for its own administrative purposes.

doctrine of merger The proposition that the contract for the conveyance of property merges into the deed of conveyance; therefore, any guarantees made in the contract that are not reflected in the deed are extinguished when the deed is conveyed to the buyer of the property.

doctrine of unclean hands A party seeking equitable remedies must have acted justly and in good faith in the transaction in question; otherwise, equitable remedies will not be available to a wrongdoer.

documentary evidence Any evidence represented on paper that contributes to supporting the legal position and/or verbal testimony of witnesses, for example, medical billing records, physician treatment notes, bank statements, and canceled checks.

do-gooder arguments Appeals to the save-the-world attitude.

domicile The place where a person maintains a physical residence with the intent to permanently remain in that place; citizenship; the permanent home of the party.

dominant tenement A piece of real property that is benefited by an easement appurtenant.

donee A party to whom a gift is given.

donor The person making a gift.

dower The provision that the law makes for a widow out of the lands or tenements of her husband, for her support and the nurture of her children.

double jeopardy Being tried twice for the same act or acts.

duces tecum A deposition notice requiring the deponent/witness to "bring with him" specified documents or things.

due process Ensures the appropriateness and adequacy of government action in circumstances infringing on fundamental individual rights. In real estate law, protection of one of two types: procedural, which provides a person a guarantee to fair procedures, and substantive, which protects a person's property from unfair governmental interference or taking.

duress Unreasonable and unscrupulous manipulation of a person to force him to agree to terms of an agreement that he would otherwise not agree to.

duty A legal obligation that is required to be performed.

duty to resell The UCC requires commercial sellers to try to resell the goods that have not been accepted by the original buyer.

duty to warn See *landowner's duty.*

E

earning capacity The ability to earn based on objective evidence.

easement A right to use another's property for a specific purpose, such as a right of way across the land.

easement appurtenant An easement created to benefit a particular piece of real property.

easement by estoppel A court-ordered easement created from a voluntary servitude after a person mistakenly believed the servitude to be permanent and acted in reasonable reliance on the mistaken belief.

easement by necessity An easement that is indispensable to the enjoyment of the dominant estate.

easement in gross An easement created that grants the owner of the easement the right to use a piece of real property for a particular purpose.

eggshell skull theory A plaintiff with a preexisting condition does not change or diminish the defendant's liability.

economic duress The threat of harm to a party's financial resources unless demands are met.

editing To delete, eliminate, or change the text of a legal document.

elective share Statutory provision that a surviving spouse may choose as between taking that which is provided for her in her husband's will, claiming dower, or taking her statutorily prescribed share.

ellipsis A form of punctuation that indicates the elimination of text from an extended quote.

embedded citation A citation placed within a sentence.

eminent domain The power to take private property for public use by the state, municipalities, and private persons or corporations authorized to exercise functions of public character.

empty promise A promise that has neither a legal nor a practical value.

en banc Appellate review by the entire circuit appeals judiciary after review by the intermediate panel.

en banc decisions Decisions by the court as a whole because of their legal significance.

encumbrance A claim or liability that is attached to property and may decrease its value.

endorsement The act of a payee of a negotiable instrument, in writing her name upon the back of the instrument, with or without further or qualifying words, whereby the property in the same is assigned and transferred to another.

entrapment An act of a law enforcement official to induce or encourage a person to commit a crime when the defendant expresses no desire to proceed with the illegal act.

enumerated powers Powers listed in the Constitution or the jobs of the particular office, for example, the president, or the branch, for example, the judicial.

equal bargaining power Both parties have the same position in terms of strengths and weaknesses.

equitable distribution Divides the assets acquired during the marriage between the parties.

equitable mortgage An agreement to post certain property as security before the security agreement is formalized.

equitable relief A remedy that is other than money damages, such as refraining from or performing a certain act; nonmonetary remedies fashioned by the court using standards of fairness and justice. Injunction and specific performance are types of equitable relief.

equitable remedies Non-monetary remedies fashioned by the court using standards of fairness and justice.

equitable servitude An agreement stipulating building restrictions and restrictions on the use of land that may be enforced in equity.

equitable title Title that indicates a beneficial interest in property and that gives the holder the right to acquire formal legal title.

equity The doctrine of fairness and justice; the process of making things balance or be equal between parties.

equity stripping A practice that involves providing a loan based on the equity of a property rather than the borrower's ability to repay.

error of fact Legal standard on appeal alleging the facts accepted by the trial court judge are incorrect.

error of law Standard of review on appeal alleging error of the court in applying the standards of the law.

escheat To pass property to the state, as is done with the assets of a person who dies without a will and without heirs.

escrow A legal document or property delivered by a promisor to a third party to be held by the third party for a given amount of time or until the occurrence of a condition.

estate The degree, quantity, nature, and extent of interest that a person has in real and personal property.

estate at will A type of estate less than a freehold estate, where land and tenements are let by one person to another, to have and to hold at the will of the lessor.

estate for years A type of estate less than a freehold estate, where a person has an interest in land and tenements, and a possession thereof, by virtue of such interest, for some fixed and determinate period of time.

estate in land An ownership interest in real property; the compilation of all a deceased's assets and debts.

estoppel certificate A signed statement by a party, such as a tenant or a mortgagee, certifying for the benefit of another party that a certain statement of facts is correct as of the date of the statement.

ethics Standards by which conduct is measured.

Euclidean zoning Type of zoning based on district and use.

evict In civil law, to recover anything from a person by virtue of the judgment of a court or judicial sentence.

evidence Any fact, testimony, or physical object that tends to prove or disprove allegations raised in a case; must be reasonably calculated to lead to the discovery of admissible evidence.

ex parte A communication between one party in a lawsuit and the judge.

exceptions to contract enforceability Legally adequate reasons for nonperformance of contract obligations.

excessive and unreasonable cost A court will only consider excusing performance based on impracticality if the additional expense is extreme and disproportionate to the bargain.

excited utterance An exception to the hearsay rule that allows a statement made spontaneously after a shocking event to be admissible at trial.

exclamation point A form of punctuation used to highlight something extraordinary.

exclusionary rule Circumstances surrounding the seizure do not meet warrant requirements or exceptions; items seized deemed *fruit of the poisonous tree* are excluded from trial evidence.

exclusive jurisdiction Only one court has the authority to hear the specific case; for example, only a federal court can decide a bankruptcy case.

exculpatory evidence Supports the possibility of the defendant's innocence.

excused from performance The non-breaching party is released from her obligations to perform due to the other party's breach.

executed contract The parties' performance obligations under the contract are complete.

executed The parties' performance obligations under the contract are complete.

executive order Order issued by the U.S. president having the force of law but without going through the typical process for enacting legislation.

executor/executrix The administrator of the estate.

executory consideration An exchange of value completed over time.

executory interest Following the termination of the life tenant's possession, other conditions or circumstances become complete at some designated future date or occurrence.

executory The parties' performances under the contract have yet to occur.

exemplary damages Punitive damages, awarded as a punishment and a deterrent.

exhaustion of administrative remedies Provision that a non-litigation process to informally resolve disputes must be attempted prior to filing a complaint.

exhibit A document attached to a pleading that is incorporated by reference into the body of the pleading.

exigent circumstances Compelling reason to believe the evidence may be destroyed or otherwise removed.

existence of the subject matter The goods to be transferred must exist at the time of the making of the contract.

expectation damages A monetary amount that makes up for the losses incurred as a result of the breach that puts the nonbreaching party in as good a position as he would have been had the contract been fully performed.

expectation-of-privacy test See Katz expectation-of-privacy test.

explanatory Oral testimony is permitted to clarify the terms of the contract.

express contracts An agreement whose terms have been communicated in words, either in writing or orally.

express acceptance Stated or, if applicable, written statement from the offeree that mirrors the offer; that is, it is precisely the same as the offer.

express conditions Requirements stated in words, either orally or written, in the contract.

express consideration Stated clearly and unambiguously.

express easement An easement expressly granted in writing and describing the use of the easement and the property on which the easement is located.

express warranty A written representation by the seller as to the nature of the goods to be sold.

extinguishment of liability Once a novation has occurred, the party exiting the agreement is no longer obligated under the contract.

F

fact pleading A style of pleading that requires you to identify all the facts necessary to allege a valid cause of action.

facts Significant objective information in a case.

fair market value The amount that a willing buyer would pay for an item that a willing seller would accept.

false imprisonment Any deprivation of a person's freedom of movement without that person's consent and against his or her will, whether done by actual violence or threats.

Fannie Mae Federal National Mortgage Association, organized for the purpose of investing in FHA and VA loans.

Federal Deposit Insurance Corporation An independent governmental agency that insures bank deposits up to a statutory amount per depositor at each participating bank.

Federal Home Loan Bank Government agency, consisting of twelve regional banks owned by savings and homestead associations, that issues bonds and notes to finance the home building and mortgage loans of their member associations.

Federal Housing Administration A division of the U.S. Department of Housing and Urban Development (HUD) which insures mortgage loans made by private lenders on residential real estate.

federal question The jurisdiction given to federal courts in cases involving the interpretation and application of the U.S. Constitution or acts of Congress.

Federal Register Pamphlet service that records the daily activity of the Congress.

Federal Rules Decisions (**F.R.D**) Contains decisions of the federal district courts relating to the rules of civil and criminal procedure.

Federal Rules Digest Digest of opinions related to rules of procedure in the federal court system.

Federal Rules of Civil Procedure (Fed. R. Civ. P.) The specific set of rules followed in the federal courts.

Federal Rules of Criminal Procedure (Fed. R. Crim. P.) Rules governing the procedural issues in criminal prosecutions.

federalism Balanced system of national and state government in the U.S. Constitution; the federal government has jurisdiction over all matters related equally to all citizens of all states and the state governments have specific authority in matters affecting only the citizens of the respective state entity.

fee simple An unlimited estate to a person and her heirs and assigns forever, without limitation or condition.

fee simple absolute A property interest in which the owner has full and exclusive use and enjoyment of the entire property.

fee simple defeasible An interest in land in which the owner has all the benefits of a fee simple estate, except that property is taken away if a certain event or condition occurs.

fee simple determinable An ownership interest in real property that is created by conveyance containing the words effective to create a fee simple and, in addition, a provision for automatic expiration of the estate upon a stated event.

fee simple on condition subsequent A type of transfer in which the grantor conveys fee simple on condition that something be done or not done to the property after the conveyance.

felony A crime punishable by more than a year in prison or by death.

FHA loans Loans that have been insured in whole or in part by the Federal Housing Administration.

fiduciary relationship A relationship based on close personal trust that the other party is looking out for one's best interests.

Field Code The forerunner to our present code of procedure; developed in New York in 1848.

final judgment The last possible order or judgment entered in the lower court; the required threshold for filing a notice of appeal.

finance charge The consideration for the privilege of deferring payments of a purchase price.

finish or scrap The seller has the option to either finish producing the partially manufactured goods or stop production and scrap the materials for their recycled value.

firm offer An option contract to keep the offer open between merchants that does not have to be supported by separate consideration in order to be valid; an agreement made by a merchant-offeror, and governed by the Uniform Commercial Code, that he will not revoke the offer for a certain time period. A firm offer is not supported by separate consideration.

first pleading Complaint.

fixed-rate mortgage A mortgage that specifies an interest rate that remains fixed for the life of the mortgage, regardless of market conditions.

fixtures Personal property that has become permanently attached to or associated with the real property.

flow A quality within or characteristic of the text that moves the reader easily through the text from point to point.

forbearance of a legal right Consideration that requires a party to refrain from doing something that he has the legal right to do.

force majeure An event that is neither foreseeable nor preventable by either party that has a devastating effect on the performance obligations of the parties.

foreclosure A legal proceeding to terminate a mortgagor's interest in property, instituted by the lender either to gain title or to force a sale to satisfy the unpaid debt secured by the property.

foreign corporation A business that is incorporated under the laws of a different state, doing business in multiple states.

foreseeability The capacity for a party to reasonably anticipate a future event.

forfeiture A loss caused by a party's inability to perform.

forgoing a legal right to sue Valid consideration as it has recognized legal value to support a contractual obligation.

form books Publications that contain complete or partial sample documents, often with sample factual situations and various alternative methods of stating that legal document.

formal contract An agreement made that follows a certain prescribed form like negotiable instruments.

forms Documents that set forth standardized language and are used as a drafting guide.

forum The proper legal site or location.

forum non conveniens Venue is inconvenient despite the otherwise appropriateness of a jurisdiction choice.

forum shopping Plaintiff attempts to choose a state with favorable rules in which to file suit.

four corners doctrine A principle of contract law that directs the court to interpret a contract by the terms contained within the pages of the document.

fragile class Group considered particularly susceptible to harm such as the very old or the very young.

fraud A knowing and intentional misstatement of the truth in order to induce a desired action from another person.

Freddie Mac Federal Home Loan Mortgage Corporation, designed to purchase and invest in mortgages.

freedom of contract The doctrine that permits parties to make agreements on whatever terms they wish with few exceptions.

freehold estate An estate interest that includes both ownership and possessory interests.

freelancer Paralegal in business for him- or herself who contracts with an attorney or law firm to perform specific tasks for a designated fee.

fruit of the poisonous tree Evidence tainted based on illegal seizure may not be used in a trial.

frustration of purpose Changes in the circumstances surrounding the contract may render the performance of the terms useless in relation to the reasons for entering into the contract.

full performance Completed exactly as set forth in the contract.

fundamental individual rights Contained in the first Ten Amendments to the Constitution, which spell out the individual rights the government functions to preserve and protect; those rights essential to ensuring liberty and justice.

future interest Right to property that can be enforced in the future.

G

general damages Those that normally would be anticipated in a similar action.

general defenses Specific responses by defendant to plaintiff's complaint.

General Demurrer A responsive pleading filed by a party attacking the legal sufficiency of a complaint.

general gift Gift of property that is not exactly identified, as in furniture.

general intent An unjustifiable act; reckless conduct.

general jurisdiction The court is empowered to hear any civil or criminal case.

general warranty deed Type of deed in which the grantor guarantees that he holds clear title to a piece of real estate and has a right to sell it; it contains covenants concerning the quality of title, including warranties of seisin, quiet enjoyment, right to convey, freedom from encumbrances, and defense of title against all claims.

gift Bestowing a benefit without any expectation on the part of the giver to receive something in return and the absence of any obligation on the part of the receiver to do anything in return.

gift causa mortis A gift made by the donor in contemplation of death.

gift inter vivos Gift made during the lifetime of the donor.

Ginnie Mae Governmental National Mortgage Association, a government corporation organized to administer special assistance programs and to work with the FNMA in the secondary mortgage market.

good consideration An exchange made based on love and affection, which have no legal value.

good faith dealing Doing the best possible to complete the contractual obligations.

good faith obligation Both buyers and sellers must deal with each other in a reasonable and fair manner without trying to avoid legitimate performance obligations.

good faith The ability, competence, and intent to perform under the contract; the legal obligations to enter and perform a contract with honest and real intentions to complete performance and other conditions; fair dealing, integrity, and commitment to perform under the contract in an appropriate, timely, and responsible manner.

goods Movable items under the UCC definition.

grantee The person to whom the property is to be transferred by deed.

grantee index An index, usually kept in the county recorder's office, alphabetically listing by grantee the volume and page number of grantees' recorded property transactions.

grantor The person who is the transferor of the property by deed.

gratuitous promise A promise in exchange for nothing.

gratuitous undertaking An act undertaken for reasons other than duty and measured with the same legal standard reasonably attributable to those with appropriate training.

guarantee An agreement in which a third party assures the repayment of a debt owed by another party.

guarantor A party who assumes secondary liability for the payment of another's debt. The guarantor is liable to the creditor only if the original debtor does not make payment.

guaranty A promise to answer for the payment of some debt or perform some duty, in case of the failure of another who is liable.

guardian ad litem A person appointed by the court to represent the best interests of the child in a custody determination.

guilty A verdict only available in criminal cases in which the jury determines that the defendant is responsible for committing a crime.

H

habendum clause A clause found in a deed that indicates what estate in real property is being transferred by the deed.

harmless error Standard of review that has not caused legal error requiring reversal of the trial court's decision.

header Text that appears at the top left margin of all subsequent pages, and identifies three elements: the person to whom the letter is addressed; the date of the letter; and the page number.

heading A line or more of text that identifies the party for whom the memorandum was prepared; the person by whom it was prepared; the date of preparation; and the subject matter.

headnote A key-numbered paragraph; an editorial feature in unofficial reporters that summarizes a single legal point or issue in the court opinion.

hearsay An out-of-court statement offered to prove a matter in contention in the lawsuit.

heirs Persons entitled to receive property based on intestate succession.

historic preservation An ordinance that prohibits the demolition or exterior alteration of certain historic buildings or of all buildings in a historic district.

holding That aspect of a court opinion which directly affects the outcome of the case; it is composed of the reasoning necessary and sufficient to reach the disposition.

holographic will A will entirely written and signed by the testator in that person's own handwriting.

homeowners' association An association of people who own homes in a given area, formed for the purpose of improving or maintaining the quality of the area.

hornbooks Scholarly texts; a series of textbooks which review various fields of law in summary narrative form, as opposed to casebooks which are designed as primary teaching tools and include many reprints of court opinions.

HUD-1 A uniform settlement statement required by the Real Estate Settlement Procedures Act for all real estate transactions that involve a federally related mortgage loan.

hyphen A form of punctuation used to draw together two or more words to form a single idea.

I

identification of the goods to the contract Once a seller has designated specific goods as the ones that will be delivered to the buyer, the buyer has a protectable interest in them.

identity or quality of the subject matter The goods to be transferred must be described with sufficient clarity to allow an outside third party to recognize them.

ignore the repudiation If the repudiating party has not permanently made his performance impossible, the aggrieved party can wait to see if the repudiator changes his mind and does perform.

illegal contract A contract that is unenforceable because the subject matter of the agreement is prohibited by state or federal statutory law and thus void.

illegal scheme A plan that uses legal steps to achieve an illegal result.

illusory promise A statement that appears to be a promise but actually enforces no obligation upon the promisor because he retains the subjective option whether or not to perform on it.

immaterial fact A fact that is unimportant to the case and its holding.

immediate right to commence a lawsuit The aggrieved party does not have to wait until the time when performance would be due under the contract term where there has been an anticipatory repudiation.

impasse The declaration by the mediator that the parties are unable to reach an agreement.

impleader The involuntary addition of a new party to the litigation; a party without whom all issues raised in the case could not be resolved.

implied acceptance Acceptance of the offeror's terms and conditions by actions or words indicating clearly the intention to accept.

implied contract An agreement whose terms have not been communicated in words, but rather by conduct or actions of the parties.

implied easement An easement that is created by the conduct of the parties to the easement and not by written agreement or express language.

implied in fact Conditions that are not expressed in words but that must exist in order for the terms of the contract to make sense and are assumed by the parties to the contract.

implied in law Conditions that are not expressed in words but are imposed by the court to ensure fairness and justice as a result of its determination.

implied warranty An unwritten representation that is normally and naturally included by operation of law that applies to the goods to be sold.

impossibility of performance An excuse for performance based upon an absolute inability to perform the act required under the contract.

impracticality An excuse for performance based upon uselessness or excessive cost of the act required under the contract.

in loco parentis In the place of the parent.

in personam jurisdiction A court's authority over a party personally.

in rem jurisdiction A court's authority over claims affecting property.

incapacity The inability to act or understand the actions that would create a binding legal agreement.

inchoate offenses Uncompleted crimes.

incidental beneficiaries Persons who may derive some benefit from the performance of a contract but who were not intended to directly benefit from the performance.

incidental or nominal damages Damages resulting from the breach that are related to the breach but not necessarily directly foreseeable by the breaching party.

indefinite pronoun A pronoun that does not specify its object.

indemnify To restore the victim of a loss, in whole or in part, by payment, repair, or replacement.

indenture A written agreement in which bonds and debentures are issued.

independent clause A clause that can stand on its own as a complete sentence.

indexing method Referencing method of the record to assist in identifying the important pieces of information, such as the transcript excerpts and pleadings, which will be used in the various parts of the appellate brief.

indictment A written list of charges issued by a grand jury against a defendant in a criminal case.

informal contract Can be oral or written and executed in any style acceptable to the parties.

information States that the magistrate determines there is sufficient cause to make an arrest and also sets forth the formal charges sought by the prosecution.

informative letter A letters that transmits information.

inheritance The ability to acquire ownership to real property due to a person's kinship to an owner of real property who has died.

initial client meeting The first meeting with a prospective client in which information will be gathered, additional information requested, and the attorney–client relationship formed.

injunction A court order that requires a party to refrain from acting in a certain way to prevent harm to the requesting party.

injunctive relief Court order to cease or commence an action following a petition to enter such an order upon showing of irreparable harm resulting from the failure to enforce the relief requested.

inquiry notice Notice attributed to a person when the information would lead an ordinary prudent person to investigate the matter further.

INS Immigration and Naturalization Service, which has been reorganized into part of the Department of Homeland Security.

insanity defense A defendant's claim that he or she was insane when the crime was committed, even if temporarily insane.

insolvency A party's inability to pay his debts, which may result in a declaration of bankruptcy and put all contractual obligations on hold or terminate them.

inspect The buyer must take steps to examine the goods to ensure they are of the type indicated in the contract. The seller must make the goods available for this purpose.

instructions and definitions A section in many forms of discovery requests that defines terms in the document to avoid confusion.

instrumentality of crime Used in committing a crime.

insufficient consideration Inadequate value exchanged to form a enforceable contract.

insured loan A loan in which a governmental agency or private mortgage insurance company will guarantee the lender that a portion of the loan will be repaid by the agency or company.

intangible property Personal property that has no physical presence but is represented by a certificate or some other instrument, such as stocks or trademarks.

intent Having the knowledge and desire that a specific consequence will result from an action.

intent of the parties Almost always the controlling factor in determining the terms and performance of an agreement.

intent to deceive The party making the questionable statement must plan on the innocent party's reliance on the first party's untruthfulness.

intentional infliction of emotional distress Intentional act involving extreme and outrageous conduct resulting in severe mental anguish.

intentional torts An intentional civil wrong that injures another person or property.

intentional Voluntarily and knowingly undertaken.

interest A charge by a lender to a borrower for the use of money.

interest in property The right that someone may have in specific property.

interference with business relations Overt act causing disruption or interruption to a business done with the intent to harm the business.

interlocutory appeal Appeal entered prior to entry of a final order by the trial court judge.

internal memoranda Objective documents that present all aspects of the legal issues involved in the matter.

internal memorandum of law An internal document that analyzes objectively the legal issues in a client's matter.

interpleader The deposit of contested funds with the court, followed by the removal of the filing party from other action in the suit.

interrogatory A discovery tool in the form of a series of written questions that are answered by the party in writing, to be answered under oath.

intervention The voluntary insertion of a third party into a pending civil action, often to resolve issues directly related to the third party's interests.

intestate The state of having died without a will.

intoxication Under the influence of alcohol or drugs which may, depending on the degree of inebriation, render a party incapable of entering into a contractual relationship.

invitation to treat A person is expressing willingness to enter into negotiations, inviting another to make an offer.

nvitees People wanted on the premises for a specific purpose known by the landowner.

IRAC Issue, rule, application, and conclusion.

irreparable harm The requesting party must show that the actions of the defendant will cause a type of damage that cannot be remedied by any later award of the court.

irrevocable offers Those offers that cannot be terminated by the offeror during a certain time period.

issue The legal problem presented or point of law or fact on which the appeal is based; questions presented; a section that identifies the legal issues presented in the memorandum of law to the trial court.

J

jargon Legalese. See legal jargon.

joint and several liability Shared responsibility, apportioned between all of the defendants, but in no case can the plaintiff recover more than 100 percent of the damages awarded.

joint custodial arrangements Detail the scope of the shared parental responsibility, whether legal, physical, or both.

joint stipulation States agreement of the parties to implement the change or other mutual agreement.

joint tenancy The shared ownership of property, giving the other owner the right of survivorship if one owner dies.

judge Trier of law.

judgment The court's final decision regarding the rights and claims of the parties.

judgment lien An encumbrance that arises by law when a judgment for the recovery of money is docketed and that attaches to the debtor's real estate located in the county in which the judgment is docketed.

judgment notwithstanding the verdict (judgment N.O.V.) Asks the judge to reverse the jury verdict based on the inadequacy of the evidence presented to support the law and the verdict.

judgment on the pleadings A motion that alleges that if all of the allegations raised in the pleadings are true and correct, the movant would still be entitled to a ruling in his favor and a dismissal of the opposition's pleadings.

judicial notice A request that a court accept evidence as fact without the necessity of further proof.

judicial opinions Analysis of a decision issued by an appellate court panel.

judicial precedent A court decision in which similar facts are presented; provides authority for deciding a subsequent case.

jump cite Same as a pinpoint citation.

jurisdiction The power or authority of the court to hear a particular classification of case.

jurisdictional clause Establishes that the court in which the action is filed is empowered to hear the case and has jurisdiction over the parties.

jurisdictional statement Section of the brief that identifies the legal authority that grants the appellate court the right to hear the case.

jurors Those people who have been selected to sit on a jury; they will consider the evidence and reach a verdict in the case.

jury instructions (jury charge) Directions for the jury regarding what law applies and how it applies to the facts of a case; also known as *points of charge*.

jury strike The removal of a jury panel member, also known as a jury challenge.

jury trial Case is decided by a jury.

jury Trier of fact.

justiciable content Genuine issue of law and fact within the power of the court to decide.

K

Katz expectation-of-privacy test Two prongs: (1) reasonableness of the expectation of privacy—the subjective prong; (2) efficacy of the expectation asserted based on community standards—the objective prong.

Key Number System A detailed system of classification that currently divides the law into more than 400 separate categories or topics.

key search terms Words or phrases used in legal research to help focus the research.

key words Terms used in legal research to identify the law related to your case's facts and legal issues.

KeyCite The Westlaw case updating and validation system, which is similar to Shepard's Citations System.

kickback A payment of money or something of value to a person for the purpose of obtaining business from that person.

knowing and intentional A party must be aware of and plan on the outcome of his words or actions in order to be held accountable for the result.

knowledge of the offer An offeree must be aware of the terms of the offer in order to accept it.

L

landlord The lessor of property.

landmark cases Interpretation of the applicable rule is overruled or changed substantially and intentionally.

landowner's duty To warn of known unsafe artificial conditions on the property.

lapse of time An interval of time that has been long enough to effect a termination of the offer.

larceny The common law crime of taking property of another without permission.

"last in time = first in right" A principle in law that favors the most current activity or change with respect to the transaction as it is most likely the most reflective of the intent of the parties.

law A set of rules and principles that govern any society.

law of equity The body of principles constituting what is fair and right; natural law.

law reviews Periodicals edited by the top students at each law school, featuring scholarly articles by leading authorities and notes on various topics written by the law students themselves.

lay the foundation The presentation of sufficient background material to establish the relevancy and competency of a particular piece of evidence.

leading Attorney objection based on the question creating the desired answer.

lease Any agreement that gives rise to a relationship of landlord and tenant or lessor and lessee.

leasehold An estate in real property held by a tenant under the lease.

legal analysis The process of examining prior case law and comparing it to your case.

legal argument A well-reasoned presentation of your position.

legal assistant Individual qualified to assist an attorney in the delivery of legal services.

legal capacity The right of persons to come into court and be bound by their own agreements.

legal custody The right and obligation to make major decisions regarding the child, including, but not limited to, educational and religious issues.

legal document assistant A specialized type of paralegal, legally able to provide assistance to clients in preparing forms.

legal encyclopedia A multivolume compilation that provides in-depth coverage of every area of the law.

legal issue The point in dispute between two or more parties in a lawsuit.

legal jargon Legalese.

legal memorandum Summary of the case facts, the legal question asked, the research findings, the analysis, and the legal conclusion drawn from the law applied to the case facts.

legal remedy Relief provided by the court to a party to re-dress a wrong perpetrated by another party; the recovery of money damages in a lawsuit.

legal secretary A secretary trained to perform specialized tasks directly related to the practice of law.

legal value Having an objectively determinable benefit that is recognized by the court.

legalese Language that is characterized by the frequent use of Latin, French, and Old English terms unfamiliar to most present-day vocabularies in legal writing; jargon.

legally significant facts Facts that are critical to the analysis of a case.

legislation Regulations codified into laws by Congress.

legislative history The transcripts of the legislative debates leading up to the passage of the bill that became the law or statute.

lessee One who rents property from another.

lessor One who rents property to another.

letter bank A depository for firm letters regarding client cases.

letter of intent/nonbinding offer A statement that details the preliminary negotiations and understanding of the terms of the agreement but does not create a binding obligation between parties.

letterhead Standard stationery.

Lexis Commercial electronic law database service.

liability A jury's determination that one party is responsible for injuries to another party; the basis for an award of damages.

liability insurance That type of insurance protection which indemnifies one from liability to third persons, as contrasted with insurance coverage for losses sustained by the insured.

libel Oral defamatory statements.

license A personal privilege to do some particular act or series of acts on lands without possessing any estate interest therein; it is ordinarily revocable at the will of the licensor and it is not assignable.

licensee One known to be on the premises but whose presence gives no benefit to the property owner.

licensure The requirement of governmental approval before a person can practice a specific profession.

lien A legal right or interest that a creditor has in another's property.

life estate An ownership interest in property for a designated period of time, based on the life of another person.

limitation of acceptance A commercial offeror may specifi-cally state that the offeree must accept all terms as set forth in the offer with no deviations.

limitation of damages An amount of money agreed upon in the original contract as the maximum recovery the nonbreaching party will be entitled to in the event of a breach.

limited jurisdiction The court is empowered to hear only specified types of cases.

limited liability company A hybrid business formed under state acts, representing both corporation and partnership characteristics.

limited partnership A partnership of two or more persons, consisting of limited partners, who provide only financial backing, and general partners, who manage the business and have unlimited liability.

limited warranty deed Deed wherein the grantor covenants and warrants only against the lawful claims of parties claiming by, through, and under the grantor.

limiting physical conditions Class considered for purposes of the standard of care to be reasonable for an ordinary person with those limiting physical conditions; for example, blindness or deafness.

liquidated damages An amount of money agreed upon in the original contract as a reasonable estimation of the damages to be recovered by the nonbreaching party. This amount is set forth in the contract so the parties have a clear idea of the risk of breach.

lis pendens (Latin for "a pending lawsuit") A notice, re-corded in the chain of title to real property, required or permitted in some jurisdictions to warn parties that certain property is the subject of litigation, and that any interests acquired during the pendency of the suit are subject to outcome.

litigants A party to a lawsuit.

litigation process Adversarial process in which parties use the courts for formal dispute resolution.

littoral right Use and enjoyment of water rights concerning properties abutting an ocean, sea, or lake rather than a river or stream.

loan-to-value ratio Ratio of the amount borrowed on a mortgage loan to the value of the real property being used to secure the loan.

local rules Individual rules for a particular court that supplement the other rules of court.

looseleaf, binder, or pamphlet service A service that publishes recently decided court decisions in looseleaf binders, such as U.S. Law Week; provides for information to be easily updated. The loose pages are used to replace the existing pages in the notebook to ensure that the most current information is available.

loss of consortium A claim filed made by the plaintiff's spouse for the loss of companionship in the marriage caused by the injuries.

lost profits A calculable amount of money that the non-breaching party would have made after the execution of performance under the agreement but that has not been realized due to the breach.

lost property Personal property with which a person has involuntarily parted possession.

M

M'Naghten Rule The defendant alleges he or she lacked capacity to form criminal intent.

Magna Carta British document (originally issued in 1215) describing the system and form of government and law upon which the U.S. Constitution was modeled.

mailbox rule A principle of contract law that sets the time of acceptance of an offer at the time it is posted and the time of rejection of an offer at the time it is received.

majority opinion An opinion where more than half of the justices agree with the decision. This opinion is precedent.

malice aforethought The prior intention to kill, or cause grievous bodily harm to, the victim or anyone else if likely to occur as a result of the actions or omissions.

malice Person's doing of any act in reckless disregard of another person.

malum in se An act that is prohibited because it is "evil in itself."

malum prohibitum An act that is prohibited by a rule of law.

mandatory authority Authority that is binding upon the court considering the issue—a statute or regulation from the relevant jurisdiction that applies directly; a case from a higher court in the same jurisdiction that is directly on point; or a constitutional provision that is applicable and controlling.

manslaughter The unlawful killing of a human being without premeditation.

marital estates (marital property) The property accumulated by a couple during marriage, called community property in some states.

marital privilege An evidentiary protection that permits married individuals to refuse to testify against one another.

market price The amount of money that another neutral party would pay for the goods on the open market.

marketable title Title that transfers full ownership rights to the buyer.

marriage A union between a man and a woman.

master plan A municipal plan for housing, industry, and recreational facilities.

material A term is material if it is important to a party's decision whether or not to enter into the contact; an element or term that is significant or important and relates to the basis for the agreement.

material alteration A change in the terms that would surprise or impose hardship on the other party if allowed to become a part of the agreement.

material breach Substantial and essential nonperformance.

material fact A fact that is essential to the case and its holding; a fact that, if different, might alter the entire outcome of the case.

measuring life Person whose life determines duration of a life estate.

mechanic's lien A claim created by state statutes for the purpose of securing priority of payment of the price or value of work performed and materials furnished in erecting, improving, or repairing a building or other structure, and as such attaching to the land as well as buildings and improvements erected thereon.

mediation A dispute resolution method in which a neutral third party meets with the opposing parties to help them achieve a mutually satisfactory solution without court intervention.

mediator Individual who facilitates a resolution by the parties using methods designed to facilitate the parties' reaching a negotiated resolution.

mediation The process of submitting a claim to a neutral third party who then makes a determination about the ultimate liability and award in a civil case.

medical authorization A form, signed by the client, that allows the legal team to review and obtain copies of the client's medical records.

medicinal side effects Under the influence of over-the-counter or prescription drugs having an impact on a person's mental capacity which may render a party incapable of entering into a contractual relationship.

meeting of the minds A legal concept requiring that both parties understand and ascribe the same meaning to the terms of the contract; a theory holding that both parties must both objectively and subjectively intend to enter into the agreement on the same terms.

memorandum at the request of a judge A persuasive memorandum of legal points requested by the trial court judge.

memorandum in regard to a motion A persuasive memorandum supporting the points and authorities in a motion.

memorandum of law Analysis and application of existing law setting forth the basis for filing the motion.

memorandum of law to the trial court An adversarial document filed with the trial court and written to persuade the trial court of a party's position on a disputed point of law.

mens rea "A guilty mind"; criminal intent in committing the act.

mental duress The threat of harm to a party's overall well-being or a threat of harm to loved ones that induces stress and action on the party of the threatened party.

mentally infirm Persons not having the capacity to understand a transaction due to a defect in their ability to reason and, who therefore do not have the requisite mental intent to enter into a contract.

merchantable Goods must meet certain standards that are required in the relevant industry.

merchants Businesspersons who have a certain level of expertise dealing in commercial transactions regarding the goods they sell; persons who regularly deal in goods of the kind specified in the agreement. They hold themselves out as having special knowledge in their area.

mere request for a change A party's interest in renegotiating the terms of the contract does not amount to anticipatory repudiation.

merger clause Language of a contract that indicates that the parties intend to exclude all outside evidence relating to the terms of the contract because it has been agreed that all relevant terms have been incorporated in the document.

merger Combining previous obligations into a new agreement.

metaphor A figure of speech that links dissimilar objects, but it is more powerful than a simile in that it equates, rather than compares, the objects.

minimum contacts The test, based on the case *International Shoe v. Washington,* that courts use to ascertain if a defendant has some contact with the state of which he or she is not a resident.

minors Persons under the age of 18; once a person has reached 18, she has reached the age of majority.

Miranda warnings Mandatory notice given detainees specifically advising that anything said while in custody can be used subsequently as trial evidence.

mirror image rule A requirement that the acceptance of an offer must exactly match the terms of the original offer.

misdemeanor A lesser crime punishable by less than a year in jail and/or a fine.

mislaid property Personal property that the owner has intentionally placed somewhere and then forgotten about.

misrepresentation A reckless disregard for the truth in making a statement to another in order to induce a desired action.

mistake in fact An error in assessing the facts, causing a defendant to act in a certain way.

mitigate damages (mitigation of damages) The obligation to offset or otherwise engage in curative measures to stop accrual of unreasonable economic damages; that is, to minimize the damage incurred through affirmative actions.

mitigate To lessen in intensity or amount.

Model Penal Code (MPC) A comprehensive body of criminal law, adopted in whole or in part by most states.

models Copies of actual complaints, obtained from your firm's files, that have a similar factual foundation.

modification A change or addition in contractual terms that does not extinguish the underlying agreement.

modifiers Words that describe a subject, verb, or object in a sentence.

moral obligation A social goal or personal aspiration that induces a party to act without any expectation of a return performance from the recipient.

mortgage An interest in land created by a written instrument, providing security for the performance of a duty or the payment of a debt.

mortgagee A person that takes, holds, or receives a mortgage.

mortgagor One who, having all or some part of title to property, by written instrument pledges that property for some particular purpose, such as security for a debt.

motion A procedural request or application presented by the attorney in court.

motion for a directed verdict A request by a party for a judgment because the other side has not met its burden of proof.

motion for a new trial Post-trial relief that requests a new trial on the same issues for specific reasons that must be clearly explained and argued in the motion.

motion for a summary judgment A motion by either party for judgment based on all court documents.

Motion for More Definite Statement A request by a defendant for additional specificity of plaintiff's complaint.

Motion for Protective Order A motion filed by a party upon whom a discovery request has been made to protect the disclosure of information.

Motion for Sanctions A motion filed by any party to counter alleged violations by another party in the case.

motion in limine A request that certain evidence not be raised at trial, as it is arguably prejudicial, irrelevant, or legally inadmissible evidence.

Motion to Compel Discovery A motion filed by a party seeking to force compliance with a discovery request.

motion to compel Request for the production of information or testimony for use at trial

Motion to Dismiss A motion that dispenses with the lawsuit because of a legal defense.

motion to suppress Asks the court to eliminate allegedly tainted evidence.

murder The killing of a human being with intent.

mutual agreement A meeting of the minds on a specific subject, and a manifestation of intent of the parties to do or refrain from doing some specific act or acts.

mutual assent Concurrence by both parties to all terms.

mutual benefit bailment A bailment created for the benefit of both parties.

mutual mistake An error made by both parties to the transaction; therefore, neither party had the same idea of the terms of the agreement. The contract is avoidable by either party.

mutual release (mutual recission) An agreement by mutual assent of both parties to terminate the contractual relationship and return to the pre-contract status quo.

mutual will Joint wills executed by two or more persons.

mutuality of assent Both parties must objectively manifest their intention to enter into a binding contract by accepting all of the terms.

mutuality of contract (mutuality of obligation) A doctrine that requires both parties to be bound to the terms of the agreement.

N

Napoleonic Code French code of law and government influencing certain aspects of our system. It serves as the model for the government and law in the State of Louisiana.

National Association of Legal Assistants (NALA) A legal professional group that lends support and continuing education for legal assistants.

National Federation of Paralegal Associations (NFPA) National paralegal professional association providing professional career information, support, and information on unauthorized practice of law.

necessaries of life Generally legally considered to be food, clothing, and shelter; necessities; goods and services that are required; basic elements of living and employment.

negligence per se Results from statutes establishing that certain actions or omissions are impermissible under any and all circumstances; the failure to use reasonable care to avoid harm to another person or to do that which a reasonable person might do in similar circumstances.

negligence The failure to use reasonable care to avoid harm to another person or to do that which a reasonable person might do in similar circumstances.

negligent Careless or unintentional act or omission.

negotiable Legally capable of being transferred by endorsement or delivery.

negotiation The transfer of an instrument in which the transferee becomes the holder.

neutral citation Uniform citation system that contains the name of the case, year of decision, court (postal code) abbreviation, opinion number, and paragraph pinpoint for references.

new law A novel interpretation of established law.

no fault divorce A divorce in which one spouse does not need to allege wrongdoing by the other spouse as grounds for the divorce.

nominal consideration The value of the things exchanged are grossly disproportionate to each other so that very little is given in exchange for something of great value.

nominal damages A small amount of money given to the nonbreaching party as a token award to acknowledge the fact of the breach.

nonconforming Goods that are not in reasonable compliance with the specifications in the contract.

noncustodial parent Parent with whom the child(ren) stays or visits some of the time but not as primary residence.

nondisclosure The intentional omission of the truth.

nonfreehold estate A lease agreement.

nonpossessory interests The holder does not have per se possession of the property but may have use interests such as easements, profits, and licenses.

nonprivileged information Discoverable information not protected by confidentiality provisions even when exchanged between parties who may enjoy privileged communications in certain circumstances.

notice of appeal Puts the trial court, the appeals court, and the opposing party on notice that the judgment entered is challenged.

notice pleading A short and plain statement of the allegations in a lawsuit.

notice statute A recording act providing that the person with the most recent valid claim, and who purchased without notice of an earlier, unrecorded claim, has priority.

novation An agreement that replaces previous contractual obligations with new obligations and/or different parties.

nuncupative will An oral will, usually made by the testator near death.

nutshell A paperback series of the law; condensed versions of hornbooks.

O

objection for cause The attorney making the objection states the reason, which must be such as to impair the juror's ability to rule impartially on the evidence.

objection to terms A merchant must state her disapproval of the offeree's new or different terms within a reasonable time, or else they are considered accepted by her.

objective Impartial and disinterested in the outcome of the dispute.

objective documents Documents that convey information and avoid bias.

objective impracticality A party's performance is excused only when the circumstances surrounding the contract become so burdensome that any reasonable person in the same situation would excuse performance.

objectively determinable The ability of the price to be ascertained by a party outside of the contract.

objectively reasonable A standard of behavior that the majority of persons would agree with or how most persons in a community generally act.

obligor The original party to the contract who remains obligated to perform under the contract.

offer A promise made by the offeror to do (or not to do) something provided that the offeree, by accepting, promises or does something in exchange.

offeree The person to whom the offer is made.

offeror The person making the offer to another party.

official reporters Government publications of court decisions (for example, 325 Ill.3d 50).

open-fields doctrine The personal residence per se is protected from unreasonable search; the open fields surrounding the property are not equally protected.

opening statement An initial statement by a party's attorney explaining what the case is about and what that party's side expects to prove during the trial.

opinion Analysis supported by emotion; a formal statement by a court or other adjudicative body of the legal reasons and principles for the conclusion of the court.

opinion letter A letter that renders legal advice.

option contracts A separate and legally enforceable agreement included in the contract stating that the offer cannot be revoked for a certain time period. An option contract is supported by separate consideration.

oral argument Oral presentation by attorney of key issues and points of law presented in the appeals documents and written legal argument.

oral deposition A discovery tool in a question-and-answer format in which the attorney verbally questions a party or witness under oath.

Order Nunc Pro Tunc An entry made by a court now of an event that previously happened and made to have the effect of the former date.

ordinance A law passed by a local government, such as a town council or city government.

ordinary person standard The reasonable behavior for an ordinary individual in a similar situation.

original jurisdiction Authority of a court to review and try a case first.

outline The skeleton of a legal argument, advancing from the general to the specific; a preliminary step in writing that provides a framework for the assignment.

output contract An agreement wherein the quantity that the offeror desires to purchase is all that the offeree can produce.

outrageous conduct Exceeding all bounds of decency and propriety.

overrule A judge's ruling in disagreement with the party who raised the objection.

overt act Identifiable commission or omission, an intentional tort requirement.

ownership The right to possess a thing allowing one to use and enjoy property, as well as the right to convey it to others.

P

PACE Two-tiered paralegal certification program requiring a bachelor's degree, completion of a paralegal program, and practical experience to qualify for the proficiency examination leading to certification.

palimony A division of property between two unmarried parties after they separate or the paying of support by one party to the other.

panel A group of people who have been called for jury duty; the final jury will be selected from this group; also known as venire.

paralegal A person qualified to assist an attorney, under direct supervision, in all substantive legal matters with the exception of appearing in court and rendering legal advice.

parallel citation A citation of a case text found in two or more reporters.

parallel construction Repeating usages to make a point, to suggest either a connection or a contrast.

Parental Kidnapping Prevention Act (PKPA) An act related to jurisdictional issues in applying and enforcing child custody decrees in other states.

parentheses A form of punctuation that unites cohesive passages.

parenthetical phrase A phrase that supplements or adds information to a complete thought.

parol evidence Oral testimony offered as proof regarding the terms of a written contract.

parol evidence rule A court evidentiary doctrine that excludes certain types of outside oral testimony offered as proof of the terms of the contract.

partial breach A failure of performance that has little, if any, effect on the expectations of the parties.

partial integration A document that contains the essential terms of the contract but not all the terms that the parties might have agreed, or need to agree, upon.

partial performance doctrine The court's determination that a party's actions taken in reliance on the oral agreement "substitutes" for the writing and takes the transaction out of the scope of the Statute of Frauds and, thus, can be enforced.

partial performance/substantial beginning An offeree has made conscientious efforts to start performing according to the terms of the contract. The performance need not be complete nor exactly as specified, but only an attempt at significant compliance.

parties The persons involved in the making of the contract.

partition The dividing of lands held by joint tenants or tenants in common.

partners Attorneys who own the law firm and split the profits and losses.

partnership Business enterprise owned by more than one person, entered into for profit.

partnership agreement The contract between the partners that creates duties, establishes responsibilities, and details benefits of the attorneys involved in the partnership.

passive voice A verb form in which the subject of the sentence is the object of the action.

past consideration A benefit conferred in a previous transaction between the parties before the present promise was made.

paternalism One person looked out for another; companies took care of their employees.

paternity action A lawsuit to identify the father of a child born outside of marriage.

payee The person in whose favor a bill of exchange, promissory note, or check is made or drawn.

payor The person by whom a bill or note has been or should have been paid.

pen register Records telephone numbers for outgoing calls.

per capita distribution The equal division of assets according to the number of surviving heirs with the nearest degree of kinship.

per curiam A phrase used to distinguish an opinion of the whole court from an opinion written by any one judge.

per curiam decision A decision that reflects agreement of all the judges on the correct disposition of the case.

per diem (Latin) "by the day" or daily.

per stirpes distribution The division of assets according to rights of representation.

peremptory challenge (peremptory jury strike) An attorney's elimination of a prospective juror without giving a reason; limited to a specific number of strikes.

performance The successful completion of a contractual duty.

performance prevented If a party takes steps to preclude the other party's performance, then the performance is excused due to that interference.

perjury A false statement knowingly made concerning a matter wherein an affiant is required by law to be sworn as to some matter material to the issue or point in question.

periodic sentence A sentence that conveys the information at the end of the paragraph.

periodic tenancy Tenancy in which the tenant is a holdover after the expiration of a tenancy for years.

permanent injunction A court order that prohibits a party from acting in a certain way for an indefinite and perpetual period of time.

permanent loan A long-term loan that finances the acquisition of real property or refinances a construction loan on improvements.

permissive counterclaim A counterclaim that is not required to be filed with a complaint because the facts do not arise out of the same set of circumstances as the complaint.

personal jurisdiction A court's power over the individuals involved in the case; when a court has personal jurisdiction, it can compel attendance at court hearings and enter judgments against the parties.

personal property Movable or intangible thing not attached to real property.

persuasive authority A source of law or legal authority that is not binding on the court in deciding a case but may be used by the court for guidance, such as law review articles; all nonmandatory primary authority.

petition for dissolution of marriage Request for an order dissolving the marriage of the petitioner and spouse.

petitioner Name designation of a party filing an appeal.

physical custody Child living with one parent or visiting with the noncustodial parent.

physical duress The threat of bodily harm unless the aggressor's demands are met.

piercing the corporate veil To show that a corporation exists as an alter ego for a person or group of individuals to avoid liability.

pinpoint citation (pincite or jump cite) The page reference in a citation that directs the reader to the cited material in the case.

plagiarism Taking the thoughts of another and presenting them as one's own without properly crediting or citing the source.

plain meaning rule Courts will use the traditional definition of terms used if those terms are not otherwise defined.

plaintiff The party initiating legal action.

plat A map of a specific land area, such as a town, section, or subdivision, showing the location and boundaries of individual parcels of land subdivided into lots, with streets, alleys, easements, units, etc.

pleadings Formal documents filed with the court that establish the claims and defenses of the parties to the lawsuit; the complaint, answer to complaint, and reply.

pledge to charity A legally enforceable gift to a qualifying institution.

pocket parts Annual supplements to digests.

point headings Headings that outline and identify the argument in the section.

points of charge See *jury instructions.*

political asylum Immigration status available under some circumstances when the party seeking asylum claims political persecution. Not commonly and broadly available without a clear showing of oppression.

polygamy Multiple marital relationships are entered while others remain intact.

poor judgment Contract law does not allow avoidance of performance obligations due to a mistake that was simply a bad decision on the part of one party.

position Analysis supported by fact.

positively and unequivocally In order to treat a party's statement as an anticipatory repudiation, the statements or actions from the potential repudiator must clearly and unquestionably communicate that intent not to perform.

possession Having control over a thing with the intent to have and to exercise such control.

power of disposition The ability of an owner to transfer the care and possession of her property to another.

prayer for relief A summation at the end of a pleading, which sets forth the demands by a party in the lawsuit.

preamble The section of a deed that identifies the parties to the deed.

precedent The holding of past court decisions that are followed in future judicial cases where similar facts and legal issues are present.

precedential value The force that a cited authority exerts upon the judge's reasoning.

precise Accurate written communication.

precision Legal writing that clearly and definitely conveys the point of the document.

predominant factor test An examination of a transaction to determine whether the primary purpose of the contract is the procurement of goods or services.

preemption Right of the federal government to exclusive governance in matters concerning all citizens equally.

pre-existing duty An obligation to perform an act that existed before the current promise was made that requires the same performance presently sought.

preliminary hearing An appearance by both parties before the court to assess the circumstances and validity of the restraining application.

preliminary matters Determining the legal issues, parties, venue, and jurisdiction.

prenuptial agreement An agreement made by parties before marriage that controls certain aspects of the relationship, such as management and ownership of property.

preponderance of the evidence The weight or level of persuasion of evidence needed to find the defendant liable as alleged by the plaintiff in a civil matter.

prescriptive easement A right to use another's property that is not inconsistent with the owner's rights and that is acquired by a use, open and notorious, adverse, and continuous for the statutory period.

present obligation The performances under the contract must not have been carried out but must still be executory in order to be available for a novation.

pretrial conference The meeting between the parties and the judge to identify legal issues, stipulate to uncontested matters, and encourage settlement.

pretrial memo Outlining the legal and factual issues, as well as the recommended jury instructions, and other matters related to trial conduct.

pretrial motions Used to challenge the sufficiency of evidence or the suppression of allegedly tainted evidence or other matters that could impact the focus, the length, and even the need for trial.

pretrial order An order, prepared by the trial judge with the input of the parties, that summarizes key issues in the case, including witness order, evidence, and other critical concerns.

pretrial phase (pretrial stage) The steps in the litigation process before trial, to accomplish discovery and encourage settlement.

price The monetary value ascribed by the parties to the exchange involved in the contract.

price under the contract The seller has the right to collect the agreed-upon price for the goods where the buyer has possession, despite the market conditions at the time.

prima facie (Latin) "At first sight." A case with the required proof of elements in a tort cause of action; the elements of the plaintiff's (or prosecutor's) cause of action; what the plaintiff must prove; accepted on its face, but not indisputable.

primary authority The original text of the sources of law, such as constitutions, court opinions, statutes, and administrative rules and regulations.

primary market Lenders who lend money directly to borrowers.

primary sources of law State the law in the state or federal system and can be found in statutes, constitutions, rules of procedure, codes, and case law; that is, the most fundamental place in which law was established.

prior or contemporaneous agreements These negotiations and resulting potential terms are governed by the principles of the parol evidence rule.

prior proceedings The previous procedural history of a case.

private adoption Parents acting on their own behalf or with the assistance of a third-party intermediary.

private necessity Invasion into property of another for purposes of protecting the property.

private reprimand The minimum censure for an attorney who commits an ethical violation; the attorney is informed privately about a potential violation, but no official entry is made.

private sale A sale between the buyer and the seller without notice or advertisement.

privilege Reasonable expectation of privacy and confidentiality for communications in furtherance of the relationship such as attorney–client, doctor–patient, husband–wife, psychotherapist–patient, and priest–penitent.

privity Mutual or successive relationships to the same right of property, or such an identification of interest of one person with another as to represent the same legal right.

probable cause The totality of circumstances leads one to believe certain facts or circumstances exist; applies to arrests, searches, and seizures.

probable cause for a search Thing(s) sought and assertions as to location, date, and time are correctly represented and researched prior to a search.

probate The court process of determining will validity, settling estate debts, and distributing assets.

probate court The court empowered to settle estates for those individuals who have died with or without a will.

procedural due process These requirements mandate scrupulous adherence to the method or mechanism applied. Notice and fair hearing are the cornerstones of due process, though certainly not the only consideration.

procedural law The set of rules that are used to enforce the substantive law.

process server A person statutorily authorized to serve legal documents such as complaints.

product liability theory The manufacturer and the seller are held strictly liable for product defects unknown to consumers that make the product unreasonably dangerous for its intended purpose.

professional corporation Business form organized as a closely held group of professional intellectual employees such as doctors.

professional duty Exercising a reasonable level of skill, knowledge, training, and understanding related to the specific profession.

profit A right exercised by one person in the soil of another, accompanied with participation in the profits of the soil thereof.

profit à prendre [Law French "profit to take"] A right or privilege to go on another's land and take away something of value from its soil or from the products of its soil.

profit interest The grantee has the right to enter the property of another and remove a specified thing or things from the premises.

promisee The party to whom the promise of performance is made.

promisor The party who makes a promise to perform under the contract.

promissory estoppel A legal doctrine that makes some promises enforceable even though they are not compliant with the technical requirements of a contract.

promissory note A promise or engagement, in writing, to pay a specified sum at a time therein stated, or on demand, or at sight, to a person therein named, or to his order, or bearer.

promissory reliance A party's dependence and actions taken upon another's representations that he will carry out his promise.

promoter A person, typically a principal shareholder, who organizes a business.

pronoun ambiguity Lack of clarity that results from an unclear indication about the noun to which the pronoun refers.

proper dispatch An approved method of transmitting the acceptance to the offeror.

property Rights a person may own or be entitled to own, including personal and real property.

prosecutor Attorney representing the people or plaintiff in criminal matters.

Prosser on Torts Legal treatise or discussion on the law of torts.

protection defense. Includes self-defense, defending another, and defending one's own property.

province of the jury An issue that is exclusively the responsibility of the jury to determine.

proximate cause The defendant's actions are the nearest cause of the plaintiff's injuries.

proxy marriage An agent for the parties arranges the marriage for the couple.

public necessity defense The invasion is necessary to protect the community and therefore is a complete bar to recovery.

public reprimand A published censure of an attorney for an ethical violation.

public sale A sale advertised to the public and subject to UCC provisions.

public use A use that confers some benefit or advantage to the public; it is not confined to actual use by the public.

publicly held corporation A business held by a large number of shareholders.

punitive damages An amount of money awarded to a nonbreaching party that is not based on the actual losses incurred by that party, but as a punishment to the breaching party for the commission of an intentional wrong.

putative marriage The couple completes the requirements in good faith, but an unknown impediment prevents the marriage from being valid.

Q

qualified domestic relations order (QDRO) Retirement account distribution's legal documentation requirement for ultimate distribution.

quantum meruit A Latin term referring to the determination of the earned value of services provided by a party.

quantum valebant A Latin term referring to the determination of the market worth assignable to the benefit conferred.

quasi-contract (pseudo-contract, implied-in-law contract) Where no technical contract exists, the court can create an obligation in the name of justice to promote fairness and afford a remedy to an innocent party and prevent unearned benefits being conferred on the other party.

quasi in rem jurisdiction The court takes authority over property to gain authority over the person.

query A string of key terms or words used in a computer search.

questions presented Section of the appellate brief that identifies the grounds upon which the decision of the trial court is questioned.

quiet enjoyment The possession of real property with the assurance that the possession will not be disturbed by superior title.

quiet title A proceeding to establish the plaintiff's title to land by bringing into court an adverse claimant and there compelling him either to establish his claim or be forever after estopped from asserting it.

quitclaim deed A deed transferring only the interest in property of the grantor, without guarantees.

R

race statute Recording act providing that the person who records first, regardless of notice, has priority.

race-notice statute Recording act providing that the person who is first to record in the chain of title without notice of a prior unrecorded deed or mortgage has priority.

ratification A step taken by a formerly incapacitated person that confirms and endorses the voidable contract and thereby makes it enforceable.

Real Estate Settlement Procedures Act (RESPA) Federal statute governing real estate closings for all federally guaranteed mortgage loans.

real property Land and all property permanently attached to it, such as buildings.

real property ownership Legally recognized interest in land, fixtures attached thereto, and right to possession, transfer, or sale.

reasonable assignment A transfer of performance obligations may only be made where an objective third party would find that the transfer was acceptable under normal circumstances and did not alter the rights and obligations of the original parties.

reasonable Comporting with normally accepted modes of behavior in a particular instance.

reasonable person standard The standard of conduct of a person in the community in similar circumstances; when objectively assessed, a reasonable person would consider the complained-of activity both unwanted and the cause of harm.

reasoning The court's rationale that sets forth the legal principles the court relied upon in reaching its decision.

rebuttal witness Refutes or contradicts evidence presented by the opposing side.

receiver A third party that is appointed by the court to take possession of the real property and take care of the real property in the event of a default on the mortgage.

reciprocal will Will in which testators name each other as beneficiaries under similar plans.

reckless(ness) Lack of concern for the results or applicable standards of decency and reasonableness.

record Documentation of the trial court, including pleadings, physical evidence, transcript, and decision of the trial court.

record notice Constructive notice of the contents of an instrument, such as a deed or mortgage, that has been properly recorded.

recuse (recusal) Voluntary disqualification by a judge due to a conflict of interest or the appearance of one.

redacted Eliminated information or material from a legal document due to privacy and security matters.

redemption The act or instance of reclaiming or regaining possession by paying a specific price; the payment of a defaulted mortgage debt by a borrower who does not want to lose the property.

redirect examination The attorney who originally called the witness asks more questions.

redundancy The repeated use of the same point or concept.

reference line A line of text that appears below the address block, and identifies the subject matter of the letter.

reformation An order of the court that "rewrites" the agreement to reflect the actual performances of the parties where there has been some deviation from the contractual obligation; changed or modified by agreement; that is, the contracting parties mutually agree to restructure a material element of the original agreement.

regional reporters Reporters that contain the cases of all the states in a particular geographical area.

regulatory law Laws passed by administrative agencies and court interpretations.

rejection A refusal to accept the terms of an offer.

release A discharge from the parties' performance obligations that acknowledges the dispute but forgoes contractual remedies.

relevance Reasonably related or associated with the ultimate facts and legal theories.

relevant fact A fact that is significant to a case and its holding.

reliability Confidence of soundness.

reliance A party's dependence and actions based on the assertions of another party.

reliance damages A monetary amount that "reimburses" the nonbreaching party for expenses incurred while preparing to perform her obligations under the agreement but lost due to the breach.

remainder interest The original owner transfers the remaining portion of the interest and property upon termination of the life estate.

remainder Right to receive property interest at some point in the future.

remainder interest The property that passes to a beneficiary after the expiration of an intervening income interest.

remand(ed) Disposition in which the appellate court sends the case back to the lower court for further action.

removal Moving a case from the state court to the federal court system.

reply The responsive pleading provided in Rule 7 to a counterclaim.

reply brief Short responsive brief of the appellant to the appellee's brief.

reporters Hardbound volumes containing judicial decisions.

request for admission (request to admit) A document that provides the drafter with the opportunity to conclusively establish selected facts prior to trial.

request for medical examination Form of discovery that requests a medical examination of an opposing party in a lawsuit.

request for production of documents (request to produce) A discovery device that requests the production of certain items, such as photographs, papers, reports, and physical evidence; must specify the document sought.

requirements contract An agreement wherein the quantity that the offeror desires to purchase is all that the offeror needs.

res ipsa loquitur Doctrine in which it is assumed that a person's injuries were caused by the negligent act of another person as the harmful act ordinarily would not occur but for negligence.

Res judicata (Latin) "The thing has been adjudicated." The principle that a court's decision on a particular matter is binding on future litigation between the parties; sometimes referred to as "res adjudicata."

resale value The nonbreaching party's attempt to mitigate damages may require that he sell the unaccepted goods on the open market. The nonbreaching party can recover the difference in price between the market price and the contract price.

rescind Cancel; revoke; terminate.

rescission and restitution A decision by the court that renders the contract null and void and requires the parties to return to the wronged party any benefits received under the agreement.

rescission Mutual agreement to early discharge or termination of remaining duties.

rescue doctrine Doctrine in which a tortfeasor is liable for harm caused to a person who is injured while rescuing the original victim.

research Process of locating law.

research memorandum Reviews case facts, presents the research question, summarizes the research findings, and answers the research question with a legal analysis of the applicable law.

residence The permanent home of the party.

residuary gift Gift of the remaining property of an estate after expenses and specific gifts have been satisfied.

respondent Name designation of the party responding to an appeal.

restatement A recitation of the common law in a particular legal subject; a series of volumes authored by the American Law Institute that tell what the law in a general area is, how it is changing, and what direction the authors think this change is headed in.

Restatement of the Law of Torts, Second An authoritative treatise that is a compilation of the key principles of tort law.

restitution damages A monetary amount that requires the breaching party to return any benefits received under the contract to the nonbreaching party to ensure that the breaching party does not profit from the breach.

restitution Returns the injured party to the same position enjoyed prior to the breach.

restrictive covenant Private agreement that restricts the use or occupancy of real property.

restrictive phrase A phrase that specifies or restricts the application of something.

retainer letter A form of correspondence that sets forth the agreement and relationship between the attorney and client.

retract the repudiation Until the aggrieved party notifies the repudiator or takes some action in reliance on the repudiation, the repudiator has the right to "take it back" and perform on the contract.

reverse(d) Disposition in which the appellate court disagrees with trial court.

reversion A future interest under which a grantor retains a present right to a future interest in property that the grantor conveys to another.

reversionary future interest Upon completion of the life estate, the property, in its entirety, passes back to the original owner.

reversionary interest Upon completion of the terms under the conditional estate, the remainder of the real property reverts to the original owner, or his or her estate, as appropriate and consistent with the type of ownership originally vested in the owner.

revert (reversion) Right to receive back property in the event of the occurrence of a certain condition.

revocation of a previous acceptance A buyer has the right to refuse to accept the seller's attempts at a cure if those attempts are still not in conformance with the contract requirements.

revoke (revocation) To take back, as in to retract an offer at any time prior to it being accepted; the offeror's cancellation of the right of the offeree to accept an offer.

RHS loans Loans that are guaranteed by the Rural Housing Service.

rhythm A pattern of writing conveyed through word choice and word placement in the sentence.

right of exclusivity The right to exclude all others from the owner's property.

right of survivorship The right of a surviving joint tenant to take ownership of a deceased joint tenant's share of the property.

right to transfer The party supplying the goods must have the legal title (ownership) or legal ability to give it to the receiving party.

riparian right The right of every person through whose land a natural watercourse runs to benefit of water as it passes through the person's land, for all useful purposes to which it may be applied.

risk management Prospectively evaluating potential problems or legal challenges in a particular situation and implementing avoidance strategies in advance to limit potential liability.

robbery The direct taking of property from another through force or threat.

Rule 11 One of the major rules under the Rules of Civil Procedure; it requires an attorney to investigate an action before bringing it.

rule of law Sources of law that control the issue.

rules of construction The rules that control the judicial interpretation of statutes.

rules of court The rules that govern the litigation process in civil and criminal proceedings.

run-on sentence A sentence that contains two independent clauses that are not joined by a conjunction.

S

sale on approval The agreement may provide that the contract for sale is not consummated until the buyer receives and approves of the goods.

sale or return The agreement provides that if the buyer is unable to resell the goods, she is permitted to return the unsold goods to the original seller.

sales contract The transfer of title to goods for a set price governed by the UCC rules.

salutation A greeting that appears below the reference line.

sanctions Penalty against a party in the form of an order to compel, a monetary fine, a contempt-of-court citation, or a court order with specific description of the individualized remedy.

satisfaction Changed agreement resulting from agreed discharge of obligations.

Savings and Loan association A financial institution—often organized and chartered like a bank—that primarily makes home mortgage loans but also usually maintains checking accounts and provides other banking services; often shortened to S & L.

SBA loans Loans made by the Small Business Administration to small businesses.

seal An impression or sign that has legal consequence when applied to an instrument.

secondary authority Authority that analyzes the law such as a treatise, encyclopedia, or law review article.

secondary mortgage market Condition that exists as to demand for purchase of second mortgages, generally by financial institutions that use mortgages as part of their investment portfolio.

security deed A legal document that conveys title to the lender in order to secure a debt.

security deposit Money deposited by a tenant with the landlord as security for full and faithful performance by the tenant of the terms of the lease, including damages to premises.

seisin The condition of having both possession and title to property.

seizure Personal exercise of the possessory right to particular property is interrupted or denied by virtue of government action.

Self-authenticating document A document that is authorized by statute and that can be used without additional offer of proof.

self-defense A defendant's legal excuse that the use of force was justified.

semicolon A form of punctuation used to indicate a break in thought, though of a different sort than that indicated by a comma.

seminal Most important, fundamental.

sentence fragment A group of words that lacks necessary grammatical information, such as a verb, that would make it a complete sentence.

separate property Property owned by a married person in his or her own right during the marriage.

separation Legally requires continuously living separate and apart for the statutorily set period.

separation agreement Contract between husband and wife to live apart; the document outlines the terms of the separation.

separation of powers A form of checks and balances to ensure that one branch does not become dominant; the doctrine that divides the powers of government among the three branches established under the U.S. Constitution.

service of process The procedure by which a defendant is notified of a lawsuit by a process server.

servicing the loan The collecting of loan payment by one entity for another entity for a fee.

servient tenement A piece of real property on which an easement appurtenant is located.

session laws The second format in which new statutes appear as a compilation of the slip laws; a bill or joint resolution that has become law during a particular session of the legislature.

settled law Established law.

settlement A negotiated termination of a case prior to a trial or jury verdict.

severability of contract The ability of a court to choose to separate and discard those clauses in a contract that are unenforceable and retain those that are.

severance The converting of a joint tenancy to a tenancy in common.

sham consideration An unspecified and indeterminable recitation of consideration that cannot support an exchange.

shareholder The owner of one or more shares of stock in a corporation.

Shepard's Citations Reference system that reports the legal authority referring to the legal position of the case and making reference to the case opinion.

Shepardizing (shepardize) Using Shepard's verification and updating system for cases, statutes, and other legal resources.

short form citation Citation used after the complete citation is used in the legal document.

short summary of the conclusion A summary that provides the reader with a quick answer to the "yes-or-no" questions raised by the issues.

signals Words that introduce additional references to the legal authority cited, such as "see" and "accord."

signature block Section of the brief for attorney's signature that includes the name, address, bar card identification, fax number, and telephone number.

signed by the party to be charged The writing that purports to satisfy the Statute of Frauds must be signed by the party against whom enforcement is sought.

silence In certain circumstances, no response may be necessary to properly accept an offer.

simile A direct comparison of dissimilar objects, for the purpose of emphasizing a common characteristic.

simple sentence A sentence that has a simple format—subject/verb/object.

Sixth Amendment Protections include a speedy trial, the right to confront the accuser, a jury trial, and the assistance of counsel.

skip tracing A general term for tracking a person who has absconded or is attempting to avoid legal process.

slander Written defamatory statements.

slang Informal expressions.

slip law The first format in which a newly signed statute appears; a copy of a particular law passed during a session of legislature.

slip opinion The first format in which a judicial opinion appears.

social guest licensee Property owner derives no benefit or economic gain from the individual's presence on, and legal use of, the property.

Socratic method Analysis and teaching tool based on questioning and discussion.

sole custody Only one of the divorcing spouses has both legal and physical custody, but the noncustodial parent may have visitation rights.

sole proprietorship A business owned by one person.

solemnization A formalization of a marriage, as in for example, a marriage ceremony.

solicitation The crime of inducing or encouraging another to commit a crime.

solicited offer An invitation for members of a group to whom it is sent (potential offerors) to make an offer to the party sending the information (the potential offeree).

special appearance A term describing a defendant's contest of jurisdiction; the defendant enters the court for the limited purpose of contesting the case, but does not submit to the court's jurisdiction for other purposes.

special damages Those damages incurred beyond and in addition to the general damages suffered and expected in similar cases.

special defenses Affirmative defenses.

specialized goods A product made for a particular buyer with specifications unique to that buyer so that it could not be sold on the general market.

specific gift A gift of a particular described item.

specific intent The mental desire and will to act in a particular way.

specific performance A court order that requires a party to perform a certain act in order to prevent harm to the requesting party.

specific reasons for rejection The buyer is under an obligation to notify the seller within a reasonable time not only that the goods have been rejected but also the reasons for the refusal to accept the goods.

speculative damages Harm incurred by the nonbreaching party that is not susceptible to valuation or determination with any reasonable certainty.

spot sale A purchase on the open market in that particular place at that particular time.

spousal payment See *alimony, support.*

standard of care Criteria for measuring appropriateness of behavior.

standard of review Guideline the court applies in evaluating the errors on appeal.

standards of good faith and fair dealing A party's performance will be judged in light of the normal or acceptable behavior displayed generally by others in a similar position.

standing Legally sufficient reason and right to object.

stare decisis (Latin) "Stand by the decision." Decisions from a court with substantially the same set of facts should be followed by that court and all lower courts under it; the judicial process of adhering to prior case decisions; the doctrine of precedent whereby once a court has decided a specific issue one way in the past, it and other courts in the same jurisdiction are obligated to follow that earlier decision in deciding cases with similar issues in the future.

star-paging A practice that enables the reader to identify the page breaks in one reporter by reviewing the decision as reprinted in another reporter.

state bar The organization that licenses and oversees the practice of law and the conduct of attorneys in the state. An attorney must be a member of the state bar before he or she will be allowed to practice in that state.

state or federal rules of civil procedure (rules of the court) Rules related to all aspects of the legal process from the proper court and judicial system for a particular dispute through each aspect, including appeals and agency proceedings.

state rights Constitutionally defined rights of individual state governments to preserve and protect individual rights of citizens of the state, providing there is no conflict with the federal Constitution.

state supremacy Constitutional principle that the individual states have sole governmental authority over matters related to only state citizens without influencing or negatively impacting federal rights and privileges.

state supreme court The final and highest court in many states.

statement of facts Section of a brief that sets forth the significant facts and information needed to analyze the issues presented.

statement of the case Section of the appellate brief that sets forth the procedural history of the case.

Statute of Frauds A collective term describing various statutes stipulating that no suit or action shall be maintained on certain classes of contracts or engagements unless there shall be a note or memorandum thereof in writing signed by the party to be charged or by his authorized agent.

statute of limitations Establishes the applicable time limits for filing and responding to certain claims or legal actions.

statute Written law enacted by the legislative branches of both federal and state governments.

statutory authority The legislature of a jurisdiction may codify certain actions as subject to punitive damages if they occur in conjunction with a contractual breach.

statutory law Derived from the Constitution in statutes enacted by the legislative branch of state or federal government; Primary source of law consisting of the body of legislative law.

stay(ed) Extraordinary relief suspending the process in one court while the appellate court reviews the legal issue, which may result in dismissal of the case from the lower court.

stipulation An agreement between attorneys and parties in a case about a procedural or factual issue.

strict liability The defendant is liable without the plaintiff having to prove fault.

strict scrutiny standard Most exacting and precise legal analysis because fundamental constitutional rights may have been unconstitutionally restricted or revoked.

string citations List of citations in the brief following a point of law cited.

structure Fundamental principle of law and social order in any government system.

structured enumeration Sequential identification of each point in a sentence.

style Also known as caption; the heading or title used in all legal pleadings.

sua sponte On his or her own motion; rarely exercised right of the judge to make a motion and ruling without an underlying request from either party.

subdivision The division of a lot, tract, or parcel of land into two or more lots, tracts, parcels, or other divisions of land for sale or development .

subheadings Headings that identify the subpoints in an argument section.

subject matter The bargained-for exchange that forms the basis for the contract.

subject matter jurisdiction A court's authority over the res, the subject of the case.

sublease A lease executed by the lessee of land or premises to a third person, conveying the same interest that the lessee enjoys, but for a shorter term than that for which the lessee holds.

sublessee A third party who receives by lease some or all of the leased property from a lessee.

submission The agreement to arbitrate a specific matter or issue raised between the parties.

subordinate clause A clause that cannot stand on its own as a complete sentence.

subpoena A document that is served upon an individual under authority of the court, and orders the person to appear at a certain place and certain time for a deposition, or suffer the consequences; an order issued by the court clerk directing a person to appear in court.

subpoena duces fecum A type of subpoena that requests a witness to produce documents.

subprime lending A type of lending in which higher interest rates and higher loan fees are extended to higher-risk borrowers.

subrogation The right to sue in the name of another.

subsequent agreements Negotiations and potential terms that are discussed after the agreement has been memorialized are not covered by the parol evidence rule.

subsequent history History of a case on appeal.

substantial beginning An offeree has made conscientious efforts to start performing according to the terms of the contract. The performance need not be complete nor exactly as specified, but only an attempt at significant compliance.

substantial compliance A legal doctrine that permits close approximations of perfect performance to satisfy the contractual terms.

substantial detriment The change in a party's position in reliance upon another's representations that, if unanswered, will work a hardship on that party.

substantial performance Most of the contracted performance is complete.

substantial-cause test Analysis of which of the possible factors was the real cause.

substantive due process Requires that legislation be reasonable in scope and limitations, and further that the statute serve a legitimate purpose, including equal impact on all citizens.

substantive law Legal rules that are the content or substance of the law, defining rights and duties of citizens.

substantive law Legal rules that are the content or substance of the law, defining rights and duties of citizens.

substituted agreement A replacement of a previous agreement with a new contract with additional but not inconsistent obligations.

substituted goods The products purchased on the open market that replace those not delivered by the breaching party.

sufficiency Adequacy.

sufficient consideration The exchanges have recognizable legal value and are capable of supporting an enforceable contract. The actual values are irrelevant.

summons The notice to appear in court, notifying the defendant of the plaintiff's complaint.

supervening illegality An agreement whose terms at the time it was made were legal but, due to a change in the law during the time in which the contract was executory, that has since become illegal; a change in the law governing the subject matter of the contract that renders a previously legal and enforceable contract void and therefore excusable.

"supplemental evidence which adds to, but does not contradict, the original agreement is admissible under the parol evidence rule" Agreements of the parties that naturally add to, but do not conflict with, the original terms of the partially integrated contract.

supplemental pleading A pleading that adds to a pleading without deleting prior information.

supplemental response Additional response to previously filed discovery because of newly found information.

support Periodic payments extending over time.

supra (Latin) Above.

Supremacy Clause Sets forth the principle and unambiguously reinforces that the Constitution is the supreme law of the land.

surety A party who assumes primary liability for the payment of another's debt.

survey A description of the boundaries of a piece of property.

sustain A judge's ruling in agreement with the party who raised the objection.

syllabus A short paragraph summary in the official reporter identifying issue, procedural history, and ruling of the court; an editorial feature in unofficial reporters that summarizes the court's decision.

synopsis A short paragraph summary prepared by the publisher in unofficial reporters that identifies the issue, the procedural history, and the ruling of the court in the instant case.

T

table of authorities Section of the appellate brief that identifies the cases, statutes, constitutional provisions, and all other primary and secondary authorities contained within the brief.

table of cases Lists of all the cases whose text appears in the associated volumes.

table of contents Road map of the appellate brief, which includes the section headings and corresponding page numbers in the brief.

tacking A term applied especially to the process of establishing title to land by adverse possession, when the present occupant and claimant has not been in possession for the full statutory period, but adds or "tacks" to his own possession that of previous occupants under whom he claims.

tangible property Personal property that can be held or touched, such as furniture or jewelry.

tax lien A legal right or interest that the government has in a delinquent taxpayer's property.

technical terms, specifications, or trade/business custom Parol evidence is permitted to explain the meaning of special language in the contract as the parties understood it if the plain ordinary meaning of the language was not intended or was ambiguous.

temporary injunction A court order that prohibits a party from acting in a certain way for a limited period of time.

temporary restraining order A court order barring a person from harassing or harming another.

temporary suspension A punishment for an ethical violation; an attorney is temporarily prohibited from practicing law or representing clients.

tenancy at sufferance A tenancy that arises when one comes into the possession of property by lawful title, but wrongfully holds over after the termination of her interest.

tenancy at will The holding of premises by permission of the owner or landlord, but without a fixed term.

tenancy by the entirety A form of ownership for married couples, similar to joint tenancy, where the spouse has right of survivorship.

tenancy for years The temporary use and possession of lands or tenements not the tenant's own, by virtue of a lease or demise granted to him by the owner, for a determinate period of time, as for a year or a fixed number of years.

tenancy in common A form of ownership between two or more people where each owner's interest upon death goes to his or her heirs.

tenancy in severalty The holding of land and tenements in one person's own right only, without any other person being joined or connected with him in point of interest during his estate therein.

tenant A person, or corporation, who rents real property from an owner; also called a lessee.

tender of delivery The seller is ready to transfer the goods to the buyer and the goods are at the disposal of the buyer.

tender of performance Acts in furtherance of performance; the offeree's act of proffering the start of his contractual obligations. The offeree stands ready, willing, and able to perform.

terminated Performance is complete and the contract is discharged.

tendering The process of admitting evidence in a trial by asking the court to rule on relevance.

terms of art Words that are commonly used in the legal profession and have an accepted meaning.

testamentary Pertaining to a will or testament.

testamentary capacity The ability to understand and have the legal capacity to make a will.

testimonial evidence Oral statements made by a witness under oath.

testate The state of having died with a valid will.

testator/testatrix The person who writes a will.

testimonium The portion of a deed that the grantor signs and that is usually witnessed or notarized.

texts One-volume treatises.

***The Bluebook: A Uniform System of Citation,* 17th ed.** Widely used legal citation resource, published by the Harvard Law Review Association, that is regularly revised and updated.

third-party beneficiary A person, not a party to the contract, who stands to receive the benefit of performance of the contract.

third-party claim A suit filed by the defendant against a party not originally named in the plaintiff's complaint.

tickler file System of tracking dates and reminding what is due on any given day or in any given week, month, or year.

time A point in or space of duration at or during which some fact is alleged to have been committed.

time for performance A condition that requires each party be given a reasonable time to complete performance.

time of the essence A term in a contract that indicates that no extensions for the required performance will be permitted. The performance must occur on or before the specified date.

timekeeping Records of the time spent and the nature of the work done for each client; a legal task for both paralegals and attorneys.

timeshare A form of shared property ownership, commonly in vacation or recreational condominium property, wherein rights vest in several owners to use property for specified periods each year.

title The right to or ownership in land.

title examination An investigation of the title made by a person who intends to purchase real estate or to ascertain the history and present condition of the title to such land.

title insurance A policy issued by a title company after searching the title, representing the state of that title, and insuring the accuracy of its search against claims of title defects.

title page Cover page of the brief.

title search A search of the abstract of title, the short history of a piece of property including ownership interests and liens.

tone Language and style used to present an argument; the way a writer communicates a point of view.

topic sentence The first sentence of the paragraph, which introduces an idea.

tort A civil wrongful act, committed against a person or property, either intentional or negligent.

tort reform law Limiting or capping the monetary awards juries can make for specific classes of tort actions such as personal injury or automobile liability.

tortfeasor Actor committing the wrong, whether intentional, negligent, or strict liability.

tortious A private civil wrong committed by one person against another that the law considers to be punishable.

torts against property Trespass to land and chattel, interference with business relations, and conversion.

torts against the person Assault and battery; false imprisonment; defamation, either libel or slander; and intentional infliction of emotional distress.

total breach A failure of performance that has a substantial effect on the expectations of the parties.

totality of circumstances test Evidence offered must be sufficient in terms of quantity or comprehensiveness.

trade fixtures Pieces of equipment on or attached to the property being used in a trade or business.

traditional (manual) legal research Uses libraries, books, and other materials in paper format.

transactional documents Documents that define property rights and performance obligations.

transactions in goods A sale or other transfer of title to identifiable, tangible, movable things from a merchant to a buyer.

transcript Written account of a trial court proceeding or deposition.

transfer of interest In a purchase agreement, a preliminary requirement is that the seller has legal title to the subject matter and authority to transfer it to the seller. If the seller transfers his interest to a third party, this preliminary requirement can no longer be met.

transferred intent doctrine The doctrine that holds a person liable for the unintended result to another person not contemplated by the defendant's actions.

transition The writer's ability to move the reader from paragraph to paragraph.

transitional function Moving the reader though the material they are reading in an orderly progression.

transmittal letter A type of confirmation letter that accompanies information sent to a designated party.

treatise A scholarly study of one area of the law.

trespass to chattel Interfering with the right to freedom of possession of chattel, or personal property, rightly owned and possessed.

trespass to land Intentional and unlawful entry onto or interference with the land of another person without consent.

trespasser One who intentionally and without privilege enters another's property.

trial courts Courts that hear all cases and are courts of general jurisdiction.

trial notebook Started and organized prior to the pretrial conference, it contains all documentary and other tangible evidence or materials used by the attorney in trial.

trial order Also called a trial schedule order; issued by the judge assigned to the case.

trial The forum for the presenting of evidence and testimony and the deliberation of guilt.

trier of fact Jury.

trier of law Judge.

TRO A temporary restraining order that is issued prior to any hearing in the court.

trustee Person holding property in trust.

Truth-in-Lending Act A federal regulation passed to protect consumers from unfair billing practices, as well as provide them with information for an informed credit use.

U

U.S. Bankruptcy Code Defines the rules related to bankruptcy filing, process, and adjudication.

U.S. Constitution The fundamental law of the United States of America, which became the law of the land in March of 1789.

U.S. Court of Federal Claims Part of the lower or trial court level of the federal court system in which disputes with the U.S. government are heard.

U.S. courts of appeals Intermediate review level of the federal court system that reviews the decisions of the district or trial court level.

U.S. district courts Trial or lower court level in the federal system.

unauthorized means The offeree accepts the offer by a method that is not the same as specified by the offeror.

umpire A person with greater authority than an arbitrator; this person has the authority to make a final and binding decision when an arbitrator has been unable to do so.

unauthorized practice of law (UPL) Practicing law without proper authorization to do so.

unconscionable contract A contract so completely unreasonable and irrational that it shocks the conscience.

unconscionable So completely unreasonable and irrational that it shocks the conscience.

uncontested dissolution Following the waiting period prescribed by statute, parties jointly file the documents required by law to dissolve the marriage, based on voluntary agreement.

under the influence Persons who do not have the capacity to understand a transaction due to overconsumption of alcohol or the use of drugs, either legal or illegal; and, who therefore, do not have the requisite mental intent to enter into a contract.

undue enrichment Gain experienced without related duty or obligation of performance.

undue influence Persons who do not have the capacity to understand a transaction due to overconsumption of alcohol or the use of drugs, either legal or illegal, and, therefore, who do not have the requisite mental intent to enter into a contract.

unfair detriment A burden incurred for which there is no compensation.

unforeseen circumstances Occurrences that could not be reasonably forecast to happen.

Uniform Child Custody Jurisdiction Act (UCCJA) An act that resolves jurisdictional issues related to child custody.

Uniform Parentage Act An act defining legal parentage and establishing parental rights.

uniform resource locator (URL) Precise location of a specific document retrieved from an electronic source or the Web address for the referenced source.

uniform statute Model legislation drafted by the National Conference of Commissioners on Uniform State Laws, dealing with areas of the law such as sales transactions.

unilateral contract A contract in which the parties exchange a promise for an act.

unilateral mistake An error made by only one party to the transaction. The contract may be avoided only if the error is detectable or obvious to the other party.

United States Constitution The fundamental law of the United States of America, which became the law of the land in March of 1789.

unjust enrichment The retention by a party of unearned and undeserved benefits derived from his own wrongful actions regarding an agreement.

unlimited liability A finding that a business owner's personal assets may be used to satisfy a judgment against the business.

unmarketable title A title that a reasonable buyer would refuse to accept because of possible conflicting interests in or litigation over the property.

unofficial reporters Private publications of court decisions (for example, 525 N.E.2d 90).

unpublished case A case decided by a court that is not published in a reporter because it does not set precedent.

unsolicited memorandum anticipating legal issues Memorandum of law prepared by one of the parties to the case in support of an anticipated legal issue.

urban renewal Redevelopment plans indicating a relationship to such local objectives as appropriate land uses, improved traffic, public transportation, public utilities, recreation, community facilities, and other public improvements.

usage of the trade Actions generally taken by similarly situated parties in similar transactions in the same business field.

utility easement The right of utility companies to lay lines across the property of others.

V

VA loans Home mortgage loans provided to veterans and their spouses that are guaranteed by the Veterans Administration.

vacate(d) Disposition in which an appellate court voids the decision of the lower court.

value of the goods as accepted The buyer is entitled to a "set-off" for the difference between the price of the goods as specified in the contract and the actual price those goods would garner on the open market.

value The objective worth placed on the subject matter in a transaction.

variance A license or official authorization to depart from a zoning law.

venue County in which the facts are alleged to have occurred and in which the trial will take place.

veracity test Meets truth or strict correctness in process and content.

Verbosity The use of an excessive number of words, or excessively complicated words, to make a point.

verdict Decision of the jury following presentation of facts and application of relevant law as they relate to the law presented in the jury instructions.

verification Acknowledgment by a party of the truthfulness of the information contained within a document.

vested Having a present right to receive the benefit of the performance when it becomes due.

vicarious liability (respondeat superior) One person, or a third party, may be found liable for the act of another or shares liability with the actor.

video deposition Videotaped version of the oral deposition; the videotape serves as an additional method of preserving the testimony, in addition to the transcript.

visitation rights The right to legally see a child, where physical custody is not awarded.

voice The sound heard in the mind of the reader, or the impression created by virtue of the words chosen.

void Describing a transaction that is impossible to enforce because it is invalid.

voidable Legally valid until annulled; capable of being affirmed or rejected at the option of one of the parties.

void ab initio Marriages that are void from the inception.

void contract Agreement that does not meet the required elements and therefore is unenforceable under contract law.

void marriage The marriage fails to meet the legal requirements.

voidable contract Apparently fully enforceable contract with a defect unknown by one party.

voidable Having the possibility of avoidance of performance at the option of the incapacitated party.

voidable marriage Valid in all legal respects until the union is dissolved by order of the court.

voidable obligation A duty imposed under a contract that may be either ratified (approved) or avoided (rejected) at the option of one or both of the parties.

voir dire The process of selecting a jury for trial.

voluntary destruction If a party destroys the subject matter of the contract, thereby rendering performance impossible, the other party is excused from his performance obligations due to that termination.

voluntary disablement If a party takes steps to preclude his own performance, then the performance due from the other party is excused due to that refusal/inability to perform.

voluntary repayment of debt An agreement to pay back a debt that cannot be collected upon using legal means because the obligation to make payments has been discharged.

W

waiver A party may knowingly and intentionally forgive the other party's breach and continue her performance obligations under the contract.

warrant Issued after presentation of an affidavit stating clearly the probable cause on which the request is based.

warrantless search Compelling reasons support search without a written warrant.

warranty A promise or representation by the seller that the goods in question meet certain standards.

warranty deed A deed guaranteeing clear title to real property.

warranty of title The seller promises the buyer that the seller has the right to transfer the title free and clear of encumbrances to the buyer.

waste Deterioration of the property.

Westclip An electronic clipping service used on Westlaw that monitors legal developments.

Westlaw Commercial electronic law database service.

will A document representing the formal declaration of a person's wishes for the manner and distribution of his or her property upon death.

witness locator service A company that provides information about a witness's former addresses, telephone numbers, employment, and current location.

words and phrases An index to a digest that construes a judicial term.

work product An attorney's written notes, impressions, charts, diagrams, and other material used by him or her to prepare strategy and tactics for trial.

writ of certiorari Granting of petition, by the U.S. Supreme Court, to review a case; request for appeal where the Court has the discretion to grant or deny it.

writ of habeas corpus Literally "bring the body"; application for extraordinary relief or a petition for rehearing of the issue on the basis of unusual facts unknown at the time of the trial.

writing to satisfy the Statute of Frauds A document or compilation of documents containing the essential terms of the agreement.

Z

Zoning The division of a region, such as a county, city, or town, by legislative regulation into districts, and the prescription and application in each district of regulation having to do with structural and architectural design of buildings within designated districts.

Index